Studia Fennica
Linguistica 17

The Finnish Literature Society was founded in 1831 and has from the very beginning engaged in publishing. It nowadays publishes literature in the fields of ethnology and folkloristics, linguistics, literary research and cultural history. The first volume of Studia Fennica series appeared in 1933.

Since 1992 the series has been divided into three thematic subseries: Ethnologica, Folkloristica and Linguistica. Two additional subseries were formed in 2002, Historica and Litteraria. Subseries Anthropologica was formed in 2007.

In addition to its publishing activities the Finnish Literature Society maintains a folklore archive, a literature archive and a library.

Editorial board
Markku Haakana, professor, University of Helsinki, Finland
Timo Kaartinen, professor, University of Helsinki, Finland
Kimmo Rentola, professor, University of Turku, Finland
Riikka Rossi, docent, University of Helsinki, Finland
Hanna Snellman, professor, University of Helsinki, Finland
Lotte Tarkka, professor, University of Helsinki, Finland
Tuomas M. S. Lehtonen, Secretary General, Dr. Phil., Finnish Literature Society, Finland
Pauliina Rihto, secretary of the board, M. A., Finnish Literary Society, Finland

Editorial office
Hallituskatu 1
FIN-00170 Helsinki

Terhi Ainiala, Minna Saarelma
& Paula Sjöblom

Names in Focus
An Introduction to Finnish Onomastics

Translated by Leonard Pearl

Finnish Literature Society · Helsinki

Studia Fennica Linguistica 17

The publication has undergone a peer review.

The open access publication of this volume has received part funding via
a Jane and Aatos Erkko Foundation grant.

© 2012 Terhi Ainiala, Minna Saarelma, Paula Sjöblom and SKS
License CC-BY-NC-ND 4.0 International

A digital edition of a printed book first published in 2012 by the Finnish Literature Society.
Cover Design: Timo Numminen
EPUB: Tero Salmén

ISBN 978-952-222-387-6 (Print)
ISBN 978-952-222-748-5 (PDF)
ISBN 978-952-222-751-5 (EPUB)

ISSN 0085-6835 (Studia Fennica)
ISSN 1235-1938 (Studia Fennica Linguistica)

DOI: http://dx.doi.org/10.21435/sflin.17

This work is licensed under a Creative Commons CC-BY-NC-ND 4.0 International License.
To view a copy of the license, please visit http://creativecommons.org/licenses/by-nc-nd/4.0/

A free open access version of the book is available at http://dx.doi.
org/10.21435/sflin.17 or by scanning this QR code with your mobile device.

BoD – Books on Demand, Norderstedt, Germany

Contents

Preface   8
Abbreviations and Symbols   11

1. Theoretical Background to Onomastics   13
What is a Name?   13
Names in Culture and Society   16
   The Many Functions of Names   16
   Changing Names and Naming Systems   21
   Categorisation of Names   23
Names in Language   27
   Names and Appellatives   27
   Meaning of Names   31
   Name Typology   35

2. Materials and Lines of Finnish Onomastics   38
Research Material   38
Research Tradition   44
   Etymological Research   45
   Cultural-Historical and Settlement-Historical Research   47
   Loan Name Research   49
   Typological Research of Toponymy   52
   Sociolinguistic Research   56
   Research on Urban Nomenclature   58
   Diversification of Research   59
   International Cooperation   60

3. Place Names   63
Introduction to Place Names   63
Grammar and Semantics   71
   Structure and Content of Names   71
   Syntactic-Semantic Classification Model   72
   Various Means of Name Formation   75
   Variation in Names   82

Name Strata over Time and across Languages   85
   Origin and Etymology   85
   Name Strata across Languages   94
Urban Nomenclature   99
   Official, Planned Names   99
   Formation of Unofficial Names   105
   Functions of Unofficial Names   109
Use of Names   110
   Knowledge of Names   110
   Children as Name Users   114
   The Many Contexts of Use   115
   Attitude towards Names   118
   Other Functions of Names   119

4. Personal Names   124

Introduction to Personal Names   124
   Personal Names and Culture   124
   Differences and Similarities in Naming Systems   126
   Anthroponymic Typology and Terminology   129
   A Changing Anthroponymy   136
   African Naming Systems   138
   Asian Naming Systems   142
Development of European Naming Systems   145
   European Pre-Christian Anthroponymy   145
   Standardisation of Christian Nomenclature in the Middle Ages   148
   From Bynames to Hereditary Surnames   152
   Name Giving Trends of the Modern Era   154
Stages of Finnish Anthroponymy   157
   Old Finnish Naming System   157
   Features of Medieval Anthroponymy   159
   Name Giving in Finland between the 16th and 18th Centuries   162
   Fennisation of Given Names during Russian Rule   163
   Formation of a Modern Surname System   166
Given Names and Surnames in 20th and 21st Century Finland   170
   General Features of Finnish Given Names   170
   Principles of Name Selection   176
   Popularity Change of Given Names   180
   Name Day Tradition in Finland   185
   Finnish Surnames   186
   What the Law Says about Finns' Names   188
Finnish Unofficial Anthroponymy   190
   Unofficial Bynames in the Finnish Naming System   190
   Bynames of Small Children and Schoolchildren   193
   Bynames of Teachers and other Professional Groups   196

Naming Systems of Linguistic Minorities   197
    Finland Swedish Personal Names   197
    Sámi Personal Names   199
    Personal Names in Sign Language   200

5. Animal Names   202
Do Animals Use Names?   202
Cat and Dog Names   204
Cattle Names   206
Horse Names   207

6. Commercial Names   210
Commercial Nomenclature as a Topic of Research   210
    Names and Trade   210
    Types of Commercial Names   211
    Factors Taken into Account in Examining Names   214
    Research Traditions of Commercial Nomenclature   217
Factors that Determine Name Giving   219
    Laws and Guidelines   219
    Commercial Objectives   223
History of Commercial Naming in Finland   226
Company Names   233
    Structural Description of Company Names   233
    Determining Language in Company Names   238
    Semantic Description of Company Names   241
    Social and Cultural Functions   243
Brands, Product Names and Trade Marks   245
On the Border Areas of Commercial Nomenclature   249

7. Names in Literature   255
Names in Fiction   255
Translating Names in Literature   261
Finnish Literary Onomastics   264

Bibliography   267
Index   281

Preface

Names are used in all languages and cultures. With names, it is easy for people to speak about individuals, certain people, certain places, certain objects or subjects, without having to describe them with a great deal of words. Without names, communication would be difficult, practically even impossible. How would we speak of, for example, Finland, if countries or any other geographic place had no name? How could we be sure that all of the participants in a conversation would be thinking about the same person, for example Jean Sibelius or Mika Häkkinen, if we had no names to use? It is a name that identifies and sets apart a referent from others of the same class.

Names are crucial words when it comes to efficient language use. On the other hand, they are also words which many emotions are associated with: a name carries all of the information we have about its name bearer such as a person, an animal, a place or object. On the emotional level, significant topics such as identity, history, tradition, kinship, ownership, power and money are associated with names. Because names are such words of special quality, they fascinate people and arouse many questions.

This book is about names and onomastics from a Finnish perspective. There has been a great deal of literature published around the world concerning names. On the one hand, there is an abundance of scholarly studies – monographs as well as individual and collections of articles – and on the other hand, there are many name guides in popular literature meant for a broader audience as well as light, humorous name dictionaries. These publications usually focus on one specific area of onomastics, for example, on hydronyms, first names, names of restaurants or dog names. There has not previously been any comprehensive, linguistic work completed in Finland covering the entire field of onomastics and there are not that many international ones either – at least not in such a compact form.

This book was originally written in 2008 in Finnish for a Finnish audience, primarily as study material for university students, covering the "basics of onomastics" as the original title *Nimistöntutkimuksen perusteet* suggests. The aim of our now translated and edited *Names in Focus: An Introduction to Finnish Onomastics* is to introduce Finnish onomastics to an international audience whilst comparing it to other (mostly European) onomastic studies. The book is about onomastic methods and findings from a contemporary research perspective. It illustrates a new type of take on research and reflects newer theoretical approaches to language, however founded on a strong, Finnish research tradition. Discussion amongst onomasticians from different countries is nowadays quite lively and so efforts have been made to take a great deal of significant international research findings into consideration in this book.

Names in Focus works as a general introduction to the world of onomastics. We hope that this book would serve readers who wish to get a general idea about onomastic subjects, key theoretical questions and research methods. It also provides the reader a glimpse at Finnish history and culture through names.

The question of terminology has come up in the creation of this book. In the past years, there has been an international need for cohesive terminology, many new terms and a clear understanding of old terms. Our book introduces terminology used in Finnish onomastics, relates it to terminology used elsewhere and also connects it to wide-ranging, international terminological discussion. The index should help the adventurous reader navigate through the vast number of terms utilised for the book.

We have divided our book into seven chapters. Its content focuses on the presentation of the most essential research data available. The first chapter discusses general questions on onomastics and the philosophy of names such as what a name is and why a name is given. Readers will also become familiar with the history of onomastics in Finland and materials used by Finnish onomasticians. Without excluding other name categories, place names, personal names and commercial names are covered in great detail and animal names and names in literature discussed rather broadly.

There is a great deal of examples in this book. Because Finnish onomastics is the subject at hand, many of the examples are naturally from Finnish nomenclature. We have given explanations of Finnish examples in glosses when the name's structure is concerned and regular translations when highlighting the name's meaning. As all of the world's languages have a morphological structure, a list of abbreviations and symbols of name formation suffixes and other morphological aspects used in the explanations of Finnish names was created. Some of the examples, however, have been modified and new ones created in English in order to help the international reader to get familiarised with the subject at hand more easily. No strict academic referencing has been applied in the citations but all of the sources used can be found in the bibliography at the end of the book. The titles of Finnish publications mentioned, for example, in the chapter on Finnish onomastic materials and lines of research have been translated into English in brackets which can help the reader get an idea of onomastic topics carried out in Finland.

In addition to the new examples created exclusively for this book, we also included brief explanations pertaining to Finnish history and culture in connection to different names, for example in street names and company names. The glosses, especially in place names, will help readers grasp the understanding of the grammar, that is, the typology of Finnish names. In addition, because they are in nature quite different from each other, the translations of place names and personal names, with the exception of derivational endings, have been handled differently. With the exception of any names that have an official English equivalent, the translated names are not capitalised. However, the translated newspaper advertisement examples in chapter 6, for example, have been capitalised to fit the style, even though these names have never had official English counterparts.

The authors of the book are onomasticians and represent specialised expertise in different areas of onomastics. Terhi Ainiala, PhD was responsible for the chapters on onomastic materials and history as well as place names, Minna Saarelma, PhD covered the chapters on personal names, animal names and names in literature and Paula Sjöblom, PhD took on the chapters on theoretical questions in onomastics and on commercial names. Linguist and onomastician Leonard Pearl, MA translated the book into English. He did not participate just as a translator but rather as an expert in the field, making many excellent editing suggestions during the translation process. As four onomastic specialists, working as collaborative co-editors, we all came to the project from different angles, all of us sharing our knowledge, ideas and genuine interest in the field of the investigation of names.

We would like to thank the Kone Foundation for financing this project and the Finnish Literature Society for taking our concept with enthusiasm and for the approval of the book in its publications. In addition, we would warmly like to express our gratitude to the anonymous examiners who gave a positive review of our book.

Terhi Ainiala, Minna Saarelma, Paula Sjöblom and Leonard Pearl
Helsinki
September 2012

Abbreviations and Symbols

The following is a list of the most frequently used abbreviations and symbols in this book. Slang suffixes, for example, in chapters 3 and 4 and any other ending mentioned only once have not been listed here but clearly noted in the chapter in question.

Fin. = Finnish
Ger. = German
Grk. = Greek
Heb. = Hebrew
Lat. = Latin
Sám. = Sámi
Swe. = Swedish

Morphological symbols:
| = Compounding marker in place names, e.g. *Saarijärvi* 'island|lake'; also used to separate name parts in company names e.g. *Musiikki | Oy | Forte fortissimo* 'music | ltd | Forte fortissimo'
\+ = Morphological affixations in place names, e.g. *Järvenkangas* 'lake+GEN|moor'; compounding marker in personal names, e.g. *Mustapää* 'black' + 'head'
← = Derived from, e.g. *Amadeus* ← Lat. 'love' + 'God'
\- = A single lexeme in Finnish that would be a collocation in English, e.g. *Hietalahti* 'fine-sand|bay'
( ) = The part of a truncated name replaced by a slang ending, e.g. *Lönkka* 'Lön(nrotinkatu)+KKA' ← *Lönnrotinkatu* 'Lönnrot street'
* = Archaic form e.g. place name **Haapalaksi* 'aspen|bay'; unaccepted form e.g. in trade names **1991*

Derivational suffixes:
ADJ = Adjective suffix e.g. personal name *Hyväneuvonen* 'good' + 'advice+ADJ'
KKI = Feminising/diminutive suffix e.g. cattle name *Talvikki* 'winter+KKI'
LA = (*la* or *lä*) Name formation suffix traditionally used for a homestead name e.g. *Mattila* 'Matti+LA': 'house of Matti'; also used as a place name suffix in general e.g. *Syrjälä* 'border+LA'
NEN = Multipurpose name formation suffix: in place names, traditionally replacing a generic name part e.g. lake name *Saarinen* 'island+NEN' ← *Saarijärvi* 'island|lake'; in personal names, typical surname suffix e.g. *Virtanen* 'current+NEN' (this suffix has multiple other nominative functions, such as a diminutive function, however these are not presented in this book)
URI = (*uri* or *yri*) Agentive suffix e.g. surname *Nahkuri* 'leather+URI'
vA = (*va* or *vä*) First active participle e.g. place name *Koliseva* 'rattle+vA': 'rattling'

Inflectional suffixes:
ADE = Adessive (*lla* or *llä*) e.g. *Saimaalla* 'Saimaa+ADE': 'on/at Lake Saimaa'
GEN = Genitive (*n*), e.g. *Kaisanmökki* 'Kaisa+GEN|cottage'
INE = Inessive (*ssa* or *ssä*), e.g. *Helsingissä* 'Helsinki+INE': 'in Helsinki'
PL = Plural (*t* or *i*) e.g. *Naistenluoto* 'woman+PL+GEN|islet'

1. Theoretical Background to Onomastics

This introductory chapter gives a comprehensive overview of onomastics as a field of study, and tackles the core question of the discipline: what is a name. It covers the philosophy of names, the history of onomastics, onomastic terminology and categorisation as well as how onomastics has developed into an interdisciplinary field of research. The chapter focuses on two main perspectives: names as a part of language and names as a cultural phenomenon.

What is a Name?

The word *name* has two fundamental meanings. On the one hand, a *name* is a word or combination of words, such as *Eero* or *Baltic Sea*, referring to one identified person, being, subject or object, in which case the term *proper noun* or *proper name* can be used. On the other hand, it can mean a word or combination of words, such as *boy*, referring to persons, beings, subjects or objects as a representative of its class, whereupon we can speak of a *common noun* or an *appellative*. *Onomastics* is a branch of linguistics in which proper nouns are examined. In this discipline, the word *name* always refers to proper noun.

The word *name* has quite an old history to it. Similar forms can be found throughout the family of Indo-European languages, for example, in Sanskrit *nāman*, Latin *nōmen*, Italian *nome*, German *Name*, Swedish *namn*, Spanish *nombre* and French *nom*. The same root can also be seen in, for example, Russian имя (*imya*) and Greek όνομα (*onyma*). Equivalents to the word *name* have also reached the Uralic languages such as Finnish and Estonian *nimi*, Northern Sámi *namma*, Hungarian *név*, Mari *lüm* and Nenets *ńum'*. It has sometimes also been speculated that the broad distribution of the word is proof of early ties between the Uralic and Indo-European language families. (Häkkinen 2004.) Be that as it may, the age of the word shows us how important a concept it is. Different items and phenomena in an environment have generally been named as long as human language has existed.

The question of what a name is has piqued the interest of linguists and philosophers for hundreds, even thousands, of years. When we speak of names on a philosophical and theoretical level, we are always speaking about both meanings found in the human mind and our external reality. As the two-fold meaning of the word *name* already shows, expressions that are categorising and those that are identifying can somehow be quite similar to one another. They are both words of a language but moreover, common to them are the recognition and naming of various, real world phenomena and beings as well as those in the imaginative world. However, due to a certain something at their essence, they are considered different from each other. The Greek philosopher Aristotle divided these notions into the concepts of individual and class. The more abstract a concept is, the more beings are included in the set. Thus, a proper noun referring to one individual would be a more concrete concept. The most abstract concepts of all are hypernyms, which Aristotle called categories. Beings, substances, are designated by both proper and common nouns. Aristotle's contemporary Plato, for one, emphasised concepts, ideas: they are unchangeable and names represent these never-ending ideas.

Efforts have been made to define proper names through the concepts of philosophy and logic later as well. Common to these definitions, generally, is that they are seen as signs which are used to refer to individuals in the extralinguisic world. However, not all philosophers wish to see them specifically as linguistic signs. For example, Saul Kripke (1972) did not want to highlight the meaning of proper names in relation to linguistic form. Instead, he preferred to emphasise a referential relationship as well as the tradition of using proper names in a language community. The referential relationship of proper names emerges in special naming occurrences, in "christenings", where a certain form is connected to a certain object. Form can be any arbitrary symbol which functions as a label. Kripke was not alone in what he was thinking because many others have ignored the fact that names are linguistic signs and a part of language. Before Kripke, the idea of labels was presented by John Stuart Mill (1906) who stated that proper names designate extralinguistic objects and thus have no meaning. The view of the meaninglessness of proper names has been widely accepted in language theories from the 19th century all the way up to the present day.

Often, when speaking about the essence of proper names, reference is made to Bertrand Russell (1956) and John Searle (1969), according to whom the name *Romulus*, for example, is not in a strict logical sense a true name but rather a kind of truncated description of its referent. This description includes all of the necessary and sufficient features with which the referent that is indicated by the name is identified. The name *Romulus* represents a person who did certain things: a person who killed Remus, founded Rome and so on. A name, so to speak, is like a straightforward equivalent to this defining description. In other words, a name equates to what it refers to. A proposal given against this concept, for example, is that different speakers, who use the same name, would probably not define the name's referent in the same way. A proper name can be used effortlessly even though one would not be able to describe the characteristics of the object indicated by it at all. A referent can therefore not be the meaning of a name.

However, other kinds of views on the nature of proper names have been proposed as well. These views often emphasise the fact that linguistic forms are always meaningful. Proper names have meaning because of the fact that they are words in language, and words always have their "exchange rate": they are mental equivalents of reality (Gardiner 1940). Meaning must be understood to a broader extend than just a classifying meaning, like that of appellatival meaning. Names are different from appellatives in that they have a different function in language use. According to Ludwig Wittgenstein's (2001 [1953]) later thoughts on language, words do not describe their referents but rather, above all, the meaning of words are seen in how they are used. There are various word classes in language in the same way as there are different tools in a toolbox which are used for different purposes. According to Wittgenstein, the word *meaning* cannot mean the object that "corresponds" to this word because then the name would be confused with the name bearer. If we say that Mr X had died, it means that the name bearer had died, not the meaning of the name. If a name ceased to have meaning, the whole sentence would make no sense. Correspondingly, the views of Edmund Husserl (1929) and Eugenio Coseriu (1987), for example, emphasise the meaning of proper names which are only dissimilar to the meaning of an appellative.

So, names, as elements in language, are quite special, however it is not easy to linguistically define them. Nevertheless, most of us language users, on the basis of our sense of language, know quite well if a word is a proper noun. It is easy to see expressions such as *Helsinki*, *Amanda*, *Johnson*, *Blackie* and *Kalevala* as proper names but can we say that expressions such as *Pearl*, *Stone*, *Owl* and *the Internet* are names and equally as clear? In written form, we can interpret them as names because they begin with a capital letter but in speech, the only opportunity we have to identify the preceding expressions as proper names is to rest on context, that is, the environment in which the words appear. Can you say if the boldfaced words in the following sentences are proper names?

(1) *Every **Tom**, **Dick** and **Harry** is on the go!*
(2) *That student is a little **Einstein**.*
(3) *I bought some new **Reeboks**.*

Basically, in drawing the line between proper and common nouns, the expression's function has been considered to be the key criterion. Proper nouns are *monoreferential* which means that they have only one outside world *referent*. Names identify their referent, its object, by differentiating it from all other referents of the same class. In their context, the boldfaced expressions in sentences 1 to 3 do not work in an identifying function. They have a classifying function: Of those present in the situation in sentence 1, there is no one necessarily named *Tom*, *Dick* or *Harry*; the words refer to people in general. The student in sentence 2 may not be identified as *Einstein*, but rather this word refers to the student's characteristics; the student is like the Einstein we know, a genius. Sentence 3 is also not a question of an identifying expression; the word *Reeboks* classifies the sneakers or trousers as an item of clothing bearing a certain label.

In the same way as the recognition of names is often dependent on context, there is always a cultural and social context behind the emergence of individual names as well as name categories. Names are created and used for a specific purpose; the foundation of name giving is in our culture.

Names in Culture and Society

THE MANY FUNCTIONS OF NAMES

Onomastics is quite young for being a field of science. It first emerged in the 19th century as a sub-science contributing to research in language history, history and archaeology. For linguists, names have shed light on the history and distribution of words. They have given historians and archaeologists a clue on the expansion, routes, economy and livelihoods as well as true bio-geographic circumstances of settlement.

People have always been interested in names. There is a great interest in names because there are words preserved in them which are otherwise no longer known. By investigating these names and their referents, we can get an idea of what those words mean. For example, many geographic appellatives (*topographic words*) in contemporary Finnish, unfamiliar to its speakers, such as *vaha* meaning 'large rock', *rauma* 'inlet' and *köngäs* 'rapids', may appear in Finnish place names. Old, Finnish surnames and bynames ending with *uri* or *yri*, such as *Kankuri* ('cloth+URI'), *Nahkuri* ('leather+URI'), *Ojuri* ('ditch+URI') and *Vakkuri* ('bushel+URI') may be of interest to Finnish lexicologists because these names can be proven to be based on old occupational titles and by investigating them, information on the age of the words can be revealed to us (Nummila 2007). The same types of names in English ending in *er* can be seen in the same way as we compare these names to, for example, the surnames *Weaver* ('one who works with cloth') and *Lederer* ('one who works with leather').

Furthermore, with a name, we may get clues about the dwelling places of a people that disappeared a long time ago. For example, there are many place names today that are associated with Finno-Ugric languages in the Russian-speaking regions of Central and Northern Russia. These kinds of names make up as much as 10 to 15 per cent in certain regions. For example, there are numerous names of bends and grasslands located in the Arkhangelsk area along the Pinega River ending in *nem'*, a word akin to the Finnish word *niemi* ('cape') or small brooks which end with the element *oja* ('ditch'): e.g. *Kuzonem'* ← *Kuusiniemi ('spruce|cape'); *Murdoja* ← *Murtoja ('break|ditch'). It is probable that a Baltic-Finnic-speaking people resided in this area before its Russification. Likewise, from its origin or *etymology*, some unclear names of Finnish lakes have given scholars reason to suspect that perhaps some unknown Indo-European language had been spoken in the area of present-day Finland (Saarikivi 2006). Names can also help in reaching the tracks of old settlement routes. Those who colonised new hunting grounds and dwelling areas have given names to important places. By examining the lexicon included in place names and the circulation of name types, it has been concluded that the Torne River Valley and Kemijoki Valley were inhabited by hunters in prehistoric times who migrated from the Häme region in Southern Finland to the north. (Vahtola 1980.)

Onomastics has, for a long time already, been profiled as a linguistic field of research but still, it is strongly associated with many other scholarly fields. In addition to linguists, other types of scholars such as philosophers, geographers, cultural anthropologists, theologians, religious studies scholars, ethnologists, historians, archaeologists, researchers of literature, psychologists and neuropsychologists, sociologists, economists and marketing researchers, jurisprudents, statisticians all for different reasons are interested in names. Onomastics is, by nature, the kind of topic of research which simply attracts those interested in interdisciplinarity. Why?

The answer is simple: names are a part of culture. Names always come about in the interaction between people and a language community as well as their environment. A person gives a name to the referents which he feels are worth naming. An individual, a place, an object or thing that has its own name is always, in some way, meaningful to a person. Domesticated animals raised in large herds are not given names but when someone would like to make an animal an individual, the animal is given one. By naming, a person takes hold of the environment, in a way slaps a label on it and thus changes it as a part of his own culture. Human culture therefore creates names. On the other hand, names, being their own, unique elements of language, produce culture. Models can emerge and new names follow them. How we are used to forming names and what it is we hope for with a name are questions connected to the surrounding society and culture through the language-speaking community. The approval and establishment of names for common use always requires a community which has a fairly similar vision of the surrounding world and, thus, the ability to understand the motivation and social function of the name.

A sociocultural perspective is fundamental when the *function* of a name is defined or why a name is given and what is done with it. Because a name is a word in a language that has only one referent, a good many different images associated with this one special referent is attached to it. Because of this unique quality, names are often words quite rich in emotion. They become attached to its referent like a face to a person: a man is known by his name and the name won't make him any worse, no matter what the name is. If something gets a name change, we would be left empty-handed and would have to start from scratch in associating the new name to all of the things associated with the referent. Names and emotion go hand in hand. It could be, for example, an inanimate object but when strong emotions are associated with it, it can be given a name. Some people give names to their trusty bicycles or to their computers with which they have a love-hate relationship. In the beginning of the 1880s, a new, fabulous means of transportation which received *Orient Express* for its name made a huge impact in the human mind, whereas the name *Enola Gay* forever left its dark imprint on the collective memory of the world after this plane dropped the bomb *Little Boy* on Hiroshima. Because of its identifying function, a name has a special relationship to identity. We can perhaps recognise the solid relationship between a name and identity easiest through a first name but giving a name to a domestic animal, business, mode of transport, a loved one or a hated object is thoroughly based on our need to humanise these entities and therefore build an identity for them.

Influential features of almost mythical origin, occurring in different cultural circumstances, are sometimes associated with names. Let us take, as an example of these circumstances, the belief that changing the name of a ship will bring misfortune to the vessel or even, the commandment in the Old Testament that states "Do not take the name of the Lord in vain", which conveys the notion appearing in many cultures that a sacred name may not be spoken out loud. This same belief indeed touches upon common names of holy and threatening subjects: for example, the finger between the middle finger and the little finger is called "nameless" in some languages (for example, Finnish *nimetön*, Hungarian *nevetlen ujj*, Turkish *adsiz parmak*, Japanese *nanashi-yubi*, Russian *безымянный палец*) because there was a belief that a vein travelled straight to the heart from it and that this finger had power which required protection. The same idea is related to the way the word *unmentionables* is used when bashfully referring to women's undergarments.

A name is therefore a word charged with emotion but on the other hand, due to its identifying nature, it is quite a handy and economical expression: names make language use easy because when we talk about a particular place or certain person, we do not need to go so in depth in describing it to a listener each time. Place names help us navigate by extracting and identifying certain locations of the environment and personal names immediately conjure an image about a certain individual.

Names are important in regard to the operation of society and furthermore, the form and use of a name can be more or less jointly steered with given laws and decrees. There can be many kinds of socio-political problems associated with names: the public approval of and attention to ethnic and linguistic minorities' as well as small indigenous peoples' own names in their own languages go hand in hand with democracy and equal rights. Similarly, the issue of the right to a name has inevitably been connected to women's emancipation: who or what defines what name a woman gets to use or ends up using? Strong international relations, global politics and trade still have brought out a problem pertaining to names of different languages. On a high international level, through the United Nations (UN) in practice, we can contemplate about how to standardise the use of names in an international context and how in these situations we can take, for example, different writing systems of languages into consideration. In the *standardisation* of place names, the principle is to make an effort to use each area's population's mother tongue names or *endonyms* (*Wien, Göteborg, Nippon, Suomi, Sverige*) instead of using foreign name equivalents or *exonyms* (*Vienna, Gothenburg, Japan, Finland, Sweden*). In practice, it may be impossible to completely follow this principle.

Place names come from needs of convention: when we speak about places, we need expressions to help us recognise them. Name planners provide names to areas where there is development. Children name their playgrounds. Farmers name the fields where they work, and fishermen name their fishing grounds. Important landmarks, mountains, hills, forests, marshes, lakes, rivers etc. have been named so that we can discuss these places. With names, we can analyse our environment, and they show us what places we perceive as central regarding our actions. Place names also function as guides: they have assisted in navigation before and they do so now in the modern world. When advice about a road is given to someone who knows the nomenclature, it is easier to ask him to turn right at the intersection of *Main Street* or to choose the left lane at *Harrods* rather than describe the environment with the help of appellatives so that there would be no danger of being mistaken.

One function of place names is to indicate ownership or user rights to certain areas. This is carried out concretely by naming a place according to an owner or user (*Anttila* 'Antti+LA', a homestead name in Finland) but on deeper level, the naming event itself is often an indication of seizing of the place. During colonisation, Europeans conquered new areas of the world and gave their own names to these places they imagined to be untouched, in other words, places which were in reality already named long ago by peoples that originally lived in those areas. Those who have resettled in new dwelling places have always taken their toponymy along to their new home countries. A good example of this can be seen in the many city, state or regional names in America beginning with *New* such as *New Orleans*, *New York*, *New Jersey* and *New England* but also inside of the borders of their own country. Aside from seizure, perhaps a name also helps preserve the memory of a former place. With a name, as it were, the spirit of the place that had been previously known and the positive factors associated with it could be transferred to the new place. The cultural function of place names furthermore includes the preservation and transference of tradition and beliefs: names send us messages, remind us of things that occurred at the place with the help of stories connected to them, they tell us about beliefs and boundaries and also sustain social order.

Similarly, personal names have, in addition to their practical function, an extremely strong sociocultural function. With personal names, it is, of course, easy to talk about different individuals. However, they function not only as a tool for identification but also a tool for the social classification of an individual. A personal name therefore tells a community who the individual is and, secondly, lets the individual know what his place in the community is. Through a patronym (e.g. *Michelson*), paternity is recognised, the surname tells us to which family the name bearer belongs. A surname can sometimes even reveal something about the individual's social position: language users may, on the basis of their experience, recognise and differentiate a nobility name, a name of learned people or a peasant name from each other. Various abusive names and names of ridicule, used behind the name bearer's back, maintain the social order of the community, put a norm violator in his place and function as a warning to other members of the community. Social values have importance in the selection of a first name: the national background, mother tongue, religious convictions, and even social status of the name giver have an affect on name giving. For example, it has been proven in certain studies (Vandebosch 1998; Gerhards 2003) that the schooled in many European countries favour traditional names in their own languages, whereas those who are competent on a low-ranking educational level prefer to give their children popular, trendy names.

A name is an important part of a person's identity in all cultures of the world. The relationship between a name and an individual in various cultures is, however, understood in numerous ways. A personal name in the Western world is mostly perceived as meaningless label, whose function is only to refer to a certain individual and work as marker or symbol of this individual's identity. In some other cultures, a name and an individual is thought of as being the same, in other words, the name is like an icon of the individual. A child becomes a person only after receiving a name and a deceased family member will be kept alive in the child who bears his name. There are cultures in which there is the belief that a name will affect the individual's personality and those in which namesakes, for example, have quite a special relationship to one another. A name can wield magical powers: it can be used for sorcery and for power over people. The magic of a name is also founded on the custom of certain cultures to keep an individual's name a secret.

Although the Western world no longer thinks of a name as a something that determines the identity of a name bearer nor confines his development and change in society, there are signs in our thinking that pertain to beliefs associated with names. Naming children after living or deceased grandparents is common – more conventional in one country than another – and, for example, there is the hope, apart from practical reasons and particularly on an emotional level, that a surname will be carried on in future generations. Different changes occurring in identity often lead to name change in the Western world: changing religions is shown through the change of a first name (*Cassius Clay → Muhammad Ali*), marriage can lead to the changing of a surname and an author is transferred from one identity to another by writing, for example, a book under a pen name (Anne Rice: *Anne Rampling* and *A.N. Roquelaure*).

The need for *identifying* and humanising or *personifying* gets us to provide names to such referents that are not human nor are they even necessarily alive. Giving a name to a pet, the family car, a computer or a toy is a linguistic phenomenon where, at its deepest, it is a question of so-called *personification*, a metaphor in which a non-human being is seen as having human traits. This kind of thinking is common in language and culture, and it is even essential. Aside from the fact that we, as a language community, realise something as an individual, we consider it completely natural. Ships, trains, fighter planes, weapons, sales products, hurricanes, events, businesses and other inanimate objects and abstract subjects can be named and these names can have many different communicative and cultural functions.

Changing Names and Naming Systems

The fact concerning what referents can be given names, what kind of names are given and in which way they are named, varies in different cultures and different time periods. Because the nomenclatures of different cultures and naming customs are different, we must remember that contacts between cultures will also always affect nomenclature. Through time, name loans have been assimilated in both personal and place names from one culture to another. Today, name loans are increasingly more common as the influences between cultures are not only passed along through data transfer but also while an entire society becomes multicultural. *Loan names*, or names taken from another language, are easily adopted in first name nomenclature but different lexical and structural influences of loaning extend to all other nomenclature, especially to the nomenclature of commercial names.

Over time, many kinds of changes happen in nomenclatures. Individual names can be preserved as they are from one century to the next (Fin. *Laatokka* 'Lake Ladoga') or they can change phonologically (*Englaland* → *England*) or completely change into something else. Individual names can also disappear from use, whereupon signs of them may remain in old written sources or other nomenclature (for example, Old Finnish personal names can be found in toponymy) or, then again, they can disappear without a trace. Names in a greater danger of disappearing are those which are used by only a small group of people. These kinds of names are called *micronyms*. However, an extensive circle of users better guarantees the preservation of a name. These names that are known by many language users are *macronyms*.

Whole naming systems can also change. When speaking of a *naming system*, we are referring to a system that is formed by certain types of names where certain structural or functional principles are dominant. As the size of a community grows and its social structure changes, an anthroponymic system, for example, can shift from being a single naming system to a system of more than one name which may also include a surname system akin to what we now know. Then again, one system may disappear: for example, the patronymic system in which people are known on the basis of their own name and father's name, as seen in Icelandic (*Tómas Guðmundsson* 'Tómas, son of Guðmund', *Erla Elíasdóttir* 'Erla, daughter of Elías'), no longer exists in Finnish. Several scholars, such as Rudolf Šrámek (1972/1973), Eero Kiviniemi (1971, 1977) and Vincent Blanár (1991, 1996), have emphasised the systemic nature of nomenclature. According to these scholars, certain *name formation models* make up the foundation of naming systems. We can understand naming systems at greater length as totalities whose parts or individual names (and their possible subsystems they form) in some way depend on one another. The whole system is always more and something

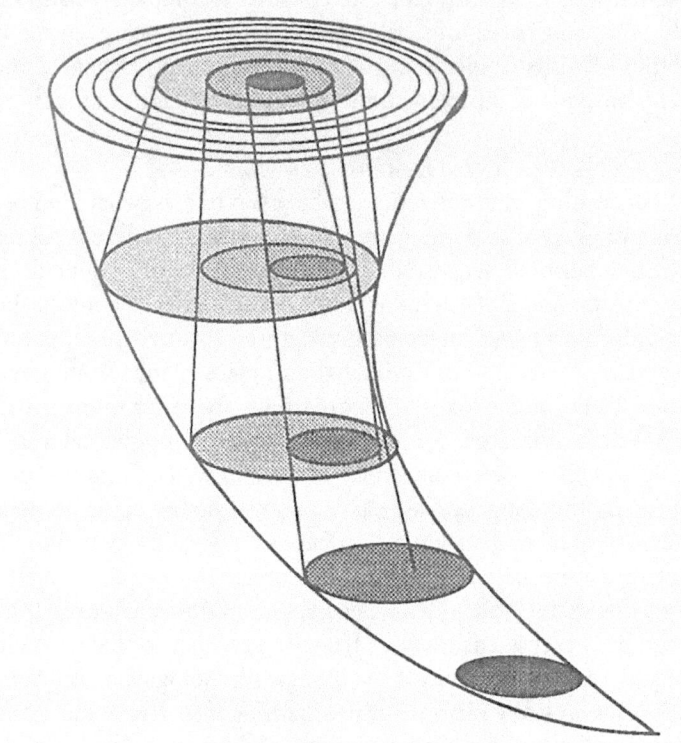

Fig. 1. Temporal strata of toponymy (Kiviniemi 1990).

else other than merely a sum of its parts. Because naming systems are open by nature, they are in a continuous state of change while being affected by the surrounding society, culture and language use.

Names form different strata over time. If we do a cross section of, for example, toponymy at a certain moment we can discover that simultaneously there are names of rather various ages in use. Eero Kiviniemi (1990) has illustratively described these place name strata of various ages in the "horn of plenty" as seen in fig. 1. The widest, upper part of the horn represents the present or a period to be examined where different, temporal name strata are viewed as "annual rings". The youngest name strata are the outermost rings and the more inward we go, the older the name strata gets. The oldest (innermost) strata are smaller by the number of names because the names have vanished during the passage of time. The levels pictured in the lower part of the horn are similar cross sections where name strata of various ages can be seen. The oldest strata of all, which is depicted by the curved shape of the horn, will not likely be seen anymore in modern nomenclature.

New names are continually emerging. A cultural and social context can be found behind both the creation of individual, new names and the development of whole name categories. The onset of a new name category is probable when a new phenomenon, a class of new referents, emerges and there is a need to individualise the members of the class by linguistic means.

Ship names would not be required if there were no ships and company names would be created only when company activity has been perceived as its own, independent entirety.

Personal names and place names are name categories which have already existed since ancient times. Many other name categories we know, however, have later emerged, some even in our recent history. However, the development of a new name category can be investigated by linguistic means by examining the ways of expression (appellatives and proper names) people begin to use for new phenomena and subjects in the environment (*onomasiology*), on the other hand by focusing attention on how the meanings of certain expressions extend and change to proprial use (*semasiology*). We can use the category of company names as an example of these different perspectives. When people, a few centuries ago, began to perceive businesses as their own independent activities and not just as an activity of individuals, the need to speak of these new subjects arose by personalising them. When we examine what kinds of expressions are used on individual businesses, it is taken from an onomasiological perspective. When we examine how some expressions have first been more appellatival, such as *Waseniuksen kirjakauppa* ('Wasenius' book shop'), and how later they gradually have developed into regular forms and contextually more and more types that have taken on proprial features, then it is a question of a semasiological perspective. Proper nouns are not necessarily required for describing new referents. Only little by little, when we speak of these referents in the cultural environment in which we live, can expressions be perceived as proper names in our sense of language. The formation of a language community's shared perception may even take quite a long time. The aforementioned instance specifically concerns the creation of a new name category. It is important to note that new names generally emerge in an existing name category directly as a name – that is, they are not developed from appellatives.

CATEGORISATION OF NAMES

What then are name categories found in onomastics? How can names be categorised? These questions are important because names are varied both by their linguistic structure and their sociocultural function. It is essential, in onomastics, that the investigator perceives the whole field of nomenclature in relation to his own topic of research, and understands what it has in common and what kinds of differences it has considering other sub-branches.

Traditionally, research in onomastics has focused on the investigation of place names or *toponyms* and personal names or *anthroponyms*, in other words, on *toponomastics* and *anthroponomastics*. The term *toponymy* is used for place name nomenclature and *anthroponymy* for personal name nomenclature. In Finnish onomastics, for example, there has been a greater focus on toponomastics, hence the classification of place names has traditionally been more centrally focused. Place names are normally divided into two groups: nature names and culture names. *Nature names* are those whose referent is a natural place (for example a sea, a mountain or a forest) and *culture names* are those whose referent is a place built or formed by humans (for example a field, a road or a house). Nature names can roughly be divided into two groups, *topographic names* (for example the name of a bog or rock) and *hydronyms* (for example the name of a lake or ditch). Culture names can be divided into *settlement names* (such as homestead or village names), *cultivation names* (such as names of fields and meadows) and *artefact names*. This last category includes names of roads, bridges, dams and other structures. Personal names of the modern Western naming system can roughly be divided into three groups: *first names* and *surnames* in the official naming system as well as *unofficial bynames*.

The changing of our habitat – the migration of people from a rural environment to cities, facilitation of movement, acceleration of communication and the globalisation of our actions – has created many new name categories and has enhanced our lives with the significance of new names that have come up in these categories. The creation of cities has once been in close connection to commerce and a large group of different nomenclature has been developed around commerce. New means of transport, many various organisations and communities as well as mass happenings are significantly important. Through media, we are interested in things which people did not know about before mass communication such as natural disasters or wars happening on the other side of the globe or the undertakings of a movie star or footballer's wife. Nomenclature often pertains to all these phenomena and we even understand it to be a part of common knowledge. This is why modern onomastics has to take many other sub-branches of nomenclature, in addition to place names and personal names, into consideration.

There are different ways to classify the whole field of names into rational sub-branches. In classification models generally presented in various research, we can start off from referents of names, in other words we can classify such phenomena in the world that can receive a name. In 1940, Alan Gardiner classified names into groups this way although the members of these groups may not even be considered proper nouns in every language. There were – indeed a bit uniquely grouped – for example, place names, personal names, animal names, ship names, house names and celestial names in his classification but also such groups as titles, names of the months and holidays. Examples such *January* and *Christmas* would be included in this latter group. However, months and holidays, for example, do not really have any specific referent and have more of a classifying rather than identifying function. Because of this, the corresponding *tammikuu* and *joulu* in Finnish are not considered proper nouns, which is why they begin with a lowercase letter. He also makes note, in his investigation, of patent medicine and commercial products as such referent groups which can receive a name.

After Gardiner, a number of scholars have presented referent-based classification models, some more randomly, others quite logically, following his chosen principle. In 1985, Gerhard Bauer classified names so, that the relation of a referent to a person was his point of view: for example, personal names are names whose referent is a person, the referent of place names is a person's habitat and the referent of an event name is a person's actions.

Swedish scholar Bengt Pamp made an extensive and quite consistent classification in 1994. He set off from names of living beings, in other words, personal names as well as animal and plant names, after which a third group made up of place names. A fourth group included concrete names of objects (aeroplanes, weapons, works of art etc.), then places more abstract names of events and eras (for example *Baroque* which may not be considered a name at all in some languages) and the last being group names which are brought together by abstraction (names of books, names of compositions, company names, trademarks).

In his classification system of names, Wilbur Zelinsky (2002) aimed at extreme accuracy. His classification included eight main classes, under which there were altogether over 130 name categories. This classification was in places up to a four tier system. His idea was to achieve a classification which would encompass the entire broad field of onomastics and thus would also enable an extensive development of nomenclature theory. At the same time however, he showed that name types are continuously being created all the time, along with society, technology and education. Basically, there were no limits to referents, which can generally receive a name. A classification system that aims at perfection in the end serves no one because, consequently, we would end up classifying the extralinguistic world and not names starting off from names themselves.

It is important to understand that the classification of nomenclature depends on many factors. Classification is unavoidably language-specific because the concept of "name" is understood in different ways in different languages. For example, as in English, many German scholars consider language and nationality terms to be proper nouns, whereas in Finnish, for example, these terms are not considered as such. Classification is also system-specific: we can examine certain naming systems and categorise the names included in them into different classes or examine the relationship of different names systems to one another. Classification ultimately always depends on the perspective the investigator himself chooses. If the foundation for classification is based upon the referents of names, the surrounding world that the names mirror will, in actuality, be classified instead of them. The ability to categorise world phenomena is a basic human trait whereupon there is also a well-founded aim to classify nomenclature on the basis of our perceived categories of these phenomena. This kind of classification can depart from, for example, a cultural point of view as seen in fig. 2 (Sjöblom 2006). If we investigate, for example, place names, this kind of classification would not necessarily satisfy us because with it, we cannot outline toponymy as a whole, as its own system. The most important thing to understand is that the investigator must always himself outline and define the relation of his own topic of research to other nomenclature and place it to a certain naming system.

As Paula Sjöblom (2006) has pointed out, a more in depth view to the classification of names unfolds when we set off from the aforementioned human tendency of categorisation itself. We can base a classification for how a person is generally accustomed to lingually analyse and conceptualise his

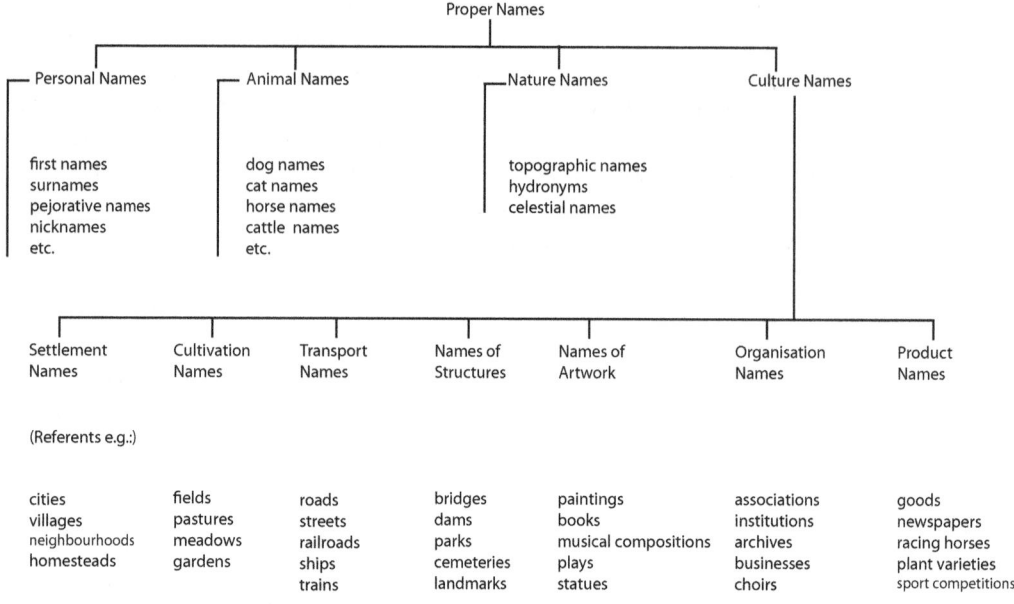

Fig. 2. Classification of proper names from a cultural perspective in Finnish onomastics.

environment. In line with certain, cognitive trends in linguistics (e.g. Lakoff 1987) is the thought that the human practice to categorise is dependent on our own corporality, hence our physical traits and interaction with our environment. On the other hand, we have the fundamental cognitive ability of empathy with which we can conceive another's experiences and which enables the awareness of ourselves as part of our environment. The same empathy, for example, leads us also to the fact that we believe that pets experience human emotion.

On the basis of the aforementioned issue, we can take off from a name itself, not its referent, in classification and consider what the basic purpose of naming is: do we want to designate the referent as an important part of human environment, that is, to categorise the referent as a place with a name, do we want to designate the referent as human (as a person or human-like) with a name or is the purpose of naming only a need to designate the referent as a distinction from other comparable referents? Place names arise because we have a need to analyse our physical environment and personal names, animal names and other such names arise because we want to reflect our own human experiences in others. However, not all names are necessarily based on these two needs. A name can merely identify. (Sjöblom 2006.) However, at the same time, the structure and/or content of a name, for example, often give a clue about to what category the name's referent belongs. This kind of *categorical meaning* included in the name itself, that is, the information included in the name on the referent's category is called *presuppositional meaning* (Van Langendonck 1997). This means, for example, that without knowing the referent, we can recognise certain names be they a man's name, a surname, a cattle name, a homestead name or the name of a restaurant.

Names are classified in this book, from the viewpoint of studies done thus far, roughly into groups according to referents: place names, personal names, animal names, commercial names and names in literature. The classification within each group can vary according to perspectives in research. For example, besides nature and cultural names, place names can be classified according to rural names and urban names or unofficial or official names. Animal names can be divided up according to species into cat, dog, cow, horse etc. names or even domestic pet names, domestic animal names, so-called breeder names (such as dog kennel names) and other animal names (*Keiko* the orca in Free Willy, *Paul* the octopus that predicted many football winners).

In the examination of names, the investigation and categorisation of their structure and content, taking a person as an individual that gives and uses names into consideration is essential. It is also necessary to take the language community and its social and cultural customs and societal needs as a context in which names are used and created. Of course, names can be examined as they are as a part of language and language use, in other words, pragmatics will always have an effect on interpretations. Anyone studying names or utilising names in their research should also always take these perspectives into consideration.

Names in Language

NAMES AND APPELLATIVES

Names are, above all, a part of language and they are a part of our shared language environment and language use. Humans have been giving names to people, and perhaps also to places, probably for as long as natural human language has existed. Names are considered universal, elements that are encountered in all the languages of the world.

Scholars have different opinions on the question of if the first words in the evolution of language were proper names that refer to one being or if they were appellatives that categorise many beings into one category. There is no unambiguous answer to this question and we will probably never arrive at one but we do know that the human brain processes proper names and appellatives in different ways. In some studies, it has been observed that first names and place names are recognised faster than appellatives or, for example, brands. In certain neuropsychological studies, it has been proven that the recognition of proper names is seen as a reaction on the right side of the brain, where information concerning a composite, complete perception is generally processed, and the recognition of appellatives is located on the left half of the brain, which generally is key regarding linguistic activities and analytical processes (Müller 2003). On the other hand, injuries to the left side of the brain, in addition to other language disorders, often also cause difficulties in remembering names.

There would seem to be a neurological difference in the processing of proper names and appellatives. Appellatives pertain to a person's tendency to categorise phenomena of his surroundings, that is, to find common features between beings, objects or things on the basis of which they can be collected as one group. This, for one, is based on the ability to break down the details and traits of different subjects. Proper names, on the other hand, are associated with a person's ability to discern the big picture: we combine the features of a certain being, object or thing as one totality in our minds and we perceive how this totality differs from comparable totalities. What is noteworthy to state is that when we use proper names, our minds also simultaneously end up categorising because while perceiving a totality, it is necessary for us to understand to what category this totality belongs. A proper noun requires or presupposes a particular category: we assume that a person named *Andrew* is male, *Rover* is a dog and *Smallville* (albeit fictional) is a town or city.

When we consider the development of proper names in language and the difference between proper names and appellatives in the human mind and human thought, one fundamental, new point of view could be provided by a study in which a child's language, especially children's language in the early stage of language development, is explained. Unfortunately, there has been little research done dedicated to children's awareness and use of names. Hopefully, there will be more research done in the future to explain language development in children with regard to proper nouns and would therefore perhaps shed some light on these research questions on the theory of names.

Appellatives are thus categorising words of a language but in a certain sense, this categorisation is associated with proper names as well. In this context, it is important for us to stop for a moment at the tendency of human categorisation as such and state that not all members of the same category can be connected to one another by virtue of certain, necessary features but instead, the fact that they resemble one another, much like family members or relatives do, is more of what unites these category members. This so-called notion of family resemblance was brought up by Ludvig Wittgenstein (2001 [1953]): for example, things which we call "games" do not have any such features which would be common to them all but rather different games (card games, board games, ball games, children's games) resemble one another in different ways and form a network of overlapping and crosswise similarities. Similarly, for example, having wings, the ability to fly, bipedalism and a beak are traits that are associated with birds but none of them are sufficient enough to categorise a being as a bird (mammals that have wings, the ability to fly, are bipedal and have a beak, also exist), and on the other hand, they are also not necessary in order for us to identify the being as a bird. A penguin is a bird although it cannot fly and a pigeon is a bird even if it would have lost one of its legs in an accident. On the basis of our ability to categorise, we have a certain conception of a *prototype* of a bird and we mirror the traits of all the potential category members in this prototype. Some beings resemble the prototype more, some do less.

Prototypicality, a concept used to quite a great extent in linguistics, is applicable to onomastics as well. Let us take a look at, for example, the category of "proper noun". What makes a prototype of a proper noun? What would people answer if they were asked to give a proper noun? To what name category would this name belong? They would quite probably give a first name, either their own or someone's name close to them, or some other first name or place name known to them. Very few people think of some name of a company or composition as their first example. What kind of form of a name would be perceived as being prototypical? Such expressions as *London* and *Landon* would probably be "more" of a proper name than perhaps *Student Village* and *Heather*. Prototypicality explains why it is sometimes difficult to draw the line between proper names and appellatives. There are expressions in language which all speakers consider to be proper names without context but there are also such expressions which are placed on the borderline of a category and whose interpretation as a proper name depends on the word's context in which it occurs.

Grammatically, names are always *definite* expressions. When looking at languages which have articles, we can note that names can equally be expressed in an indefinite (*Lund*, *Smith*) as in a definite (*Expressen*, *The Post*) form, depending on the language and the name; however, the element expressing definiteness does not have a normal grammatical function (Dalberg 1985). Such names which do not take an article cannot get one either because a name as such tells us that it is a question of some specific, known referent. Therefore, we cannot normally say **The Tom came by train.* However, nicknames, such as *The Donald* which famously refers to Donald Trump, are an exception to this due to the phenomenon associated with unofficial bynames. It is also grammatically characteristic for names to have a singular function in a sentence even though their surface form may be in plural. This can be seen in the lack of verbal and pronoun congruency in a sentence such as ***The United States is*** *sending **its** representative to the conference* and this lack of congruency is also featured in other languages such as Finnish.

Basically, recognising and distinguishing a name from appellatives is usually clear. In practice, however, we can encounter different demarcation problems. These are roughly divided into three: 1) The expression, taken without context, is clearly a proper noun but seems to have, in one way or another, a classifying meaning in certain contexts. 2) The expression is used monoreferentially but, at the same time, the expression can refer to different referents in an individualising way in different situations. In some sentential contexts, we can think that the same expression, at the same time, has several different referents whereupon the expression will be given a classifying tone instead of definiteness. 3) The expression, completely regardless of context, is possible to interpret either as individualising or classifying.

The first problem concerns the cases seen in example sentences 1 to 3 on page 15 in which the expressions would be, without context, perceived as proper names but which, in these particular contexts, are presented as appellatives. This is possible if we think that the proper noun is, in our minds, in connection with other words of the language. When we have common images that are linked with the name *Einstein*, it is possible to use the word as an appellative too, whereupon the expression gets the classifying meaning of 'brilliant, inventive' through a metaphor. When the title "New Chernobyl Unlikely" appeared in 2005 in a local newspaper, it did not mean that it is unlikely that the city of Chernobyl will be rebuilt or go under some other kind of restoration but that a new, immense nuclear accident is, in general, not likely expected to happen anywhere in the world. The name *Chernobyl* has received a classifying meaning of 'nuclear disaster of catastrophic proportions'. Product names, for example, can get an appellatival meaning in the same way. Sometimes, appellatival use even leaves the original propriality completely in its shadow. *Xerox* is a trademark of photocopiers of the Xerox Corporation but the word *xerox* completely became an appellative synonymous with the terms 'photocopy' and 'photocopier'.

There are names which are apparently *polyreferential*, in other words, they have a number of different referents. These include, for example, many first names and surnames (we can point out many *John Smiths*), some place names (there are several places with the name *Pyhäjärvi* 'sacred|lake' in Finland) and all product names (*Marimekko* curtains or *IKEA* furniture can be found in many homes). Context, however, will generally indicate if it is a case of a monoreferential expression referring to one individual, or a polyreferential appellative including a classifying meaning. The examples in sentences such as 4 through 6, which are modified examples of the name *Cambridge* given by Klaas Willems (2000), pose this problem. *Pyhäjärvi*, presented in all of these, seems to be monoreferential but it is clearly a proper noun in sentence 4 only. By its basic nature, a proper noun is a definite expression. Words that express definitiveness in connection with *Pyhäjärvi* such as *this* or *the same* give reason to presume that the expression that is defined by them also has an indefinite and classifying meaning, a certain kind of class of Pyhäjärvis. In this case, the solution for interpretation is hidden in its context.

(4) We have a cottage in **Pyhäjärvi**.
(5) **This Pyhäjärvi** has clear waters.
(6) We are not speaking of **the same Pyhäjärvi**.

The opposite can happen in language use: an indefinite article or some word expressing indefiniteness can be added to a definite name such as in example 7 or a numeral as in example 8. The expressions in these two aforementioned examples are perhaps easier to interpret as proper names than those in examples 5 and 6.

(7) There's **a** Maria Svensson on the phone.
(8) There are **three** Edwards in the class.

Such expressions which can, regardless of context, be interpreted as proper names or appellatives (example sentence 9) make up the third problem group. They can function in language use like proper names, that is, referring to one specific referent. However, if their form exactly corresponds to some appellatival word and the referent corresponds to the meaning of the appellative, the information on the situation will not necessarily even help us interpret if the speaker meant for the word to be a proper name or appellative. As a matter of fact, the speaker himself will not necessarily think about it or can even say.

(9) Nähdään **Ojalla/ojalla** kello kolme!
'See you **in Oja / by the ditch** at three o'clock!'

Names which have an appellatival, visually similar equivalent or *homonym* (such as *Oja* a place name and *oja* 'ditch'), or elements included which can be recognised as words of a language, are lexical-semantically *transparent*. These kinds of names include, for example, the place name *Land's End*, the Finnish male given name *Veli* (*veli* 'brother') or the horse name *Shooting Star*. Names such as the place name *Oulu*, the surname *Huxtable* or the company name *Nokia* can be lexical-semantically *opaque*. Most transparent names are easily recognisable as names because they could not have exactly the same semantic homonym. Hardly one would very easily use appellatives in Finnish such as *koivulahti* 'birch|bay' or *rautavaara* 'iron|hill', which are quite common as proper names. Moreover, such useful expressions as appellatives such as the *White House* are identified as proper names based on word stress (cf. *the white house*) and, in Finnish, on grammatical inflection of the morphemes of the name or word (*Korkeasaaressa* 'high|island+INE': 'on Korkeasaari' or *korkeassa saaressa* 'high+INE island+INE': 'on a high island').

Meaning of Names

A name works in a name's identifying function regardless if we recognise the elements included in the name or not. When thinking of a name's identifying function, whether or not the name is transparent or opaque is insignificant. Because of this, certain onomasticians (such as Zilliacus 1997) have emphasised that a name's linguistic content has no meaning. Supporting an extreme viewpoint are the notions that a name has no meaning at all (Mill 1906) or that names do not belong to linguistic units although they are indeed needed in communication (Nicolaisen 1997).

According to the opinions of a number of academics, proper nouns are nevertheless considered to be genuine words of a language. Words of a language are always, in one way or another, indeed significant. According to the classical definition, a linguistic sign is a unit which simultaneously includes an expression made up of sounds, mental content or meaning as well as an extralinguistc counterpart, that is, a referent. On the basis of this definition, we can already consider that a proper name must have some kind of meaning situated in the human brain, although this meaning cannot be described in the same way as, for example, the appellative *cat* can be described in a dictionary.

When speaking of the meaning of a name, we often think about the *lexical meaning* of words included in it, in other words, the dictionary meaning of appellatives used in name formation. Most names at the time of name giving are, thus, motivated expressions that are descriptive of their referents. For this original, semantic content of a name, that is, what an expression understood as a name meant at the time of name giving, we can use the term *etymological meaning*, or sometimes also *identifying meaning*. Etymological meaning is interesting when the names are interpreted from the name bearer's point of view, whereas regarding the name's context of use, etymological meaning is irrelevant.

It is easy to show examples in which the meaning of name elements are also interpreted in a situation of language use and the meanings connected to the form of the name are relevant regarding the use of the name. The name *Venus* can refer to many different referents, one of which is a planet that orbits the Sun, like Earth. This Venus is also known in everyday language by two other names: the *Morning Star* and the *Evening Star*. All three of these different names have the same referent. However, a name cannot be used in just any kind of way. It would be strange if someone would remark, when gazing at the dark, star-filled sky at night, how bright the Morning Star is shining today. On the other hand, it would hardly be feasible to talk about anything other than Venus in a scientific paper. A name, therefore, includes lexical-semantic and stylistic boundaries of usage. Likewise, for example, name changes of companies such as when changing the line of business (for example, *Postipankki* 'post bank', a public limited company that started in 1887 as a bank run by the Finnish government, became a financial group called *Leonia* in 1997) shows how we can think of the meanings connected with a form of a former name as somehow being "wrong". A name of ridicule (such as *Lazy Larry* or *Skinny Vinnie*) is meant to be understood – it is not insignificant what the lexical meaning of the name elements is because without this meaning, a name of ridicule would not work in the function of this type of name.

A name's referential relationship to its referent is called *denotation*. We should know that there are different meanings associated with the word in linguistic and onomastic research literature but in Finnish onomastics, the term is usually defined in the aforementioned way, whose origin stems from the definition provided by semanticist John Lyons (1984). The second term, misleadingly used in different meanings, is *connotation*. In onomastics, this could be defined as contents of information, images or associations pertaining to a name. A name can include such common meanings to language speakers that have no point of reference to the words included in the name. These associations can be common to language speakers or completely subjective, one person's own image. Connotations pertain to all the information which we have gathered on the name's referent. Every one of us, of course, creates our own connotations about a name but there are many connotations which are common to every group of speakers, such as a family or an entire language community, and the appellatival use of names, for example, is precisely based on these connotations. As the name *Marilyn* conjures an image of a sexy blonde, it is a question of a connotation common to language speakers but if the name *Rainer* brings a caretaker or janitor to mind, it is a question of connotation based on subjective experience.

In addition to the aforementioned presuppositional meanings, lexical-semantic associations and connotations founded on information, names can, to some extent, also include common emotionally based or *affective meanings*. Generally, however, these meanings are a great deal more subjective than categorical presuppositions, lexical associations aroused by name elements or informational connotations.

Because a name, as a genuine linguistic sign, has semantic content in the human mind in addition to a linguistic form and an extralinguistic referent, it is natural that people sometimes try to "explain" names that seem strange with some story associated with them. These kinds of interpretations are called *folk etymologies*. They are folk-type explanations to a name which have been lexically changed into opaque ones or whose original reason for naming has somewhat been obscured either in the referent or in the name itself due to some change that occurred. For example, people can interpret the Finnish lake name *Oijärvi* as having the interjection *oi* 'oh' with *järvi* 'lake' when in fact it is a phonetic contraction of the original *Ojajärvi 'ditch|lake' (Kiviniemi et al 1974). Another example is that the story of seven royal huntsmen whose horses drank from a stream in a suburban area of northeast London is not connected to its name *Seven Kings* but in fact is most likely derived from a Saxon place name *Seofecingas*, the settlement of Seofeca's people (Mills 2001).

The question of ambiguity, *polysemy*, is also associated with the meaning of names. In the case of Finnish onomastics, there has traditionally been the thought that because monoreferentiality is included in a name's essence, every name with a similar appearance that refers to a different referent is a different name. Let us take the name *Kivijärvi* ('stone|lake') as an example. It is natural for Finnish speakers to think that because this name is used both for the lake and the municipality (located in Central Finland), it is a question of two different names. Because, in Finland, a lake name existed first, its name is a *primary name*, and the residential centre that sprung up in the vicinity of the lake was named after it. This is a *secondary name* and as a name it is one of *metonymic transference*, a name that has been transferred from one adjacent location to another. The referents of these names are clearly different from each other. Another kind of situation, however, is when some name of a specific referent is used for a part that is inseparably and closely included in it. Someone could say "I was in *London* for the weekend" and specifically mean by this that he stayed at his own dwelling located in the city area and did not, for example, go shopping in the City of London. In this case, the name *London* refers to a dwelling place but it would be appropriate to think that it would not be a question of another *London* but rather a case of flexible extension or compression of the name's meaning, a certain kind of polysemy. In short, a name is polysemic when it is used for a referent closely associated to another but it is a question of two different names if they are used for clearly different referents. (Sjöblom 2006.) However, this does not hold true, as such, for personal names for which polyreferentiality is natural: personal names that refer to different human beings (*Susanne, Johnson*) are understood as the same name.

Many aforementioned notions on the linguistic nature of names reflect the views of broad-based cognitive language theory and partly functional language theory as well. *Cognitive linguistics* is a discipline of linguistics that came on the scene at the end of the 20th century, according to which, language is inextricably connected to cognitive structures of the human mind. Language is not examined as a disconnected, autonomous system but rather examined in relation to a person, a person's information structures or cognition, circumstances of communication and social interaction. Deviating from certain preceding language theories, meaning has a central status in the cognitive description of language. The starting point is that the function of language is to produce meanings that, at the same time, always have some function. In cognitive linguistics, language is perceived with the help of *symbolic units*. They are complete totalities, automatically used by speakers and form is united with the meaning in these totalities. A symbolic unit can be word in a language, but it can also be, for instance, a totality broader than a word, even the saying *it's on the tip of my tongue*. An important concept in regard to onomastics is a *cognitive domain*, our storage area of information where the meanings of expression are proportioned. We can consider the fact that proper names can arouse connections to different cognitive domains, such as a personal name to the image of a person's appearance, voice, walking style, temperament, position in his family, society and so on. A name is a common indicator of all these meaning relationships. Units of a language form a network of meanings in our minds, in which their meanings are connected to one another. Against this theoretical background, it is easy to see names as being language units equal to other words. Cognitive linguistics has been utilised in onomastics by Willy Van Langendock (2007), Antti Leino (2007), Staffan Nyström (1998) and Paula Sjöblom (2006) among others.

Over time, different theoretical viewpoints in linguistics have had an effect on onomastics, the most visible perhaps being generative theory, which divides a language system into clearly separate sub-systems. This theory operates on the idea that expressions in a language are formed according to strict and all-inclusive rules. In regard to description, syntax is foundational and semantics only interprets it. According to the theory, an expression has a semantic *deep structure* which, with rules, can be phonologically transformed to a *surface structure*. This kind of outlook to language has had an especially strong influence on Finnish toponymy in which Kurt Zilliacus and Eero Kiviniemi in particular have utilised generative theory; Swedish scholar Bengt Pamp is also a self-confessed supporter of the *generative linguistics* point of view. Connecting – according to the basic notion of generative grammar – meaning as a separate component to a model emphasising linguistic form and sentence structure has lead us to think of meaning in a dictionary-like way and stress the meaninglessness of a proper name. On the other hand, we have been able to semantically analyse transparent names in a novel way by examining the *principles of naming*, that is, the grounds according to which a name is given. These principles of naming are, as it were, semantic deep structures to which surface structures, that is, the existing name forms, can be recovered. In this way, we can get to know why a name giver has given the referent in question precisely this specific name. This point of view is decidedly not the same as in earlier 1960s onomastics, in which conceptual spheres or categories of lexical elements included in the name were only explained.

The notion of principles of naming includes the concept of identification. It must still be noted, while speaking of these principles, that discrimination is essential in naming: names are given so that the same types of referents can be differentiated from one another. Because of this, each trait that is common to referents is generally not good enough for the principles of naming. What is common in culture or society is often in rare nomenclature and vice versa. The foundation for naming is such a special feature which clearly enough, from the language community's perspective, differentiates one referent from others. Two similar, equally widespread known names cannot occur in the same community either. If, for example, all the lakes in some region would be full of whitefish, it is quite unlikely that one *Muikkujärvi* 'whitefish|lake' would be named in the area. On the other hand, *Riihilahti* 'drying-barn|bay' works as a name of a bay even if it wouldn't be the only bay in the area whose shore has a drying barn, if the other bays of the area have been named in some other way. (Kiviniemi 1978.)

Name Typology

In onomastics, it is important to highlight, on the one hand, the individual that uses language, and on the other hand, the language community's perspective. Naming and the interpretation of names are always the action of both the individual and the community. The name giver is an individual and the first who uses a certain expression but approving the expression as a name requires the community, a group that starts to use this expression in the function of a name. So-called *planned names* make up an exception to this practice as these names are those formed for official use. They are approved in official decision-making processes and adopting them does not therefore require the approval of the entire language community.

Of course, a name giver is himself always a member of the language community. He lays the naming foundation for names already in existence used by the language community, name models. These models can be structural (for example, Finnish town or city names ending in la or lä, such as *Kokkola* and *Rääkkylä*) or lexical (for example, Finnish hydronyms starting with *Väärä* such as *Vääräjoki* 'crooked|river' and *Vääräkoski* 'crooked|rapids'). Naming is *analogous*, which means that some other nomenclature, in one way or another, acts as a model for new names. Using names and their interpretation at their moment of use are also all the time linked to name giving. All the names we know make up our mental storage of names or *onomasticon*.

The notion once presented by Gottfried Wilhelm Leibniz, that names had originally been appellatival expressions, only concern either the early stages of language development, whereupon the difference between appellatives and proper names were still not clear, or the emergence stage of a new name category. When a new name emerges in an existing name category, it emerges in a set naming system model. While creating a new name, an expression according to dominating *name formation rules* is formed, which is recognised as a proper name on the basis of specific distinguishing features and which can not easily be confused with appellatives. In place of rules or the grammar of names, we can speak of *name typology* which refers to a name's classification into different types on the basis of structural circumstances. Language speakers recognise these different name types of the language and analogously form new names, complying with typological name models.

The typological information of names includes information on what the names phonologically, morphologically, syntactically and semantically are. Phonological information includes information on the sound structure of names, such as the fact that most names ending with *a* are female first names. Morphological information helps us recognise the features of the name's form, for example surnames ending in *son* or place names ending in *ville*. The syntactic information tells us how a name's elements are connected to one another and in what kind of syntactic relation they are in comparison to each other. For example, there are such compound names as *Chapel Hill* or *Jamestown* whose initial parts can be recognised as either being in the nominative or genitive case which syntactically modifies the nominative formed word that is the final part of the name. Semantic information is the information on the content of meaning which, on the one hand, can be information on what kind of meanings are included in the words being name elements, on the other hand why a certain kind of name is given to a certain referent.

In Finnish onomastics, there are two concepts that have been used for quite some time now that have been proven to be advantageous in the structural analysis of names: *name element* (*nimenelementti*) and *name part* (*nimenosa*). We should point out that what is known as the frequently used term *name element* in international onomastics is what we call *name part* in this book. In our view, the terminological classification utilised in Finnish clarifies and systematises the analysis of names which is why we propose that it be introduced here. All of the separate morphological elements that are included in a name make up what is called a *name element*: words, derivational affixes and endings. We can apply this approach to an English example. For instance, we can separate the name *King's Road* into three different name elements: *King*, genitive case ending *'s* and *Road*. The term *name part* is used in the syntactic approach to the analysis and refers to an expression included in the name which signifies one feature characteristic to the referent. There are thus two name parts in *King's Road*: *Road*, signifying the type of place and *King's*, which signifies a special feature of the place.

Names are structured from different name elements, that is, words, inflectional endings, derivational affixes and also compounding. In the typological analysis of names, it can be noted that their name elements syntactically play different roles in comparison to one another. The Finnish name *Hietalahdenkatu* ('Hietalahti+GEN|street' ← *Hietalahti* 'fine-sand|bay') has three words (and one genitive ending) being name elements but these words have different roles in comparison to one another. The appellative *katu* 'street' signifies the place itself and the place name in the genitive *Hietalahden* qualifies it. Hence, there are two name parts in this name: *katu* is the structural *generic part* of the name and its preceding place name is its *specific part*. We previously distinguished the term *name element* used in Finnish onomastics from its international use. In turn, the terms *generic element* and *specific element* are also quite frequently used in international onomastics. However, in this book, we shall use the terms *generic part* and *specific part* to coherently be in accordance with the Finnish onomastic term *name part*.

When name typology is examined, information is provided on what kinds of structural features, which lexical elements and what kinds of relationships between names belonging to naming systems are common in nomenclature. In a typological study of names it is important to clarify the general structure of the nomenclature with the help of vast materials. Quite unlike it could have been considered in the early days of Finnish onomastics, regular, common names are nowadays thought of as interesting because with them, information can also be available on rare and special names. It is important to know what kinds of lexical elements for a name in a name category are generally preserved and what makes the most common names. It is also interesting to examine what kinds of structures are prototypical in various nomenclatures. For example, typological information of names concerning toponymy can easily reveal which region or part of the region the name comes from on the basis of place names of just one area. Likewise, on the basis of this knowledge, an investigator can make conclusions on subjects from the history of the area. When we know what is commonplace in an area, it is easier to discover exceptional names and start to explain the background of these names. These kinds of exceptional place names are often a key to, for example, historical deductions on settlement.

The contribution of the typological information of names has been raised as one of the main roles of onomastics (Kiviniemi 1990). In Finnish onomastics, a clear picture of toponomy has already been created and the typology of, for example, surnames and company names have also been subjects of examination. As far as those name categories that have been less examined thus far are concerned, it is essential that a meticulous typological investigation of names will be further carried out. The typological information, which applies to place names, would not necessarily at all pertain to, for example, unofficial additional names, product names or animal names. Observing the special features of a name category is thus essential in this type of study.

2. Materials and Lines of Finnish Onomastics

This chapter gives a thorough overview on the background of Finnish onomastics as a topic of research. The reader will become familiar with research materials and methods carried out in Finland as well as significant scholars, pioneers, in the field. In gaining insight on the types of materials there are in Finnish onomastics, a clear picture of Finnish research strongly resting on empirical data will emerge. It also covers where Finnish onomastics fits in international research.

Research Material

An important foundation of Finnish onomastics includes first-rate and diverse materials. The most comprehensive are topographic and anthroponymic materials.

Different materials are required in toponomastics which can be either collected from living language use or from written sources. The former is often a result of field work; the researcher has collected the names from his research area by interviewing local inhabitants. This kind of material from the field has primarily been collected in Finnish rural areas. In Finland, the place name collections that encompass the entire country are in manual form, found in the Names Archive of the Institute for the Languages of Finland in Helsinki. In all, there are approximately 2.6 million name entries on card files in the archive.

The collections also include names from outside the borders of Finland, mostly from the Karelia region of Russia that was ceded to the Soviet Union in 1940. There are also Finnish place names from the Finnish-speaking areas of Norway and Sweden, East Karelia, Viena Karelia, Aunus Karelia, the Vepsian regions, as well as Ingria and Estonia. The collections in the archive were predominantly collected by Finnish language researchers or students.

The card file entries include information not only on the name itself but the place the name refers to (plate 1). The information on the card contains the search item in standard Finnish, its dialectical variant and the locative case and other endings used in inflection (for example, *Kupittaalla*

Plate 1. Card file from the Names Archive for the name Näkyväluoto *'visible|islet' with its case ending (*Näkyvälläluojolla *'visible+ADE |islet+ADE'), location (in Ähtäri in Central Finland) and other information (the islet is visible at low tide; it has one deep side and one shallow side) as well as the name collector (Terhi Ainiala).*

Näkyväluoto

näkyväluoto : näkyvälläluojolla

989 Ähtäri, Ähtärinranta
2242 01: 48/56 1

Luoto
Ähtärinjärvessä Lehtosaaren eteläpuolella. Luoto näkyy, kun vesi laskee, ei korkean veden aikana. Luodon toinen puoli on matala, toinen syvä.
Erkki Ollikkala 1928, Reetta Väyrynen 1923.
Näkyvänluodonkivet (rinn.)

ÄHTÄRI
Terhi Ainiala 1994

'Kupittaa+ADE': 'in Kupittaa'). Municipality and village names are given as the locative data of the referent, sometimes also a homestead name with numeric, specific positioning with cartographic reference. The locations of the names have been marked on maps (on base maps with a ratio of 1:20000). After the locative data, there is a description of the type of referent. In addition to all of this basic data, the card contains various other information that the collector found on the name and the place. The name of the person who has provided this information is also often mentioned.

Roughly half of the collections in the Names Archive were compiled in the 1960s and 1970s. A guide to collecting the data called *Nimestäjän opas* was compiled by Terho Itkonen in 1961 which encouraged name collectors to large-scale collecting and, at the same time, provided practical instructions on this work. All place names were subject to collecting: municipality and village names, dwelling names, names of cultural features such as fields, meadows, pastures, barns, roads, paths, bridges and fishing grounds and also names of natural features such as hills, rocks, forests, bogs, lakes, bays and islands. In such an area of name collecting, the aim was to compile the most comprehensive collection as possible. The goal was to go to each permanently populated dwelling and by interviewing its residents, shed light on the names of the homestead and its cultivated lands and other places as well as other nomenclature of the area. The essential objective of compiling was to obtain old and native toponymy. After the mid-20th century, Finnish rural areas were noticeably changing and quickly becoming desolate in certain areas and so "saving" this nomenclature was considered to be a matter of urgency. The aim was to find old residents of the area for interviewing. Male farmers of the older generation of these areas were considered the best name guides. The compiling of names during this period was not to clarify the nomenclature used by various residents and those of different ages and variants of these names. The objective was to obtain mostly old and traditional place names.

Toponymic field compilation in Finland originally stemmed from the 19th century principle of national awakening, the same as elsewhere in Europe.

With place names, efforts were made to show the value and age of the culture of the Finnish people. The Finnish Antiquarian Society already publicised a place name collection programme in 1876. According to its national romantic principles, the focus of interest in Finland particularly included such special, often etymologically opaque names, that were seen to illustrate old times and the earliest settlement. As result of this, two manuscripts were written: one on place names and local stories entitled *Paikannimiä ja paikallistarinoita* and a place name dictionary compiled by O. A. F. Lönnbohm.

In 1907, the Finno-Ugrian Society publicised a programme for the collection of place names. In 1915, an updated version of these guidelines and instructions for collecting place names called "Kehotus ja ohjeita paikannimien keräämiseen" set by the Place Name Committee of the Federation of Finnish Learned Societies had begun. The programmes covered the names of all types of places and aimed at the compilation of systematic name collections thus by establishing detailed orthographical guidelines for the material. The card file had to include information on the kind of place, a description of its terrain, its possible names in other languages, the local form of the name as well as tradition pertaining to it. These guidelines set the standard to Itkonen's guide. However, it was only Itkonen who provided name collectors detailed and concrete instructions on compilation.

The collecting of names reduced rather much after the 1970s. The main part of the collecting had been a repeat of earlier covered areas and also collecting pertaining to research projects. The field work of place name collecting in the Finnish countryside has nevertheless continued on to a lesser extent in the 21st century.

It has been considered that the Names Archives may cover up to 95 per cent of all of Finland's traditional place names. We must however point out that these estimations can concern only a central and also, at least, a rather established nomenclature. Toponymy is multilayered and, according to the useful needs of particular inhabitants, a changing and varied totality so that no perfect nomenclature of an area can be compiled. When utilising the collections in the Names Archives we should remember that they illustrate the toponymy of the Finnish countryside that was in use in the beginning 20th century. It is a question of a time when the rural toponymy had most likely been at its largest. Other nomenclature than in rural areas is more dispersed in the Names Archive collections.

In addition to Finnish, there are Sámi place names in the Names Archive. All three Sámi languages in Finland are represented in the collections: Northern Sámi, Inari Sámi and Koltan Sámi. Approximately 30,000 Sámi-language names can be found in the collections. The material has been collected in Enontekiö, Utsjoki, Inari, Kittilä and Sodankylä which covers the entire Sámi-speaking area of Finland. In addition, Koltan Sámi names outside of Finland have been entered. The collecting of Sámi names began primarily in the 1960s.

Moreover, Swedish toponymy of Finland has been entered in the collections. There is a name part register of place name collections taken from Swedish-speaking areas of Finland on archive at the Institute for the

Languages of Finland. This register is arranged in alphabetical order according to the name's initial part and second part. It is also an important source to Finnish-language onomastics because there is old toponymy of Finnish origin in these areas and there is still a living bilingual toponymy around their linguistic border. Original Swedish name collections are kept in the archives of the Society of Swedish Literature in Finland in Språkarkivet. The collections include some 300,000 name data. The collecting of Swedish place names began at the same time of Finnish place name collecting, in other words, in the late 19th century.

On the basis of collection data, Swedish toponymy in Finland was systematically investigated in the *Finlands svenska ortnamn* project which began in the 1970s and ended at the beginning of the 21st century. The results of this project were published along with its Swedish materials in four books. The subject of *Namn på åkrar, ängar och hagar* (1990) by Gunilla Harling-Kranck was cultivation names, the subject of *Finlandssvenska bebyggelsenamn* (2001) by Lars Huldén was settlement names, the subject of *Terrängnamn i Svenskfinland* (1998) by Ritva Valtavuo-Pfeifer was topographic names and the subject of *Skärgårdsnamn* (1989) by Kurt Zilliacus was the toponomy of the southwest archipelago. All of these books were published by the Society of Swedish Literature in Finland. We should also note Kurt Zilliacus and Michaela Örnmark's database on Swedish-language toponymic materials, *Namnledslexikon* (2000). This database includes all non-unique name parts, suffixes and endings that appear in Finland Swedish place names.

Different maps and, above all, base maps with their names form one key and an easily available collection of toponymic materials. The National Land Survey of Finland had begun its basic survey in 1947 after which the surveyors interviewed the local population while going around the terrain to clarify the nomenclature of natural and cultural places. Because the names collected this way has still been examined on the basis of the Names Archive collections, the nomenclature in Finnish base maps is, in reality, used by the local population. This nomenclature can be found on the Internet at http://kansalaisen.karttapaikka.fi.

The majority of entries in the collections of the Names Archive, approximately 2.6 million place names, are mainly in manual form but the most central part of toponymy in Finland is available digitally. It is a question of the nomenclature of base maps which have been digitally entered in the *Finnish Place Name Register* of the National Land Survey of Finland. The materials of the register are largely included in the Names Archive collections as well. There are all together approximately 800,000 place names in the Place Name Register, over 722,000 of which are Finnish. Approximately 75,000 are Swedish names and together roughly 10,000 Northern Sámi, Inari Sámi and Koltan Sámi names. In addition to the name itself, other information is available on each name: for example, the type of place and its location (including its coordinates). The Place Name Register comprehensively includes the nomenclature of central places, however, the names of smaller user groups and minor places are only randomly represented. For example, the register is an excellent source for those investigating Finnish lake names but when it comes to those investigating cultivation names or names of rocks and hills, these sources are incomplete.

Another important digital toponymic source is the *Atlas of Place Names*. This atlas, which can be found in the materials services Kaino (http://kaino.kotus.fi/nikar/index.php) of the Institute for the Languages of Finland, above all serves those who wish to examine the distribution of various place names. With the atlas, the user can check, for example, what the distribution of name starting with *Nälkä* ('hunger') is or how widespread names beginning with *Akka* ('old woman') are in Finland. The atlas materials are comprised of over 230 place name elements and approximately 92,000 different place names. The name data has been taken from the Names Archive collections.

The *Toponyms Data Bank* should also be mentioned when speaking of digital materials of traditional place names in Finland. As data of the Institute for the Languages of Finland and based on the Names Archive collections, the Toponyms Data Bank includes approximately 90,000 place names from 18 different municipalities which are Alajärvi, Enonkoski, Hailuoto, Hankasalmi, Kihniö, Kiikoinen, Mäntsälä, Nokia, Nurmijärvi, Oulunsalo, Pirkkala, Pori, Rautjärvi, Sauvo, Sodankylä, Suonenjoki, Taipalsaari and Velkua. Name data that has been carefully analysed both structurally and semantically is available in this database.

Planned, official names have been entered in municipality registers and maps and the official minutes of council meetings. There have been books primarily written on the largest cities in Finland which include information on their street names with their principles of naming. These include the three-part series *Helsingin kadunnimet* (1971, 1979, 1999) on Helsinki street names, the book *Lahden paikannimistö* (Laapotti 1994) on the toponymy of Lahti, *Oulun paikannimet – mistä nimet tulevat* (Toropainen 2005) on Oulu place names, *Tampereen kadunnimet* (Louhivaara 1999) on street names in Tampere and *Turun katuja ja toreja* (2011) on street names in Turku.

Many scholars of toponomastics – for example those investigating the origin, borrowing and formation of names – require old spellings of names in their work. These can be found in various documents and maps. There are documents starting from the 16th century and maps from between the 17th and 18th centuries kept in different archives. Although the materials have been compiled for administrative requirements, they include useful data for the onomastician as well.

The oldest documents in Finland are from the 13th century, the beginning of the era of Swedish rule, and they are in Latin. Up until the mid-19th century, the language of documents was the official language of Finland, that is, Swedish. Moreover, the officials who wrote up the documents were Swedish-speaking, which is why the spelling of the Finnish place names in these documents may seem rather strange. We cannot get a complete picture of the toponymy of that time on the basis of old documents because only individual place names in different contexts were entered in them. It was not until the mid-16th century when a complete toponymic group could be seen in cadastral maps because the main Finnish settlement names, that is, names of parishes and villages, were entered in these documents. Homestead names systematically appeared much later, starting in the early 18th century.

Some old documents were published in print within the research of history. Older, medieval documents include the series *Bidrag till Finlands historia I–V* and *Finlands medeltidsurkunder I–VIII* as well as *Registrum ecclesiae aboensis* or *Turun tuomiokirkon mustakirja*. A key set of settlement names had been entered in some tax books and cadastral maps which were published from old documents. Finnish place names had for the first time been entered in early 16th century maps, for example, in the 1539 *Carta marina* by Swedish Olaus Magnus which describes the Nordic countries. Finnish names in this map, as in other maps made outside of Finland of this early period, are strangely spelt and difficult to interpret. The first maps to actually benefit onomasticians are regional maps drawn up by Finland's first surveyors from the 1630s. There is quite an abundance of place names in these maps and their spellings are recognisable.

The most central cartographic materials of toponomastics in Finland include the maps of the Great Partition (Fin. *Isojako*) from the late 18th century that was drawn up by village. The Great Partition was a method of land consolidation whose task was to merge narrow strips of fields dispersed according to the open field system of homesteads into less frequent and bigger sections. The toponymy of villages in maps of the Great Partition appears more diverse than it was prior to it. In addition to homestead names, the names of fields, meadows and forests as well as the most significant natural places have been entered in the maps and in detailed accounts.

In regard to onomastics, valuable, old cartographic materials have not really been published but they are available in the Finnish National Archives and in regional surveying archives. Individual old maps have been published as an atlas, for example, the book *Kuninkaan kartasto Suomesta 1776–1805* edited by Timo Alanen and Saulo Kepsu covering Southern Finland, which was taken from war maps drawn up in Sweden.

A key source for a researcher in anthroponomastics is the data of the Finnish Population Register Centre (*Väestörekisterikeskus* VRK, www.vaestorekisterikeskus.fi). The Population Register Centre personal information system contains data on the given names and surnames of all Finnish citizens alive in 1965 and those born afterwards. There is a free-of-charge Name Service on the VRK webpages which has a given name and surname search. Through this service, one can look up the numbers of given names and surnames in Finland. Moreover, one can investigate the statistics of the most common names from different time periods. The population of the entire country is cohesively on hand in the VRK materials whereupon, for example, Finnish and Swedish names are available in the same database.

Valuable materials for those studying Finnish given names and surnames can be found in the HisKi database, located on the webpages of the Genealogical Society of Finland (www.genealogia.fi). It includes the so-called history book data of parishes, mostly lists of christenings, marriages, burials and removals until the late 19th century. The oldest information is in places from the 17th century but for the most part from the 18th century. There is also information on name changes on genealogia.fi.

Research Tradition

The majority of onomastics has focused on toponymy and anthroponymy. This is natural because it is people and places in particular that have long been identified the most in different languages and cultures. Research on other nomenclature has been quite marginal both in Finland and elsewhere. However, more systematic studies, especially on commercial nomenclature and names in literature, have started since the latter half of the 20th century.

The lines of Finnish onomastic studies will be illustrated in this section. These studies will be examined through choices that were made in them: for what reason the study has found its way to specific fields, how it has changed and developed over time and what circumstances can be found behind these changes. This examination, first and foremost, follows Finnish lines of research but a chronological development will also be highlighted. The main focus of onomastics in Finland has been in toponomastics, at least partly because in comparison to anthroponymy, there has already early on been a vast and comprehensive amount of material available on toponymy. Moreover, theoretical questions on onomastics have, above all, been researched in Finnish toponomastics. For these reasons, a much greater emphasis on toponomastics will be given in this section than on other onomastic areas. The general development of onomastics will also be discussed, however not focussing on its exact details. We will mostly take a look at a period of so-called modern research: the main focus being on research after the 1960s.

When taking a look at individual studies, we should remember that only in rare cases would a concrete study examine only one research question and follow one line of research. For example, it is quite rare that a study would focus exclusively on etymology – it could examine the structure and typology of names. In practice, a Finnish study of names would therefore not strictly have representatives of one line of research but rather just different emphases.

The examination of names was, up until the 19th century, quite random and sometimes even arbitrary. The unique, historical documentary value of nomenclature was noted in linguistic and historical research during this time period. Because there may have been earlier linguistic features preserved in nomenclature, names can function as a valuable source of language history. The value of nomenclature as including linguistic, cultural-historical and settlement-historical material has been even greater in Finland than in many other countries because the historic source material concerning Finland and its language is relatively young and even limited. Onomastics was thus originally more of a sub-science of language history and historical research. At the end of the 19th century, however, onomastics already began to emerge as a separate field, for example, in Germany, Scandinavia and also in Finland.

ETYMOLOGICAL RESEARCH

The investigation of the origin of names, in other words, *etymological research*, is the most traditional part of onomastics. The etymological study of names has rather been in abundance even in Finland. The general non-linguistic notion may be the idea that the explanation of a name's origin is entirely the most central, and sometimes even the only question in onomastic research. Onomasticians most often also hear questions concerning the emergence of names, such as "Where does the name *Helsinki* come from". However, the task of onomastics is, as is well known, more extensive, and etymological research can also be considered more extensive in terms of its goals and the field it covers. Hence, the study of the origin and background of nomenclature is also a key part of, for example, the semantic and grammatical study of names because the grammar of names cannot be explained without knowing their content.

The first dissertation on Finnish onomastics even embodied etymological research. This study was published in 1891 by A. V. Forsman, entitled *Pakanuudenaikainen nimistö: tutkimuksia Suomen kansan persoonallisen nimistön alalla*, and it aimed at describing what pre-Christian anthroponymy in Finland had been like. According to Forsman, up to a few thousand different pre-Christian personal names (*Ilma, Kauka, Toiva*) have been especially preserved in Finnish toponymy and family names. For a long time, it was the only study exploring the topic, as the second extensive study on the same subject was not published until 1964. This was D.-E. Stoebke's dissertation, published in Germany, *Die alten ostseefinnischen Personennamen im Rahmen eines urfinnischen Namensystems* which dealt with Old Baltic-Finnic personal names within a Proto-Finnish naming system.

The etymological study of names has later on been a central part of Finnish anthroponomastics as well. The most extensive etymologies of Finnish given names are included in *Etunimet* by Kustaa Vilkuna, and later, in its newest edition published in 2005, edited by Pirjo Mikkonen. After Vilkuna's book – and greatly based on the information presented in it – many other name dictionaries shedding light on the background and origin of Finnish given names have been published in Finland. The most extensive of these include Pentti Lempiäinen's *Suuri etunimikirja* (third, revised printing 2004) and *Suomalaiset etunimet Aadasta Yrjöön* (2007) by Anne Saarikalle and Johanna Suomalainen. Given names amongst the Swedish-speaking Finns are illustrated by Marianne Blomqvist's *Dagens namn* (2002) and *Vad heter finlandssvenskarna?* (2006). Pirjo Mikkonen and Sirkka Paikkala's book *Sukunimet* offers a well-founded presentation on the etymology of Finnish surnames, whose newest edition was published in 2000. The explanation on the origin of many Finnish people's first and surnames can be found in these books.

In addition to this, the first extensive investigation of Finnish place names was predictably an etymological study. This was Viljo Nissilä's dissertation entitled *Vuoksen paikannimistö I* (1939). The majority of this study, which deals with the names of natural places associated with the Vuoksi River, covers the etymological explanation of individual names. Moreover, on the basis of all of his research material, Nissilä had also aimed at different syntheses, including the classification of etymological research results, among other things.

In its purest form, *Suomalainen paikannimikirja* (2007), a dictionary of Finnish place names, offers findings on Finnish etymological toponomastics. This dictionary includes information on the origins and backgrounds of the names of significant places in Finland, containing over 4,700 headwords, including a reference search. Out of these headwords, there are approximately 3,800 definite name entries in alphabetical order, from *Aakenustunturi* to *Östermyra*. The names for this reference work had been selected on the basis of the centrality and other well known factors of the location, upon which included, for example, all the names of municipalities and names of the highest fells and the largest lakes. As for the book *Nimet mieltä kiehtovat: etymologista nimistöntutkimusta* (2003) on etymological onomastics by Alpo Räisänen, the origin of two types of names (names including the derivational ending *nkV* such as in *Jaalanka* or *ua* such as in *Lentua*) and some individual names are examined.

We should still point out one issue about Finnish etymological toponomastics. Besides being etymological work, namely Nissilä's dissertation and many extensive place name studies are also *regional monographs* in which the entire toponymy of some area or the names of a certain class of an area are discussed. These studies are based on the analysis of the etymological origins of individual names and the findings of this etymological research have been systematised according to the classification of naming principles. Thus, the aim was to explain with what various *principles of naming* (for example, location of the place, characteristics of the place) places have been identified. A large part of regional monographs includes Master's theses which normally discuss the entire toponymy of one village. More extensive regional monographs are often done from a historical research perspective. These regional monographs include dissertations, such as Saulo Kepsu's study (1981) which examines the village names of Northern Kymenlaakso, located in South-Eastern Finland. With place name materials, the goal has been to shed light on the past of the research area, especially the stages of settlement as well as culture, from which the place names have emerged.

One objective of regional monographs has been the diverse depiction of regional naming systems. This includes Laila Lehikoinen's dissertation *Kirvun talonnimet: karjalaisen talonnimisysteemin kuvaus* (1988) on Kirvu homestead names in Karelia which, at the same time, is the first extensive study concerning settlement names in Finland. Not only are officially documented names of homesteads the subject, but also their unofficial names that are exclusively used orally. The materials consist of all the homestead names collected from the rural municipality, that is, the former parish of Kirvu, located on the Karelian Isthmus, nearly 2,000 names. The theoretical basis for the study is a depictive model based on syntactic-semantic structural analysis which will be described later. Instead of being restricted to homestead names in one parish, this study serves as a systematic model, extending to depict the naming system of the entire province of Karelia.

Characteristic of the Karelian homestead naming system is that a majority of these names includes a personal name that conveys the owner. These personal names are varied: first names, surnames, bynames, occupational titles, and different combinations of them.

An etymological approach can also be firmly found in many investigations which have aimed at giving a more extensive explanation of settlement history. A more detailed account on these studies will be given in the following section.

Cultural-Historical and Settlement-Historical Research

Names are always emerging at some point in time and in connection with some form of culture. When names are examined particularly as part of local history and they are used as a source of information on local history, we can speak of cultural-historical onomastics and/or settlement history onomastics. In many local histories and similar types of work, an area's past and settlement history have been examined or often just described with a name. Generally, with individual names, conclusions may however be rather unfounded because the effect a nomenclature's systematic nature on name giving hasn't been taken into account in the interpretation. This kind of study is also etymological because the central objective is to explain the background and origin of the names. When the investigation is first done, the names can be set as part of a broader, historical development and thus conclusions can be made on cultural and settlement history.

Cultural-historical and settlement-historical objectives are significant in many place name studies. There has occasionally also been an aspiration for more extensive cultural-historical perspectives in anthroponomastics. Viljo Nissilä, the first in Finland to bear the title of Professor of Onomastics, has aimed to answer questions on history and the history of settlement with the help of nomenclature in his vast number of books and articles. As for toponymy, he has written articles for publications on the history of parishes intended for the general public in which he charts the stages of settlement and former lifestyle of the region on the basis of place name lexical elements. The book *Suomen Karjalan nimistö* (1975) on Finnish Karelian nomenclature also took a cultural-historical and settlement-historical viewpoint. In this work, Nissilä presents a synthesis of his own toponymic and anthroponymic studies of the province of Karelia. A good example of how the modern research of onomastic data can be used in the history of parishes includes the article *Rautalammin varhaishistoriaa paikannimistön näkökulmasta* (1985) by Eero Kiviniemi, an all-round scholar who followed in the footsteps of Nissilä as Professor of Onomastics. From a toponymic perspective, this article examines the early settlement of the Rautalampi region in Eastern Finland and the notions about its formation presented at different times. This was done on the basis of onomastics as well as archaeology and historical research.

Eero Kiviniemi gives a general and principled discussion on the value of the settlement-historical documentation of place names in his article *Nimis-*

tö Suomen esihistorian tutkimuksen aineistona (1980) using names as research material of Finnish prehistory. He evaluates the prospects of the existence and identification of loan names of different linguistic origins in Finnish nomenclature. Kiviniemi presented many causes of uncertainty related to settlement history conclusions drawn on the basis of old place names. For example, the contents and factual background of names often remain ambiguous, which is why drawing direct conclusions on the basis of the distribution and typological criteria is often misleading. Kiviniemi emphasises that it is only possible to draw reliable settlement history conclusions on the basis of extensive data from basic research of place names.

In his dissertation on the origins of settlement in the Torne and Kemi River Valleys *Tornionjoki- ja Kemijokilaakson asutuksen synty. Nimistötieteellinen ja historiallinen tutkimus* (1980), historian Jouko Vahtola aims at the analysis of the stages of settlement in Northern Finland, using place names as his material. Vahtola's research is the first systematic onomastic study done in Finland from a settlement-historical perspective. The author has studied each name collected from the research area, a total of 90,000, of which he has chosen 900 place name types which seem to offer evidence on settlement history. His research method is comparative: the emergence and distribution of the name types on the basis of these comparisons. Vahtola himself calls his method typological-geographic research. On the basis of these analyses, Vahtola is able to present, very convincingly, the strata with different origins of the settlement in Northern Finland and their chronology. According to the study, the settlement – excluding the indigenous Sámi settlement of the area – relocated to the northern, newly settled areas first and foremost from different parts of Southern Finland.

The studies *Pohjois-Kymenlaakson kylännimet* (1981) on village names in northern Kymenlaakso, *Valkealan asuttaminen* (1990) on the settlement of Valkeala, *Uuteen maahan: Helsingin ja Vantaan vanha asutus ja nimistö* (2005) on old settlement and nomenclature of Helsinki and Vantaa and *Espoon vanha asutusnimistö* (2008) on old settlement names of Espoo by Saulo Kepsu and Timo Alanen's study *Someron ja Tammelan vanhin asutusnimistö: nimistön vakiintumisen aika* (2004) on the oldest settlement names of Somero and Tammela also have settlement history objectives. Kepsu and Alanen also base their conclusions largely on the geographic distribution of place names. Archaeological and historical facts as well as genotype data on the settlement has been used as background information. The strongest evidence for the regions of origin is provided by individual names which the new settlers seem to have brought with them from their old home territories to the new areas. For example, according to Kepsu, the first settlers came to Helsinki from the Häme region and the place names would give a clue about it, such as the present-day neighbourhood named *Konala*. This name's original form would be *Konhola* whereupon the settlement may have originated from the village of Konho in the old municipality of Akaa in the province of Häme.

Kaija Mallat's dissertation *Naiset rajalla: Kyöpeli, Nainen, Naara(s), Neitsyt, Morsian, Ämmä ja Akka Suomen paikannimissä* (2007) can be considered a cultural-historical, however not a settlement history study. The topic of research includes Finnish place names that start with the words *kyöpeli* ('witch'), *nainen* ('woman'), *naara(s)* ('female'), *neitsyt* ('virgin'), *morsian* ('bride'), *ämmä* ('hag') and *akka* ('old woman') along with their variants. This study analyses the grounds for why places are given these multi-orientated names as they are interpreted. A part of these names seem to be mythological. These types of names can convey information about the social norms against women and the names may have been associated with regional, territorial borders. These names could have been seen as restrictions on the movement of women. Thus, for example, *Naistensuo* ('woman+PL+GEN|bog') and *Naaraskallio* ('female|rock') may have functioned as signs of direction and caution to places which were prohibited to women. Above all, the norms of the community could have been depicted and validated with mythological names, regulations, warnings and prohibitions imparted, a story preserved and it could have been believable by connecting it to this certain place.

As for anthroponymy, Sirkka Paikkala's dissertation *Se tavallinen Virtanen: suomalaisen sukunimikäytännön modernisoituminen 1850-luvulta vuoteen 1921* (2004) closely studies personal names as a part of cultural and social development. It concerns the *Virtanen* surname type and the modernisation of Finnish surname practices from the 1850s to 1921. In this investigation, the Finnish surname system is approached as a system which had been developed from many old ones concerning surnames and bynames. This system however is, neither functionally nor characteristically, not a sum of their old systems. Päivi Rainò's dissertation in general linguistics *Henkilöviittomien synty ja kehitys suomalaisessa viittomakieliyhteisössä* (2004) analyses how personal name signs in Finnish sign language has developed. Along with language establishment and sign language development, personal name signs have changed from expressions that describe the name bearer gradually more to opaque expressions.

Loan Name Research

The study of loan names has been established as its own field in onomastics. Discussion on the study of loan names has been prevalent in toponomastics but naturally, the borrowing of names and name elements from one language and culture to another is a noticeable and central topic in anthroponymy and commercial nomenclature as well. Generally, different borrowing and loaning from foreign languages is seen in all nomenclature, for example in literary onomastics. The study of loan names could also of course be seen, at least partly, as a part of cultural and settlement history research because, when analysing the encounter of names and naming systems of different periods and the influence they have on one another, a more extensive, historic framework must inevitably be covered as well.

Toponomastics in Finland offers excellent opportunities for the study of loan names because there are two language contact areas in the country. One of them is northernmost area of Finland, where the Sámi languages and Finnish come into contact with each other, and the other is the western coast and the archipelago whose toponymy includes a large number of Finnish

Swedish loan names. The best known and most investigated names of the Finland Swedish areas are *substrate names*, that is, names of an area based on an earlier spoken language.

There has been a great deal of investigation of Finnish Swedish loan names, carried out as cooperative work between onomasticians of both languages. This included a research project called *Kieliraja-alueiden paikannimistöt* which dealt with place names in linguistic border areas. This project started in the early 1970s and was led by Eero Kiviniemi and Kurt Zilliacus. It concerned bilingual place names in the linguistic bordering areas between Finnish- and Swedish-speaking settlements. The subject of interest was primarily the linguistic form of loan names and also the structure of the individual names and the nomenclatures. The aim was to analyse, on the basis of eight partial studies, what the nomenclatures by different language groups were and how they had been loaned from one language to another over time, which factors had affected the ways of loaning and how common the ways had been (Kiviniemi et al. 1977; Zilliacus 1980). The main result of the study was the classification of different loan names and the terminology concerning it. A general feature of loaning was that the vernacular toponymy had been loaned from one language to another mostly through phonetic adaptation, however only rarely by translation.

Ritva Liisa Pitkänen's dissertation *Turunmaan saariston suomalainen lainanimistö* (1985) is a regional monograph of Finnish loan names of the Turunmaa archipelago. Its research materials include the oldest place names of the southwest archipelago in Finland, the Finnish substratum names included in the Swedish-language nomenclature of the area. The study aims to describe these loan names as such, together with their historical and cultural background. In her work, Pitkänen disproves the established notion of the origins and historical background of Finnish loan names: since the 12th century, Swedish settlers borrowed names from the Finnish-speaking population that already lived in the archipelago, instead of borrowing them from Finnish hunters that had come to the area on their hunting trips, as it had previously been assumed.

Finland's oldest Swedish-language place names are from the Middle Ages, the oldest between the 12th and 13th centuries when Swedish settlement began to arrive on the country's western shores. This element, loaned from even older Germanic languages, is what appears in Finnish nomenclature. However, there has not been much investigation on this nomenclature. In the early 20th century, at the time of the language conflicts between the Finnish- and Swedish-speaking populations, a few Finland Swedish linguists (Ralf Saxén 1910, Hugo Pipping 1918 and T. E. Karsten 1921, 1923) tried to prove, by virtue of place names, that Finland had been settled by Swedish peoples since prehistoric times. Finnish linguist Heikki Ojansuu (1920) protested against their interpretations of these names. The names were interpreted equally as arbitrarily and tendentiously by all the parties involved in the conflict. As a result of this debate, the search for Germanic names in a Finnish study, especially in regard to toponymy, had been actually quite limited for many decades.

Viljo Nissilä's research should also be noted regarding anthroponymy. In these studies, he searches for the Germanic roots of personal names included in many Finnish place names, the most predominant being *Germaanisen nimiaineiston etymologista ryhmittelyä Suomen nimistössä* (1980). Moreover, Jouko Vahtola has, in his article *En gammal germansk invandring till västra Finland i bynamnens belysning* (1983), mostly aimed to explain what personal names of Germanic origin may be in Western Finnish settlement names. Jorma Koivulehto, a researcher of Germanic loan names, has highlighted the origin of presumably proto-Germanic place names as such in his article *Namn som kan tolkas urgermansk* (1987).

Sámi nomenclature in Finland, the names of the current, bilingual Sámi Finnish areas in particular, has been investigated less as compared to the toponymy of Finland Swedish areas. In line with documented data, the Sámi peoples used to live in an area considerably more southern than where they do now. Place names with traces of Sámi settlement left behind can successfully be found in inland Finland. Ante Aikio investigated the most extensive Sámi substrate names in his article *The Study of Saami Substrate Toponyms in Finland* (2008).

Settlement as well as place names of Finnish origin can also be found in the Finnish-speaking areas of Norway and Sweden. Tuula Eskeland has investigated the toponymy of Finnish origin of the Finnskogen area of Norway in her dissertation *Fra Diggasborra til Diggasbekken: finske stednavn på de norske finnskogene* (1994), which was reviewed at the University of Oslo. Janne Saarikivi did a study predominantly on Finno-Ugric substrate nomenclature in Russia in his dissertation *Substrata Uralica: Studies on Finno-Ugrian Substrate in Northern Russian Dialects* (2006), focusing on the Arkhangelsk area. This study not only presents this substrate but also examines the research method of substrate nomenclature. One of the most significant results of the study shows that the area where Finno-Ugric languages are spoken has been significantly more widespread in the Middle Ages than it is today.

In regard to anthroponymy, cultural contacts and loaning is highlighted in Minna Saarelma-Maunumaa's dissertation *Edhina ekogidho – Names as Links: The Encounter between African and European Anthroponymic Systems among the Ambo People in Namibia* (2003). This study examines the turning point in the anthroponymy of the Ambo people in 20th century Namibia. This defining moment was influenced by both European colonialism and the adoption of Christianity. Due to Finnish missionary work, Namibia also had adopted an abundance of Finnish first names and at the end of the 20th century, approximately every fifth Ambo had a first name of Finnish origin (for example, the male names *Eino*, *Toivo* and the female names *Rauha*, *Tuulikki*). When these names were loaned, they were often subject to adapt according to the phonetic system of the Ambo language (*Vilhelm* → *Vilihema*). In their research project that began in 2006, Minna Saarelma and Gulbrand Alhaug, from the University of Tromsø, analysed the influence of Norwegian and the Norwegian personal naming system on the first names and surnames of residents in Norway with a Finnish background (Alhaug

& Saarelma 2007). Elin Karikoski has studied the stock of surnames of the Kven people predominantly in Northern Norway (1996, 2001).

Language and cultural contacts are global in an era of information networks and the notable influence of English is bound to have an impact on nomenclature as it does on other aspects of language. English and other foreign languages can be seen in, for example, Finnish company names. Paula Sjöblom has examined this phenomenon in her article *Linguistic Origin of Company Names in Finland* (2009).

Typological Research of Toponymy

Since the later decades of the 20th century, research aimed solely at examining the etymological origin of names has been put to the sidelines. Instead, efforts have been made to construct an overall picture of Finnish nomenclature. Onomastics became its own independent discipline in the field of linguistics. The core issues of toponomastics have been the exploration of the structure of names and naming systems as well as the examination of the principles of name giving and their semantic classification. Questions concerning the use of names have come forth as well. Onomastics has also begun strong interaction with other cultural and social research and it has become more interdisciplinary than ever before.

This section will cover the development that has progressed in onomastics towards present day research. Toponomastics will mostly be the centre of discussion because it is precisely this field in which methods and tools for a comprehensive, linguistic analysis of names have been developed by Finnish research. Afterwards, these methods that were developed for toponomastics have been utilised in other onomastic studies and they have been adapted to fit their needs.

Besides etymologising toponymy, early regional monographs aimed to classify it in different ways. This made it necessary to show the results of etymological analysis with the classification of naming principles. This was natural because for etymological analysis, there was already a need to know how to analyse and divide names into different parts.

The first to classify the principles of naming was Viljo Nissilä with his aforementioned dissertation *Vuoksen paikannimistö I*. Nissilä's classification model was adopted from Swedish Ivar Modéer's *Småländska skärgårdsnamn* (1933) on the names of the archipelago of Småland. Nissilä lists 21 different principles of naming: terrain and water, the soil, location, size, shape, colour, comparison, verbally expressed characteristics, plants, fish, birds, other animals (excluding domestic animals), hunting, fishing, agriculture and haymaking, domestic animals and cattle breeding, traffic and transportation, borders, buildings, et cetera, terms referring to people as well as houses and villages. Nissilä's classification is mostly lexical-semantic. These categories, such as domestic animals, fishing, hunting or cattle breeding neither constitute actual principles of naming, nor relate to the ideas of identification. This classification is also unsystematic because it includes not only lexical but also morphological categories. All in all, Nissilä's model of classification could be characterised as being more philological-historical rather than linguistic. Its purpose was not to study nomenclature, as such, as its own system. A central element in Nissilä's classification and his entire approach to the study is its cultural-historical and settlement history documentary value. Nissilä's model, together with a philological aspect in general, dominated Finnish onomastics until the 1960s. Nissilä himself presented his model in his book on Finnish onomastics *Suomalaista nimistöntutkimusta* (1962). He applied this model again in the aforementioned work *Suomen Karjalan nimistö* (1975). The model covered the etymological analysis of the names and the lexical-semantic classification of the material, but the basic principles of naming were left aside.

A new research trend, based on the *syntactic-semantic analysis model* and a classification model, was introduced in the 1960s and 1970s. A new school of onomastics can be seen to have emerged during this period. Onomastics was, above all, considered linguistic research. Eero Kiviniemi defined onomastic objectives and work thusly (translated from Finnish): "The objective of onomastics is to clarify name formation and the use of names as a part of language and language use" (1979). The structure of names and naming systems became central, as the subject of earlier research had included individual names or name elements and their etymologies.

This new approach is first seen in Kurt Zilliacus' study *Ortnamnen i Houtskär. En översikt av namnförrådets sammansättning* (1966). This study concentrates on the entire toponymy, including a good 6,600 names, of one Swedish-speaking archipelago parish, Houtskär. Such a corpus of one parish – or one village – can be considered suitable for a systematic study of place names. According to new, systematic onomastics, an individual name must be, that is to say, studied as a part of a system, the whole picture of the nomenclature of a specific area. Thus, the nomenclature of one village or even one parish can form a natural and suitably sized cohesive system. In his book, Zilliacus presents a new method for the analysis and categorisation of place names and gives a summary of these principles of the new method in his Finnish article on onomastic syntheses titled *Nimistötieteellisten synteesien aikaa* (1972).

Zilliacus created a method with which he was able to bypass the weaknesses of Nissilä's classification. The departure and preconditions for Nissilä's classification had been the viewpoint that names are descriptive and express the most typical features of a place. According to Zilliacus' view, names are, above all, identifying, not descriptive, nor do they necessarily express features typical to a place at all. The core element is the name giver's perspective: a name giver does not name a place just to describe its culture or nature but instead to identify it. Initially, names have been, of course, descriptive but afterwards, in practice, this descriptiveness is no longer essential.

A prerequisite for onomastics is the understanding of the linguistic structure of names, as for which, requires the understanding of the names' semantics. These two go hand in hand in interpreting names: it is not possible to perceive the structure of a name without understanding its semantics and vice versa. Zilliacus created a new syntactic-semantic analysis model for the understanding of the structure and semantics of names. In this model, names, from a syntactic-semantic perspective, are first divided into syntactic, structural components, name parts, and then, these name parts which signify a special feature are both lexical-semantically and syntactic-semantically classified. Later on, the classification model was reworked. Close cooperation between Finnish and Finland Swedish research had emerged in onomastics. The models were developed together and a new descriptive model was applied to Finnish onomastics in particular, and, above all, Eero Kiviniemi perfected Zilliacus' model. The end result was a classification which had ten principles of naming, whereas Nissilä had 21. In line with the new model, naming principles can be divided into four main groups: location of the place, characteristics of the place, what exists or appears there and the relationship the place has to people.

The work of the new school of onomastics continued strong in the 1970s. Two key works that had established a trend in research came up at that time. The first of these was *Nimistöntutkimuksen terminologia – Terminologin inom namnforskningen* (1974) which was a cooperative work by Eero Kiviniemi, Ritva Liisa Pitkänen and Kurt Zilliacus. The book was the first of its kind including Finnish onomastic terminology. It became an established feature of the usage of terms. There had not been an earlier, cohesive set of terminology, instead everyone used terms in their own way; a model was taken mostly from Scandinavia or Germany. The new terminology was somewhat more precise than Scandinavian terminology. A number of new terms had been created for syntactic-semantic analysis. The book presented and defined over 300 terms in both Finnish and Swedish both of which were given equivalents in the other language. Then, Eero Kiviniemi's book *Paikannimien rakennetyypeistä* (1975) on structural types of place names instilled the new syntactic-semantic analysis model in Finnish onomastics. As the syntactic-semantic model first started to be used for place name analysis, it gave way to general typological information on names and their composition for the first time. The question of the percentage of different structural types of names and how large a part of the names are, for example, single part names such as *Luoto* ('islet'), *Kalaton* ('fish+TON': 'without fish') and *Kapeinen* (narrow+NEN) was somehow able to be answered. Kiviniemi's book above all touches upon single part names because there had not been enough typological foundation for interpreting them.

With much thanks to Eero Kiviniemi, a shift had been made in Finnish toponomastics from the study of individual names to the analysis of broader entities, the research and description of naming systems. The interpretation of names remains incomplete unless we take other names of the same type into account and, in many cases, nomenclature that reflects the same principle of naming. In addition to the analysis model of names and the classification model of its results, Kiviniemi also introduced analogy and the lexical elements of names to this classification.

Eero Kiviniemi introduced the concept of analogy into Finnish onomastics in his dissertation *Suomen partisiippinimistöä. Ensimmäisen partisiipin sisältävät henkilön- ja paikannimet* (1971) which focuses on Finnish anthroponyms and toponyms that include the first active participle. This book marks the beginning of new, truly linguistic onomastics in Finnish-speaking Finland. On the Swedish-speaking side, Kurt Zilliacus had published his groundbreaking work a few years earlier (1966). The objective of Kiviniemi's study was to identify the maximum possible number of names that includes the Finnish first participle, to analyse the names' content and attempt to shed light upon the creation process of the names by investigating their distribution and age. The most typical of these include *Koliseva* ('rattle+vA': 'rattling'), *Töriseva* ('growl+vA': 'growling') and *Kohiseva* ('roar+vA': 'roaring') and other hydronyms derived from verbal derivations with the frequentative *ise* suffix. These types of names, for the most part, are based either on sound or movement. All in all, nearly half of the place names including the first participle proved to have emerged in line with a model of already existing names of the same type and having the same root. A model provided by other names, *analogy*, is therefore a strong factor which creates and modifies nomenclature. Never before had the share of analogy in name formation been surveyed, not to speak of understanding how great its importance was. However, it should be noted that analogous names are generally not without descriptive content. Although a name has been given according to the model, it still has not been given without naming principles.

Eero Kivinimi also investigates the role of analogy in toponymy in his book *Väärät vedet: tutkimus mallien osuudesta nimenmuodostuksessa* (1977) concerning name formation and in his article *Analogisk namngivning och den toponomastiska teorin* (1991). In his research, Kiviniemi shows how central the role of analogy in name formation is and how strong name modes can be. The emergence of models is naturally affected by the need for naming: for example, a model can only materialise when there is a need to name previously unnamed places, for example, as new areas are being settled.

The systematic, Finnish-language investigation of lexemes or words included in toponymy, gained strength at the threshold of the 1990s, even though it had been one of the objectives of new, systematic onomastics launched in the 1960s. One of the reasons why the systematic investigation of basic parts happened so late was that Finnish-language name collections were arranged according to the beginning of the name. Thus, it was not easy, nor in all respects possible, to examine the latter parts of the names.

The first detailed study of Finnish-language lexemes in toponymy is Eero Kiviniemi's *Perustietoa paikannimistä* (1990). This work covers the basics of Finnish toponomy and is considered one of the cornerstones of Finnish onomastics. It provides the principal, lexical features of toponymy: the most frequent generic parts in Finnish place names, appellatival specifiers and the most common Finnish place names. The objective was to determine approximately one thousand of the most common specific parts and one thousand most common place names. The most common specific part has been proven to be 'big'–'small' opposing pairs along with their synonyms.

Sociolinguistic Research

The sociolinguistic study of names primarily includes the investigation of their use and variation. Sociolinguistic onomastics can be called *socio-onomastics* and *socio-onomastic research*. The socio-onomastic approach takes the social and situational field, where names are used, into consideration.

Socio-onomastic research gained strength in Finland with regard to toponymy in the 1990s. It was based on the tradition of fieldwork and a strong concentration on collected material, both of which had had a historically strong position in Finnish onomastics. Thus, researchers had a close relation to the concrete use of names. Socio-onomastics was also a natural continuation to the systematic research that was introduced in the 1970s. It was already then that the necessity of studying the usage of names was taken into account. Kurt Zilliacus, for example, called for the analysis of the variation and differences of nomenclature in different idiolects. He presumed that the nomenclatures, in this respect, would not be proven as unified and unambiguous as they had previously been believed to be. This has also successfully been proven in later studies.

Socio-onomastic research of the 1970s in Finland focused mostly only on Swedish-language nomenclature. The true pioneering work in the field was the sociological study on toponymic competence *Sociologiska namnstudier* (1973) by Peter Slotte, Kurt Zilliacus and Gunilla Harling. This study covered the toponymy of three villages. Each onomastician previously collected the names of their respective villages and clarified in what way men and women from different age groups knew the names of their home villages. The claims of the study proved to hold true: older residents knew more names than young ones, and men more than women. Peter Slotte further investigated the use and knowledge of names of inhabitants in his article *Ortnamns räckvidd; namnbruk och namnkunnande* (1976). This study was particularly focussed on *name districts* (Fin. *nimireviirit*) whereupon the span of their areas from which names are known and the reasons for knowing a name are examined. According to Slotte's discovery, there are five different reasons for knowing a place name including the place's ownership, usage, event, location and the form of the name.

One of the earliest studies examining Finnish-language users' toponymic competence is Saulo Kepsu's article *Toponymie des Dorfes Kepsu* (1990) which covers the toponymy of the village of Kepsu in Southern Finland. In this article, he analyses the toponymic competence of three different generations of one family. This study shows that place names are largely handed down from one generation to the next. However, approximately half of the oldest generation's names is vanishing because the younger ones no longer require them. Ritva Liisa Pitkänen analyses the effect of profession on toponymic competence in her article *Viljelijän kylä – kalastajan saaristo: ammatti nimitaidon taustana* (1996). Toponymic competence between a fisher and farmer in a Southwest Finland village are considerably different. Water and archipelago places are significant to a fisher, whereas the farmer has a good command of the names of cultivated lands and other cultural names.

The first Finnish-language study on toponymic competence, extensively observing social variables, is the article *Paikannimien käyttö ja osaaminen – nimitaito Pälkäneen Laitikkalassa* (2000) by Terhi Ainiala, Johanna Komppa, Kaija Mallat and Ritva Liisa Pitkänen. This investigation covers the knowledge and use of place names in Laitikkala in the parish of Pälkäne in Southern Finland. It analyses the knowledge individuals from different age groups, different genders and different professions have on the place name in their home village. There are great differences between the villagers. The men know on average more names than the women and the older residents more than the younger ones. However, toponymic competence cannot solely be explained by age and gender because individual differences are considerable. Professions and pastimes often affect toponymic competence more than age and gender.

The socio-onomastic perspective came forth in the 1990s in studies on the change in place names as well. These studies showed that traditional toponymy changed and disappeared faster than expected. The first thorough investigation on the change in toponomy was the dissertation *Muuttuva paikannimistö* (1997) by Terhi Ainiala. This study investigated to what extent and in what way place names have been preserved, changed, varied and disappeared in roughly the past two centuries in two villages: Kurhila in Asikkala, in the Häme region and Närhilä in Ristiina, in southern Savo. The same objectives, however a shorter examination period, were included in a research project summarised by Ainiala in her article *Paikannimistön muuttuminen* (2000). The project analysed the changes in traditional place names used in the countryside. The collection from the Finnish Names Archives included the period from the 1960s and 1970s to the present in nine different villages. There are rather large differences in toponymy change in different villages that are located in different parts of Finland and dissimilar in development. On average, approximately half of the villages' place names have disappeared, the minimum about one third and the maximum as much as two thirds. Place names often disappear as a result of a changed need for identification. When a way of life or environment has changed, places no longer have the need to be identified in such a detailed manner as before. The fact that a name has no longer sufficiently described its referent may have also affected the disappearance of names. For example, the name *Riihipelto* ('drying-barn|field') may have been replaced by *Puimalanpelto* ('threshing-house+GEN|field'), as a drying barn that used to be on the outskirts of a field had been torn down and replaced by a threshing house.

A sociolinguistic perspective in anthroponomastics has also come forth stronger than before since the 1980s. In 1982, Eero Kiviniemi's book *Rakkaan lapsen monet nimet: suomalaisten etunimet ja nimenvalinta* was published which examines, on a foundation of extensive computerised data, the Finnish population's collection of given names that were in use at that time and the choice of first names and the variation in which names were favoured. Kiviniemi's later published books *Iita Linta Maria: etunimiopas vuosituhannen vaihteeseen* (1993), a guide to given names for the new millennium, and *Suomalaisten etunimet* (2006), on given names of Finnish people, represent the same approach. There were many theses completed on these themes at different Finnish universities. The extension of first name innovations in Finland at different times has also been examined from the sociolinguistic perspective (for example Lampinen 1997, 1999 and Mustakallio 1995, 1996). Similarly, a favourite subject of Master's theses has been the examination of the Finnish call names and additional names.

A part of socio-onomastics also includes *folk linguistics*. Folk linguistics examines language users' attitudes towards names and the sentiment concerning them. Paula Sjöblom has investigated commercial names from a folk linguistic perspective in her article *Namnens tolkning som en kognitiv process: exemplet kommersiellt namnförråd* (2008) which looks at the meaning and interpretation of names as a cognitive process. This paper discusses what images of a company's business are conjured in people's minds merely on the basis of a company name. As for anthroponymy, there are some theses in the works which take a folk linguistics perspective. The most extensive folk linguistic approach appears in research on urban nomenclature. These studies will be covered in more detail in the following section.

Research on Urban Nomenclature

Finnish toponomastics has historically focussed on the study of rural nomenclature. The reason for this, naturally, is Finland's history as a rural and agrarian country. Place names have been collected almost exclusively in the countryside and its villages, whereas place names from cities and other urban areas have hardly been compiled at all. As Finland became urbanised in the late 20th century, a city or densely populated area that replaced a rural village became the landscape and home district for more and more Finns. This led onomasticians to gradually realise how little they knew about urban nomenclature. There was little study on urban nomenclature and then again, it was limited almost solely to official names, above all street names. Extensive studies on street names have been published, particularly on these names in Finland's largest cities. Moreover, guides for assisting in name planning have been published, the most important which should be mentioned being *Yhteinen nimiympäristömme: nimistönsuunnittelun opas* (1999), edited by Sirkka Paikkala, Ritva Liisa Pitkänen and Peter Slotte.

A more systematic study of nomenclature used by city dwellers in their everyday speech, mostly being unofficial toponymy, was begun in the 2000s. The first, extensive study was carried out as a joint project between the Institute for the Languages of Finland and several different universities. The results of this study have been compiled for a collection of ten writings on urban nomenclature edited by Terhi Ainiala entitled *Kaupungin nimet: kymmenen kirjoitusta kaupunkinimistöstä* (2005). Ainiala examines the core and composition of urban nomenclature in her article *Kaupunkinimistön tutkimuksen perusteet* (2003). Both official and unofficial names offer a number of significant topics for research. City dwellers use official and unofficial names in their everyday speech whereupon it is often natural to take the entire nomenclature in use as a subject for investigation in a study as well.

Socio-onomastic perspectives and methods have been key in the investigation of urban nomenclature. One has been the folk linguistics perspective whereupon, for example, residents' attitude to the nomenclature of their living environment has been examined. As for official urban nomenclature, these themes have been covered in, for example, Tiina Aalto's article *Osoitteena Osmankäämintie: tutkimus eräästä ryhmänimistöstä* (2002), which covers street naming using plant names, and Maria Yli-Kojola's piece of writing *Kurvinpussi vai Torikatu? Kouvolalaisten mielipiteitä kadunnimistä* (2005), which discusses how Kouvola residents feel about their street names.

Research on urban nomenclature has become more interdisciplinary than before. For example, the goal of the joint project on the transformation of the onomastic landscape in the sociolinguistically diversifying neighbourhoods of Helsinki called *Nimimaiseman muutos Helsingin sosiolingvistisesti moninaistuvissa kaupunginosissa*, launched in 2004 by linguists and geographers, was to produce new, empirical data and a theoretical view on urban place names and their use in the context of social change, urban development and multiculturalisation. The most fundamental research problems pertain to the appearance of different historical stratum in place names used by residents, the role of place names in the perception of urban space and also the meanings of place names in the construction of urban identities. Its subjects included official and unofficial place names in two Helsinki neighbourhoods used by the residents in their everyday speech, these neighbourhoods being Kallio and Vuosaari. The research material was primarily collected in thematic interviews and small groups being the interviewees. Thus, the manners in acquiring the materials are new: in collecting names, the materials have primarily been compiled in individual interviews and have focussed on acquiring the names of different places. Now, the goal is to receive more extensive data on the use of names in their contexts where the methods of conversation analysis and variation studies have become helpful tools. Above all, two articles by Terhi Ainiala and Jani Vuolteenaho shed light on the perspectives and methods of the aforementioned research project: *Urbaani muutos ja kaupunkilaiset identiteetit paikannimistön kuvaamina* (2005) on urban change and the identities of city dwellers described by toponymy, and *Urbaanin paikannimistön haasteita: kielitieteen ja maantieteen tieteenalatraditioista arkiseen käyttönimistöön Helsingin metropolialueella* (2005) which covers the challenges of urban toponymy from disciplinary traditions of linguistics and geography to the daily use of nomenclature in the metropolitan area of Helsinki. Moreover, Ainiala's article on names in Helsinki, *Helsingin nimet* (2006), examines the same questions.

Diversification of Research

In the 2000s, new disciplines have been taken as cooperative and conversational partners in onomastics, one of the most essential being geography. In addition to other disciplines, perspectives have also diversified trends in linguistics, the strongest being cognitive linguistics and construction grammar, both of which having a profound effect on onomastics. An example of this is Antti Leino's dissertation *On Toponymic Constructions as an Alternative to Naming Patterns in Describing Finnish Lake Names* (2007) which analyses extensive materials of traditional toponymy moreover with computer science methods. Paula Sjöblom also investigates nomenclature with cognitive research methods. Her dissertation *Toiminimen toimenkuva: suomalaisen yritysnimistön rakenne ja funktiot* (2006) which covers the structure and functions of Finnish company names is, also on an international level, the first of its kind. This study explores the structure and function of Finnish company names under the cover of extensive material and also creates a survey of the emergence of the category of company names and a look at their development. Sjöblom's dissertation is a good indication of how the field of Finnish onomastic research has developed and also expanded by subject. This phenomenon has happened at the very least upon entering the 21st century.

The start of onomastics is thus in etymological research. Etymological research has no doubt been preserved as a central part of onomastics but there have been better tools for its study in that the whole picture on nomenclature has been fine-tuned. The structure of names, name formation and name typology rose to the core of Finnish research in the 1960s and 1970s and focus on the usage of names, that is, sociolinguistic onomastics came into being since the beginning of the 1990s.

The onomastic field has, in the 21st century, expanded as the systematic study of urban environment nomenclature and commercial names have begun. Moreover, the investigation of names in literature has gradually been started more systematically in Finland than before (e.g. Bertills 2003). Names in literature have internationally already been a central subject for quite some time but there really hasn't been much in Finnish research until the 21st century. All in all, Finnish onomastics has adapted new perspectives and methods.

There is more and more philological research that analyses names at the core of onomastics in many countries. Toponomastics in particular rests a great deal on etymological and philological research in, for example, Sweden, Norway, Germany and partly in England. However, onomastics in the United States has been more culturally and socially orientated. This is partly due to the fact that there has naturally been no European nomenclature on the "new continent", and the only names to be etymologically investigated have mostly been Native American nomenclature.

A cultural, social and sociolinguistic approach has gained strength, in the 21st century, in European research as well, whereas there has not been as much etymological and historical investigation as before – this trend could be observed, for example, at international conferences on onomastics. Finnish onomastics already set off to party tread other various roads besides etymological research decades earlier.

International Cooperation

International cooperation has been carried out in onomastics for quite some time now. Because there are names in all languages and cultures, it has been natural to examine them together regardless of linguistic borders. The international, cooperative body in onomastics is the *International Council of Onomastic Sciences* or *ICOS* (www.icosweb.net). ICOS organises international congresses of onomastic sciences every three years, the first of which was in Paris in 1938. In Finland, it was held in Helsinki in 1990. The 24th congress was held in Barcelona in 2011. Articles based on presentations at the congresses have, for the most part, been published in books and book series. For example, the articles based on those at the 2002 congress held in Uppsala, Sweden have been published in the book *Proceedings of the 21st International Congress of Onomastic Sciences*.

ICOS does not only organise congresses. It also works to otherwise represent and diversify onomastics. ICOS publishes its own onomastic periodical called *Onoma*. The first issue of Onoma came out in 1950 and by the 21st century, nearly 50 were published. New topics include, for instance, urban nomenclature and commercial nomenclature. In addition to this, international onomastic terminology and a common bibliography is developed within ICOS.

The onomastic organisation corresponding to ICOS in the Nordic countries is *Nordiska samarbetskommittén för namnforsking* or *NORNA* (www.norna.org). The main task of this body, which was established in 1971 for representing Nordic onomastics, is to organise Nordic congresses of onomastic sciences approximately every five years. The 15th congress was held in 2012 in Askov, Denmark. In addition to congresses, NORNA organises symposiums with focus on a specific theme (for example, Names and Cultural Contacts in the Baltic Area, Influence of Christianity on Nordic Name Giving). Articles based on the congresses and symposiums are mostly published in the series *NORNA-rapporter*. As is the case with ICOS, there is other work carried out in NORNA in the area of onomastics such as putting out annually published bibliographies on its website and reviews published in the journal *Namn och Bygd* as well as considering terminological questions. There is a committee selected at the congresses made up of representatives from each Nordic country. This committee is responsible for practical work.

There are several scholarly journals in the field of onomastics published in different countries. The most significant Nordic publications include *Namn och bygd: tidskrift för nordisk ortnamnsforskning* on toponomastics published in 1913 and *Studia anthroponymica Scandinavica: tidskrift för nordisk personnamnsforskning* on anthroponomastics published in 1983. Articles, summaries and book reviews appear in these journals which are annually issued and edited in Uppsala, mostly in the Nordic languages. Aside from *Onoma*, the most essential international periodicals include *Names* from the United States and *Beiträge zur Namenforschung* from Germany. Other onomastic series include *Nomina: journal of the Society for Name Studies in Britain and Ireland*, *Journal of the English Place-name Society*, *Nomina Africana* from South Africa (published by Names Society of Southern Africa), *Naamkunde* from the Netherlands (published by Instituut voor naamkunde te Leuven), *Rivista Italiana di Onomastica* from Italy, *Namn og Nemne* from Norway (published by Norsk namnelag), *Namenkundliche Informationen* from Germany, *Österreichische Namenforschung* from Austria, *Acta Onomastica* from the Czech Republic and *Onomastica Canadiana* from Canada. Finno-Ugric onomastics and the nomenclature of these languages are presented in the series *Onomastica Uralica* which is published in Debrecen, Hungary and is done in cooperation between scholars from different countries.

The most extensive and comprehensive series of books of international onomastic sciences is the three-part *Namenforschung: ein internationales Handbuch zur Onomastik – Name Studies: an international Handbook of Onomastics – Les noms propres: manuel international d'onomastique* (1995, 1996). Approximately 2,000 pages, this comprehensive work is comprised of articles from almost all the areas of onomastics, which include, for example onomastic methods, theory, grammar, semantics, pragmatics, the origin of names and the historic development of names in different countries. In addition to this, there are articles in the book on personal names and various types of place names of different countries and linguistic areas. Over half of the articles are in German; other articles are published in English or French.

3. Place Names

As toponomastics plays an exceptionally significant role in Finnish onomastic research, this chapter provides in-depth coverage of Finnish place names. The reader will gain a comprehensive understanding of Finnish place name categories and the syntactic-semantic structure of Finnish place names. In addition, it covers the roles of Swedish and Sámi in Finnish toponymy. A picture of the Finnish urban onomastic landscape will also emerge as name planning and official and unofficial naming have an important part in Finnish toponomastics.

Introduction to Place Names

Place names are expressions with which places are identified and differentiated from others. When we hear, for example, names such as *Lake Erie*, *Palm Springs* and *Piccadilly Circus*, we know what places we are talking about or we can at least look up these places on a map. Lake Erie thus would not be confused with the nearby Lake Ontario nor the city of Palm Springs with the region of Palm Desert in California. Even if we have never been to Piccadilly Circus in the City of Westminster, we can look on a map where to go if a friend suggests meeting at a place so named. There would be a noticeably greater danger of getting lost if we only would have received directions to meet at a place that is "about 1 kilometre northeast of Wellington Arch".

Place names are normally formed from ordinary linguistic elements, words and derivational affixes, but, at the same time, names follow their own grammar, their own structural principles. Not just any expression can be a name: expressions such as *Green* or *That Plaza behind the Post Office* would not be known as established names in English. On the other hand, a name cannot be used as any other word. For example, *park road* is not a compound lexical expression that would be used for all roads that run alongside a park. The name *Park Road*, however, can be used – at least if we want to be understood – only for those roads whose true name it is.

The term *toponym* can be used to mean a place name and the term *toponymy* can be used for a collection of place names, that is, its nomenclature. Moreover, when speaking of the study of toponymy, the recommended term to use is *toponomastics*. These terms stem from the Greek words *topos* 'place' and *onyma* 'name'.

Place names are universal, that is, there are place names found in all known cultures and languages. The need to identify places and linguistically differentiate them from each other is therefore common to all languages. The question of how a place name is formed naturally varies. The characteristics of each language and culture have an effect on what structurally and contexually makes place names. Many Western languages have, for instance, compound expressions, made up of two elements, one which signifies the class or type of place and the other signifying certain special features: *Queensland, Long Island, Alice Springs, Östersjön, Nötholmen, Schwarzwald* and Finnish names *Hämeentie, Korkeasaari*. There are also several names in many languages with only one element, such as *London, Oslo, Vättern, Pretoria, Lima* and Finnish *Oulu* and *Päijänne*.

Place names in the Slavic languages, for example, are structured in their own unique way. In Finnish toponymy, the most typical are two-part compound names, whereas names in these languages include various derivational affixes. For example, the most common affixes in Russian are *ov* (*Rostov*), *in* (*Erzin*) and *ka* (*Novopokrovka*).

When speaking about foreign place names, how should they appear in, for example, English or Finnish texts? And how are places of foreign countries generally spoken about in the contexts of different languages? These questions can be shortly examined here. On an international scale, these matters go to the United Nations (UN) whose primary objection of place name work is the harmonisation of place name spellings for the facilitation of international interaction and cooperation. The goal is to standardise the official spellings for all place names in each spelling system. For this purpose, the United Nations Economic and Social Council has organised the Conference on the Standardisation of Geographical Names every five years since 1967. Decisions of the Conference are implemented and prepared by UNGEGN, that is, the United Nations Group of Experts on Geographical Names. The group has members from numerous countries, including Finland.

According to accepted views, the spelling of names must be based on their local pronunciation. These kinds of internationally accepted names are generally fine as they are for all languages that use the same writing system. A more difficult matter is the transference of names from one writing system to another, that is, their *transcription*. The recommendation, among others, is that only one international Latinisation be selected for each non-Latin writing system. Thus, for example, the spelling for the capital of China should be *Beijing* and not *Peking*.

In looking at where names come from, it is clear that a large number of place names have spontaneously emerged everywhere in the speech of a people. The need to name a place is found behind the origin of a name: a community requires a name for such places when there is reason to speak about them. Names have been given to all places which are important in regard to inhabitance, movement, navigating the landscape, working and other activity. These kinds of names can be called *traditional place names* and, for example, all place names appearing in the oldest strata are included in them.

Traditional, spontaneously created place names have generally fulfilled the needs of small communities. They originated, for example, in a community of a few dozen or a few hundred people that have been in movement or lived and worked together. Later on, many names have become widely or at least more widely known. However, these kinds of names are thus only extensively learned, not having originated in a large community.

The majority of Finnish toponomy are traditional place names. For instance, *Naarkoski* ('female|rapids') and *Savijoki* ('clay|river') are names which have been created to refer to East Uusimaa waterway sites located in the area of Pukkila in Southern Finland. These names originated as they have been used by early inhabitants of the area or even those who travelled in the region prior to them, as these places became so important that they had to be spoken about in an established way. It is impossible to trace the names' precise time of origin and the way they came to be. Names have been preserved for centuries as they have been used because there has continuously been a reason to speak about places.

In addition to traditional names, there are official names. *Official place names* are names sanctioned by a legally constituted names authority and applied within its jurisdiction. These kinds of names, above all, can be found in the urban environment, including, for example, names of streets, parks and plazas but they can be found in rural areas as well, mostly as names of roads and dwellings. There are certain types of Finnish names that are a part of this latter group, such as *Onnela* ('fortune+LA'), *Tyynelä* ('calm+LA') and *Rauhala* ('peace+LA'), which have been given to new settlements. These names describe the name givers' wishes on their settlement and, even more broadly speaking, on life in their own space.

Nevertheless, one should remember that the distinction between traditional and official names is not necessarily clear-cut. Traditional names may have gained the status of official names. Thus, not all official names are names created by naming authorities but only sanctioned by them.

There is, still, quite a significant difference between the toponomy of rural and urban settings. Official names in an urban environment and the variants created on the basis of them are a significant part of all of its nomenclature, as in a rural area, they are in the minority. In an urban setting, various names of businesses are also used as place names more than in a rural area simply because there is an abundance of these kinds of locations. Urban nomenclature is also generally more stratified and varying than rural nomenclature because urban inhabitants, as name users, are not only a concretely larger but also more heterogeneous group.

Place names that have emerged in a natural way have originally been those that describe places. Place names include linguistic elements which have appeared in the language at the moment of name giving. All place names, therefore, have had some semantic content. This descriptive content, however, no longer necessarily carries any meaning regarding the use of the name. For example, names such as *London* and *Päijänne* or *Long Island* and *Pihlajamäki* ('rowan|hill') work just as well as place names even though we may not even understand their original content.

According to the size of the user community, place names can be divided into micro- or macrotoponyms. Such names, which are only used in a small-scale user circle, are called *microtoponyms*. Typical microtoponyms are names of cultivated land in a rural area which often are included in the onomasticon of one family and are farm-specific. As for an urban environment, microtoponyms can be, for example, names used by certain sports club members for places to play or compete.

In terms of widely known names, these are called *macrotoponyms*. Macrotoponyms are generally names of larger places or, at least, major ones. These kinds of names include, for example, names of lakes, other natural sites and important settlement and dwelling areas. For example, in the urban environment, names of neighbourhoods and important streets and squares are macrotoponyms. Naturally, many names of tourist destinations (*Koli* and *Aavasaksa* in Finland), for example, are also macrotoponyms, even from a national perspective. The line between microtoponyms and macrotoponyms cannot be too carefully drawn; the user community at hand perceives what names make micro- and macrotoponyms. Nevertheless, a large number of the entire toponymy of Finland includes microtoponyms.

In line with the nature of the named place, there is a tendency to divide traditional place names into two groups: culture names and nature names. *Culture names* are names of cultivated places, that is, places developed by people and *nature names* are those of natural places. This kind of division of names, according to the type of place, is actually a classification of named places.

The main group of culture names includes settlement names, artefact names and cultivation names. *Settlement names* are names of areas including, for example, names of cities and municipalities (*Tampere*) and districts, neighbourhoods, regions, densely populated areas (*Töölö, Hervanta*) as well as names of dwellings, that is, for example, names of houses, farms and cottages (*Mattila* 'Matti+LA', *Alatalo* 'lower|house', *Kaisanmökki* 'Kaisa+GEN|cottage'). *Artefact names* include, for example, names of roads (*Hämeentie* 'Häme+GEN|road'), lanes (*Rantapolku* 'shore|lane'), bridges (*Pitkäsilta* 'long|bridge'), barns (*Perälato* 'rear|barn') and other structures. As for *cultivation names*, these include, for example, names of fields (*Kotopelto* 'home|field'), meadows (*Kiviniitty* 'stone|meadow') and pastures (*Hevoshaka* 'horse|pasture'). The main group of nature names includes topographic names and hydronyms. *Topographic names* include, for example, names of hills (*Palomäki* 'fire|hill), rocks (*Rajakallio* 'border|rock'), forests (*Takametsä* 'behind|forest'), moors (*Kettukangas* 'fox|moor') and bogs (*Sammalsuo* 'moss|bog'). *Hydronyms* include, for example, names of bays (*Mustalahti* 'black|bay'), islands (*Lammassaari* 'lamb|island'), lakes (*Päijänne*) as well as rivers and ditches (*Kemijoki* 'Kemi|river', *Mätäoja* 'rot|ditch').

Culture and nature names can be split up differently in various settings. There are more culture names in many areas than nature names. Three fourths of the names in a rural setting can be made up of culture names. There are more nature names than culture names in such areas where settlement is rare and where waterways are a central part of the setting. The number of culture names can be compared to the dominance of the culture setting: the denser the populated and developed and also cultivated the setting is, the more culture names there will be.

The same classification can be used, at least when applicable, in urban toponymy as well. There are notably more culture names in the urban environment than there are nature names. Out of all the named places in the urban environment, as much as over half may be buildings or sections of them and the various businesses located there. Areas, passageways and structures make up an average of one third of named places, whilst parks and other similar areas about one tenth and natural places only a few percent. All in all, the number of nature names in an urban setting is quite low as compared to culture names.

Place names can be structurally divided into two main groups: single part and two-part names. Let us examine here a common type of place name, a compound name such as *Saarijärvi*. The latter part of the name, that is, the generic part (*järvi* 'lake'), signifies the place's class or type; it is an appellative that characterises the place. The initial part, that is, the specific part (*saari* 'island'), signifies some special feature of the place. As far as traditional toponymy is concerned, Eero Kiviniemi performed a detailed investigation on the lexical elements in Finnish toponymy in his book *Perustietoa paikannimistä* (1990), noting the most common generic parts, appellatival specific parts and the most common Finnish toponyms. The objective was to uncover approximately one thousand of the most common specific parts and one thousand of the most common place names. The following is an account based on Kiviniemi's findings.

The number of appellatives that characterises a place, which appear in a Finnish name's generic part, has reached approximately one thousand. The most common of these generic parts include the appellatives *pelto* ('field'), *mäki* ('hill'), *niemi* ('cape'), *suo* ('bog'), *saari* ('island'), *lampi* ('pond'), *lahti* ('bay') and *niitty* ('meadow'), depicting the general landscape of the Finnish countryside. A majority of all these terms pertain to natural places, which is due to the fact that topographic places are more varied than cultural places whereupon a broader lexicon is required for their identification. All in all, places are characterised by both common and special terms which have been created on the basis of more local needs for expression. On average, common terms often seem to be sufficient for larger referents, whereas a relatively small sized place would easily require a special term. For example, the most common generic part for Finnish lakes and ponds are *järvi* ('lake'), *lampi* ('pond') and *vesi* ('water'), whereas smaller bodies of water have been given generic parts that refer to smaller ponds, pools and puddles, for example, *allikko, jorpakko, krotti, lantto, lutakko, passi, pauni, pukama* and *ropakko*. Quite often, a common term is chosen as a generic part, although there is an abundance of other possibilities. The reason for this is, above all, that the identification of places has always happened through the perspective of small communities. In this way, a regular, common term serves to differentiate the place.

The most common lexical elements in specific parts are proper names. Their share can be nearly half of all specific parts and out of these, place names appear roughly three times more than personal names. This is understandable because the naming of places on the basis of their location is, regarding a toponymic system, an economical feature in relation to names that already exist. For example, it is appropriate to give the bog surrounding *Haukijärvi* ('pike|lake') the name *Haukijärvensuo* ('Haukijärvi+GEN| bog') and the ditch from there *Haukijärvenoja* ('Haukijärvi+GEN|ditch'). Consequently, dwellings are most often named according to an inhabitant (*Antintalo* 'Antti+GEN|house'). A name based on a nomenclature that already exists – either toponomy or anthroponomy – is called a *deproprial* name, that is, a name based on a proper name.

Names based on appellatives are *deappellatival* names. The most common appellatival specific parts include 'big'–'small' opposing pairs: *Iso*, *Suuri* and *Pieni*, *Pikku*, *Vähä*. This is not unexpected because a place's relative size is the most natural foundation of all for differentiating. Other common qualifiers include those that describe the relative location *Ala*, *Ali* ('lower', 'low') and *Ylä*, *Yli* ('upper', 'high'), the adjective *Pitkä* ('tall, long'), tree terms *Mänty*, *Honka* and *Petäjä* (all 'pine'), terms of natural places *Kivi* ('stone'), *Ranta* ('shore'), *Mäki* ('hill') and terms of culture places *Koti* ('home'), *Riihi* ('drying barn') and *Mylly* ('mill'). The most common specific part that refers to a natural place is *Kivi* which may come from the fact that stones or rockiness is a labelling feature of many places regarding movement in this setting or cultivation. Out of cultural places, a home, a drying barn and a mill are such places in relation to which other places are identified the most. However, places have been named after churches and mills relatively the most because there have been less mills and churches in particular than names with *Mylly* and *Kirkko* ('church').

When examining the specific parts of toponyms, we can also see that different types of places are often named in different ways. For example, fields are often named according to their location. The most common field names are *Riihipelto* ('drying-barn|field'), *Kotipelto* and *Kotopelto* (both 'home|field'), *Peräpelto* and *Takapelto* ('rear|field' and 'back|field'), *Rantapelto* ('shore|field') and *Metsäpelto* ('forest|field'). Location is a natural principle of naming mostly because fields are not really different from one another by other characteristics, such as appearance. The most common lake names are *Valkeajärvi* ('white|lake' also *Valkeinen* 'white+NEN'), *Vähäjärvi*, *Pikkujärvi* and *Pienijärvi* (all 'small|lake'), *Saarijärvi* ('island|lake'), *Särkijärvi* ('roach|lake') and *Pitkäjärvi* ('long|lake'). Lakes, in most cases, have been named on the basis of the characteristics of the place. Field names are mostly always microtoponyms, farm-specific names. The same names can many times be replicated in the same village. Lake names, on the other hand, are often macrotoponyms, more extensively known and used. These same names cannot be replicated as those given by the same user community. The same community will by and large not intentionally give the same name to different places of the same type because, although this kind of naming, as far as the motivation of names are concerned, would seem well-founded and natural, it would go against the identifying function of names.

A layperson particularly may sometimes wonder, for example, that if there is something commonly seen in nature and in his setting, why would it not be better seen in names as well. This may serve as a basis for the explanations of names too. However, when interpreting names, we must bear in mind a name's basic function, that is, individualisation. Individualising is also differentiating so that something rare will always characterise a place better than something common. Thus, for example, *Haapa* ('aspen') is a common specific part in Finnish nomenclature, even though, as a tree, an aspen is quite uncommon.

All in all, there is a notably great deal of common elements in toponymy. Regarding the use of names, frequency and rareness aim at an optimal balance. In line with calculations, one thousand of the most common names cover roughly one third of deappellatival names and one thousand of the most common specific parts would be sufficient for over one half of deappellatival nomenclature. The most common Finnish place names are settlement names ending with *la* or *lä* – five of the most common settlement names are *Mäkelä* ('hill+LA'), *Rantala* ('shore+LA'), *Peltola* ('field+LA'), *Heikkilä* ('Heikki+LA' ← male given name *Heikki*), and *Ahola* ('glade+LA') – and cultivation names with the generic part being *pelto* ('field'). The most common Finnish place name of all, around five thousand locations that have appeared in Finland, is probably *Riihipelto* ('drying-barn|field'). Cultivation names and names of settlements are the most common because there are relatively few naming models of farm names and cultivation names are usually microtoponyms that originate in farm-specific use whereupon the replication of the same names is not a problem.

How many place names then are there in Finland? This question will most certainly raise much interest but it is impossible to give an absolute answer. Toponymy is always a changing and living system. The number of names primarily depends on the number of locations to be identified: how many and what kind of places are in need of identification. It has been estimated that the number of traditional rural place names had been at its largest in the first decades of the 20th century whereupon the various names in Finland would have reached around three million. The number of traditional place names was most likely smaller than this in beginning of the 21st century. However, there is an abundance of names in rural nomenclature which were still not in existence one hundred years ago – part of the locations of current names, such as many settlements, buildings and roads, is a later stratum.

A vast, complete picture has been formed by urban environment place names in 21st century Finnish toponomy. There are several hundreds of thousands of planned names in the current urban environment and densely populated areas. In addition to this, there are an abundance of different unofficial names in use.

The regional number of toponyms can indicatively be calculated and a *name density*, in other words, the number of place names in the area of one areal unit, can be determined. These kinds of calculations have been done regarding the traditional toponomy of rural areas. Because the breadth of the toponym collection in the Finnish Names Archive is known, approximately 2.6 million place names, we can also estimate how these names are distributed in Finland. The average name density would be, in this way, roughly seven place names per square kilometre. It is of course clear that these names are not distributed so evenly. There are different regions in the area of the same municipality: more frequently settled centres are usually more specifically named than sparsely settled wildernesses. Exact calculations have been made on name density at locations of some municipalities or villages and have ended up at even noticeably larger calculations. At the most, one square kilometre can have about thirty place names or even more. It is easier to get to greater numbers in areas where name collecting has been completed quite precisely than in regions where name collecting has been more disorganised.

Settlement density and the age of settlement have a key role in the effect on name density. When there is dense settlement, a great deal more names are required for different places. The names that are used may have been preserved for a long time in an area of old and permanent settlement and there might be name strata of various ages in the nomenclature. Moreover, the natural circumstances of the area will have an effect on name density. When there is topographic variation, it is clear that there will be more locations to be named. Then again, the average name density is smaller in later and scarcely settled areas. For example, name density in some Lapland municipalities may be to the tune of one or two names per square kilometre. There is still a decreased number of place names in these kinds of spacious and sparsely settled settings due to the fact that the locations to which the names refer are often wide-ranging.

Not only will the number of locations for naming affect concrete numbers but also the number of different name types. The more the same kind of places there are in an area which requires naming, the more naming models are often required. For example, in an area where there is an abundance of lakes and ponds, there are also more ways used to name these places than in areas where there is little water.

There is, thus, no balance to the number of place names. Toponymies are not permanent nor are they unchangeable. This matter can also be examined from the perspective of just one place name and we can see what the life span of this place name is. To begin with, a name is given to a place when it needs a name and the need to name a place comes about in a community. Secondly, a name remains in use for as long as there is a need to use the name. Thirdly, a name is forgotten when the there is no longer a need to talk about the place.

Grammar and Semantics

STRUCTURE AND CONTENT OF NAMES

The basic requirement of onomastics is the understanding of the linguistic structure of names and this, in turn, requires their semantic understanding. These two also go hand in hand in the interpretation of toponyms: the structure of a place name cannot be perceived without understanding its semantics and vice versa. A name's semantics here especially refers to a name's factual background, that is, the specific principles of name giving with which a name giver has identified a place.

When studying individual names, we also must take the regional nomenclature as a whole into consideration. A regional toponymy forms a functional totality and practical system regarding its name users. For example, the explanation of the rock name *Kanakallio* ('hen|rock') may be that close to it is *Kukkokallio* ('rooster|rock'). So, the similarly shaped but smaller rock formation, close to *Kukkokallio*, received *Kanakallio* for its name. When interpreting the lake names *Valkeajärvi* ('white|lake') and *Vähä Mustajärvi* ('small Mustajärvi'), it is again good to point out that there is a lake called *Mustajärvi* ('black|lake') nearby. *Valkeajärvi* may be a name given in relation to *Mustajärvi* because its water is lighter than the water in the adjacent lake Mustajärvi. The explanation of *Vähä Mustajärvi* can be that this lake is smaller than the nearby Mustajärvi.

Many place names are compound expressions formed with two parts. These are called *compound names* such as the aforementioned *Valkeajärvi*. These names have two name parts: a *generic part* and a *specific part*. The term *generic part* (Fin. *perusosa*), may sometimes be replaced with the term *principle element* (Fin. *edusosa*) in other linguistic studies on Finnish compounding (such as the comprehensive book on Finnish grammar *Iso suomen kielioppi*). The generic part is typically an appellative which signifies the class or type of named place, for example, *järvi* 'lake'. The name giver has noted the type of place and described the place by virtue of *topographic words* included in his language. These types of words indicate how the environment is perceived in the local language. For example, the Finnish words *harju* ('esker'), *kallio* ('rock'), *kero* ('bare fell top'), *kukkula*, *kullas*, *kumpu*, *köykkä* and *töyry* ('river bank') can be used for various hillocks, knolls or land elevations, not all of which are necessarily known in all Finnish dialects. Besides the nature and traits of a land elevation, the choice of topographic word depends, of course, on what kinds of words are known in the local dialect.

A generic part alone naturally is not sufficient for being a place name because then it only combines places of the same class. Because the function of a place name is to identify a place, that is, differentiate it from other places of the same class, the name still requires an identifying name part. Thus, this name part is called a *specific part* (Fin. *määriteosa*).

Compound place names, such as *Saarijärvi* ('island|lake') and *Pitkäsilta* ('long|bridge'), are the most common type of Finnish place names. There are, of course, other structural types in Finnish nomenclature, such as single part names (*Saarinen* 'island+NEN', *Harju* 'esker', *Saimaa*) and exceptional compound names to the typical ones (*Vähä Saarijärvi* 'small Saarijärvi', *Alempi Pitkäsilta* 'lower Pitkäsilta'). We will be acquainted with these types later.

When we examine the semantics of a place name, we explore its original semantic content and search for the answer to what the semantic content is, in other words, the factual background which the name giver has given a place. Each traditional place name has had this kind of semantic content although we, as contemporary language users, can no longer interpret all of them. Place names have therefore been comprehensible expressions when they originated. Names that are contextually obscure and opaque include, for example, *Häme* and *Tampere*. The fact that we do not understand the content of these and many other place names is mostly due to the fact that these names are usually rather old. They have been given through culture which we do not have enough information on (agriculture, fishing, hunting). Names can include an old vocabulary or names that have disappeared. The form of a name could also have linguistically changed over time.

However, many place names are contextually transparent such as the aforementioned lake of white waters named *Valkeajärvi* and the name of the long bridge *Pitkäsilta*. These kinds of names can, in two respects, be interpreted in one way. First of all, we understand the meaning of the words included as well as what the words in the name mean. These names are *lexically* unambiguous. Secondly, we can understand the factual background regarding these kinds of names whereupon they are also *syntactic-semantically* unambiguous.

However, many place names, by their semantic content, are not as unambiguous and transparent as *Valkeajärvi* and *Pitkäsilta* nor, on the other hand, are they as opaque as *Häme* or *Tampere*. Place names can be placed on a continuum from transparent to obscure. Names which certainly include familiar vocabulary can be found between *Pitkäsilta* and *Häme* but in spite of this, we cannot – without more detailed investigation – interpret their original semantic content. An example of this is *Kirkkokallio* ('church|rock') whose factual background can be a "rock where a church is located", a "rock from where you can see a church" or a "rock which looks like a church". These kinds of names may be lexically unambiguous however syntactic-semantically ambiguous. Another type of example we can look at is *Akanniemi* ('old-woman+GEN|cape') which is both lexically and syntactic-semantically ambiguous. The word *akka* could refer to an old woman, a grandmother or a woman in general. Names with *akka* can also be mythological (Akka is a female deity in Finnish mythology), referring to the ritualistic or historic nature of the place. There can, thus, be lexically ambiguous names including words that have many of these types of meanings and these multiple meanings are possible regarding the name's factual background.

SYNTACTIC-SEMANTIC CLASSIFICATION MODEL

The *syntactic-semantic classification model* was created in a study for understanding the structure and semantics of Finnish place names (Kiviniemi

1975, Zilliacus 1966). The syntactic-semantic classification model aims at taking the name giver's perspective for examining what factual bases can be found behind naming. The model first outlines names from a syntactic-semantic perspective into structural, that is, name parts. The concept of *name part* (Fin. *nimenosa*) refers to the syntactic "part of a name" which has the function, regarding name formation, of characterising or identifying a place. For example, the lake name *Valkeajärvi* has two name parts: the generic part *järvi* 'lake' characterises the place whereas the specific part *valkea* 'white' identifies it. Name parts are usually divided with a slash: *Valkea/järvi*.

Name parts are threefold. Firstly, a name part can be a component that *signifies the type of place* (***Valkea**/**järvi***, ***Pitkä**/**silta***). The function of a name's generic part generally is exactly this: an appellative that classifies the place is its generic part. The name part conveys what the type of place is – if it is, for example, a lake (*järvi*) or a bridge (*silta*).

Secondly, a name part can have a *designating* function, either by the generic part or the specific part. Such proprial name parts, that is, those which include a name that have no function of signifying a special feature, are designating name parts. This name part, therefore, does not signify the type of place nor describe the place on the basis of special features. There are three kinds of designating name parts. The first are loan names (Fin. **Porvoo** cf. Swe. *Borgå* 'castle|river') which, in regard to the borrowing language, has no content. Moreover, there are such names which have undergone a structural change in which a generic part that clarifies the type of place is added to a single part name (*Valkeajärvi* → *Valkeinen* white+NEN → *Valkeisenlampi* 'Valkeinen+GEN|pond') and these names include a designating name part (***Valkeisen**/lampi* 'a pond whose name is *Valkeinen*'). In addition to this, name parts of so-called specified entities are considered designating name parts (*Iso / **Valkeinen*** 'bigger lake out of those named *Valkeinen*'). Designating name parts in place names are not as common as other name parts. As a term, *designating name part* (Fin. *nimittävä nimenosa*) is not necessarily the most effective because it does not precisely describe what the issue in the name part is all about. Because the term, however, has been established in Finnish onomastics, it would not be practical to change it.

The third point is that a name part can be one that *signifies special features* (***Valkea**/järvi*, ***Pitkä**/silta*). This kind of name signifies something about the place to which the name refers; for example, the name part *valkea* which signifies a special feature in the lake name *Valkeajärvi* indicates that the issue at hand is a white (watered) lake. The entire name can be one that signifies a special feature. If the name *Valkeajärvi* had been given to a house located on the shore of the lake Valkeajärvi, *Valkeajärvi* as a house name would be a single part name and it would signify a special feature, in this case, the location of the place and it would not have a name part that signifies the type of place.

Name parts signifying a special feature generally appear as specific parts in names (***Valkea**/järvi*, ***Pitkä**/silta*). They could also be expressions included in a single part name (*Valkeajärvi* as a homestead name, *Katinhäntä* 'cat+GEN|tail' as a long and narrow name of a field whose shape looks like a cat's tail). This kind of special feature actually refers to the idea on the basis of which the particular place has been identified, that is, differentiated from other (similar types of) places. In a way, the principles of naming the place is the issue here, which indicates why a certain name has been selected for the place.

If a name has only one name part, it is a single part name (*Niemi* 'cape', *Porvoo* ← Swe. *Borgå* 'castle|river', *Saarela* 'island+LA'). In studies, it has been said that these kinds of names have been formed from merely a generic part. By its function, the generic part can either signify a type (*Niemi*), designate (*Porvoo*) or signify a special feature (*Katinhäntä*, *Saarela* 'the object on the shore of the lake Saarijärvi').

Two-part place names are more common in Finnish than single part names. The overwhelmingly most common type of name is the two-part compound name whose specific part signifies a special feature of the place and the generic part signifying the type of place (*Saari/järvi* 'island|lake', *Mylly/mäki* 'mill|hill'). Other two-part name types (*Vähä Saarijärvi* 'smaller lake out of those named Saarijärvi', *Saarijärven Mattila* 'Mattila which is at Saarijärvi') are clearly less common.

In syntactic-semantic analysis, names are first divided into name parts. The next phase is the syntactic-semantic and lexical-semantic classification of name parts that signify a special feature (also those appearing as single part names). This classification is shown in Fig. 3 with examples.

In syntactic-semantic classification, we examine the question of what the principles of naming are. When naming a place, the name giver has had some *principle of naming*, that is, a certain kind of idea for naming and he has given the place a name in relation to this idea. A principle of naming is a subject regarding extralinguistic reality, such as the shape of a place. These principles are also shown in fig. 3.

Principles of naming are divided into four main groups: location of the place, the natural qualities of the place, what occurs or appears at the place and the place's relationship to people. When analysing the principles of naming, it is worthwhile to *paraphrase* the name, that is, present the name in an explanatory form. Thus, for example, the name *Saarijärvenkangas* 'Saarijärvi+GEN|moor' can be paraphrased as 'a moor which is close to the lake Saarijärvi' (the principle of naming is its precise location), the name *Pihlajakari* 'rowan|rock' is 'a rock on which rowan grows' (the principle of naming is what occurs at the place) and the name *Matinpelto* 'Matti+GEN| field' is 'a field owned by Matti' (the principle of naming is ownership). Sometimes, one name can have more than one principle.

Lexical-semantic classification signifies the lexical category from which the expression for the principle of naming has been signified. For example, the naming principle of the aforementioned *Saarijärvenkangas*, that is, its name part signifying a special feature (*Saarijärven-*) has been expressed using a proper name, more precisely saying, a place name and even an entire place name. The same place could be given, with the same principles, for example, the name *Järvenkangas* 'lake+GEN|moor', whereupon the principle for naming would have been expressed using a part of the place name (*Saari/*

järven- → *Järven-*). In the aforementioned name *Pihlajakari*, the principle for naming (*Pihlaja* 'rowan') is a tree term, or phytonym, and more precisely said, a wild plant. In the name *Matinpelto*, the name part signifying a special feature (*Matin* 'Matti+GEN': 'Matti's') is expressed with a personal name or more precisely said a given name. Lexical-semantic classification with examples is shown in fig. 3.

The model of syntactic-semantic analysis has extensively been used in Finnish toponymic interpretation, for example, in many theses. The entire toponymy of one village has generally been the material for this kind of study, or the names of certain kinds of places of a larger area, for example, names of lakes or ponds. In general, a majority of the place names, up to over 90 per cent, were able to be interpreted, that is, placed for categorisation. The interpretation worked out so well particularly because a majority of all the place names are unambiguous in its motivation. However, it is impossible to reach 100 per cent interpretation because we cannot get a definite answer on the background and naming principles of all names. Moreover, there are more principles of naming than the aforementioned four principles of classification and thus their number is not limited. For this reason, the classification can never be completely comprehensive. It would be impossible to construct a classification that would include all of the syntactic-semantic relationships that could possibly occur in identifying expressions and on which the motivation behind the place names are based. Because the identification of places is also the differentiation of places of the same type from one another, some naming principles regarding certain referents are more central than others. In general, place names can be interpreted correctly only as a part of a certain name system and certain world view. In the case of transparent names, information is required because the explanations could otherwise be completely off the mark.

As shown, the structure of a name has briefly been covered and the interpretation of toponymy with syntactic-semantic classification analysed. In the following section, we will examine the structural features of place names in more detail and get acquainted with different structural types and various means of name formation more specifically. Because structure and semantics in the interpretation of names go inseparably hand in hand, they will overlap here as well.

Various Means of Name Formation

Direct naming. The most typical thing about place names is that they are informative. In this case, there is a *direct meaning relationship* between a name and a place. We can also speak about *direct naming*. The names provide "direct" information about its referent, for example, location or characteristics. The aforementioned *Valkeajärvi* informatively and descriptively conveys a message about its referent: the named location is a place of white waters (at least in relation to other adjacent waters). There were already several examples of direct naming given earlier; for example, *Saarijärvenkangas*, *Pihlajakari* and *Matinpelto* are names in which there is a direct meaning relationship between the name and the place.

Saarijärvenkangas is a place name which includes a name of an adjacent place (*Saarijärvi* 'island|lake' → *Saarijärvenkangas* 'Saarijärvi+GEN|moor'). Other toponymy is also exploited in name giving: many place names include an existing name of a place. This kind of name formation is economical and practical. Providing the moor located in the surroundings of the lake Saarijärvi with the name *Saarijärvenkangas* is advantageous. This kind of place name is called an annexe. The process has also been called *inductive naming*. An *annexe* is a place name which has been formed referring to the name of some nearby place thusly that it either partly or completely includes this name. For example, the annexe of the lake name *Saarijärvi* can, in addition to *Saarijärvenkangas*, include *Saarijärvenpuro* ('Saarijärvi+GEN|brook'), the bay name *Saarilahti* ('bay of the lake Saarijärvi') and the area of *Järvenperä* ('back of the lake Saarijärvi'). The lake name *Saarijärvi* itself can be called the *root name*. The root name along with its annexes form a *name cluster*.

In keeping with means of formation we can distinguish different annexes. When an annexe includes the entire root name as its specific part (*Saarijärven/kangas*), it is a question of a *full annexe*. If the annexe only includes the specific part of the root name (*Saari/lahti* 'bay of the lake Saarijärvi'), then it is a question of a *specifying annexe*. We can speak about a *generic part annexe* when the annexe includes the generic part of the root name (*Järvenperä* 'back of the lake Saarijärvi'). We cannot always recognise these generic part annexes from the nomenclature because corresponding names could have originated independently without the name of the nearby place. In all, there are many annexes in nomenclature, up to half of some area's toponymy. This is understandable because with these names, new, well-localised names are conveniently being developed.

One certain kind of annexe is a *specified name*. This is a question of a name that is associated with a specifying modifier. A specified name is, for example, *Vähä Saarijärvi* ('small Saarijärvi'): this lake is located near a lake named *Saarijärvi* but it is smaller. According to this model, the name *Saarijärvi* could also, and probably for the purpose of clarity, be called *Iso Saarijärvi* ('big Saarijärvi'), which would also, of course, be a specified name. This kind of name is structurally a two-part name in which the specifying modifier is a name part signifying a special feature (*Vähä* 'small', *Iso* 'big') and the name's generic part, the root name, is a designating name part (*Saarijärvi*). We can state, however, that in a way, there is an element in these names that gives a clue, not only to the type of place but to its location: there is always another referent located close to *Pikku Saarijärvi* ('small Saarijärvi'), whose name includes the element *Saarijärvi*.

There are various single part names in Finnish toponymy in which the meaning relationship between the place and the name is direct, in which case the name can include only an appellative or, in addition to an appellative or proper name, a derivational suffix.

A place name can include an appellative only. Sometimes, an appellative signifying the type of place is sufficient for the identification of a place which then would function as its name, as a proper name. The usage of these kinds of expressions could have begun, as the place was the only one of its kind or quite central. For example, *Kirkko* ('church'), *Harju* ('esker') and *Tori* ('market square') can be sufficient to identify the region's only or most important church, esker or market square. In concrete language use, it can sometimes be difficult to decipher if these aforementioned types of expressions here are identifying proper names or just the place's classifying appellatives. Only names that include an appellative can originate from two-part place names if the name's specific part has undergone an apocopic dropping from the name (*Hailuoto* 'Baltic-herring|islet' → *Luoto* 'islet'). Names that include a composition or collocation signifying location of the place (*Suontaus* 'bog+GEN|behind', *Mäenalus* 'hill+GEN|under', *Järvenperä* 'lake+GEN|rear') are also those that only include an appellative.

Names which include a name formation suffix are also considered single part names which express a direct meaning relationship. In name formation, a derivational suffix used in place of a principle part is called a *name formation suffix*. These include, for example, the suffix *la* or *lä* with which many settlement names are formed on the basis of personal names (*Mattila* 'Matti+LA', *Anttila* 'Antti+LA'). There are other suffixes used in Finnish names: such as *nen* typically used in lake names in Eastern Finland (*Saarinen* 'island+NEN', *Valkeinen* white+NEN'). Sometimes the generic part of a two-part name has been replaced with a name formation suffix. In this case, for example, instead of *Valkeajärvi* ('white|lake'), we can speak of *Valkeinen*.

Indirect naming. Not all place names originate as a result of direct naming. There can be an *indirect meaning relationship* between a name and its referent in many place names. We can also speak of *indirect naming*. In this case, a place received its name on the basis of associations aroused by the place. These names are metaphoric and metonymic and they can be called *associative names*.

Metaphoric names are founded on paralleled associations between a place and a concept (*Katinhäntä* 'cat+GEN|tail' as the name of a narrow field and in Finland, *Ghetto* as a name of a crude, compact area populated by those with foreign backgrounds). These have also been called *comparative names* in onomastics. Metaphoric names are structurally most often single part names but they can also be two-part names (*Satula/kivi* 'saddle|stone': 'stone with the appearance of a saddle', *Alttari/kallio* 'altar|rock': 'rock with the appearance of an altar'). A place can be compared with some object or, for example, an animal or a part of it (*Katinhäntä* 'cat+GEN|tail', *Hauenkuono* 'pike+GEN|snout', *Häränsilmä* 'bullseye', *Puuronsilmä* 'porridge+GEN|eye'). For example, the pond named *Häränsilmä* can be compared to a bullseye due to its depth and darkness and the small and drying pond named *Puuronsilmä* can be compared to a dot of butter, the "eye", on top of porridge.

A named place can also be compared to some named place, already known or imagined by the name giver whereupon the place gets its name in relation to this. These names are rather abundant in Finnish nomenclature both in traditional rural nomenclature (*Amerikka* 'America', *Betlehem*

'Bethlehem', *Kaanaa* 'Canaan', *Siperia* 'Siberia') and younger, spontaneous urban nomenclature (*Bronx, Harlem, Monaco*). A broad field, located far away from a house and perhaps sensitive to frost can be called *Siperia* and a field with fertile soil can be called *Kaanaa* or even *Kaanaanpelto* ('Canaan+GEN|field'). In the urban environment, for example, an area where there is a block of flats kept with a racy reputation can be called *Bronx*. The phenomenon of metaphorical, comparative names given in relation to an already named place has been called a *name of comparative transference*.

The second main group of names that are founded on an indirect meaning relationship include *metonymic names*. These names are based on a relational association. Metonymic names can be split up into two different groups. The first group includes names which are founded on an appellatival expression. These are, for example *Yksipihlaja* ('one|rowan') 'an island where a rowan can be seen' and *Kapulasilta* ('duckboards') 'a bog that has duckboards'. The second group of metonymic names are formed by names which are founded on a name of an adjacent place. In this case, it is a question of the fact that the name of an adjacent place begins to be used for the place. When, for example, a house located on the shore of the lake Valkeajärvi, has begun to be called *Valkeajärvi*, this house name is a metonymic name. This phenomenon has also been deemed a *metonymic transference*. These names are given on the basis of location.

Names of metonymic transference are not always considered to be their own independent names. This, for example, is seen in Scandinavian research which, instead, holds the view that it would be a question of one name (*Valkeajärvi*) that has two referents (a lake and a house). It would, however, be appropriate to consider that it would be a question of two different places and simultaneously two different names. Named locations by nature are clearly different and also, by their referents, indisputably separable from one another. It is at least a question of a name's *polysemy*, that is, the extension of its meaning, as we speak of *Valkeajärvi* not only as a name of a lake but also the surrounding region of the lake. This is common in language use: we can, for example, "go picking blueberries at *Valkeajärvi*" in which case, it is most natural to consider that it is question of one place and its one name.

An indirect meaning relationship between a place and its name also occurs in such metonymic, variation names. To begin with, *variation names* are those that have been given according to the name of an adjacent place thus so this name will be phonetically and semantically varied. If, for example, some rapids, perhaps smaller, located close to the rapids Kohiseva ('roar+vA': 'rushing') were to be called *Köhisevä* ('rasp+vA': 'rasping') or a smaller hillock located in proximity to Kukkotörmä ('rooster|river-bank') were to be called *Kanatörmä* ('hen|river-bank'), these would be variation names. Secondly, names called *opposing names*, that is, *contrastive names*, which are those that have originated on the basis of opposing association, are variation names. The aforementioned *Kukkotörmä* and *Kanatörmä* may also work as an example of opposing names. Other examples include *Valkealampi* ('white|pond') and *Mustalampi* ('black|pond') or *Kissalampi* ('cat|pond') and *Koiralampi* ('dog|pond') or *Naistenluoto* ('woman+PL+GEN|islet') and

Miestenluoto ('man+PL+GEN|islet'). Generally, a location named first has received its name according to the natural qualities of the place and later, an adjacent location (or locations) of the same type has been named according to the first one. The principle of naming is thus at least location but sometimes also characteristics. When for example, *Valkealampi* has received its name on the basis of its white waters, location (in proximity to Valkealampi) is the principle for naming of the adjacent *Mustalampi* and perhaps the colour of the pond's water (in comparison to Valkealampi).

These opposing names can also easily originate on the basis of an existing nomenclature exclusive of the fact that the opposition between the places is especially visible. Opposition is always relative: *Mustalampi* is not necessarily an especially black watered pond but in comparison to *Valkealampi*, its waters are, however, perhaps darker. Moreover, adjectives are used when speaking about a place only as references to certain types of traits that label Finnish places. The use of adjectives in nomenclature is also more constricted and different than in language in general. For example, the opposite of *paha* ('evil') is more often *kaunis* ('beautiful') than *hyvä* ('good') and the opposite of *kuiva* ('dry') usually *vesi* ('water') and not *märkä* ('wet'). The adjective *kylmä* ('cold') in hydronymy usually is not given an opposite nor do names usually have *lyhyt* ('short') as the opposite of *pitkä* ('long'). For example, *Pitkälahti* ('long|bay') is one of the more common bay names in Finland but its opposing qualities have predominantly been expressed by the names *Laajalahti* ('wide|bay') and *Leveälahti* ('broad|bay').

Analogical name giving. Place names are often given according to existing nomenclature. An example of this includes, for example, the aforementioned name *Mustalampi* according to *Valkealampi* and the aforementioned *Kissalampi* in relation to *Koiralampi*. When the model of name giving is some other nomenclature, we can speak of *analogy* and *analogical name giving*.

The percentage of analogy in Finnish name formation can be seen by virtue of place names which include a participle, as examined in the dissertation (1971) by Eero Kiviniemi. The research material was 387 sets of names which includes over 1,800 name clusters or individual names. This name type is based on expressiveness: over half of the names are based on an onomatopoetic or descriptive verb. The most typical of these are hydronyms with the frequentative *ise* derivational ending of which the largest sets are *Koliseva* ('rattle+vA': 'rattling'), *Töriseva* ('growl+vA': 'growling') and *Kohiseva* ('roar+ vA': 'roaring'). Most of these names are based on the sound or movement of water or watery soil. This study proved that up to at least half of the place names with the first participle have emerged in line with a model of already existing names of the same type and having the same root. Although a model provided by other names can be found behind many names, analogical names are nonetheless generally descriptive of a place. They have not been given without a principle of naming. In most cases, there is some similarity amongst a place that has provided and received a model.

The need for naming naturally has an influence on the emergence of models: a model can be created only when, for example, there is a need to name previously unnamed places in the expansion of settlement. Moreover, the environment also creates preconditions for the occurrence of names of a certain type. It is clear that, for example, hydronyms are required in those places where there is an abundance of waterways. There have been certain types of name formation models at different times and in different population groups; hence, name formation models are connected to settlement history. The models have usually been included in the language of the population which inhabits the area. Depending on if these names given in line with the model occur in an early or later inhabited area and if they are names of small or larger locations, we can make a conclusion on the age of a name type. The names that occurred in early inhabited areas and as names of large places are nearly without exception old. If names are associated with small locations, they have been given when the largest ones have already been named.

The Main Features of Syntactic-Semantic Analysis

Alphabetic and numeric codes are utilised in this analysis. The results of the analysis are expressed as a uniform code whereupon it includes (a) a structural identifier (A, B or C) and – if there is a name part signifying a special feature in the name – (b) information on the principles of naming (10, 11, 12 etc.) and on (c) the lexical category from which the expression for the principle of naming has been signified (letters and combination of letters S, N, NP, NK etc.).

- From a syntactic-semantic perspective, names are first arranged in syntactic, structural components, name parts. A name part = a 'part of a name' whose function is to classify or identify the place in regard to name formation. The name part signifies one feature characteristic to the referent.

The syntactic-semantic function of a name part can:

A = signify the type of place (*Musta*/*lahti* 'black|bay')
B = designate (*Iso / Mustalahti* 'great Mustalahti'; *Porvoo*)
C = signify a special feature (*Musta*/*lahti* 'black|bay')

The name part signifying a special feature is usually the specific part of a compound name or an expression included in a single part name. This kind of special feature actually refers to a concept, on the basis of which the place has been identified, in other words, distinguished from other places (of the same type). It is thus a question of the place's principle of naming.

Principles of Naming

10. Location, status of the place
11. Precise location (*Ahvenlahden/kari* 'Ahvenlahti+GEN|skerry', *Ranta/pelto* 'shore|field')
12. Relational location (*Ala/suo* 'low|bog', *Etelä/pelto* 'south|field')

20. (Natural) characteristics of the place
21. Topographic dimension or shape (*Laaja/lahti* 'broad|bay', *Vähä/mäki* 'small | hill', *Koukku/järvi* 'hook|lake')
22. Nature or characteristics of soil, water or material (*Musta/lahti* 'black|bay', *Terva/järvi* 'tar|lake', *Hieta/lahti* 'fine-sand|bay')
23. Other characteristics (*Vanha/kylä* 'old|village')

30. Existing or occurring at the place
31. Individual referent (*Riihi/mäki* 'drying-barn|hill')
32. Collective referent (*Haapa/niemi* 'aspen|cape', *Ilves/kallio* 'lynx|rock')

40. Relationship of the place to people
41. Ownership, usage, residence (*Anttila* 'Antti+LA', *Antin/pelto* 'Antti+GEN|field')
42. Use, activities, origin (*Onki/kivi* 'fishing-rod|stone', *Tanssi/kallio* 'dance|rock', *Laidun/mäki* 'pasture|hill')
43. Incident (*Surma/luoto* 'death|islet', *Riita/maa* 'conflict|land')

The upper-level numeric codes (10, 20, 30, 40) are used when if we can decided that the principle of naming is, for example, the relationship of the place to people (40) but we cannot be sure if it is, for example, ownership or use of the place.

- In order to get a more specific picture of the lexical structure of names and their semantics, name parts (also those appearing as single part names) signifying a special feature are classified more specifically according to sentential semantic.

Lexical Analysis and Lexical-Semantic Classification

Lexical-semantic classification (that is, based on the meanings of name elements) expresses the lexical category from which the expression for the principle of naming has been signified.

Noun
N   Proper name
NP   Place name
NK   Whole name
NO   Place name part

NH   Personal name
NHE   Given name
NHS   Surname
NHL   Byname
NM   Other proper name
SA   Non-proprial noun, as a referent:
SP   Place, artefact etc.
PL   Natural place
PK   Cultural place, artefact
PM   PL/PK

MVI Natural element (land, water, snow, ice; weather phenomena)
SK Flora
KL Wild plants
KK Cultivated plants
KP Place defined by flora
SE Fauna
EL Wild animals
EK Domesticated animals
EY EL/EK
SH People, community
HK Cultural product (object, instrument, weapon, material etc.)
HE Social life (work, leisure, conflict, beliefs, emotions, time periods etc.)
D (Compound) adjective
B Compound adverbs of place or locative postposition
V Compound verb, participle
X Numeral, prepositional expression
SS Collocation signifying location
SM Other collocation

Examples

Saari/järvi 'island|lake' CA 31 (or 32) PL "a lake which has (an) island(s)"
Saarinen 'island+NEN' C 31 (or 32) PL
Saarijärvi (homestead name) 1 C 11 NK "adjacent to the lake Saarijärvi"
Saarijärvenkangas 'Saarijärvi+GEN|moor' 2 CA 11 NK "a moor which is adjacent to Saarijärvi"
Saari/kangas 'island|moor' 2 CA 11 NO
Iso / Saarijärvi 'big Saarijärvi' 2 CB 21 D "a Saarijärvi that is larger"
Saarela 'island+LA' (homestead name) 1 C 11 NO "adjacent to the lake Saarijärvi"
Siperia 'Siberia' 1 C 22 (or 23) "(a field which is) reminiscent of Siberia"
Katinhäntä 'cat+GEN|tail' 1 C 21 EK "(a field which is) reminiscent of a cat's tail"
Ykspihlaja 'one|rowan' (island name) 1 C 31 KL "(an island where) a rowan exists / is visible"
Kapulasilta 'duckboards' (bog name) 1 C 31 PK "(a bog which has) duckboards"
(*Häränsilmä* 'bullseye' →) *Häränsilmän/lampi* 'bullseye+GEN|pond' 2 BA "a pond whose name is Häränsilmä"

Fig. 3. *The main features of syntactic-semantic analysis.*

Variation in Names

A place name does not necessarily have an established form. Instead, several different forms can be used for the same name. Sometimes a structural change has occurred in a name: *Valkeajärvi* could have become *Valkeinen* and *Hailuoto* became *Luoto*. The different forms of the same name may be asynchronous whereupon it would be a question of name change. However, it may at the very least be just as common that different forms are concurrently used for the same name. A change in a place name and the variation of different forms cannot always be distinguished from each other because change and variation are partly overlapping phenomena. The following will examine variation in place names: structural variation and briefly phonetic as well.

Both single and two-part forms can be used for a Finnish place name. In this case, it is a question of structural variation. Firstly, a two-part name can become a single part name and vice versa. When a two-part, compound type name may be shortened to a single part name, it is a question of an *ellipse*. An ellipse of either the specific part or generic part can occur. Should a name's specific part disappear (*Hailuoto* 'Baltic-herring|islet' → *Luoto* 'islet') the result is a single part name form signifying the type of place. This expression only functions as an identifying component when the name's referent is one of the most central places of its kind in the user circle, the places to which the generic part in question refers.

A generic part ellipse is more common than an ellipse of a specific part. Elliptic possibilities of a generic part depend a great deal on the lexical structure of the name. For example, it is not likely for the lake *Kalajärvi* ('fish|lake') to be shortened to the form *Kala* ('fish') nor *Mustalampi* ('black|pond') to become *Musta* ('black'). With certain distinctive features, the specific part, as such, must be able to be recognised as a proper name. For example, the forest name *Monikkalankorpi* ('Monikkala+GEN|woods') has possibly been shortened to *Monikkala* and the meadow name *Närviäistenniitty* ('Närviäinen+PL+GEN|meadow') to *Närviäinen* as any other *Monikkala* or *Närviäinen* is no longer known in the area. These kinds of single part forms work well as names because they do not get confused with the appellative or another proper name.

An elliptical change can also occur in a reduction. A *reduction* refers to the ellipse of an element featured in the middle of a name. This kind of change is mostly possible in a whole annexe whereupon, for example, *Haukijärvenvuori* ('Haukijärvi+GEN|mountain' ← *Haukijärvi* 'pike|lake') can become *Haukivuori*. Of course, the mountain adjacent to Haukijärvi could have directly been given the name – a specifying annexe – *Haukivuori*, whereupon it would not be a question of a reduction.

The opposite of an elliptical change is an epexegesis. In an *epexegesis*, the name has been supplemented with a generic part which explicates its referent. An example of an epexegesis would be if, for example, the pond name *Valkeinen* were to get a specifying, generic part and its resulting form would be *Valkeisenlampi* ('Valkeinen+GEN|pond'). Epexegetical forms emerge mostly when there is a need to supplement what kind place is at hand. This kind of change can also initially occur in two-part names if, for example, the name's latter part is no longer recognised as a component that signifies the type of place or if there is the desire to explicate the type of place. For example, the name of the Southern Savo ditch *Raitinpuru* ('village-road+GEN|brook') has been supplemented with the principle part *oja* ('ditch') and the final form *Raitinpurunoja* ('Raitinpuru+GEN|ditch'), as the appellative *puru* ('brook'), which previously had been a part of the local dialect then afterwards nearly disappeared, is no longer perceived to mean a ditch.

If *suffixation* occurs in a name, a two-part name signifying the type of place will become a single part name that includes a name formation suffix. Suffixation is a question of, for example, when the generic part *järvi* ('lake') in the original two-part lake name *Saarijärvi* (island|lake) is replaced with the suffix *nen* whereupon the result becomes *Saarinen* (island+NEN). With suffixation, shorter, single part forms can be achieved and, above all, become expressions that can be recognised as proper names when an ellipse, as a means of change, is impossible.

Up to this point, we have shown cases in which a name's structure has undergone a change. Variants that are distinguishable from one another in other ways can also be used for place names. For example, the generic parts in a two-part name can be interchangeable. Alongside *Likovuori* ('soaked|mountain'), we can speak of *Likokallio* ('soaked|rock') and with *Ränskälänkorpi* ('Ränskälä+GEN|marsh') we have *Ränskälänsuo* ('Ränskälä+GEN|bog'). The generic parts, in this case, are full or close synonyms in the local dialect.

Morphological variation can also occur in toponymy. A Finnish name can have both singular and plural forms whereupon, for example, *Rainionpelto* ('Rainio+GEN|field' ← surname *Rainio*) and *Rainionpellot* ('Rainio+GEN|field+PL') can simultaneously occur. The case of a place of a name's specific part can also vary: the specific part can, for example, appear either in the nominative (in Finnish, its basic form, that is, an unmarked or zero-inflection case ending) or genitive (in Finnish, marked with *n*) case. The name *Kupparipelto* ('cupper|field') can exist alongside of *Kupparinpelto* ('cupper+GEN|field') and *Kettumäki* ('fox|hill') alongside of *Ketunmäki* ('fox+GEN|hill'). The specific part of a Finnish place name is always either in the nominative or genitive case – or both are recognised for the same name as seen in the aforementioned examples. It is impossible to provide precise rules on the choice of case in specific parts but many can however say which specifier is more common in different names. The specific part is in the genitive case in names that signify the location of the place which include another place name (*Haukijärvenoja* 'Haukijärvi+GEN|ditch'), when the name signifies an owner or user (*Matinpelto* 'Matti+GEN|field') and when the name is epexegetical (*Valkeinen* 'white+NEN' → *Valkeisenlampi* 'Valkeinen+GEN|pond'). Some names which signify an entity located at a place are often qualified with the nominative case (*Riihimäki* 'drying-barn|hill', *Haapaniemi* 'aspen|cape'). The specific part in the nominative case also occurs when the name describes the place on the basis of, for example, size or shape (*Pitkäniemi* 'long|cape', *Laajalahti* 'wide|bay').

A phonetic aspect in the variation of names can be seen in, for example, the forms *Säiniönjoki*, *Sääniönjoki* and *Säyniäjoki* used for a river name in the Eastern Finland municipality of Ristiina. The name includes the dialectical forms, and forms created from them, of the word *säynävä* ('ide', *Leuciscus idus*, a freshwater fish in the family Cyprinidae). Diversity can thus stem from dialectical variation, dialectic change or the obscurity of the name's origin. For example, the name *Vellinkimäki* ('Vellinki|hill') in the Southern Finland municipality of Asikkala may include the personal name

Velling. As the name's origin is unclear, the form *Vellitmäki* has come into discussion. As for *Pukarajärvi* ('Pukara|lake'), from the same municipality, this name has become *Pukalajärvi* as the word *pukara* which refers to an irregular shape has been deemed unknown. (Ainiala 1997.)

When different forms are used for the same name, these forms of the same name are each other's *parallel forms.* Variation and parallel form are quite common in toponymy. In the name data (excluding settlement names) of the village of Kurhila of the Häme municipality of Asikkala, more than every fifth place name has structural parallel forms (Ainiala 1997). Phonetic parallel forms are hence not included in this figure. In reality, there may be an abundance of even more variation than this because all of the different names and name variants will never be obtained in the compiling of material.

The same place can also completely be called by different names, in which case it is a question of parallel names. *Parallel names* are different names of the same place, given by different principles. The same field can be called *Kivipelto* ('stone|field') and *Mäkeläntakuinen* ('behind the farm named Mäkelä') and the same rock *Akankallio* ('old-woman+GEN|rock') and *Lehmänkallio* ('cow+GEN|rock'). Parallel names also include such settlement names in which the same inhabitant is referred to with different names. Thus, for example, a cabin inhabited by Eetu Matikainen can be referred to by two different, that is, parallel names *Eetunmökki* ('Eetu+GEN|cabin') and *Matikaisenmökki* ('Matikainen+GEN|cabin').

The aspect of parallel names averages out to be the most common in settlement names. In the data including settlement names in the village of Kurhila in Asikkala, each dwelling has an average of 1.9 names. Out of many parallel names, surnames are used as dwelling names. Because settlements are often named in relation to an inhabitant, they can receive new names in line with new inhabitants. The use of old names can also be preserved. Moreover, different names given according to location can be provided. However, all of the names of the same settlement are not necessarily used simultaneously. For example a house originally named *Mattila* ('Matti+LA'), after the owner *Matti*, also began to be called *Ala-Mattila* ('lower Mattila') when the house was split into two as *Ala-Mattila* and *Ylä-Mattila* ('upper Mattila'). The house can also be called *Kivisoja* (the house is located by the ditch Kivisoja) according to its location and as *Kivisojan Mattila* ('Kivisoja+GEN Mattila': 'Mattila of Kivisoja'). It is also known by the owner's surname *Lehtinen*. (Ainiala 1997.)

Name Strata over Time and across Languages

Origin and Etymology

We cannot always grasp the semantic content of all place names. This is apparent under many old names which are often contextually obscure. In Finland, these names include, for example, many city names: *Espoo, Helsinki, Kajaani, Oulu, Tampere, Turku, Vantaa* and several others as well.

When we examine the *etymology* of place names, their origin is analysed. The key point of departure is the knowledge on how all traditionally emerged place names have originally been completely comprehensible linguistic expressions and also, in some way, descriptive of the place. The subject of etymological research, thus, includes what a name's original semantic content had been which had existed at its moment of emergence. When examining etymology we also seek information on what the name consists of and what these linguistic elements mean as well as what the name's original form had been. It is never always perfectly clear what the original language of a name had been and the investigation must first be able to decipher this. For example, the Finnish lake name *Päijänne* has be suspected to be of Sámi origin but many studies have regarded the name to be of an unknown ancient language.

Etymological research aims at dating a name as precisely as possible. To assist in this, early document notations of names are used which indicate when a name had at the latest been in use. The earliest Finnish documents and maps are generally just from the 16th century, thus, it is not possible to reach far into the past – the dates of origin of many names – with written sources. In finding the age of names, information on the natural state of locations and their environment and also their changes can, however, be useful tools.

The etymology of place names and, secondly, their semantic examination go closely hand in hand. However, the semantic investigation of place names is a more extensive subject than etymological research because it aims at deciphering a name's factual background and principle of naming. Many Finnish place names are transparent to such an extent that this principle of naming can be rather reliably found. For example, the principles of naming for the island name *Korkeasaari* ('high|island') or the hill name *Koivumäki* ('birch|hill') are quite clear – at least when the names are truly given to be descriptive of the place – without any investigation. With regard to many opaque names and also lexically and syntactic-semantically ambiguous names, the analysis of the principles of naming is, however, not necessarily easy. In this case, there is often a reason to attempt to etymologise the name.

Traditional place names have always originated in a local community and have been structured from elements of the local language. If we do not know the circumstances under which a name has been given in its time, it is difficult for us to analyse its origin. Contemporary linguistic circumstances and its current setting may be quite different from that in which a name had been given a long time ago. The linguistic elements which are included in a name could have been left out of the local language. In this case, we no longer would recognise the content of the name although it was, of course, quite clear to the name giver. For example, the historically known transitive verb *neitää* and intransitive verb *neityä* ('leak, drip through; get wet') may be behind the village name *Neittävä* ('leaking, dripping') in the Northeast Finland municipality of Vaala. The area is located on a low land between two waterways upon which the name would be semantically well suited for the place. A word originally included in a name may have been small-scale in its distribution. The Häme village name *Letku*, in Southern Finland, is an example of this. This name only includes the narrowly distributed known dialectic word *letku* which means 'undulating land'.

Through time, different structural or phonological changes could have occurred in a name whereupon the name has become incomprehensible by its form. There could have been an apocopic change in the end of the name's specific part, that is, phones disappeared from the end of a word appearing as a specifier. This kind of change can be explained in the emergence of the name forms of *Hailuoto* (← *Haililuoto* 'Baltic-herring|islet') and *Koijärvi* (← *Koivujärvi* 'birch|lake'). In their interpretation, it is difficult to confirm the names *Haukjärvi* (← *Haukijärvi* 'pike|lake' or *Haukkajärvi* 'hawk|lake') and *Lehlampi* (← *Lehmilampi* 'cow|pond' or *Lehtilampi* 'leaf|pond'). Only a vowel has undergone an apocopic change in the end of the specific part whereupon the name has often remained comprehensible (*Korpjärvi* ← *Korpijärvi* 'woods|lake', *Rautjärvi* ← *Rautajärvi* 'iron|lake', *Riihmäki* ← *Riihimäki* 'drying-barn|hill'). The final forms after an apocopic change are naturally regular in many dialects. Also, a name's generic part could have also gradually vanished whereupon for example *Mustajoki* ('black|river') became *Mustio* and *Kotaoja* ('hut|ditch') became *Kotaja*.

When investigating a name's origin, we must be familiar with its old forms included in documents and maps. From these, old spellings and, in this way, perhaps the name's earlier forms can be revealed as well. For example, the name of the Padasjoki village community *Mainiemi* of Southern Finland is quite unclear to speakers of today but a documented form from 1511 reveals that the spelling at that time was *Mayenemi*. This means that the name is a shortened form of *Majaniemi* and behind this could simply be the word *maja* meaning 'cottage' – in conclusion, *Mainiemi* could be 'cottage|cape'. On the other hand, many names in this area beginning with *maja* are shortened forms of *majava* ('beaver') names whereupon the name would refer to a beaver nesting at the place. In addition, the origin of the village name of *Vaistenkylä*, in the part of Maaria in the city of Turku, is clear through old documented notations (*Wayuas* 1359, *Vaywastinkylä* 1453, *Vaijvaisten kylä* 1540): the original form of the name being *Vaivaistenkylä* ('cripple+PL+GEN |village').

Names do not originate independent of other nomenclature; when new names emerge, they are always formed as part of an existing one. Names are greatly formed in line with a model of an already existing nomenclature as well. For this reason, when examining a name's etymology, it is necessary to take the kind of name system into account and the whole nomenclature to which the name being examined has belonged. For example, the form *Joutsenne* has been used for the name known as *Joutsenjärvi* ('swan|lake') in Padasjoki. This name form, which includes the ending *nne*, may have come about in accordance with the names of the large nearby lakes *Lummenne* and *Päijänne*. We often also notice that names have been given according to existing names and that they simultaneously give information, for example, on the distributive orientation of settlement. For example, the Häme parish name of Hattula, whose name stems from an old Germanic personal name, can be seen in the Kymenlaakso names *Hattustensaari* and *Hattusenmaa*. In this case, we can conclude that settlement from Hattula had come to the area.

There are also loaned names or name elements from other languages in Finnish names. For example, many settlement names include personal names of Germanic origin. Various Germanic influences have come to Finland starting in the Bronze Age (from Proto-Scandinavian) and more extensively in the Middle Ages (Old High German, Low German). These inhabitants brought their anthroponymy which the original population would thus adopt. These names have been speculated to be included, for example, in the following settlement names appearing in the areas of Southern Finland: *Asikkala* (← *Asicka*), *Halikko* (← *Halick*), *Kyötikkälä* (← *Gödicke*), *Laitikkala* (← *Laidich*), *Masku* (← *Masco*) and *Pyynikki* (← *Byniki*).

Dating place names. Discerning the age of place names can be a difficult task. In practice, there are not too many ways to find out the time of emergence of individual names. With names entered in old maps and documents we can achieve the dating "before a certain time": if a name has been entered in a source dating at the end of the 18th century, we can say that the name has been in use then but we do not know when it came about before it.

The difficulties in dating place names are greatly due to the fact that their linguistic form or content do not give a many clues that can be used to even relatively date the emergence of names precisely. There are such names (*Haukijärvi* 'pike|lake', *Saarijärvi* 'island|lake'), particularly in natural places which, regardless of their transparency, can just as easily be two hundred or two thousand years old.

In regard to settlement names, dating is relatively easier because these names often include such personal names or terms referring to a person, which can be given a rough estimate on the time. As many Finnish personal names are of Christian origin (*Antti* 'Andrew', *Jaakko* 'Jacob', *Mikko* 'Michael'), we can state that, for instance, homestead and village names, including these personal names, have been given, at the earliest, during the establishment of Christianity in Finland. In addition to this, information is generally more easily available on the age and history of different dwellings, and, for example, there is research data largely on settlement history. The oldest Finnish cadastres are from the 16th century and thus, they reliably account for the settlement of that time.

There are not as many sources and research data on the age of cultivation and artefact names as there are for settlement names. However, there is detailed documentary information on cultivation names from the time of the the land consolidation realignments of the Great Partition in Finland which began in the beginning of the late 18th century. Cultivation and artefact names are usually a younger stratum than settlement names. Their age is, of course, in direct relation to the age of settlement because cultivation had been established and artefacts fabricated only when the area had already had settlement.

In setting off to date place names, we must first examine the principle of naming and the lexical element on which the principle has been signified. If a name includes, for example, a plant or animal term, which we know appeared in the area only for a certain time period, we will get a rough idea of the name's age. For example, the field name *Peorhaaro* in the municipality of Kalanti, located in Southwestern Finland, can be reconstructed as **Peurahaudat* ('reindeer|grave+PL', noted as *Peurahautij* in a 1783 document); a dialectical form has appeared as *peorhaora*. It is probable that this name, associated with reindeer hunting, had emerged before the 13th century because it is known that the wild reindeer, to which these names refer, became extinct in Finland by the 13th century. (Mallat 1997.)

The changes of the location to which a name refers, and its environment, help each other in dating the name. Post-glacial rebound on the coast and archipelago is one of the earliest criteria of dating place names. As the velocity of post-glacial rebound is rather strictly known, in keeping with map contour lines, it is possible to reconstruct the features of the setting at different times. At the beginning of the Common Era, the archipelago, for example, could have differed from what it is today, and many of today's islands could have been under water. However, with contour lines, we can figure out when the islands have emerged from under the water and thus conclude the earliest when these places could have been given names ending in *saari* ('island').

Questions on settlement history are also connected to the dating of names. With place names we can explicitly make settlement history conclusions. The distribution of place names here is central. When, with extensive name materials and collections, we examine where a certain name or name element appears, we can make a conclusion on something about the distributive orientation of names. This can thus be connected to the distribution of settlement.

When making conclusions on settlement history, there are names that have a central status, whose words included in them extend beyond their geographical distribution of dialect. The distribution of place names is primarily the same as the distribution of a word included in it. For example, a majority of names that include the word *keiju* ('swing') are known (*Keijumäki* 'swing|hill', *Keijukallio* 'swing|rock') in an area where the word itself is also known, in other words, in the region of Northeast Häme and Päijät-Häme. This, however, is not always the case. For example, names beginning with *Hyypiö* are located in Northern Finland and the areas of Lake Saimaa even though the appellative *hyypiö* ('eagle-owl') is unknown there. We can also conclude that the names have been distributed to these regions by their regions of origin from Southwest Finland and, at the same time, from Southern Karelia through settlement. (Mallat 2007.)

Moreover, how the distribution of names has crossed its dialectic distribution can be shown with the case of names including *Salin*. *Salin* originally is a variant of the word *sadin* ('hunting trap') in Häme dialect. The name *Salin* is found in nomenclature in a clearly more expansive area (through Northern Savo and Northern Ostrobothnia) than the word *salin* in its region of use. The Häme population that knew this word were hunters and game trackers who, in their travels, had named places starting with *Salin* after the traps they were familiar with and used. With names that include *Salin*, for instance, we can uncover how Häme settlement has extended from the Häme region more extensively to Finland and taken these names with it. We can also conclude that these names had been given during its subsequent time when the Häme population went on hunting trips and when the voiced dental fricative of the Häme region ([ð], predecessor to the standard Finnish [d]) had changed to [l]. Scholars have dated this to the 13th century at the latest but possibly even earlier to the 11th century.

The most central place names in Finland and their etymologies can be seen in the dictionary of Finnish place names *Suomalainen paikannimikirja* (2007). This book contains information not only on the etymology of names, that is, their origins and age, but also different information on the places themselves. Under a good many entries, a familiar subject is encountered in their etymological examination: we can never be absolutely sure about the origin of a name. We often have to end up being satisfied with pointing out which interpretation or interpretations in previous investigations are possible, which again, according to research data, appears more unreliable. Many names may thus receive an alternative interpretation but not one of these may necessarily be correct. The task of the study is to divide etymological work and critically review the findings of earlier investigations and search for new possibilities. The following examines the etymologies of a few well-known place names in Finland with the information of the aforementioned dictionary of Finnish place names.

Suomi
This endonym meaning 'Finland' earlier had only meant the country's southwestern part which later became known as *Varsinais-Suomi* (Finland Proper or Southwest Finland). The oldest known spelling of the name may be *Somevesi* in the Treaty of Nöteborg (also known as the Treaty of Oreshek) meaning '*Suomenvesi* that referred to the Bay of Vyborg or its bottom' (*Suomenvesi* 'Suomi+GEN|water'). There have been many suppositions on the origin of the name *Suomi*. Petri Kallio's etymology is considered the most probable, according to which, the name's basis may have developed from a word from an Indo-European root that meant 'human'. The members of the Indo-European Battle-Axe peoples that migrated amongst the early Proto-Finns and assimilated with them over time may have used the word to refer to themselves. The word may have been descended in the form of *ćoma to the early Proto-Finnish ancestors as a term used about themselves as well. The later phonetic development of the word led to the form *sōmi and further on to its current form *suomi*. This explanation is not only linguistically plausible but also possible due to its factual background: national or tribal terms used by peoples related to the Finns and even other peoples about themselves originally are based on words that have meant 'human' or 'man' and many of these terms are loans adopted from a language of (conquering) peoples of foreign origin.

Häme

The earliest written records of this province's name are from the 15th century. The newest etymology of the name has been provided by Jorma Koivulehto, according to whom, its starting point is a Proto-Germanic word meaning 'dark' which took the form *šämä in early Proto-Finnish. The Proto-Finns that inhabited Finland, that is, the coastal regions of Southwest Finland, borrowed the word from the Germanic peoples who migrated amongst the Proto-Finns one thousand years before the turn of the Common Era. The costal inhabitants began to use the term *šämä/hämä to refer to the darker complexioned Sámi neighbours inhabiting the inland and these peoples perhaps also adopted the already obscure word as its own term *šämä/sápmi. As the inhabitants began to migrate inland from the coast to the old Sámi region in the subsequent Iron Age, after the beginning of the Common Era, the region in the migrants' language was *Hämä and they became known as hämäläinen, that is, the 'Hämä people'. The indigenous Hämä, that is, the Sámi people, who withdrew to more remote areas to make way for them, started to be called lappalainen ('Lapp') and their dwelling area Lappi ('Lapland'). The subsequent stages of the word's loaning have been examined, above all, by Unto Salo in his research focusing on archaeology, cultural and settlement history.

Päijänne

The first written record on the name of Finland's second largest lake is from 1474 (*Peijendaranda*). The name includes the derivational suffix *nne* which appears in certain other contextually obscure hydronyms (*Tarjanne*). Many interpretations have been presented on the name's origin, none of which has been very plausible. It is possible that the name originated in some unknown old language which loaned the word to Finnish through Sámi. At some point in its history, the name was included in the Sámi languages, however it probably did not originate from them.

Saimaa

The earliest records of Finland's largest lake have not been available until the 17th century: *Saimas wesi* 1646, *Saimas selkä* 1646. The name's original form was thus *Saimasvesi* ('Saimas|water') or *Saimasselkä* ('Saimas|open-waters') which eventually was shortened to *Saimas*. On the basis of how certain Finnish words ending in *s* are morphologically inflected in the paradigm of case endings (*Saimas* → *Saimaa-* → *Saimaalla* 'Saimas+ADE': 'on/at Saimas'), the name developed to its current base form *Saimaa*. The Sámi word *sápmi* – which was already covered in the section on Häme – which in English, became *Sámi* or *Sami* (in Finnish *saame*), may be behind the name. There was a Sámi people that inhabited the area, thus this explanation is plausible.

Tampere

Finland's third largest city, founded on the edge of the Tammerkoski rapids, received its name from these rapids (e.g. *Tamberkoski* 1544) and from the village of the same name that was built up around it. According to the most common explanations, this body of water may have received its name from the Old Swedish word *damber* which meant 'dam' or 'mill', that is, oak. The Finnish word *koski* 'rapids' may have been added afterwards. Lars Huldén however gave his explanation which states that the name's origin may have come from the Old Norse word *þambr* 'strained, thick-bellied'. This would have been descriptive of the rapids where the masses of water crash and bubble against the wider basin.

Turku
The name of Finland's former capital most likely originated when it was founded in the 13th century, although its oldest written record was not available until 1543 in Mikael Agricola's, the father of literary Finnish, primer *ABC-kiria*. The name indicates that the city had been built as an old trade centre, a point of contact of the main roads where a market square, a *turku*, took shape. The word *turku* signifies connections to the east. It was borrowed from the Old East Slavic word *turgu* 'trade centre' which found its way along with Novgorod merchants.

Kuopio
The name of the capital of the Northern Savo region is a shortened form of the longer name *Kuopionniemi* (*Coopianiemi* 1549, 'Kuopio+GEN|cape'). It has been considered that the name includes the Karelian Orthodox male name *Prokopij* – the name stemming from the Greek saint's name *Procopios* – the Fennicised adaptation being *Kuopio*.

Pyhäjärvi
There are dozens of lakes named *Pyhäjärvi* ('sacred|lake') in Finland. Many of these are placed at different borders, in which case their names include the word *pyhä* 'sacred, holy' which originally meant 'an enclosure, an area separated from something'. Later, the word *pyhä* may have become a term that was given to a conquered area as a name and it designated topographic places acting as the area's borders. There was a belief that there were powers in places that were separate, that is, sacred, which would harm anyone who would approach them without warning. However, all of the places beginning with *Pyhä* are not boundary markers. Instead, for some other reason, they have been sacred places in an old community.

Temporal Stratification
Toponymy is made up of name strata of various ages. The oldest names of a region can be equally as old as the oldest settlement of the area or even older, in other words, they can come from a time when there had still been no permanent settlement in the region. In this case, the oldest names may be the first in the region or at least at an early stage given by those who travelled about there. The oldest Finnish name stratum is associated with hunting culture. First, the areas' most significant and central locations are usually named which, for example, have been important regarding travel. These are, for instance, lakes and other significant natural locations. The general rule

of thumb is that there are on average less macrotoponyms, names of more widely known locations, than there are microtoponyms, names known in only a small user community. The more significant and extensive the name of the location is, the older it usually is.

A central place, a large lake for example, does not necessarily always have an old name. A name may have changed whereupon a new name has replaced the original name. For example, many Finnish names with *Kirkko* ('church') are, as expected, relatively young, the earliest given at the coming of Christianity, and may have replaced an earlier name. Many lakes presently known as *Kirkkojärvi* ('church|lake') were known by a different name but the proximity to the church has given reason to rename the lake whereupon an earlier name gradually was forgotten.

Places today thus do not necessarily bear their original names. A part of old names may have been lost or replaced by new ones. The names of such places which we no longer need to speak about may have completely become forgotten. As for new names, they can emerge both in new, previously unnamed places and in places that already have had a name.

Change in Finnish toponymy has been examined under the scrutiny of materials from different time periods. These studies have shown that a notable part of place names may disappear in a rather short amount of time, a few decades. Terhi Ainiala's (1997) research on names from of the time of the Great Partition, approximately 200 years back, in the Häme village of Kurhila in Asikkala and in the Southern Savo village of Närhilä in Ristiina, shows that 71 per cent of place names in Kurhila disappeared and 84 per cent of place names in Närhilä disappeared by the end of the 20th century. Between 1920 and 1930, 50 per cent of the names in Kurhila disappeared and 43 per cent disappeared in Närhilä. In the 1960s, no fewer than 43 per cent, nearly half, of the names used in Kurhila had disappeared. The names in these calculations include artefact names, cultivation names, topographic names and hydronyms, however no settlement names.

The preservation of place names that had been used in rural villages between 1960 and 1970 has been examined to a great extent in a total of nine different villages located in different parts of Finland (Ainiala 2000). Of all the names (excluding settlement names), about half on average have disappeared from the 1960s and 1970s until the 1990s, the minimum approximately one third and the maximum up to two thirds. Susceptible to disappearing are the names of small user circles, microtoponyms, out of which the names of changed places, in particular (by way of use), have often remained in use. Alternatively, the names of central places, macrotoponyms, rarely disappear. The need to identify these kinds of more notable places will not generally disappear, even though, for example, the settlement of the region may significantly be shrinking. The differences in the disappearance of various names by their range of use also become evident when examining the disappearance of names of places of different types. Microtoponyms can, above all, be found in cultivation names and artefact names. Cultivation names are those that have suffered the most disappearances: roughly 50 to 90 per cent of cultivation names of various ages have disappeared. A majority of artefact names have also disappeared. On the contrary, nature names have predictably been better preserved: on average, less than one fourth of hydronyms and one third of topographic names have disappeared.

A change in lifestyles and environment – a country setting itself – has usually caused the disappearance of place names. The number of inhabitants in rural villages has nearly diminished everywhere and of all those living in rural areas, fewer than before are getting their livelihood from agriculture. Traditional means of livelihood and methods of production have been replaced by new ones. Many dwelling places have become desolate, fields have become covered with trees and many places, barns, bridges and lanes for example, have vanished. The entire number of rural toponymies has diminished and there are no longer so many names needed for speaking of these places as before.

The fact that a name no longer is sufficient enough to describe its referent could have sometimes affected the disappearance of a name. Although a name does not need to characterise its point of reference, the loss of descriptiveness can be fatal to a name, in which case a name can change: for example *Laitumenlähde* ('pasture+GEN|spring') has changed to *Isolähde* ('large|spring') after grazing has ended.

There are various temporal strata in toponymy. As a general rule, we can state that the longer settlement has continued without any breaks, the more multi-layered the toponymy is. The fact that place names can be preserved at all of course requires that the area has continuously been included in the habitat or sphere of interests of a community or communities. In rural toponymy, the stratum of the youngest, that is, stratum emerged during the last few centuries, is on average the most extensive because an abundance of names had been required in agriculture-intensive culture. Nevertheless, in many aspects, the oldest stratum associated with hunting culture or a time of older manors is most interesting because it always represents the oldest linguistic tradition of the region and also the oldest verbal communication used on places. This most likely includes nomenclature particularly associated with old roads and older dwelling places. These are central hydronyms but also such place names which may have historically been associated with different roads and routes. We can also naturally presume that other kinds of places (hills, large marshlands and others), more notable in their own kind or otherwise significant, have received their name quite early.

Name Strata across Languages

There are not only strata of various times but also strata of various languages in toponymy. If we are able to discern what language a name or name element is, we can often make a conclusion on the time of name giving. This is, of course, due to the fact that we know which era and in which regions Sámi or Swedish speaking settlement, for example, has been in Finland.

For quite some time, there have mainly been three languages spoken in Finland: in addition to Finnish, there is Swedish on the coasts and in the archipelago and Sámi in northernmost Finland. As the inhabited areas of linguistic groups have changed over time, an abundance of loan names has emerged in linguistic border areas. In the old Sámi areas, the Finnish people had adopted Sámi nomenclature. There is also Finnish nomenclature in the Swedish areas in southern Finland and nomenclature that had been provided by Swedish-speakers at the time in their adjacent Finnish-speaking areas. Loan names in linguistic border areas usually have originally been names of natural places. Later, with the addition of settlement, many of them have progressed to settlement names.

The best known and studied nomenclature includes *substrate names* of Finnish Swedish areas, that is, those names which have been used in these areas before a later settlement of different linguistic backgrounds had arrived. Moreover, there have been loan names in Finnish nomenclature of an earlier period which have been primarily Germanic, mostly Scandinavian, names. The term *loan name* is defined as being a loan from one language to another as a name of the same place. As for *substrate name*, this is a name that is based on an earlier language spoken in some country or area.

When examining loan names, we should be familiar with the rules of the loaning language's word formation and linguistic history. The same goes for the search for substrate names: there must be a command of the stages of the originating language and in what ways the name in the language could have changed must be understood. In the loaning of names, we must also take note of the fact that nomenclature does not necessarily follow phonological rules in the same way and as equally as strict as other vocabulary.

In a way, some foreign component indirectly reached Finnish toponymy because in the formation of place names, elements of foreign origin have also been used as part of them. For example, names with *Kupitta(a)* in Southwest Finland probably include the word *kupitsa* 'boundary mark', an Estonian loan, the word however no longer appearing in modern Finnish. However, the original language of a name is not the same as the language of a name element, word or derivational affix. In Finnish, there can be an element included in a name known as a word whereupon the name in itself is not, by its original language, of foreign origin. It is, however, not easy to draw the line in all cases and a loan name could have also disappeared from the language.

Nomenclature of the Finnish- and Swedish-speaking linguistic border area. During the 12th and 13th centuries, settlement began to migrate from Sweden to the coasts of Finland whereupon the oldest Swedish-language place names are roughly from that period. These names are presumably amongst the settlement names of, for example, Åland. Old Swedish settlement earlier reached a broader and more inland coastal area than today and a reminder of this can be seen in the loan names of Swedish origin included in modern Finnish-language toponymy.

For example, there is an abundance of old place names of Swedish origin in the Finnish-language toponymy of the municipality of Kustavi in Southwest Finland. These include *Pukkeenluoto* ← **Bockön* and *Lankoora* ← **Långör*, which have been phonetically adapted in the borrowing process. Moreover, there are numerous examples of place names of Swedish origin in the nomenclature of the Southwest Finland municipality of Kaarina. These place names as used by the Finnish-speaking population have received an adapted form in Finnish, and include, for example, the cultivation names *Kuhenki* ← **Skogängen* ('forest|meadow'), *Överi* and *Överinki* ← **Överängen* ('over|meadow'), sound name *Reevsunti* ← **Rävsundet* ('fox|sound') as well as the cape name *Vaaksnainen* and bay name *Vastnainen* ← **Kvastnäs* ('bone|isthmus'). These kinds of names borrowed from Swedish could have remained in use even when the areas began to become unilingually Finnish-speaking.

The oldest settlement of the Helsinki region, for example, is also Swedish whereupon its old toponymy is linguistically Swedish as well. For instance, currently known names of neighbourhoods such as *Botby* (Fin. *Vartiokylä*), *Brändö* (Fin. *Kulosaari*), *Gamlas* (Fin. *Kannelmäki*), *Munksnäs* (Fin. *Munkkiniemi*), *Nordsjö* (Fin. *Vuosaari*), *Skatudden* (Fin. *Katajanokka* and *Åggelby* (Fin. *Oulunkylä*) are originally Swedish language names. These Finnish-language names shown here were later adapted phonetically or (partly) translated on the basis of the Swedish ones, at the latest in the drafting of official names.

The toponymy of many Finnish-speaking areas thus includes old Swedish-language names. Moreover, the toponymy of Swedish-speaking areas includes old Finnish-language place names. These names had originated before the arrival of Swedish settlers, thus they are the oldest in the costal toponymy of Finland. The centrality of names of Finnish origin is proven by the fact that many of them had been taken for a parish or village name in the area. These include, for example, the Ostrobothnian parish names *Malax* ← **Madelaksi* ('burbot|bay'), *Kvevlax* ← **Koivulaksi* ('birch| bay') or **Kuivalaksi* ('dry|bay') and *Terjärv* ← **Tervajärvi* ('tar|lake'). Beginning in the 12th century, the Swedish settlers that arrived had borrowed these names from the Finnish-speaking population who permanently inhabited the archipelago and coastal regions at that time.

In addition to this, there are names of Finnish-language origin in the Helsinki region which have been borrowed by the Swedish-speaking inhabitants. In many cases, modern Finnish-language names of places are newer ones formed for official use. For example, the name of the neighbourhood and railway station *Huopalahti* stems from the Finnish-language name **Haapalaksi* ('aspen|bay'). The name's principle part *laksi* 'bay' preceded its contemporary form in Finnish *lahti*. To Swedish-language speakers, *Haapalaksi* was pronounced *Hoplax* [huːplaks] whereupon the official Finnish-language name *Huopalahti* was adapted from this. Similar, initially Finnish-language names include district names in Espoo *Köklax* (today in Finnish *Kauklahti*) ← **Kaukalaksi* ('long|bay') and *Sökö* (today in Finnish *Soukka*) ← **Soukko* ('narrow, slim').

The bilingual toponymy used in the linguistic boarder areas between Finnish and Swedish-speaking settlements has been extensively researched in Finland. The means of loaning names has also been examined in detail on the basis of this nomenclature. For this reason, the loaning of names is presented here, although the same rules of loaning naturally holds true for other sets of loan names. When a name is borrowed from one language to one's own language, the name can be adapted to the borrowing language as a whole or partly or the name can be translated. Fig. 4 shows the means of Finnish place name loaning.

1. The name loaned as a translation:
Fin. *Laajalahti* ('broad|bay') → Swe. *Bredvik* ('broad|bay')
Swe. *Bredvik* → Fin. *Laajalahti*

2. The name loaned as a phonetic adaptation:
Complete adaptation:
Fin. *Laajalahti* → Swe. *Lalax*
Swe. *Bredvik* → Fin. *Preiviikki*
Epexegetical adaptation
Swe. *Bredvik* → Fin. *Preiviikin/lahti*
Partial adaptation:
Swe. *Bredvik* → Fin. *Prei/lahti*

Fig 4. Means of Finnish place name loaning.

The fact that names in traditional toponymies have been phonetically loaned from one language to another has been proven as a general feature of loaning in the Finland Swedish linguistic boarder area, whereas translation had been uncommon. On the contrary, translation in loan names formed by Finnish authorities has been a common phenomenon. For a long time, the guidelines were that a Swedish-language name was sufficient for a place as long as it is easy to pronounce and, in line with pronunciation, easy to write (*Kilo, Tali*). Efforts were made to otherwise translate names (*Sköldvik* → *Kilpilahti* 'shield|bay') or if this did not work out, phonetic adaptations may have been created (*Billnäs* → *Pinjainen*, *Gumböle* → *Kumpyöli*). However, under 21st century Finnish Name Management guidelines, names in bilingual areas should not be synthetically translated. The aim is to preserve old place names in their original form with no translation, whenever at all possible.

Germanic loans. According to archaeological evidence, Germanic settlement arrived in Finland from the Bronze Age on, hence starting from the second prehistoric millennium. There is no trace of this settlement in coastal Finland Swedish toponymy which has no Proto-Scandinavian name types. On the other hand, it is possible that Finnish toponymy may include Germanic loan names that are older than Early Medieval Swedish settlement in those Western areas where the settlement could have been proven, on the basis of archaeological evidence, to have continued for thousands of years. Attempts have been made to find these old Germanic place names in Finnish toponymy.

Jorma Koivulehto (1987), a researcher of Germanic loan words, considers it possible that old Germanic name elements may have been preserved in Finnish toponymy. Germanic etymology can be found, for instance, in the municipality names *Harjavalta*, *Hauho*, *Vammala* and *Eura*. Of these names, for example, the word **hauha* 'high' can be found behind *Hauho*. The name may include an old personal name of Germanic origin from which the forms *Hauha*, *Hauho* and *Hauhia* had become established in use in Finland during the Middle Ages. Another different interpretation that has been considered a possibility is that the name may have had a connection to the high terrain of the region. As for the name *Eura*, it may include the word **etra* meaning 'vein' as well as 'water vein' and 'water system'.

Sámi substrate names. Today, the Sámi people of Finland reside in the northernmost part of the country only, but according to documented data, they earlier had inhabited areas more notably south, even in the province of Savo in the 17th century. Because Sámi settlement had gone on for so long, we can presume that its place names left behind would be found in inland Finland. A study of this nomenclature as a whole has not thus far been reached because the identification of mere Sámi substrate names amongst other toponymy would require the systematic examination of the entire toponymy of extensive areas. It has, however, been possible to prove that there is toponymy of Sámi origin in nearly all of the areas of inland Finland, the most being in Savo and Kainuu in Eastern Finland. These include, for example, the lake names *Kiesimä* ← Sám. *keässim* 'drawing in of a (fishing) net', *Maaninka* ← Sám. *maaṅṅij* 'large whitefish' and *Sonkari* and *Sonkajärvi* ← Sám. *sonke* 'nook, corner' or *suongeri* 'fish or net drying rack' (Aikio 2008). Municipality names that have been considered to be of Sámi origin include *Lieksa*, *Posio*, *Puolanka*, *Siilinjärvi*, *Utajärvi* and *Vaala*.

Nomenclature of Sámi origin can be found in more southern areas of Finland. It is presumed that the Häme and Satakunta regions may have been inhabited by the Sámi people early on in the Finnish Iron Age. It was not until later when Finnish settlement, which initially extended from the coast up to the Kokemäenjoki River, displaced it. There is evidence of this in many place names that have been interpreted as having Sámi origins, for example *Konta-*, *Kontan-*, *Kontaa(n)-* ← Sám. *goddi* 'wild reinder' (*Kontaa*: a residential area in Nokia, *Kontankallio*: a rock in Hollola), *Kuk(k)as-* ← Sám. (attributive form) *guhkes* 'long' (*Kukkanen*: a lake in Nastola, *Kukainen*: a village in Uusikaupunki), *Posio-* ← Sám. *boaššu* 'rear of a hut' (*Posionlahti*: a bay in Tyrväs), *Runo(n)-* ← Sám. *rotnu* 'reindeer doe which has not calved' (*Runonnokka*: a cape in Vammala, *Runosmäki*: a neighbourhood in Turku), *Siita-*, *Siiti-* ← Sám. *siida* 'Sámi village' (*Siittanlahti*: a bay in Hauho, *Siitama*: a village in Orivesi), *Suono-* ← Sám. *suotnju* 'watery bog' (*Suonojärvi*: a lake in Vesilahti) and *Tolva(s)-* ← Sám. *doalvi* 'wild reindeer trot' (*Tolvasniemi*: a village in Joutsa). We can take all of these concrete names as examples because places names of Sámi origin beginning the same way can be found elsewhere. Moreover, place names with *Vuo(s)sio*, *Vuotso* and *Uotso* (found in Mouhijärvi, Pornainen, Kiikka) and even *Uossu* in Vammala and *Outsola* in Mouhijärvi, for example, are based on the Sámi word *vuohččiu* meaning 'narrow, watery bog'. (Aikio 2008.)

One of the most well-known Southern Finland place names of Sámi origin may be the village and outdoor area name *Nuuksio* in Espoo. The village apparently received its name from the lake whose vicinity the settlement was built around. The lake name, now known as *Pitkäjärvi* ('tall||lake'), may have originally been **Nuoksujärvi* or **Nuoksijärvi*. The name may include a Sámi word for 'swan' which is *njukča* in Northern Sámi. (Suomalainen paikannimikirja 2007.)

There is not much evidence of many place names of Sámi origin in Southwest Finland as there are in Häme and Satakunta but the reason for this may be a lack of investigation. In any case, the place names of Sámi origin that are in this area include the aforementioned *Runosmäki* in Turku and *Kukainen* in Uusikaupunki. In addition to these, *Livonsaari* (in Askainen) ← Sám. *livva-* 'resting of (wild) reindeer' and *Joksunmäki* (in Perniö) ← Sám. *juoksa* 'bow' have been considered to be other examples. This shows that Sámi settlement may have preceded Finnish settlement here as well.

Urban Nomenclature

Official, Planned Names

Names in an urban environment are essentially similar to those in rural areas. The earliest and oldest places names in an urban setting are so-called traditional place names. These names spontaneously emerged out of the needs of users and they have been given to various, important places regarding work and travel. The number of oldest names can reach the hundreds or even up to the thousands. However, an urban, constructed and compact environment has created the need to provide planned names as well. These names differ from traditional names in that the local inhabitants have not had the role of name giver, instead some official, for example, has created them. These planned names and, in addition to them, names that have emerged through the speech of the people in the urban environment – often on the basis of planned names – will be examined in this section.

Urban nomenclature can be divided into official and unofficial names. *Official names* have been planned for a special area (for a detailed plan, for example). Official names are typically those regarding neighbourhoods or districts, streets, market squares, plazas and parks. There are also planned names in places other than planned areas of an urban setting. *Name planning* includes the planning of official toponymy, that is, the official names of cities and the nomenclature of roads of rural, dispersed settlement areas. *Planned nomenclature* is set up by authorities and includes authenticated, official city names and nomenclature of roads in dispersed rural settlement areas.

In Finland, both detailed plans and official names are matters under municipal power. The Finnish Land Use and Building Act (*Maankäyttö- ja rakennuslaki*, enacted 1 January 2000) obliges municipalities to give numbers to districts and neighbourhoods and blocks of buildings and to give streets and roads names. There is no requirement to give names to neighbourhoods and other common areas but in practice, they are always named. Names are needed because they primarily have a practical function of guidance. Name planning in Finnish municipalities is a part of the technical industry in which sometimes a name committee, or sometimes an architect, engineer or surveying technician, takes care of this practical job. There is a trained, full-time name planner in Espoo and Helsinki only; earlier, there had also been one in Vantaa.

There are various issues taken into account in Finnish name planning. One key principle is the fact that the entire area of the municipality or city or even the area of many municipalities – such as the Greater Helsinki area – are dealt with as a whole where two similar names or names that seem to look like one another in a confusing way cannot be given. Moreover, an official name must be succinct and easy to remember, write and pronounce. Official names shall be implemented in both languages in bilingual areas, for example Finnish and Swedish names in Helsinki (Fin. *Huvilakatu* – Swe. *Villagatan* 'villa|street', Fin. *Kansakoulukatu* – Swe. *Folkskolegatan* 'Volksschule|street') and Sámi and Finnish in Enontekiö (Sám. *Heahtágeaidnu* – Fin. *Hetantie* 'Hetta+GEN|road', Sám. *Junttebálggis* – Fin. *Juntinpolku* 'Juntti+GEN|path' ← personal name *Juntti*).

Many street names are structurally two-part names (*Museokatu* 'museum|street', *Sinettikuja* 'package-seal|alley', *Välitalontie* 'Välitalo+GEN| road' ← homestead name *Välitalo*) and their generic parts signify the nature of a street. The generic part *katu* 'street' has been reserved for the streets of the downtown area in many Finnish cities, whereas the more common generic part in the suburbs is *tie* 'road'. In Helsinki, for example, the guidelines had earlier been that the generic part *katu* was to be used only in the downtown area. In general, Finnish name management recommends that the appropriateness of generic parts must be taken into account: *väylä* ('passage'), *katu* ('street'), *tie* ('road'), *kuja* ('alley'), *rinne* ('slope') and other generic parts must form a logical system. It is also a good idea to use generic parts variably as all of these names do not need to end with *katu* or *tie*.

An area's old toponymy is considered the point of departure in the planning of official names. In this way, the traditional toponymy used is preserved and forgotten names can be implemented. The cultural tradition carried by names hence continues its life. These names also localise its location well and bring historical and cultural stratification to the nomenclature. Efforts are made to make old place names, usually village names, primarily regional names. For example, many neighbourhood names in Helsinki are originally medieval village names of Swedish origin (*Baggböle* → *Pakila*, *Kottby* → *Käpylä*, *Hertonäs* → *Herttoniemi*, *Gumtäkt* → *Kumpula*). Usually, homestead names and names of natural places, sometimes even cultivation names, are used for street names. For example, there are names of natural places (*Haapasaari* 'aspen|island' → *Haapasaarentie* 'Haapasaari road', *Kivisaari* 'stone|island' → *Kivisaarentie* 'Kivisaari road', *Käärmeniemi* 'snake|cape' → *Käärmeniementie* 'Käärmeniemi road', *Lokkisaari* 'sea-gull|island' → *Lokkisaarentie* 'Lokkisaari road', *Mustalahti* 'black|bay' → *Mustalahdentie* 'Mustalahti road') and names of houses and villas (*Furumonkuja* 'Furumo alley', *Harbonkuja* 'Harbo alley', *Solvikinkatu* 'Solvik street', *Uutelantie* 'Uutela road') found in the street names of the district of Vuosaari in Helsinki.

Names only used in a small group that are not widely known are not generally favoured in street names.

Old toponymy is thus widely exploited in official names. In addition to this, there are naturally other kinds of official names. One central group includes names that describe such places which have been formed in line with regular principles of naming. These principles include the location of the place (*Rantatie* 'shore road'), something that exists or appears there (*Koivukatu* 'birch street', *Kirjastonkatu* 'library street'), characteristics of the place (*Kaartokatu* 'curve street', *Lyhytkuja* 'short alley', *Uusikatu* 'new street') and the relationship the place has to people (*Ohikulkutie* 'bypass'). The most typical of these types of names include *Asemakatu* ('station street'), *Hallituskatu* ('government street'), *Kauppakatu* ('market street'), *Kirkkokatu* ('church street') and *Koulukatu* ('school street') which are common in the centres of old cities. These names can be quite old and often have spontaneously emerged from the natural need for naming. As there was a need to determine the location of a place, the road that travelled along side of a church, for example, naturally started to be called *Kirkkokatu*. The same types of names found in older street name strata include types such as *Hämeenkatu* ('Häme street') and *Hämeentie* ('Häme road') which indicate that the road in question had went from Turku or Helsinki towards Häme.

The oldest data on Finnish street names are from medieval Turku. *Hämeenkatu* (Swe. *Tavastgatan*) is first mentioned in documents from 1426 (as the name *Tauastagathu*). Another one of the most significant streets was *Karjakatu* ('livestock street', Swe. *Fägatan*) which was the old main road of Uusimaa. The name stems from the fact that the city dwellers at the time drove their cattle along the road to pastures located outside the city. Other old street names reveal location. Several streets ran parallel to the Aura River, the main river in Turku: the closest to it being *Jokikatu* ('river street', Swe. *Ågatan*), further away *Kirkkokatu* ('church street', Swe. *Kyrkogatan*), *Luostarin välikatu* ('convent mid street', Swe. *Kloster mellangatan*) and the furthest away *Luostarin yläkatu* ('convent high street', Swe. *Kloster övergatan*).

The third main group of official names includes *commemorative names*, that is, names that have been given in memory of some person, event or other occurrence. The specific part of these names in Finnish, a personal name, is always in the genitive: these names include, for example, *Mariankatu* ('Maria+GEN|street': 'Maria street') and *Dagmarinkatu* ('Dagmar+GEN|street': 'Dagmar street') in Helsinki, based on Russian empress Maria Feodorovna and Maria Sofia Fredrika Dagmar. There are numerous other imperial names given during the reign of Emperor Alexander I and confirmed in 1820. Today, these names include *Aleksanterinkatu* ('Alexander street'), *Annankatu* ('Anna street'), *Katariinankatu* ('Catherine street'), *Liisankatu* ('Elisabeth street'), *Maurinkatu* ('Maurice street'), *Mikonkatu* ('Michael street'), *Sofiankatu* ('Sophia street') and *Yrjönkatu* ('George street'). Part of the names of the time of Russian rule were changed to new names associated with Finnish culture for example *Nikolainkatu*

('Nicholas street') became *Snellmaninkatu* ('Snellman street' ← Johan Vilhelm Snellman, a Fennoman), *Vladimirinkatu* ('Vladimir street') became *Kalevankatu* ('Kalevala street' ← Kalevala, the Finnish national epic) and *Konstantininkatu* ('Constantine street') became *Meritullinkatu* ('maritime customs street'). In addition to this, *Aleksanterintori* ('Alexander market square') in Turku was changed to *Kauppatori* ('market square') after 1917 and *Aleksanterinkatu* in Kajaani was changed to *Kauppakatu* ('market street').

Commemorative names reflect honour of their time and convey authority and ruling power. For example, the central streets in former socialist countries may have had their names changed several times. Since 1859, street names in Riga, Latvia were changed up to seven times: for example, the street known as *Brīvības iela* ('freedom street') in the 21st century and in the 1920s and 1930s was named 'Adolf Hitler street' in 1942 and 'Lenin street' in 1950.

There are also monarchs, scholars, artists and other influential persons pertaining to the history of a city or of national significance that are commemorated in street names. For example, these kinds of names in Turku include *Agricolankatu* ('Agricola street' ← Mikael Agricola, the "father of literary Finnish"), *Brahenkatu* ('Brahe street'← Per Brahe, Governor General in Finland), *Flemiginkatu* ('Fleming street'← Claus Fleming, a governor of Finland) and *Porthaninkatu* ('Porthan street' ← Henrik Gabriel Porthan, the "father of Finnish history"). Commemorative names in Helsinki of various time periods include *Aleksis Kiven katu* ('Aleksis Kivi street' ← Aleksis Kivi, author of *Seitsemän veljestä* (Seven Brothers)), *Arvo Ylpön puisto* ('Arvo Ylppö park' ← Arvo Ylppö, a Finnish paediatrician), *Kaj Franckin katu* ('Kaj Franck street' ← Kaj Franck, a Finnish designer), *Runeberginkatu* ('Runeberg street' ← Johan Ludvig Runeberg, national poet of Finland) and *Urho Kekkosen katu* ('Urho Kekkonen street' ← Urho Kekkonen, eighth president of Finland from 1956 to 1982). Notable street names in Vaasa include, for example, *Klemetinkatu* ('Klemetti street' ← Heikki Klemetti, composer), *Peltokankaantie* ('Peltokangas road' ← Oskar Peltokangas, light infantry lieutenant who died in the Finnish Civil War of 1918), *Teirinkatu* ('Teiri street' ← T. E. Teiri, City Council Chair) and *Wolffintie* ('Wolff road' ← Commercial Counsellor C. G. Wolff). Nowadays, the objective is to express the whole name of the individual, both the first name and surname, but there are many commemorative names that include only the first name or surname of the individual, particularly in earlier nomenclature.

In keeping with Finnish name planning recommendations, commemorative streets or areas are not to be given to living persons. For example, in 2004, the City of Helsinki Naming Board agreed on guidelines to be followed when there is a proposal to name streets, plazas or other locations in relation to or in memory of a person, business or community. According to the main guideline, a place can be named after a person provided "the person and his or her actions are generally recognised as being worthy of being commemorated". The person must additionally be connected to the place in a noteworthy and positive way, must have been at least living in Helsinki or must be a Finn who has done his or her remarkable life's work nationally or internationally. The person must also have been deceased no less than five years.

The fourth and quantifiably extensive – in many urban areas the most extensive – main group of official names is made up of *group names*, that is, *thematic names* which include street names formed on the basis of some subject matter (a collective set of trees, professions, agriculture, etc.). Street names planned for a certain area this way form a cohesive totality by a subject. These names structure an image of the city, make it easy to remember and facilitate the pinpointing of locations. An important reason for creating these names is also that the old toponymy is not sufficient to fulfil the needs of official names. Names that describe a place or commemorative names also can be only rarely given.

A large number of thematic names have been given in many places. For example, the majority of Helsinki official names are thematic names, on average two thirds and in the suburbs no fewer than 80 to 90 per cent. The classification of group names in Helsinki has also been prepared as an aide to its name planner. The main classes include nature, society, livelihood, science and technology, art and architecture, concepts, tales and beliefs, pastimes and recreation as well as proper nouns.

Subjects that are considered to be fit for these names are those which, in their own particular way, bring about local features. These are, for instance, subjects brimming with local culture, local history and livelihood carried out in the region. For example, old professions of the inhabitants of the Vaasa area have been exploited in street names (*Leipurinkuja* 'baker's alley', *Maalarinkuja* 'painter's alley', *Muurarinkuja* 'mason's alley', *Savenvalajankuja* 'potter's alley', *Vaatturinkuja* 'tailor's alley', *Välskärintie* 'barber surgeon's road', *Vänrikinkuja* 'pilot officer's alley'). In the area of Vuosaari in Helsinki, a foundation on the theme of 'seafaring and seamarks' (*Keulatie* 'prow road', *Kompassitie* 'compass road', *Poijukuja* 'buoy alley'), 'rowing and sailboats' (*Airoparintie* 'oars road', *Melatie* 'paddle road', *Purjetie* 'sail road') and 'fishing' (*Katiskatie* 'fish trap road', *Pitkänsiimantie* 'longline fishing road', *Verkkotie* 'fishing net road') has been provided by marine livelihood and the sea.

Sometimes, a theme has come about on the basis of a neighbourhood name. An example of this can be seen in the Helsinki neighbourhood of Myllypuro ('mill|brook') where names such as *Käsikiventie* 'treadwheel road', *Myllytuvantie* 'mill cabin road', *Myllärintie* 'miller's road' and *Tuulimyllyntie* 'windmill road' have been given under a mill theme. In the Helsinki district of Kannelmäki (*kannel*, a synonym to *kantele*, Finnish national stringed folk instrument), a theme in line with instruments, playing music and musical performers has also been produced from its name. Examples of this include *Fagottipolku* 'bassoon trail', *Kitarakuja* 'guitar alley', *Klaneettitie* 'clarinet road', *Pelimanninpolku* 'musician's trail', *Soittokuja* 'music alley' and even *Kaustisentie* 'Kaustinen road' and *Vimpelinpolku* 'Vimpeli trail' based on the "musician parishes" of Kaustinen and Vimpeli in Central Ostrobothnia.

There have not always been enough local name themes or searching for such themes for the content of the names perhaps never came up. In this case, liberties have been taken to put faith into chosen themes or thematic groups which do not specifically or at all connect to the area. Many of these types of regularly used thematic groups can seem ordinary or unimaginative. For example, street names based on the national Finnish works *Kalevala* or *Seitsemän veljestä* (*Seven Brothers*) have, at the time, been considered fashionable names which do not highlight any local, special feature. There are many streets in Finland that are named in this way. For example, there are street names given on the themes of either *Kalevala* or *Seitsemän veljestä* in Vaasa: street names with a *Kalevala* theme include *Ilmarisenkatu* (Ilmarinen, mythical smith), *Pohjolankatu* (Pohjola, mythical land of the North), *Tapionkatu* (Tapio, forest deity); road names with a *Seitsemän veljestä* theme include *Eerontie*, *Juhanintie*, *Laurintie* (Eero, Juhani and Lauri, three of the seven brothers).

A great number of names with plant, animal and nature themes have also been given. For example, there have been names given in Pori that include a Finnish bird term: *Hiirihaukantie* ('buzzard road'), *Kirjosiivenkatu* ('speckled wing street'), *Sinisiivenkatu* ('blue wing street'), *Viiriäisentie* ('quail road'). The plant-themed group of names in the neighbourhood of Tikkurila in Vantaa is exceptionally broad and diverse: a group of over 200 names is in the majority of street names of the area. The names, for example, include *Kielotie* ('lily-of-the-valley road'), *Kortetie* ('horsetail road'), *Kuminatie* ('caraway road'), *Osmankäämintie* ('cattail road'), *Neilikkakuja* ('clove alley') and *Rantakukantie* ('purple loosestrife road') – the first of these may be the most popular flower-themed road name in Finland. Although these official names that are unrelated to a place are not recommended in name planning, it seems that the inhabitants generally take to them positively. Name users often associate names to the place they refer to and believe that they describe their locations even though this would not have been the point of departure in name planning. For example, we can imagine dandelions growing in the vicinity of a road named *Voikukkatie* ('dandelion road').

The naming of streets has become a more and more important part of urban planning. A great deal of street names is thus required: for example, there are approximately 4,000 street names in Helsinki. The aim is for official names to be more and more commercially appealing, to be somewhat of a brand. As a neighbourhood and its residences are marketed to possible inhabitants, the images created by their names are also key, as attractive and pleasant images may consciously be created with these names. A good example of this includes street names given at the turn of the 21st century in Vuosaari in Helsinki, whose thematic group is, for example, rose varieties in keeping with the local rose garden (*Juhannusruusunkuja* 'burnet rose alley', *Nukkeruusunkuja* 'shining rose alley'), apple varieties in keeping with the local apple orchard (*Keltakanelinkuja* 'cinnamon striped apple alley', *Syysviirunkuja* 'autumn striped apple alley') and even fairy tales by Zachris Topelius (*Adalmiinankatu* 'Adalmiina street', *Kultakutrinkuja* 'Goldilocks alley', *Lintu Sininen* 'blue bird', *Pilvilinnankatu* 'cloud castle street').

Street names make up the largest group of official urban names. Other names are also included in official urban nomenclature. Company names are counted amongst this which in their official form – or at least these names' identifying part – are used as place names. These names are common in the urban environment because, for example, we speak of shopping centres, department stores, restaurants, cafés and other businesses a great deal and we moreover identify these places with their names. We can meet at the shopping centre *Hansa*, in front of the *Sokos* hotel or contemplate going to the café *Strindberg* or *Café Picnic*. These kinds of names are seen in the cityscape, often on the walls, windows or name plates of the buildings in question. From the name user's perspective, these names can be compared with street names: they are planned names which have been given by a proprietor or authority who, with his position, is entitled to provide various registers with official names for registration.

As toponyms of the urban environment are divided up into official and unofficial names, such traditional nature names, which appear on a base map or similar, are considered official names. These include, for example, the park *Mäntymäki* ('pine|hill'), the brook *Mätäoja* ('rot|ditch') and water area of *Kruunuvuorenselkä* (*Kruunuvuori* 'crown|mountain' → 'Kruunuvuori+GEN|open-sea') in Helsinki. These types of names can otherwise be parallel with other official names because from the city dweller's perspective, they are names provided by "the powers that be".

Formation of Unofficial Names

Unofficial urban names are all place names in the urban environment which are not official. The most typical unofficial name is formed on the basis of the official name of a place (*Mäkkäri* ← *MacDonald's*, *Atski* ← *Ateneum*) but sometimes irrespective of it (*Bronx* and *Ghetto* as names of neighbourhoods in Helsinki seen as harsh and perhaps populated by those with foreign backgrounds). Sometimes a place which does not even have an official name may have received an unofficial name: for example a street corner, a canopy or some other structure may be used as a meeting point. This includes, for example, the car park area on the perimeter of Turku Market Square given the name *Varikko*, a 'paddock'. One and the same place can have, and quite often in practice they do, more than just one name.

On the basis of the way they are formed, Finnish unofficial names can be divided into two main groups. Unofficial names created, on the basis of the way they are formed, in relation to an official name (*Lönnrotinkatu* 'Lönnrot street' → *Lönkka*, neighbourhood *Roihuvuori* → *Roihis*) are *secondary*. Names given that in some way depict a place irrespective of the official name (*Romuranta* 'junk shore' as a name of a shore full of various junk and scrap, *Slummikylä* 'slum village' as a name of a compact dwelling area including structures of poor condition, *Väritalot* 'colour buildings' as a name for colourful blocks of flats) are called *primary*.

Unofficial urban names resemble slang and they can also be seen as a part of it. Slang can be defined as language of certain user groups, and with this language, a group includes those who consciously isolate themselves from others. There is a variety of slang: the language of school-aged youth represents regular slang. Sometimes the terms *slang place name* and *unofficial place name* have been used concurrently but a slang place name can really be seen more as a sub-group of unofficial place names. Not all unofficial names are slang but all slang names can be counted amongst unofficial names.

Secondary names. There are more secondary names, those formed on the basis of official nomenclature, in unofficial urban nomenclature in Finland than there are primary names. Secondary names are formed most often from official names by shortening or by adding a derivational element to the truncated root. Shortening primarily concerns compound names (*Kaivo/puisto* 'well|park' → *Kaivari* 'Kaiv(opuisto)+ARI', *Kulttuuri/talo* 'culture|building' → *Kultsa* 'Kult(tuuritalo)+SA'). Two-syllable slang name equivalents are usually not any shorter than the original names (*Vantaa* → *Vantsku* 'Vant(aa)+SKU') and then again they can even be longer (*Töölö* → *Töli(k)ka* 'Töölö+I(K)KA').

Finnish derivational suffixes used in unofficial place names are the same as what are generally used in slang. A slang derivational suffix has no semantic function in slang and slang names. In a manner of speaking, a slang suffix only "translates" a name into slang. The most common slang suffixes in Finnish place names are *ari* or *äri* (*Flemari* 'Fleminginkatu', *Hämäri* 'Hämeentie') and *is* (*Vaasis* 'Vaasankatu') which are affixed to the shortened form of the name. Compared to other slang vocabulary, the *is* ending is favoured more than *ari* or *äri* in the nomenclature of cities. Some of the most common suffixes appear in the following names of neighbourhoods in the Helsinki region: *Kruni(k)ka* 'Kruununhaka' ('crown+GEN|pasture' → 'Kruun(unhaka)+I(K)KA'), *Laajika* 'Laajasalo' ('wide|woods' → 'Laaj(a)+I(K)KA'), *Mylli(k)kä* 'Myllypuro' ('mill|brook'→ 'Myll(ypuro)+I(K)KA'), *Hietsu* 'Hietaniemi' ('fine-sand|cape' → 'Hie(taniemi)+TSU') and *Herde* 'Herttoniemi' ('duke|cape' or surname 'Hertoghe | cape' → 'Her(ttoniemi)+DE').

Sometimes, a Finnish unofficial name can be formed only by shortening its official name. For example, the name of the park *Sepän/puisto* ('blacksmith+GEN|park') in Helsinki has become *Seppä* and the name of the restaurant *Ilo/kivi* ('joy|stone') in Jyväskylä has become *Kivi*. A so-called summarisation of names can occur with abbreviated forms, that is, a phonic assemblage of letters. These include, for example [ɑː koː] for *Aleksis Kiven koulu* ('Aleksis Kivi school'), [ɛː gɛː] for *Everybody's Gym* and *CM* [sɛː æm] for *CityMarket*. Abbreviations consisting of consonants only can easily be supplemented with vowels (*Emski* ← MsK 'Merisotakoulu, Naval Academy', *Tere* ← Tre 'Tampere').

Adaptations are names borrowed from one language to another which have either completely or partly been adapted to the phonetic system of the other language. For historic reasons, there is already an abundance of these types of names in the Helsinki region and in other bilingual areas. Names of Swedish settlement were earlier more common in slang because the slang of the beginning of the 20th century was otherwise strongly of Swedish origin. These place names in slang form, based on Swedish-language name forms, include many neighbourhood names: *Berga*, *Bergga* (Swe. *Berghäll*, Fin. Kallio), *Brendika*, *Brendis*, *Brändika*, *Brändis*, *Bräntsika* (Swe. *Brändö*,

Fin. Kulosaari), *Drummis, Drumssa, Drumssika, Rumsa* (Swe. *Drumsö*, Fin. Lauttasaari), *Ogeli* (Swe. *Åggelby*, Fin. Oulunkylä), *Skaatis, Skatta* (Swe. *Skatudden*, Fin. Katajanokka) and *Sörkka* (Swe. *Södernäs*, Fin. Sörnäinen). Many of these names are known by numerous variants formed by different derivational endings and with varied phonetic features. Part of earlier used names of Swedish settlement have later been cast aside but part of them still exist (*Ogeli, Skatta, Sörkka*). As for younger stratum, examples include *Monsas* (Swe. *Månsas*, Fin. Maunula) and *Mosa* (Swe. *Mosabacka*, Fin. Tapanila).

Different language play and contortion is typical for young people's slang in particular. Also, by playfully translating place names in different ways, different kinds of name adaptations can be formed. This includes, for example, *Hattulantie* ('Hattula road', *Hattu* an old Germanic personal name or *hattu* 'hat') becoming *Stetson Street*. On the other hand, non-Finnish names – English names in particular – can be "translated" into Finnish, thusly resulting in, for example, the restaurant *Many Faces* as *Naama(t)* ('face(+PL)') and *The Body Shop* directly into *Ruumiskauppa* (*ruumis* meaning both 'body' and 'corpse').

In addition, various *phonetic conversions* can be formed on the basis of an official name. These usually carry some ironic, pejorative or obscene meaning and include, for example *Käkimäki* 'Kannelmäki' (*käki* 'cuckoo', metaphorically 'drunkard'), *Nordenskikkeli* 'Nordenskiöldinkatu' (*kikkeli* 'willy, penis') and *Pyllymuro* 'Myllypuro' (*pylly* 'bum, bottom'). Words in a name can also be replaced by words with the same or similar semantic meaning. For example, the neighbourhood of Makkaramäki ('sausage hill') has received the name *Nakkikukkula* ('frankfurter hill').

One feature typical to slang and slang names is concatenation. Numerous variants and conversions can be formed – without complying with any certain rules – on the basis of one name. Long associative chains, name clusters, may be formed from names. For example, the café in Tornio in Northern Finland called *Roosamaria* is also known as *Roosa, Rosis, Rosku* or *Roskis*.

Primary names. A majority of names in unofficial urban nomenclature are secondary names, formed on the basis of the official name of a place. In addition to these, there are also names found that are formed irrespective of the official name of a place, that is, primary, unofficial urban names. They can be divided into names that signify the type of place and those that signify a special feature of the place. Names that signify the type of place alone are sufficient enough to identify places as long as these expressions are not ambiguous as regards to what they refer. For example, the names *Bar* or *Kiska* 'kiosk' can, in some circumstances, be used individually for one's own neighbourhood bar or kiosk. The propriality of these expressions, however, is not always clear.

Names that signify a special feature can be divided into subgroups on the basis of their principles of naming. The principles of naming include the location of the place, something that exists or appears there, characteristics of the place and the relationship the place has to people – these are naturally the same principles of naming as in the classification of traditional toponymy. The realisation of unambiguous principles of naming in unofficial urban nomenclature can be trickier than in traditional toponymy. The reason for this is that different motives and explanations are often connected to name giving in unofficial urban names. There is often a desire to bring about several principles and bases on one and the same name.

Location of the place and something that exists or appears there may be amongst the more uncommon naming principles in unofficial Finnish urban nomenclature than in rural nomenclature. In keeping with location, shops in an area can be called *Alakauppa* ('lower shop') or *Peltokauppa* ('field shop'). Location is additionally common in names of such places which have no official name. Typical of this are various *kulma* '(street) corner' names (*Sokkarinkulma* '(street) corner at Sokos department store', *Mäkkärinkulma* '(street) corner at McDonalds', *Torinkulma* '(street) corner at the market square' and *Museonkulma* '(street) corner at the museum').

Many playgrounds have been given unofficial names in accordance with something that exists or appears there. These kinds of names include *Köysiratapuisto* ('zip-line park'), *Polkupyöräpuisto* ('bicycle park') and *Sydänpuisto* ('heart park', a heart-shaped pattern in the playground structure) in Joensuu. The name of a block of flats in Kuopio called *Pentutalot* ('kid buildings'), for example, is also included in this group; the name stems from the fact that a notable number of children has lived in these structures.

More common naming principles in unofficial urban nomenclature include the characteristics of the place and the relationship it has to people. Characteristics of a place can include its size, shape, colour or that the place resembles someplace else. Names given according to the characteristics of the place can be comparative of certain structures, for example, *Heinälato* ('hay barn'), *Sardiinipurkki* ('tin of sardines'), *Maitopurkit* ('milk cartons') and *Flyygelitalo* ('grand piano building'); due to their appearance, these buildings seem to resemble these items. Many places have received a name of comparative transference (*Bronx, Harlem, Monaco*). For example, the name *Bronx* has been given to unobtrusive areas or areas of tenements that are regarded as looking rather crude and these areas have also perhaps been regarded as having a poor reputation. These kinds of names are often also certain kinds of fashionable names which have spread all throughout Finland. A street in Joensuu has been given the name *Helsinkikatu* ('Helsinki street') because, according to the name givers, the buildings along the street are reminiscent of buildings in Helsinki.

As a principle of naming, the relationship a place has to people is included in such names in which there is reference to the owner or user of the place. These include, for example, the name of the residential area *Rikkaidenrinne* ('rich people's slope') and park names *Juoppopuisto* ('boozer park') and *Narkkaripuisto* ('junkie park'). These names give an indication to what kind of people are believed to reside or exist in these places. A name can also highlight the use of the place such as *Juoruristeys* ('gossip crossing', name givers habitually stop at a road crossing and gossip before heading home), *Kutukukkula* ('lovemaking hill', *kutea* 'have sex', 'make love') and

Syöpämonttu ('cancer pit', schoolchildren's smoking area). Sometimes, a name can refer to some event occurring at the place such as the name of the woods *Pihkapaikka* ('resin place', trousers get resin on them when smoking in the area). Many of these types of names are microtoponyms, that is, names only known by a small user circle.

Functions of Unofficial Names

Unofficial urban names have been given to both places that already have an official name and places which do not. There are usually various reasons for giving a name in these two groups. Should a place have no official name, an unofficial name would primarily be given so that the place can be identified. Many places that are named in this way include various meeting points, for example, street corners, canopies, benches, other structures, yards, rocks, stones and trees. At the same time, these kinds of names indicate how places in the urban environment have been taken over by naming, places which, according to official name givers, have not required a name.

A large part of unofficial urban names, however, have been given to places which do have an official name, in which case the reason for name giving is not merely identification. This is because identification would really work out by using an official name. A place can receive an unofficial name because it would hence become more "idiolectic", a part of one's own daily language usage. Planned names, given by the powers that be, are not always practical in everyday use, and in this case, forms shorter and more accessible than an official name can be created.

Unofficial names also emerge due to language play and the desire to invent new expressions. Thus, for example, *Amin grilli* ('Ami's grill') becomes *Kriminaali* ('criminal'), the restaurant *Freeway* becomes *Riivaajat* ('demons') and the residential area of *Soukanjoki* in the city of Seinäjoki becomes *Sukkajoki* ('sock river'). This kind of innovation and creation of new, colourful expressions is also one characteristic of slang.

Unofficial urban names can often be seen as a kind of nickname. Many of these have emerged in a community whose members are well acquainted with each other and share in a common activity. Different unofficial names are a part of a group's own language, so that by using language, a group spirit of 'us', a group identity, is created and confirmed. In this way, the group is distinguished from others, the group's set of values is embodied and mutual understanding and solidarity are reinforced.

The number of unofficial names increases the desire to highlight different associations and attitudes connected to a place. A name can designate, for example, warmth, familiarity, respect, derogation or labelling towards a place and its users. These kinds of names include, for example, the names of restaurant and dance clubs *Humppahelvetti* ('humppa hell', humppa is the Finnish version of oom-pah music), *Teknohelvetti* ('techno hell') and *Vahakabinetti* ('wax cabinet (room)'). Negative and dismissive images are clearly highlighted much more than positive ones; perhaps this can be seen as a typical feature of the language of young people.

Unofficial place names in the form of slang do not only appear in the urban environment. These names can also be found in sparsely populated rural areas. As slang has extended mostly as a language of young people to places other than cities and has become neutral in its expansion, names in the form of slang and their means of formation have also reached different parts of Finland. Similar "unofficial" nomenclature has indeed earlier been in use elsewhere than in the urban environment. For example, different artisan, industrial or even army areas have had a group's colloquial toponymy used in a compact community. The urban environment is not required for the emergence of names, just inventive name givers and appropriate locations.

In onomastics, there are two types of urban names: official and unofficial. However, language users do not separately categorise these types of names in their minds. Instead, an individual's or community's repertoire of names is a totality which includes all the names the language user needs. A city dweller therefore uses both official and unofficial names which appear in different ways in different contexts.

Use of Names

KNOWLEDGE OF NAMES

The examination of the use of place names is known as *sociolinguistic onomastics* or *socio-onomastics*. The variation of place names is primarily examined in a socio-onomastic investigation. A socio-onomastic research method takes the social and situational field where names are used into account.

We need place names so that we can speak about places and because of this, not one community could get along without them. Names are also in use as much as they are needed. This need, and thus the number of place names as well, varies in different areas, different communities and also between different people. Not everyone needs the same amount of place names nor do all the inhabitants of the same region need to speak about the same places. A person will name such places which need to be spoken about and will also use his required nomenclature. Individual differences in the use of names can therefore be quite large.

Each one of us is familiar with names, at least names for such places we need to speak about. We can also know and be acquainted with such names that refer to places which are not so important to us in the environment, for example, regarding orientation, movement, work or pastimes. For one reason or another, we become familiar with places and their names. A name can contextually or structurally be in some way exceptional and memorable whereupon a name is known even though we do not necessarily need to speak about the place itself. For example, the name of the road *Hiljaistenmiestenlaakso* ('silent men's valley'), located in Kangasala is known by many Finns. This name refers to the fact that there were three men living in the area in the early 20th century who were regarded as exceptionally silent. Similarly, many may know that *Äteritsiputeritsipuolilautatsijänkä* (*Äteritsi/puteritsi/puoli/lautatsi/jänkä*, *jänkä* 'swamp-like, bog area') is the longest place name in Finland but, on the contrary, not many know that this bog area is located in the Lapland municipality of Savukoski and even less would need the name itself in order to speak of the place.

Everyone's individual *toponymic competence*, that is, the knowledge of names, includes both names that are in everyday use and names that are used less frequently. In terms of their degree and frequency of use, names can be placed on a continuum ranging from names that are used every day to names that are used only rarely.

When we in socio-onomastics study people's toponymic competence, we try to find out how many and what types of place names people of different ages, professions, and genders know in their home districts. Moreover, we are interested in studying why people's toponymic competence differs from each other, that is, why they use different place names.

Studies on the use of Finnish toponymy have primarily been been carried out on rural areas. Out of these studies, the earliest are from the 1970s and a majority from the 1990s. It has been observed that individual variation in toponymic competence may be considerable. One presumption has often been that the older inhabitants of a traditional rural community know more names than young inhabitants and that men know more names than women. For example, the study carried out by Peter Slotte, Kurt Zilliacus and Gunilla Harling (1973) in three Swedish-speaking municipalities showed that gender affects toponymic competence more than age. Namely, adult men knew about one fourth more names than women of the same age. Middle aged and old men on average knew approximately 60 to 80 per cent of the village's nomenclature as women of the same age knew approximately 30 to 60 per cent.

Let us examine these claims more closely. Age definitely affects the use of names and toponymic competence, at least on average. It is natural that the longer a person lives in an area, the larger his toponymic competence grows and the greater his need to use different names is. Additionally, a native inhabitant of an area who has lived his childhood and youth often knows more names of the area than an adult who had just moved there. We easily learn to become familiar with an area and its nomenclature gradually, starting from childhood. For a long time already, one who lives in a region knows and is familiar with the phases and history of the area and may be familiar with and use names which later have been disregarded. A native inhabitant may have also become attached to his home district in a different way than someone who would later move there whereupon the region would be known more precisely and extensively.

However, there is not necessarily any significant difference between the genders in the understanding and use of names. It is of course true that men in traditional, rural culture have often travelled more extensively than women, for example, in cultivation work, hunting and fishing. Women may have lived and functioned in a more small-scale environment. However, this cannot be explained as a difference between the genders but rather something associated with profession and movement. Moreover, if there is evidence showing that women know fewer names than men, we can presume that one reason for this can be hidden behind the methods of material collection. As the nomenclature used by different inhabitants has been compared to earlier collected nomenclature of the same region, the data has been accumulated under established guidelines of that time. These guidelines gave instructions to collect names mostly from middle-aged men and preferably from male landowners. In initial data collection, nomenclature included in the environment in which women lived may have thus been given little consideration.

In more recent studies concerning the use of place names, the issue has been examined more thoroughly. For example, the study by Ainiala, Komppa, Mallat and Pitkänen (2000) has observed that the nomenclature used by youth and women in rural villages is emphasised on culture names, settlement names in particular. Settlement names are also the most central village nomenclature, and often, nearly all of the villagers know the names of the most prominent houses and spaces. As for men, they know more nature names than women mainly because they move about in the country more than woman. For example, elk hunting can be a significant elucidator of a significantly broad onomasticon. In this case, there is often an extensive *name district*, that is, the span of an area from which names are known. The names of natural features can illustrate a person's toponymic competence – the more names of natural features a village dweller knows, the broader his toponymic competence often is. Moreover, macrotoponyms are naturally best known from nature names.

It is not necessarily – at least fully in detail – worth it to examine the use of names by user group. There are namely great differences in the individual use of names. Profession and pastimes seem to have an effect on the use of names more than age or gender. Those who move about in the terrain and are more interested in the region itself use and are also familiar with more names.

As different *reasons for toponymic competence* have been sought, it has been observed that place names are known for several different reasons. Additionally, many reasons can have an effect on the knowledge of one name. Various reasons for toponymic competence include – briefly stated – at least ownership, use, work, occasion, location, an inhabitant, conversations and the form of a name. As it has been studied, the most common of these include ownership, use, work and location of the place. The most widely carried out research on the reasons for toponymic competence in Finland is the Master's thesis by Ulriikka Tiitola (1992). This investigative point of view was carried out in a rural community: the community of the Saarikylät villages in Kangasala in Southern Finland.

Ownership means that the place partly or completely belongs to the proprietorship of a family or community. For this reason, cultivation names, for instance, are known. When a name is known due to use, it is a question that the place is used in activity relating to some interest, for example, fishing, berry picking and swimming. Children know the names of places because they play there. If work is a reason for toponymic competence, different jobs have been done at the place, such as field, forestry or construction work.

As a name is known because of location, the location of the place is central from the inhabitant's point of view. The place can be quite close to one's home or a notable landmark in the setting of one's home region. Additionally, many central places regarding moving about are, of course, known primarily because of location. Then again, many names are known because the inhabitant, in one way or another, is quite familiar with the place and it has a personal relationship to him.

A notable and significant incident, usually from the community's perspective, often leaves its mark on a place name. For example, names beginning with *Surma* ('death') have been given to places where a death has occurred. Many names may be known because of this reason. A name of a place has sometimes caught on to one's use or at least to the onomasticon from the speech of other people, that is, conversations with others. One reason for toponymic competence is also its form. If there is somehow, something special about it, then there can be a reason for the knowledge of the name.

The aforementioned reasons for toponymic competence are partly the same as principles of naming. This is of course natural. Names of the oldest name stratum have been given to noteworthy places in regard to moving about or orientation, to important places in regard to livelihood, to places where something unique has happened and to places which are connected to some person.

Regardless of the fact that there are great differences in the use of inhabitants' nomenclature in a rural village, for example, this does not exactly hinder mutual communication. It is easy to speak about central and important places because these names are well-known to everyone, or at least to many. There are names used that are also known to the members of certain smaller groups (families, groups of common interests). Because an elk hunter, for example, must know and be familiar with hunting grounds and other such places, he must also know their names. One who does not need to know and be familiar with these names and places will not acquire these names or start to use them. Everyone learns a name no more than the extent to which he needs to. Respectively, through different kinds of work, jobs, pastimes and interests, a necessary nomenclature is learned.

The same names are usually known in families: the youngest family members mainly use the same names as their parents and grandparents. There are some places which are spoken about amongst family members and relatives, and so everyone needs a mutual user nomenclature. Families thus have, in a way, their own macrotoponymies. Generally speaking, the youngest generation will nevertheless not know all of the names a parent knows. It has been noted that approximately half of the names from the oldest generation may be disappearing in a rural village. In this respect, the tendency for this on the individual level is the same as on the scale of the village – many cultivation names and topographic names, in particular, are prone to disappearing.

The knowledge and use of place names are connected to name change: names which are no longer needed are disappearing. However, the amount of names being used is not necessarily decreasing – at least in the same relation – while going from the oldest to the youngest generation. In fact, young people will give names to new places and come up with new ones for places that have had names used by their parents.

Children as Name Users

In traditional collecting of names, efforts have been made to record an area's oldest and most important nomenclature. For this reason, representatives of the oldest generations have been selected for interviews. Young people and children in particular have not really been interviewed. In turn, quite little has been entered, for example, in the place name collections of the Finnish Names Archive on nomenclature used by children and youth. However, some studies have been made on the subject (e.g. Tikka 2006).

Because a child's world is small and limited in comparison to an adult's world, many appellatives signifying the type of place are sufficient enough for being a name. Regarding their own environment, children would be familiar with, for example, only one school, shop or park. Thus, the appellatival terms *Koulu* ('school'), *Kauppa* ('shop') and *Puisto* ('park') often work as names for these places. Names that signify just the type of place alone are typical as children's names and their share of the entire toponymic competence is generally larger than that of an adult. As a child's world gradually expands and the environment is taken over more extensively than before, the child's toponymic competence also grows and diversifies.

A small child has naturally already used other names than just those signifying the type of place. A child learns the names of his surroundings just like any other part of language. He thus becomes familiar with those which, for example, his parents or siblings use. Moreover, a child learns from a young age that there are names in his environment in various written forms, for example, road signs, building walls and advertisements. A child who reads will also easily acquire these names should these be the types of places which need to be spoken about. We learn to become familiar with well-known shops, kiosks, service stations, schools, day care centres and other places by their correct names – indeed along side of them, we can speak about these places in other ways. There is fewer written nomenclature in rural areas but children there also learn road names from signs and can even discern other places in the setting in relation to roads. Although road names become known through signs, names of other places that appear in these names can be quite alien to them. For example, a child who knows the name *Hernevaarantie* ('Hernevaara road') may not necessarily know that Hernevaara ('pea hill') is an existing place, one of the quarters of a village.

In addition, a child will often use his own nomenclature. A part of these names refer to places where children play which have no other names. On the other hand, a part includes names made up by children for places which already have another name used by adults. Names given by children are often quite "concrete" and convey, for example, what is done at the place or what appears there: dogs taken out are on *Koirapolku* ('dog path'), ducks swim in *Sorsalampi* ('duck pond') and a great echo is heard in *Kaikumetsä* ('echo forest'). Children's images of places and worlds of play express many names, for example *Ihmepuut* ('wonder trees'), *Kummitustalo* ('haunted house'), *Menninkäismetsä* ('goblin forest') and *Taikalampi* ('magic pond'). All in all, names given and used by children tell us how children perceive and lingualise the world. Many of the names given by children are short-lived but some may remain to be used more permanently and transfer over to adult language.

Children's place names are also – as are names of other user groups – communal names, that is, names which are used in a specific community and through which a group identity is created. For example, a certain school or class may use its own names for all places that need to be spoken about in school work or on break. These names are learned after coming to school and they often are inherited by the new generation of schoolchildren. A part of the names is known by the entire school, and a part used by smaller communities, for example, by circles of acquaintances and friends.

The nomenclature of Finnish primary schoolchildren and, above all, the names of places of play have been investigated in the Master's thesis by Kaisa Tikka (2006). This study was carried out at Vista School in Paimio in Southwest Finland. She also explored the use and familiarity of names. The most used and familiar place names of play on the schoolyard proved to be, for instance, *Hämähäkkiverkko* ('spider web', a climbing net), *Maanvalloituskenttä* ('conquest field', for game of conquest) and *Palloseinä* ('ball wall'). These names refer to places that are not only used most often in play, but also unique and clearly defined in the schoolyard. *Hevosystävienpuu* ('tree of the friends of horses'), *Salakäytävä* ('secret passage') and *Takametsänmaja* ('back forest hut') are various names used by small groups. The naming of these kinds of secret shelters and imaginary places of play confirms the solidarity of group members.

The Many Contexts of Use

Different variation appears in the use of names. There are two kinds of this onomastic variation – as any variation in language: *user-specific*, that is, *social variation* and *situation-specific*, that is, *situational variation*. User-specific variation has already been dealt with previously. Nomenclatures of language users and user groups mostly differ from one another due to the need to name places. Additionally, different communities, such as professional groups, workplaces, pastime groups, need and use their own toponymy.

Situational variation refers to the fact that the use of nomenclature varies according to situation, in other words, contextually. Different names and name variants can be used on the same places. Names must fulfil different needs in different circumstances of language use. User-specific and situation-specific variation can overlap each other: one and the same speaker can speak about places in different contexts and, at the same time, can often be a member of various user communities.

As situation-specific variation is examined, we can note that what names and the kinds of names and name variants that are used in different situations are at least affected by the members of the spoken situation and its formality. There is always an aim at standard language in official situations whereas people can communicate more freely in a familiar group. Moreover, the question of what places are spoken about and what their types are must be taken into account. Should, in a familiar and intimate situation, we speak of places which are partly or completely alien to the speakers, "correct", that is, official names, or those in the standard language, will naturally be used. When speaking of familiar places, we can naturally use "intimate" and, for example, shorter forms for longer names. For example, members of a family in a rural environment can use single part names (*Harju* 'esker', *Järvi* 'lake') that signify the type of place or other types of single part names (*Mäentaus* 'hill+GEN|back'), should everyone know what places are being referred to. With people who are less familiar with these places, appropriately "correct" names (*Kuoppaharju* 'pit|esker', *Haukijärvi* 'pike|lake', *Mäentauspelto* 'Mäentaus|field') can be used in conversation.

A common phenomenon is that the same name can have both short single part and longer two-part forms. The longer form is used when speaking with someone unfamiliar with the place in which case, he would be able to interpret the expression as a name of a certain type of place. The use of this kind of form amongst one's own family would be impractical. It is practical to use shorter name forms as we frequently speak of a place. In regard to their identifying function, the fact that place names are expressed as short as possible is in accordance with the economical principles of language.

Sometimes, there are official names (for example, the afformentioned *Hämeentie, Kulttuuritalo, Oulunkylä*) used in the urban environment and sometimes there are unofficial variants (the afformentioned *Hämis, Kultsa, Ogeli*). Sometimes, we speak of places which do not even have an official name (*Bägis* 'stairs behind the Paloheinä Library in Helsinki'; *Hutilo* 'a bench in Vuosaari in Helsinki'). Official names are common in formal use and at least in the standard language. A part of Finnish unofficial names are in standard colloquial form and are broadly extensive and then again part is quite narrowly extensive and used only, for example, in some small group's own language.

For example, a part of Helsinki unofficial names in slang can be almost characterised as standard Finnish. These include place names of the city centre such as *Aleksi* 'Aleksanterinkatu' ('Aleks(anterinkatu)+ı': 'Alexander street'), *Espa* 'Esplanadi park and the streets Eteläesplanadi and Pohjoisesplanadi' ('Esp(planadi)+A': 'esplanade'), *Freda* 'Fredrikinkatu' ('Fred(rikinkatu)+A': 'Fredrick street'), *Kaivari* 'Kaivopuisto', *Manta* 'Havis Amanda' ([d] → [t], a statue in Helsinki), *Roba* 'Iso Robertinkatu' ('Rob(ertinkatu)+A': 'greater Robert street') and *Stokka* 'Stockmann' ('Stock(man)+A', *c* = [k]). These may often be more favoured than their official variants and may often appear in official contexts as well. At the same time, numerous neighbourhood names and, for example, names of places known as travel destinations are widely known outside of Helsinki and the Greater Helsinki area. These include, for example, *Itis* 'Itäkeskus' ('It(äkeskus)+ɪs': 'east centre', an eastern quarter of Helsinki), *Sörkkä* 'Sörnäinen' ('Sör(näinen)+ккᴀ', a Helsinki neighbourhood) and *Lintsi* 'Linnanmäki' ('Lin(nanmäki)+тsɪ': 'castle hill', a Helsinki amusement park). In this way, many will learn to be familiar with such places in contemporary Finnish culture; these names therefore cannot be considered to be Helsinki names exclusively.

Some unofficial names in slang can be so strongly labelled in the minds of those who have migrated to the Greater Helsinki area as names included in the regional slang and even as those used only by natives, that there is a tendency to avoid using them. The name *Stadi* (← Swe. *stad* 'city' cf. Ger. *Stadt*), which refers to Helsinki or its centre, is seen as an example of this. As those who have moved from elsewhere do not feel that slang is a part of their language and label it as more of the language of teenagers or of those born and bred in the area, they also avoid using slang place names. At the same time, they are often also aware of how the use of slang for non-natives may not seem genuine. Moreover, they steer clear of the use of slang names partly because of the fact that they are unsure of the forms of some slang names. For example, even though *Sörkka* and *Sörkkä* (ending in [ɑ] or [æ]) are known for the Helsinki neighbourhood of Sörnäinen, the question of which form is "correct" now and again comes up. One who has moved to Helsinki from elsewhere perhaps may consider it wiser to avoid using slang altogether so that they would not accidentally use the "wrong" name form.

Many older city dwellers may, for one, consider slang and also slang place names to be the language of young people, as these names would not be included in their own language use. On average, an older generation would also take a slightly more cautious approach to the use of slang names – as with slang in general – than young people. According to the Master's thesis by Tiina Karbin (2005), which was a study on the use of slang names and their suitability in Vuosaari in Helsinki, up to half of young people (19 respondents out of 39) believed that slang names can be used in just about any situation. Many young people, however, pointed out that the use of slang names would not be appropriate for all situations. The following are some comments given on the use of slang names:

> Yeah, sure, they're appropriate except if you speak with some guy from the countryside who just wouldn't understand them.
> With friends, yeah, but if you show people the places for the first time, then they're not appropriate.
> Well, not always. You can't speak in slang to little old ladies. They won't understand you.
> They're appropriate when you're off the clock but not really at work.

Additionally, adult respondents believed that slang names are primarily a part of young people's language. However, 10 adult respondents out of 29 also believed that slang names are, in fact, appropriate for some situations.

Thus far, a few studies concerning the differences in slang use in various age groups confirm that the percentage of slang vocabulary is greater amongst young people than amongst middle-aged or older people. The same naturally also goes for slang names. Young people also both continuously create new slang names alongside of official names and give them, for example, to significant meeting points which do not even have official names. Young people most often express their own identity by using slang words and place names in slang whereas this type of language use is mainly foreign to older people. Indeed, there are also always individual differences in the use of nomenclature.

The nomenclature in the urban environment makes up a multilayered entirety in which different names and name types have different users and situational uses. Users of names have their own kind of form of language, a part of which includes names. A speaker of slang in most cases speaks about places using slang names, whereas a city dweller using standard language perhaps would not actually use slang or other unofficial names. A slang speaker can also speak about places using official names in an official context whereas a speaker of standard language can recognise slang names as well and may, in some certain context, even use them.

Every language user has his own onomasticon, a part of which, that is, the most well-known names of central places, he shares with nearly all of the area's inhabitants and a part perhaps with only a small group. A user of nomenclature utilises names appropriately; places are spoken about so that they can be identified and so that the listener knows what place is being referred to. The same speaker can speak about the same place in different contexts in different ways: for example, a person from Helsinki can refer to the neighbourhood of Kannelmäki as *Kannelmäki*, *Kantsu* ('Kan-(nelmäki)+TSU') or *Mafiamesta* ('Mafia place'). With a choice of name, the inhabitant perhaps shows his linguistic and cultural communality and even the meanings and images he associates with the place.

ATTITUDE TOWARDS NAMES

When attitudes and positions associated with names and their use are examined, the nomenclature is analysed from a *folk linguistic* perspective. Folk linguistics is one dimension of sociolinguistics. For example, different attitudes of language users can be illustrated by unofficial urban names. Images associated with places and those who frequent them can be revealed by some names (*Peräjunttila* 'rear|hick+LA', *Porvarikoulu* 'right-wing school', *Teinihelvetti* 'teenage hell'). As for other names, some slang names in particular, some user group can be so strongly labelled by them that not everyone would want to use these names.

Attitudes and images related to place names and their use can be studied from a folk linguistic perspective, analysing what kinds of characteristics and attitudes language users associate with names. For example, a group of place names could be presented in a questionnaire and the respondents could be asked to take a position on whether they would use the name or not (for example on a scale of 1 to 5; 1 = I would not use, 5 = I would use). Moreover, the images conjured by these names can be examined with the help of different adjectives (contemptuous, humorous, childish, masculine, feminine) and the respondents may be asked to select the answers that describe the name. Various open questions may also be given in which perspectives associated the names and their use can be examined.

One interesting topic is to examine what kinds of attitudes are geared towards official names. In this case, how inhabitants react to regional official names can thus be examined and what kinds of names they consider to be good ones, what kinds are bad and why. Many of these types of studies (e.g. Aalto 2002, Ainiala 2004) have noted that a name's descriptiveness is considered an important characteristic.

Maria Yli-Kojola (2005) has analysed the attitude of Kouvola residents towards official names in their environment. Many city dwellers believe that it is important for a name to convey something about a place or its inhabitants. From this point of view, one respondent believed that *Tietotie* ('information road') is an example of a good street name; this road is located alongside the respondent's school. Moreover, no one would like the names in an area of detached houses, for example, to be the same as those of blocks of flats in the city centre. Consideration has also been given to the fact that an area's possible change in the future would be taken into account. For example, some street names including an agricultural term could seem unnatural as names in urban trading centres.

Thematic names have generally been considered to be good because with them, it is easy to pinpoint a street to a specific neighbourhood. Many have hoped that these names would describe the city. For example, the respondents considered the railroad to be an appropriate theme for a name in Kouvola and would hope for more street names based on it: "The city was founded around the railroad but we're still missing streets", "Kouvola is an important railroad crossing and it's famous for it". In general, Kouvola residents expressed the desire for simple themes for the area, such themes "which bring about good memories and pleasant images". Additionally, different associations about a name have an effect on whether someone likes it or not. For example, a boy who lives on *Vesakuja* (*Vesa* commonly known as a male name, *kuja* 'alley') in Kouvola does not like street names that include personal names. In reality, the name is included in certain group names with a nature theme (*Vesa* ← *vesa* 'young tree').

Other Functions of Names

The most central function of a name is identification. Place names thus emerge when a community has the need to speak about a certain place. However, place names are given for other reasons as well and the use of place names has other functions than identification. One and the same name often has several functions. Moreover, the kinds of functions different names have vary by speaker. The same name can also have different functions for different people. The various functions of place names in the nomenclature of the Helsinki neighbourhood of Kallio have been examined, for instance, in Riikka Eskelinen's Licentiate study (2008).

Practical function. When an intimate community speaks about places it is familiar with, it is common to use shorter and most often single part name forms rather than longer, two-part names. These name forms have a clear *practical function*. For example, a farmer at home can say that he will be leaving to go plough *Hoimelanraja* ('Hoimela+GEN|border' ← Hoimela, a farm) or *Mäentake* ('hill+GEN|behind') because the family specifically knows what fields are named this way. These fields can appear as *Hoimelanrajapelto* ('Hoimela+GEN|border|field') and *Mäentaustanpelto* ('hill+GEN|background+GEN|field') in an account entered for a European Union report on these areas. Moreover, a circle of friends may say they are leaving to go skiing at *Selkä* or *Putis* instead of saying *Saariselkä* ('island|open-waters') and *Pudasjärvi* ('clean|lake').

Many places in urban nomenclature have been given shorter names than their official names which are more practical in speech. It is easier and more economical to speak of, for example, the aforementioned *Itis* instead of *Itäkeskus* and *Aleksi* instead of *Aleksanterinkatu*. Moreover, single part names signifying the type of place (*Assa* ← *asema* 'station', *Kirjasto* 'library', *Tori* 'market square') are often more common in normal, daily speech than official, longer names of places. They too are thus functionally practical.

Social function. The identity of a user community is created and confirmed by many names. A group identity is confirmed by using one's own nomenclature as part of a group's language. In this case, names work in a *social function*. Different communities use their own language and their own nomenclature which confirms membership to the group. Many communities may also have the need to speak of such places which are not important to others.

Sometimes, a rather small group can be the user of a name whereupon the names are part of an inner circle's language. The meanings of these names and even the places they refer to often remain completely obscure to outsiders. For example, a certain section of a market square or street corner can become a significant place to some urban youth because the subject of a crush has been encountered there. A street corner known by a few girls as *Tomipaikka* ('Tomi place') had received its name due to the fact that there was a chance meeting with a certain boy named *Tomi* there and from there, the place was spoken about using this name. To other city dwellers, this place would hardly be so significant that there would be a need to speak of it with one's own identifying name. This kind of spontaneously originated user nomenclature confirms a spirit of 'us' and identification as a member of a specific group.

Some names may have been altered from the basis of official names whereupon the place has, at the same time, been given its own individual meaning. The following conversation extract includes an example of this. A place important to a small group of friends has received an altered name on the basis of its official name. The use of this name expresses a spirit of 'us'.

> Pekka [talking about his favourite eateries]: It was *Pizzeria La 'Gote* but then we named it *Goethe*… It totally became *Goethe* when we all had a, this sort of like, terrible hangover morning, and to ease our suffering, like the philosopher, one of us wanted to go to *Pizzeria La Goethe*.

Marja: You all named it, but you haven't gotten other people on board with the name more than that?
Pekka: No, no. It's really only known in our small group.
Interviewer: Is it still *Goethe* to you even though it's called *El Nino* now?
Pekka: Yeah, it is.

Affective function. As images, meanings and attitudes geared towards a place or its users are shown with place names, we can speak of the *affective function* of names. This often closely goes hand in hand with the social function of names. This is due to the fact that one way to emphasise the spirit of 'us' in a group is to designate separation from others. As "other" non-members of a certain group are offended and ridiculed, its positive identity at the same time is reinforced. Many unofficial names can be interpreted to represent negative attitudes and images of those using these names towards some places and those using these places.

It is worth exercising caution when interpreting biased names and the affective functions of names. It is not possible to make too many straightforward and definite conclusions on meanings given by the users themselves based on merely the mentioning of a name. Ambiguity is typical for giving unofficial names; we often also want names to be interpreted in different ways and want them to include various motives and principles of naming. Moreover, some of the expressions classified as affective and biased can be so neutralised that speakers would not even notice that they include bias when they use them. Expressions in frequent use quickly become daily expressions and no vulgar or derogatory tones included in them are necessarily noted.

The subject of negative attention in toponymy most often seems to be the inhabitants of a specific area or users of a place, that is, usually people. Sometimes contempt seems to be geared towards the physical setting and its being aesthetically unappealing. For example, *Betonikylä* ('concrete village' signifying 'no nature') and *DDR* ([dɛː dɛː ær], 'a building that looks like concrete bunkers') as names of certain neighbourhoods are reminiscent of unattractive and dreary architecture. Several names can be used for one and the same neighbourhood. For example, the same neighbourhood in the Western Finland municipality of Pirkkala, studied by Hanna Sirén (2005), is known as *Ikiroudanmaa* ('permafrost land'), *Käpykylä* ('pine cone village'), *Nälkälaakso* ('hungry valley'), *Ryysyranta* ('rag shore'), *Siperia* ('Siberia'), *Syrjälä* ('border+LA') and *Tumppukylä* ('mitten village'). These names mainly refer to the location and characteristics of the place. However, social characterisations and descriptions associated with the physical place itself usually are together intertwined with stereotypical images of the place. Let us take Finnish names with the word *Slummi* ('slum') for example. These names refer to both a harsh environment as well as its inhabitants and the basis for naming these includes, for example, blocks of flats in poor condition and the inhabitants residing there with non-Finnish backgrounds.

Finnish names given in respect to problem users of alcohol are common for names that include an affective function, referring to the users and inhabitants of a place. These include names beginning with *Juoppo*, *Spuge* and *Spurgu*, all referring to 'alcoholic', 'drunkard, boozer', however slang words *spuge* and *spurgu* also refer to a man that consumes surrogate alcohol. These names include, for example, *Spugela* ('drunkard+LA'), *Spurgula* ('drunkard+LA'), *Spugepuro* ('drunkard brook'), *Spugeläävä* ('drunkard pigsty') and *Spugelandia* ('boozerland'), given to neighbourhoods and areas of a city and also *Spugerinki* ('drunkard circle') and *Spugetori* ('drunkard market square') for market squares and plazas. Besides an affective tone, these names also include perhaps humorous and ironic tones towards alcoholics in public, urban spaces and those that stand out from others in appearance. In these kinds of place names used by young people, "drunkards" quickly become defined as "others", a group to which the young user does not belong. At the same time, it is perhaps shown that named places in such a way are also rather a part of others (that is, alcoholics) than oneself. A number of other such "others", those who are pointed at and labelled, for example, different nationalities and sexual minorities, are naturally found in unofficial nomenclature.

Negative attitudes towards a surrounding environment and the conditions dominating there are strongly highlighted in names given to schools and used by school-aged youth. School can be criticised by young people, for example, when it is called *Laitos* ('(mental) institution') and *Keskitysleiri* ('concentration camp'). However, these kinds of names – the same as many other descriptive and biased unofficial names – are not necessarily true place names which would be used when speaking about school as a place. These expressions are mostly terms of ridicule and depicters of the place. In regular, daily conversation, reference to 'school' is made more often by using, for example, the names *Koulu* or *Skole*.

Attitudes are generally expressed quite directly in many unofficial place names. However, they do not always appear so clearly but instead circumlocutions may be used or subtly be hinted at. Additionally, attitudes can appear through exaggeration or an understatement in which case, the names can often be humorous or ironic. The realisation of humour and irony is usually only possible when one knows what the named places are in reality. Additionally, these kinds of names can be seen to be functionally affective. For example, young residents in Pirkkala in Hanna Sirén's (2005) research may call the small football field located in the Takamaa playground area *Stade de Takamaa* and the Killo football field *Killon stadion* ('Killo stadium'). In this case, they convey with irony that the football fields, in their opinion, are quite unassuming. All kinds of play and different semantic changes are otherwise a part of the common characteristics of unofficial nomenclature and through this play and these changes, different attitudes, often humorous, that are geared towards places and their users are often also seen.

Attitudes held in par with place names are often negative. This characteristic can also be seen as a part of slang, the central part of which includes these kinds of names. Negative attitudes are often intertwined with irony and even humour. Indeed, there can be positive attitudes and different forms of affection expressed by names. The general fact, that important and significant places to a speaker will be given different unofficial names, often conveys a warm, emotional bond to the place.

Informative function. We can speak of a name's *informative function* when a name provides people with some fundamental information concerning a place. From the modern person's perspective, many place names can seem to have this kind of function because many names, by their appearance, may already reveal something about what the place is (*Hietalahti* 'fine sand bay', *Mustikkakangas* 'blueberry moor'). However, it is often more appropriate to speak of an informative function in a more limited sense in research. As the actual or imagined semantic content proves to be meaningful, in one way or another, in conversation, the informative function of names is crucial. Some name users are familiar with the origins of names better than others and can understand a name's informative function better in this way too.

The following excerpt is an example of the informative function of names and its meaning to inhabitants.

> Interviewer: Do you usually think about place names or what they mean?
> Ritva: Oh yeah, a lot, I think about from where… *Kallio* [*kallio* 'rock'] is pretty clear, all of Kallio [the neighbourhood of Kallio in Helsinki] was carved out of a rock. And I often wonder where some place got its name from, I'm terribly interested in history.
> Aila: But then there are those, these streets, they've been named like that, well of course some theme, for example there's Agricola and Porthan and Franzén [surnames of important figures in Finnish history]
> Ritva: Streets of great men…

4. Personal Names

This chapter on personal names delves deep into naming systems in Africa, Asia and Europe. A cross-cultural and historic approach is taken to provide the reader with insight on how people in society attain their names. It thoroughly examines the Finnish anthroponymic system, providing historical, statistical and social features of given names, surnames and bynames of Finnish people.

Introduction to Personal Names

Personal Names and Culture

Alexander the Great, Cleopatra, Sitting Bull, Joan of Arc, Mao Zedong, Indira Gandhi, Winston Churchill, Nelson Mandela – when we hear or read these names, we know right away who is being spoken about. A person's name and his or her identity inseparably belong together. So, to the question "Who is he?", we generally respond by saying the name of the person in question: "He is Peter Newman".

In onomastics, the term used for names to referring to people is *personal name*. In addition to this is the onomastic term *anthroponym* which originates from the Greek words *anthropos* 'human' and *onyma* 'name'. The study of personal name nomenclature or *anthroponymy* is called *anthroponomastics*.

Personal names, or anthroponyms, are culturally universal. This means that names, under specific rules or established practices, are given to people in all cultures of the world. An individual's *identification*, that is, distinguishing him from other members of a community, has traditionally been regarded as the main function of a personal name. With a name, an individual can be addressed and he can be referred to without any descriptive expressions. Instead of us having to say "Hi you little redheaded girl!" or "that man with a black beard that lives in the yellow house near the sports field" we can simply use these people's names, that is if they are known to us. So, it would be "Hi Ellen!" or "Robert Hill". A personal name is also a certain kind of label which refers to the individual and identifies but not necessarily describes him.

Because personal names are cultural universals, such cultures in which people are not named are unknown. Some historical sources – such as travelogues of European colonisation – may indeed have given an account of exotic groups of people which might not have any personal names at all. However, in these accounts, it is certainly a question of the fact that the culture in question was unfamiliar to those examining it. There is a custom to give community members in many world cultures *secret names*, that is, names which are not used in daily speech but are only known in the individual's circle of acquaintances. In place of these secret names, people are often addressed by nicknames or terms of kinship, such as "older sister", "little brother" or "grandmother", which highlights the individual's role as a member of his community.

Personal names are a part of the language used by a community in all world cultures. They are thus not only culturally but also linguistically universal. However, personal names are not just isolated, separate elements in any language or its nomenclature but rather they always form an *anthroponymic system* which includes several different sub-systems. These sub-systems include, for example, the *first name system* and *surname system* of the European languages or the *clan name system* of some African languages (a *clan* is a unit, formed by several families which sees itself as being descendent from the same, often mythical, ancestors; each clan has its own *clan name*). Each language thus has an anthroponymic system but what sub-systems it is comprised of is language- and culture-specific.

German onomastician Volker Kohlheim (1998) has emphasised that although an anthroponymic system is a part of language, it is always also, in many ways, connected to the extralinguistic environment – the same as with other language components. In addition to their basic function, that is, identification, personal names can have many other social and cultural functions which are nevertheless secondary to the main function of names. While the basic function of personal names is the same in all cultures, their secondary functions may vary quite a bit, depending on the culture.

In addition to the fact that a community has the need to distinguish individuals from each other to facilitate communication, names help in the community's need to often classify people as belonging to various social groups, such as members of immediate families, kins and clans. For example, Mr Jones belongs to the Jones family and kin. A name also has another key function in an anthroponymic system beyond identification: classification. As such, personal names do not only identify a person but also they make him a member of a group and provide him with a social identity which is often also explicitly gendered.

In all cultures, giving a child a name means that he is accepted as a member of the community. Richard Alford (1988) has shown that personal names actually express the identity of a person in two ways: in the first place, they tell the other members of the community who the individual in question is and secondly, they tell the community who he is or who he is expected to be. Personal names thus have a significant role in building a person's individual and social identity. At the same time, they express different religious, political and other values associated with groups of people. It is often said that personal names are hallmarks of the cultural identity of individuals.

A person's name is, therefore, not just a meaningless tag which only differentiates him from other people of the same community as contemporary national identity numbers do. Valuable information on different cultures and their history have often been hidden in personal names, the same as information on people's religious, linguistic and ethnic background. This is why historical researchers, cultural researchers and sociologists continuously regard these names as subjects of great interest.

Differences and Similarities in Naming Systems

A common feature of most Western anthroponymic systems is that a person has one or more given names and a surname. In addition to this *official personal name*, a person can have various unofficial bynames. However, this system is not common to all countries. The number of different anthroponymic systems in the world is nearly as many as there are cultures.

Because the naming of people is a universal phenomenon, the anthroponymic systems of different cultures are nonetheless reminiscent of one another in many respects. To begin with, one universal fact is that people are given one or more names in all cultures. A name giver is often also well-defined: it can be a child's mother, father or some other individual. At the same time, names are usually given according to certain, established practices, not at all arbitrarily. In many cultures, name giving can include a special public or private *name giving ceremony*. The differences in name giving is evident in how many names a child receives, are they *unique names* or names often recurring in the naming system, or are they semantically transparent expressions of the language, that is, *transparent names*, or contextually obscure.

Onomasticians have noted that we are often led to similar anthroponymic systems in similar cultural environments whereas the differences between different naming systems are further explained by their various environmental factors. So, for example, there is a great deal of common features in the name giving of small agricultural communities, and respectively name giving in modern urban cultures largely complies with the same rules.

Richard D. Alford (1988) conducted a study on name giving in sixty different cultures in different parts of the world; however, his materials do not include modern, industrialised societies. His study reveals many interesting features both on the similarities of anthroponymic systems and the differences between them.

According to Alford, the connection of social significance to name giving is a common feature; a child is usually perceived as a legal member of the community only when he has been named. Together with name giving, the child may be dressed or adorned in some special way as a sign of this, which conveys that his social status has changed. Name giving in many cultures also confirms the status of a mother and father as the child's parents. In some cultures, a name is given immediately at childbirth or within a few days or weeks. In some cultures, a name is given only when the child is a few months or up to a few years old – or when he, for example, learns to walk or otherwise shows some signs of vitality. Name giving, nonetheless, most often occurs during the baby's first month of life (75 per cent of cultures).

Name giving is the exclusive right of the father in many cultures but a mother, aunt or uncle, grandparents, religious authority, an old or wise individual or some other person can also solely be a *name giver*. However, in most cases, name givers vary and in two thirds of cultures, either the child's mother or father or both act as the name giver.

There are special name giving ceremonies in a majority of cultures (74 per cent). They are particularly common in agriculturally intensive cultures (99 per cent). A large group of people, for example the people of an entire village community, can be called to attend this type of celebration, which is often a rather developed ritual. Large name giving celebrations are typical to more populous and, by their social structure, multi-tiered communities. On the other hand, in smaller communities, more modest occasions are favoured where the child's close relatives mostly attend and where the ceremony itself is simpler. The purpose of a name giving celebration includes announcing the child's coming into the world, presenting him to his kin and wishing him luck in life. Sometimes, special cleansing or sacrificial rituals are carried out with the celebration, aiming towards a positive future together with these rituals.

The basis for the selection of a name is different in different cultures. A common *principle of name giving* is to name a child after a relative, such as a grandparent, aunt or uncle; this often happens in a specific order. Names can also describe the child or express desired traits for him. These names often are associated with the moment of childbirth or events previous to it. They can also refer to the order in which the child was born or his special position in the family; for example, the naming of twins is carefully regulated in many cultures. In some cultures, the name of a child is determined according to a dream or some other sign.

Onomasticians presume that personal names in all cultures have originally been semantically transparent, linguistic expressions, but over time, their meaning has often become obscure due to language development. Over two thirds of the cultures in Alford's data are those in which a name has a clear lexical meaning. The most typical of these include names depicting a child's appearance or nature, names referring to animals or plants, names concerning the events of the child's birth and names referring to places. Sometimes, a child's name can include a name giver's message geared towards another community, whereupon the name is used in the community as a means of communication. In some cultures, a child is given derogatory or otherwise semantically negative names so that evil spirits would not be interested in the child nor cause him death. The semantic transparency of names is most typical for small hunter-gatherer cultures. Names in densely populated agricultural cultures are often semantically obscure.

The expression of gender in names is also typical for many cultures – however, not for all. 43 per cent of the cultures in Alford's data are those in which a name always reveals an individual's gender. 15 per cent of these cultures do not make any difference between male and female names. There is often reference to the name bearer's gender by various linguistic markers or the name's semantic content. For example, an Ambo boy born in Namibia in the morning may receive the name *Angula* whereas the corresponding girl's name is *Nangula*; both names are based on the Oshiwambo word *ongula* 'morning'. Similarly, an Ambo boy's name can refer to a frog hunter and an Ambo girl's name can refer to one who grinds corn; these names refer to the roles of boys and girls in this culture. (Saarelma-Maunumaa 2003.)

Anthroponymic systems also differ from one another regarding if they consist of unique names or if *name sharing* is allowed in the culture. 12 per cent of the cultures in Alford's data are based on the complete uniqueness of names: the names that both living and deceased members of the community bear are unique. On the other hand, 16 per cent of the cultures in the data are those in which only the names of living members of the community are unique. Many communities that have rules of naming children after relatives make sure that one name at a time has only one living name bearer. Unique naming is typical in the organisational structure of relatively small societies, such as small fishing and horticulture communities, in which the number of names required is quite minimal.

Name sharing occurs in 72 per cent of naming systems. This also refers to the fact that the function of personal names in a naming system is not always merely identification but also classification. As people are named after living or deceased relatives or other respected people, such as religious role models, they are simultaneously associated with these people. Sharing the same name gives rise to the fact that the naming of children is *systematic* in certain situations: for example, twins may always be given specifically determined names. Moreover, the fact that certain linguistic expressions have been developed as traditional personal names, whereupon a child's name is selected as it were from a ready-made onomasticon, has transpired in many cultures. Name sharing is sometimes random: for example, names with reference to the moment of childbirth often produce similar names ('thunderstorm', 'night').

According to Alford, different social and religious functions are connected to bearing the same name, that is, a *namesake relationship*. A namesake relationship in every fifth culture in Alford's study is perceived as quite a special relationship whereupon namesakes usually also have strictly regulated social obligations towards each other. It is also believed that namesakes quite often have common traits. Sharing the same name in many cultures also concerns the notion of preserving the memory of an ancestor or even his reincarnation back into the family. Sometimes, it is understood that namesakes will also fill the same place in the network of relatives. It is clear, that name sharing in this kind of community emphasises the common features of namesakes and draws attention away from their individuality.

Naming systems are also structurally different from one another. People have an individual name in all cultures but besides this, some established byname is used in a majority of cultures (60 per cent): for example, a father's name, a *patronym*, clan name or other hereditary name in a family or special given "holy" or "great" name is used in addition to an individual name. In agricultural cultures, names are often required for inheriting land and these names link an individual to his kin and the rights to land. Sometimes, only the most distinguished families of a community will have a surname whereas others are without one. In some communities, people can be given both a *public name* and a secret name. A secret, usually a "holy" or "great" name is generally perceived as the actual name of the individual whereas a public name used daily in a way works as an alias. In the reaming cultures (40 per cent), people only have their own individual name. These are, by their social structure, generally simple hunter-gatherer and fishing cultures.

Moreover, *nicknames* and *names of ridicule* are characteristic of personal naming systems, which signify different emotions or social messages geared towards the name bearer. It also seems that it is more common for men to have these types of names than women. 75 per cent of the cultures in Alford's data include those where men's nicknames and names of ridicule are either common or random, whereas only 68 per cent of the cultures include these names for women. Approximately half of these names include derogatory names and the remainder either positive or neutral. A majority of them refer to a person's appearance or behaviour.

It is typical that people's names can also change in life for many different reasons. A *name change* is realised in many cultures when a person moves on to a new phase in life, or his role in the community changes, for example, due to growing up, marriage, a first-born child or even in the reception of an important social task. An individual may receive a completely new name in this way or he will regularly begin to be named after some other person. For example, after childbirth, the parents will often begin to be called "so-and-so's mother" or "so-and-so's father". So-called *teknonymy* is seen in approximately one third of the cultures in Alford's data. With changing a name, efforts can be made to change one's fate, for example, in connection to a relative's death or serious illness. In this way, the change of an individual's identity is expressed directly in his name.

Because Alford's data includes no industrialised society whatsoever, his research naturally does not give a comprehensive overview of anthroponymic systems of the entire world. The naming systems of contemporary Europe and North America, the same as other industrialised societies, differ in many regards from the naming systems of traditional agricultural, fishing and hunter-gatherer cultures. European naming systems will be examined more closely in the section *Development of European Naming Systems*.

Anthroponymic Typology and Terminology

There have been many kinds of classifications presented in the history of onomastics on the various name types in anthroponymic systems. The classification presented in this section is a version applied to Finnish onomastics based on the classification by German onomastician Konrad Kunze (2003). Because the key functions of personal names in several naming systems include identification and classification, personal names can be divided into two main classes: firstly *individual personal names* and secondly *collective personal names* which refer to different groups of people (figs. 5 and 6).

Individual personal names include those referring to humans (*Cleopatra, Nelson Mandela*) and other human-like beings, such as mythological figures

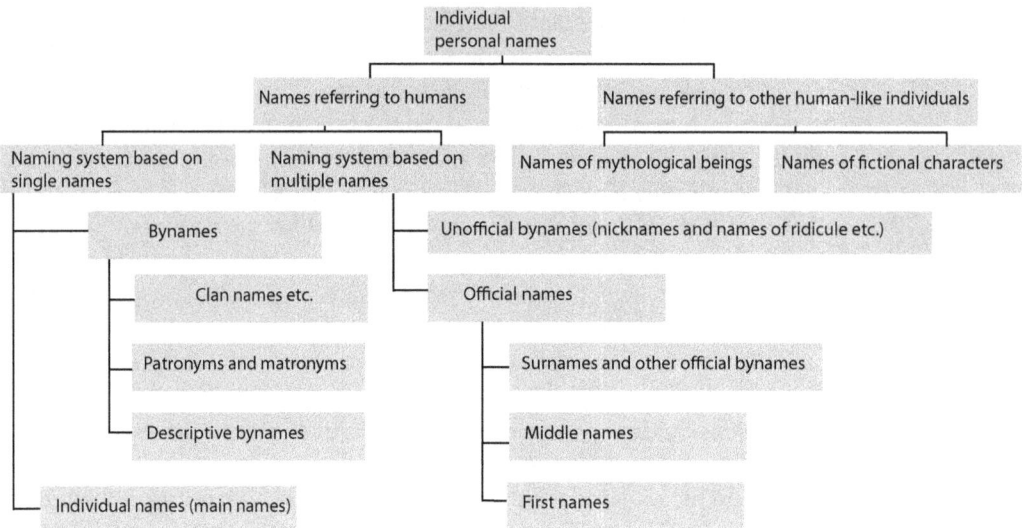

Fig. 5. Individual personal names.

(*Zeus*, *Thor*) or names in literature and other fictive characters (*Sherlock Holmes*, *Homer Simpson*). Kunze also includes names of animals in this group. Often, the naming of animals is really a question of humanising, that is, personification (cat *Fluffy*, dog *Spot*, cow *Bessie*). This inclusion is natural in both German and English, where the term *personal name* refers to the term *persona* (Ger. *Personenname*), whereas animal names are not included in the classification of personal names in Finnish onomastics. This is because the Finnish term for a personal name, *henkilönnimi*, includes the word *henkilö* ('person') which refers to humans or human-like beings only.

Names referring to humans can be divided into two groups whether the naming system is based on having *single* or *multiple names*. *Naming systems based on single names*, in which each individual has only one true name, are typical for small hunter-gatherer and fishing cultures but also for some larger agricultural cultures. The main name types of these naming systems include *individual names* (*main names*) and possible *bynames*. *Descriptive bynames* often refer to the individual's appearance (*Harald Fairhair*), character (*Ivan the Terrible*), profession (*Anders Seppä*, *seppä* 'blacksmith'), origin (*Friedrich Holländer*) or place of residence (*Desiderius Erasmus Roterodamus*). *Patronyms* (*Andersson*, *Tuomaantytär*) or *matronyms* (*Finnbogadóttir*) that are based on an individual's parents' names are also used as bynames – these have later developed into official surnames in many naming systems. When a patronym or matronym refers to an individual's mother or father, we can speak of *primary patronyms* and *matronyms*. If it is a question of a more distant ancestor, we can speak of *secondary patronyms* and *matronyms*. Moreover, the same as other bynames that refer to family or other group of people, clan names (*MacKenzie*, *Madiba*: Nelson Mandela's clan name) are included in this group when they do not develop into official surnames but rather function as unofficial bynames.

Naming systems based on multiple names are, on the other hand, typical for larger, and by its organisational structure, multilayered agricultural and industrial cultures where the functionality of the society requires specific identification of people in written sources. These kinds of naming systems include both *official names* and *unofficial bynames*.

An individual's official name is mostly made up of one or more *given names*, *first names* or *forenames* (the terms *baptismal name*, *christening name* or *confirmation name* can be used to refer to these names that are included as a part of Christianity) as well as some bynames that have received official status. The most typical structure of an official name is the European system of a first name and surname which is different in different countries. The terms *first name*, *given name* and *forename* are by and large interchangeable but when more than one of these names can be given to a person, as in the Finnish naming system, we should speak of *given names* and *first given names* and *latter given names*: the first given name is the first of these names, the latter given names are those that come after the first one. The term *first name* can be defined as the main name of the person which is situated before the surname of his official first name and surname combination. On the other hand, given names in Hungarian, for example, always appear after the surname (*Fehér Laszló*). Hungarian names in texts of other languages than Hungarian may be presented the other way around (*Laszló Fehér*), so the term *first name* when speaking of Hungarian personal names is also well-grounded.

The terms *surname*, *family name* or *last name* can be defined as a byname which is situated after the individual's main name, that is, first name – or given names – in a first name and surname combination. A surname is a hereditary byname, or meant to be hereditary according to certain rules in a family, and it can be determined in different cultures in different ways. In some naming systems, a woman, for example, regularly assumes her husband's surname, her *married name*, after marriage, whereas sometimes she can keep her *maiden name*, that is, the name which she had before getting married, or she can make her surname a *hyphenated name* which means that she takes her husband's surname after her maiden name with a hyphen. In many countries, a man can also take his wife's surname after marriage whereupon we can also speak of a man's *maiden name* or even a *bachelor name* (Swe. *pojknamn*); however this is not such an established term in English and the term *maiden name* is more often than not exclusively thought of as referring to women only. The Finnish term *poikanimi*, based on the Swedish word, is also not well-established. The term *birth name* is well suited to be used for such a surname which a person receives right after being born.

There can also be a so-called *middle name* between a first name and surname in some European naming systems. These middle names are often based on other surnames, for example a name on the mother's side or the woman's own maiden name (*Hillary Rodham Clinton*). Middle names are common, especially in such naming systems, where the surnames are relatively few in number.

Other kinds of official naming systems are represented by, for example, the Chinese naming system where a person's name is comprised of a *surname* and a two-part individual name (*Jian Ze-min*). In some countries, such as Iceland, a person's official name can consist of a first name and a patronym or matronym (*Haraldur Vilmundarson, Vigdís Finnbogadóttir*). An individual's official name in many African cultures is made up of a first name and clan name (*Nelson Mandela*). Both actual surnames and other bynames that have received some official status, such as patronyms, clan names or middle names, can thus function as *official bynames*.

Unofficial nomenclature of naming systems based on having multiple names is represented by various *unofficial bynames*. All of the names that refer to an individual, which are not first names, can be defined as bynames in a naming system that includes a first name and surname. Along these lines, a surname is the individual's official byname. Unofficial bynames include all such bynames which have not received any official status in the naming system. This group includes both *hypocoristic bynames* (*Ari Uusimäki* → first name *Arska* and surname *Uusis* in slang form) from a person's official name and other nicknames or names of ridicule that describe a person's appearance (*Kuulapää* 'baldy') or behaviour (*Hitler*), the same as, for example, so-called *foetal* and *newborn nicknames* (*Pikku Myy* 'Little My' from the Moomin books) and *pet names* or *nursery nicknames* (*Anna* → *Annuliini* 'sweet little Anna', *Nassukka* 'cutie pie'). In addition, it also includes bynames used in various social groups, such as *scout names* (*Kirppu* 'flea') or authors' *code names* or *pen names* (Charles Lutwidge Dodgson better known as *Lewis Carroll*; Agatha Christie who wrote romances under the name *Mary Westmacott*), the same as, for example, code names in Internet chat groups or *pseudonyms* (*Cinderella -92, Pettynyt äänestäjä* 'disappointed voter') used for letters to the editor in a newspaper. Unofficial bynames can include the official name of an individual (*Henkseli-Heikki* 'suspenders Heikki', *Silli-Salminen* 'herring Salminen') or be completely independent of it (*Eino Nurminen* → *Obelix*). Bynames based on an individual's official name are called *secondary bynames* and others are known as *primary bynames*.

The classification and terminology of bynames has been quite colourful in onomastics. The following terms are frequently used in the depiction of modern Western anthroponymic systems:

Byname
All names referring to persons, which are not official first names, are bynames. Bynames can either be official (surnames) or unofficial.

Primary byname
An unofficial byname which is not based on a person's official first name or surname but rather formed in some other way, for example, is descriptive of the person (*Fatso, Sherlock, Skyscraper*).

Secondary byname
A person's unofficial byname completely or partly based on an official first name or surname (*Jennifer* → *Jenny*, *Salminen* → *Silli-Salminen* 'herring Salminen').

Hypocorism
A name form from a certain root name, which either received official status (*Johannes* → *Giovanni, Ivan, Johan, John; Juha, Jukka, Jussi*) or unofficial (*Leonard* → *Lenny, Heikki* → *Hese, Mäkeläinen* → *Mäkkäri*).

Hypocoristic byname
A person's unofficial byname based on the hypocorism of a first name or surname (*Jennifer* → *Jenny, Valtonen* → *Valtsu*).

Descriptive byname
An unofficial byname descriptive of the name bearer which can refer to, for example, the person's appearance (*Punapää* 'redhead'), character (*Miss Sunshine*), typical activities (*Tuhisija* 'snorter'), nationality (*Svensson* 'Swede') or profession (*Posti-Matti* 'postman Matti').

Nickname
An unofficial byname of the name bearer used in informal contexts often in colloquial language. Nicknames often reflect either positive or negative emotions towards the name bearer (*Four Eyes, Stud Muffin*).

Foetal nickname, newborn nickname
An unofficial byname which refers to an unborn or newborn child before an official name is given (*Peikkotyttö* 'goblin girl', *Sittiäinen* 'dorbeetle').

Nursery nickname
An unofficial byname of affection which is used for babies or small children while caring for them. The name can be based on the person's name (*Iida* → *Iidukka*) or formed in some other way (*Prinsessa Ruusunen* 'Sleeping Beauty').

Pet name, term of endearment
An unofficial byname which designates affectionate and intimate emotions towards the name bearer, for example towards a child or loved one (*Honeybunch, Snookums*). The name can be based on the person's name or formed in some other way.

Name of abuse, name of ridicule, pejorative byname
An unofficial byname which designates negative emotions towards the name bearer (*Skitso* 'schizo', *Ääliö* 'moron').

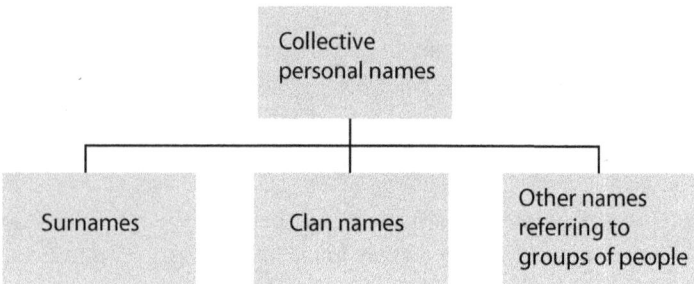

Fig 6. Collective personal names.

Behind-the-back nickname
An unofficial byname which is used only when the name bearer himself is not present and which designates negative emotions towards him (*Mutanttisormi* 'mutant finger', *Pulloperse* 'bottle-ass').

Call name, name of address
A name used when speaking of a person, which can be either an official name (first name or surname) or unofficial name (a hypocoristic byname based on an official name or some other unofficial byname).

In different languages, different terms are used for bynames. Swedish anthroponymic terms for a byname include *binamn*, *smeknamn*, *tillnamn*, *vedernamn* and *öknamn* and in German onomastics, the terms *Beiname*, *Kosename*, *Nachname*, *Nebenname*, *Rufname*, *Spottname*, *Übername* and *Zuname* are used. It is clear, that these terms cannot always be directly translated from one language to another. However, they account for themselves best in their own language environment and in the naming systems of that environment.

The second main group of personal names, in addition to names referring to an individual, includes collective names, in other words, names referring to various groups of people (fig. 6). Collective personal names in European cultures are mostly surnames (*Halonen*, *Smith*) and clan names (*MacDonald*) when they refer to these groups as a whole. However, many other names referring to groups of people, such as names of sports teams (*Manchester United*, *Mighty Ducks*) and names of artist groups (musical group *Abba*, choir group *Vienna Boys' Choir*), are often interpreted as names on the borderline of commercial rather than personal names. Collective names outside of European cultures include, for example, *initiation group names* concerning rites of passage in African cultures or *generation names* in the Chinese naming system which unite individuals of the same generation to each other.

Surnames in figs 5 and 6, which are based on Konrad Kunze´s (2003) classification, are placed in two separate locations: on the one hand as part of an official name referring to an individual, on the other hand as a name referring to a group of people. This means that a surname can have two different functions in a naming system: it can refer to both an individual and a group. Moreover, Belgian onomastician Willy van Langendonck (1995) has emphasised that a surname can work both as an individual name and as a collective name in a naming system.

Kunze also includes names of peoples, that is, *ethnonyms* (*Deutsche, Sioux, Zulu*), in his classification of collective names but these are not considered to represent personal names in Finnish onomastics. Unlike, for example, in English or German, ethnic groups and groups of peoples are not written with capital letters in Finnish which can be an indication of this. Finnish uses words such as *saksalainen* ('German', lit. 'a person/item from Germany'), *sioux-intiaani* (lit. 'Sioux indian') and *zulu* ('Zulu' or 'Zulu language') and the basis for this is that these words primarily classify and not identify their referents.

Personal names can indeed be classified on many other bases than what is described in figs 5 and 6. Should personal names be examined from the name bearers' perspective, we can speak of, for example, *male names* and *female names*, *unisex names* applied to both genders, *saint's names*, *nobility names*, *bourgeois* and *artisan names*, *monarch names*, *solider names*, *artist names* and so on. Should the point of view be the principle of name giving, we can speak of, for example, *nature names* referring to nature, *literary names* referring to characters in literature, *political names* that reflect the name giver's political point of view and so on.

A linguistic perspective to personal names brings about such terms as *mother tongue names* (a name in a naming system based on one's own language), *foreign language names* (a name in a naming system based on a language outside one's own language), *translated names* (a name in a naming system translated from one language to another), *truncated names* (a name based on another name, created by shortening), *compound names* (a first name which has two names, united by a hyphen), *hyphenated* or *double-barreled names* (a surname made up of two surnames, united by a hyphen), *double names* (a combination of two separately written first names used as a name of address), *root names* (a name on which some other name is based), *Scandinavian names* (a name, that has a linguistically Scandinavian background), *Celtic names* (a name, that has a linguistically Celtic background) and so on.

Should names be examined from a perspective of temporal or regional *popularity change*, we can speak of, for example, a *fashionable name* (a name in fashion at a certain point in time), a *top name* (the most popular name at a certain point in time), a *revived name* (an old name that has regained popularity), a *unique name* (a name which has only one name bearer in the naming system) and so on.

Many of these are quite established onomastic terms but more of these types of terms are all the time being created for various needs in the study of names. It is clear that different naming systems also generally require different terms for facilitating their exact description and analysis. So, for example, terminology created for the analysis of European naming systems may not be sufficiently applicable to describe, for example, African or Asian anthroponymic systems.

A Changing Anthroponymy

It is characteristic for anthroponymic systems to not be static – they are in a constant state of change. Many linguists have stated that names – and personal names in particular – are loaned from one language to another notably more easily than other language elements. This has been explained by the fact that foreign names do not usually make such an impact on language and its structure whereupon they are linguistically less radical than many other elements loaned from foreign languages. Loaned names are also often seen as independent lexical elements which can either be suitably adapted into the new language or remain in its original form.

The departure for this examination is that the anthroponymy of a specific language always forms an organised system which works according to its own internal rules. Each element has its own function which is often necessary regarding the functioning of the whole system. Should one part of the system change, it may result in changes elsewhere in the system as well.

An anthroponymic system can change for reasons both internal and external to the language. Changes that happen in language reflect in the anthroponymy especially in such systems that have semantically transparent names. In language change, these names can either become semantically obscure – whereupon the names remain the same but they are not comprehensible – or they will change according to linguistic changes whereupon they will preserve their semantic transparency. Moreover, changes can happen within the naming system itself and as a consequence of these changes, the nomenclature of the language will get reorganised in a new way: for example, a place name can become a surname, a surname can become a first name and so on. However, these kinds of changes are usually so small and individual, that they will not have an effect on the functionality of the anthroponymic system as a whole.

Sometimes, however, a whole name category can get a new function in a naming system: for example, a patronymic system or clan name system can develop into a surname system. In these cases, the whole organisational structure of the naming system will change, not just the individual names. Different extralinguistic, social factors are usually behind these kinds of large changes. For example, a surname system may have evolved as a result of a certain social development which has included the growth of cities, a population register required by a developed government and the clarification of inheritance as well as many other factors. A similar cultural development thus often leads to changes along the same lines in the anthroponymy as well.

When there is a truly large change in a naming system, we should speak of the replacement of one whole naming system with another. Thus, for example, the *Old Finnish anthroponymic system* – that is the pre-Christian anthroponymic system of the Finnish people – is not the same naming system as the contemporary Finnish anthroponymic system, although this system has developed from the old one as a result of multi-stage, historical development.

Anthroponymic systems can also change when two different naming systems or cultures encounter each other. This process has often been examined on the basis of the theory of acculturation applicable to cultural changes. Certain elements are loaned in the *acculturation process*, first as *innovations* from one specific culture or naming system to another. They spread in their new environment in a certain order, both in a social hierarchy and geographically (*diffusion*) and cause different changes in the anthroponymic system of the receiving culture, both in the nomenclature and in the structure of the naming system itself.

As new elements of cultural features are adopted from another culture, the old elements will either be marginalised or be found alongside the new ones, perhaps in quite a new role. Elements borrowed from another culture often transform into something suitable for a new culture but they can also remain as it had been before. Sometimes, their function may be formed into something else than in the source culture: for example, the surname *Nixon* may have been adopted in Africa as a first name. We should note that many elements become dismissed in the receiving culture.

The meeting of two different cultures and anthroponymic systems is always a dynamic process and the changes that have resulted from it are not easily predictable. Anthropologist Bronisław Malinowski (1945) has even noted that the results of the meeting of two cultures can never be predicted by first examining the distinguishing features of each culture separately. Instead, the meeting of cultures always results in something new. At the same time, when two anthroponymic systems encounter each other, this process does not always mean just the addition of new options in the language's onomasticon but rather the result may be a whole new kind of anthroponymic system. However, we should be aware that this new system is not usually explained by the influence of merely another culture and its anthroponymic system. Instead, it is influenced by numerous, simultaneous internal factors of the anthroponymic system and the culture that surrounds it.

There are also always several different internal and external processes running in cultural breakthroughs. Sometimes, their influence is also indirect: for example, the language of another culture may first have an impact on the language of the receiving culture and only through it, its anthroponymic system. All in all, we can state that there are at least six different sources for changes in an anthroponymic system and they are often simultaneously influential:

1. The internal factors of the anthroponymic system
2. The linguistic environment, in other words, the name and language system that the anthroponymic system is part of
3. The extralinguistic environment, in other words, the culture that the anthroponymic system is part of
4. The anthroponymic system of another culture
5. The language system of another culture
6. Another culture

African Naming Systems

In today's multicultural Europe, more and more citizens are involved with the anthroponymic systems of different immigrant groups, both in schools and other various official contexts and in normal, everyday life. That is why knowing their naming systems would be quite beneficial to many. Moreover, it is good for an onomastician to be familiar with other anthroponymic systems than what he himself investigates. Becoming familiar with foreign naming systems not only helps in seeing the distinguishing features of one's own topic of research but also to recognise the universal features of name giving.

To begin with, this section, based on Saarelma-Maunumaa's (2003) analysis, will cover the traditional naming systems of African cultures whose many practices are still prevalent in different parts of the continent, especially amongst the rural population. However, we should note that Africa is not a uniform area in relation to name giving: various naming practices and naming systems are on this vast continent as much as there are different cultures. Nevertheless, some common features can be seen in the name giving of their cultures.

All over Africa, a name's meaning is traditionally quite significant and the relationship between a person and his name is perceived as being nearly inseparable. It has been said that while according to European thinking, a name *refers* to a person, a name in African thinking *is* a person. A name is thus not only an arbitrary "tag" that is related to a person, which only identifies its referent, but according to African thinking, a name makes a human a person. So, for example, the dead are thought to have personality only for as long as someone remembers them by name.

Because the relationship between a person and his name is thoroughly inseparable in African cultures, there is a wide range of beliefs connected to the use of the names. Speaking a name out loud may be avoided because of the fear that evil spirits could get a hold of a person's soul by using a name. The rules of name avoidance are often quite complex and the use of words resembling names of certain relatives is forbidden in some communities.

Name giving all around Africa is quite a significant event and much attention is given to the choice of a name. This is understandable because of the fact that names in Africa usually carry meaning, in other words, they are semantically transparent. Name giving in different parts of the continent is traditionally carried out approximately within one week of childbirth. Sometimes, however, a name may already be given before the child is born or immediately with the birth – and sometimes much later. When, in some cultures, a child is born, he will be given a *temporary name* or a so-called *birth name* and only later his actual individual name. This temporary name often refers to the child's moment of birth ('wind', 'night') or describes the child ('long legs', 'potbelly'). The child can be given a semantically belittling or derogatory name ('I am ugly', 'pile of manure') immediately after being born so that evil spirits would not be interested in him. These kinds of *derogatory-protective names* are common in different parts of Africa.

In connection to name giving in African cultures, there is usually some kind of ceremony in which the child's relatives, neighbours and friends participate and in which the child is introduced to his community. These celebrations usually include various religious rituals: the child may be presented, for example, to his dead ancestors or the moon. Sometimes, there are two naming ceremonies: the first is held soon after birth for giving a temporary name and a second for giving an actual name. In some cultures, name giving can occur without any special celebrations.

It is often the child's father who has the role of name giver in Africa. This is explained by the fact that by giving a name, the father in a way acknowledges his obligations to the child. In some cultures, a name is given by the child's parents or with the eldest members of the kin, by some other relative or, for example, by the head of the tribe. Suggestions for a name are also often given by other members of the community.

The number of given names varies a great deal in different communities. There is often one given, sometimes two, one of which can be a secret name, the other public. Secret names are particularly common in West Africa. In some cultures, the child will receive one name from the father's side and a second from the mother's. A name may be replaced several times during one's life in many countries, particularly in circumstances pertaining to a change of life. For example, kings and other rulers will often receive a new *monarch name* which indicates their eminence ('valiant lion'). New names are often given with rites of passage and simultaneously names used in childhood would no longer be used. Moreover, teknonyms are common in Africa: when, for example, a man becomes a father, he may be addressed as "so-and-so's" father afterwards. Many Africans change their names when experiencing various difficulties; by changing a name they believe they will change their destiny too.

There are also varied principles of name giving in Africa. Giving a *namesake*, that is, naming a child after other individuals, such as relatives, friends or deceased ancestors, is quite common. As a child is given a deceased ancestor's name, this ancestor is also thought to return amongst his family. Sometimes being named after family is quite systematic. The tendency, for example, is that the first son will always be given his father's father's name and the daughter will be given the father's mother's name whereas the next are named after the mother's parents and so on.

A namesake relationship is quite significant in several African cultures. There is often a complete correlation between namesakes which is reflected in addressing practices: a child, for example, will call his grandfather's namesake his grandfather no matter how young or old he may be. It is believed – and hoped – that the features of a namesake will be passed on to a child because, according to African thinking, the name may influence the bearer's personality. The obligations of namesakes often include helping one another in different ways in the course of life. These social relations are also quite significant during the community's difficult times.

When a child is not named after an individual, the principle of naming often pertains to the child's moment of birth. A child may, for example, be given the name of the day of the week on which he was born ('Friday'). These *weekday names* are quite common in West Africa. Similarly, a child may be given a name after the season or time of day at his moment of birth ('dry season', 'night'). A name may also convey a wide variety of events associated with his time of birth: the community has suffered from hunger, it has been a rainy day or the child's father had been hunting or at war. A name can also signify the emotions of the name giver, such as fear or gratitude, or it can simply describe the child ('small gazelle').

Names often also convey expectations geared towards a child. Sometimes, the name giver can attach a message to the name, a kind of social comment, meant for another community or a certain member ('be quiet', 'where is he from?'). There are also different philosophical ideas or proverbs included in the names in many African cultures. *Proverbial names* are typical, for example, in the nomenclature of the West African Yoruba people (*Aghorunse* ← *A ka gho urun ji a ri se* 'examine something closely before you act').

Name giving in certain circumstances have been carefully regulated. Such is the case with twins who are often systematically given certain names. This is due to the fact that the birth of twins in many African cultures has been regarded as a sign of great misfortune and in many places they – or at least one of them – are even killed. Giving birth to twins is seen as a non-human trait because it is reminiscent of animals calving litters. On the other hand, twins have been thought of to work as special messengers between people and their ancestors. These kinds of "predetermined" *systematic names* are also often given to the firstborn, to children born legs first or to children whose mother died during childbirth.

Various descriptive nicknames and pejorative names are also typical to African anthroponymic systems. These names may change quite a bit during the individual's lifetime. Special bynames may have also been adopted when the individual leaves for war (*solider name*), a hunting trip (*hunting name*) or some other long journey (*wandering name*) or when he is associated as being a member of a new community. There are also special *dance names*, *social names* and *praise names* in many African cultures which the young people use in their leisurely activities. Moreover, young people receive various *initiation names* in rites of passage which are often temporary by nature. In many cattle raising cultures, people have a tendency also to be named after their oxen (*ox name*).

In addition to a person's actual name, quite well-established patronyms and matronyms are used in many African cultures; in others, a person's clan name is used. There has also been a clan system for a long time developed in several cultures according to which, a member of a community is a member of a clan – for example the Hyena Clan, the Snake Clan or the Lion Clan. Moreover, other groups of people, such as groups of soldiers, professionals and initiations, often have their special names. These collective names are generally used in addressing all of the people that belong to these groups.

The names included in traditional African naming systems can be classified in the following groups:

1. Birth name (temporary names descriptive of the child or names according to the time of birth, derogatory-protective names etc.)
2. Individual name (main name)
    a. Names given in a name giving ceremony (namesakes, names according to the time of birth, systematic names, names descriptive of the child, names of aspiration, proverbial names etc.)
    b. Names given/adopted later in life (initiation names, monarch names, teknonyms etc.)
3. Bynames referring to an individual (nicknames, pejorative names, war names, hunter names, wanderer names, monarch names, dance names, society names, praise names, initiation names, ox names)
4. Collective names (clan names, soldier group names, initiation group names, professional community names etc.)

Changes have naturally always been a part of African anthroponymic systems. However, not until the extension of Christianity and European colonisation did they truly begin to revolutionise the African naming systems starting at the end of the 19th century – the same as traditional cultures that otherwise ended up getting completely made over. Upon getting christened, being in school or enlisting in European service, many Africans were given biblical or European names (*Ester, Rosemary*; *David, George*) which became their official names in colonial administration. The adoption of these foreign names signified a change in the African naming systems whose names had traditionally been semantically transparent.

The Europeans that had arrived in Africa favoured the use of biblical and European names in the colonies because African names were difficult for them to pronounce. Many European missionaries also considered them to be "pagan" names and thus inappropriate for Christian Africans. On the other hand, many Africans regarded these new, European names to be progressive and eagerly adopted them especially in the beginning of the 20th century. A new name of foreign origin symbolised them both as becoming Christian and moving over from the "primitive" to the modern world. European names had also been given in naming systems based on a namesake relationship because of the fact that Christian Africans have had the desire to have Christian Europeans for their namesakes. This is, for instance, explained by why there are so many Finnish names in Namibia. (Saarelma-Maunumaa 2003.)

African personal names became popular again in the 1950s and 1960s when African nationalism gained strength and the colonies began to become independent in different parts of the continent. Personal names became one visible way to indicate a new African identity. Today, African and European nomenclature and naming practices coexist with each other in many African countries. European names may be used at workplaces and other areas of public life whereas African names are mostly used amongst family and friends. On the other hand, more and more Africans are selecting an African name for their official name. African names that are mostly of

Christian content and semantically positive ('blessing', 'gift', 'He loves us') have become popular in many countries.

Moreover, the European surname practice has replaced the traditional practices of bynames in different parts of Africa. Because colonial administration required detailed identification of people in various employment papers and other documents, patronyms, matronyms and clan names were begun to be systematically used alongside of a person's individual name. These names developed into European-type, hereditary surnames in many African countries – however, not everywhere.

The development of African naming systems can be described by the following periods:

1. Period of traditional naming system
2. Coexistence of traditional and new names
3. Replacement of African names
4. Renaissance of African names

The first of these periods can be placed in a time preceding colonialism, hence mostly before the mid-19th century. The second period is a time of active seeds of colonialism and Christian missionary work which dates back to the end of the 19th century and beginning of the 20th century. The third period depicts the strongest degree of the Europeanisation of African cultures before World War II. The replacement of African names had not been completely implemented in any African naming system. Still, many Africans today only bear European names, especially in such cultures where the convention of patronyms is followed. Should the individual name of both the father and son be European, the son's entire name will inevitably become European (*Thomas Hans*). The fourth period, in other words the Renaissance of African names, started in several African countries after World War II and was generally at its strongest in the 1960s when many former colonies became independent from their parent countries. The use of African personal names was even made compulsory in Zaire in 1972. The Africanisation of names is still a strong trend in different parts of the continent.

The swift urbanisation of 21st century Africa has also changed the anthroponymy in an interesting way. Scholars have noted that the selection of African names in an urbanised community has essentially decreased and name giving has not been as creative as before. The nomenclature of African countries had thus begun to be more and more reminiscent of anthroponymies of other industrialised countries.

Asian Naming Systems

Traditional Asian anthroponymic systems are in many regards reminiscent of African naming systems, although there are of course differences. Chinese naming systems have been examined by Liao (2000), among others. In Chinese culture, both in mainland China as well as in Taiwan, a child is all the time given traditional Chinese names which are contextually meaningful, hence semantically transparent.

The traditional Chinese anthroponymic system was comprised of several different name types which included, for example, a small child's *milk name*, a person's official name and in written sources a *pen name*, a *stage name* used by artists, a Buddhist *religious name*, an ancestral *posthumous name* and various nicknames. Today, the Chinese have one official registered name which is made up of a surname and an individual name; the latter cannot be called a first name according to Western customs because it is a name combination given just after the surname. Nearly without exception, there are three syllables in the official name or characters of which the first is the surname and the second and third form the individual name, for example *Zhang Peng-fei*. The first part of the two-part individual name has traditionally been the so-called generation name which is common to all male siblings and cousins of the same generation and the second part is the true individual name. Apart from an official name, the Chinese also use various unofficial bynames. Only in some families, is it still a custom to give small children a milk name; ancestral posthumous names are nowadays quite rare.

Chinese culture has had the traditional belief that a person's surname and individual name as a whole has, in many ways, an influence on the person's future: his marriage, career, property, family life and relationships. A name is therefore the same as a person's fate, not just a symbol which differentiates one individual from another. For this reason, names are always carefully selected. In general, the Chinese favour rare and even unique names. The most important rule is that a name must not be phonetically reminiscent of words which have some meaning regarded as evil.

The number of brushstrokes or pen strokes in the characters of Chinese names is similarly an important issue. The fewer strokes there are, the "more fortunate" the name is considered to be. Moreover, there is an aim at the balance of *yin* and *yang* in these names, that is, elements pertaining to masculinity and femininity. Each Chinese character is understood to be representative of either yin or yang. Because of these beliefs, many Chinese turn to name experts when selecting a name for their child and, as a result, name guidance has become a profitable form of business. Should a name be proven to be poor, changing it afterwards – and, at the same time, changing of one's destiny – is possible.

In Chinese culture, boys are usually given names which bestow luck, health, wealth and wisdom upon them, whereas girls' names reflect wishes that they would become beautiful, like grass. All in all, the Chinese wish to give their children names which have a positive meaning, that are elegant, whose characters have few strokes and which are easy to pronounce.

Chinese boys' names
Zhong-yi   'faithful' + 'just'
Shi-zhan   'world' + 'expand'
Wei-cheng   'great' + 'journey'
Chang-xian   'substantial' + 'wise'

Chinese girls' names
Chun-hsing   'spring' + 'almond'
Ming-chien   'bright' + 'smile'
Yu-fen   'jade' + 'balm'
Mei-chu   'beautiful' + 'pearl'

The practice of surnames is unknown in many other Asian naming systems and instead, people may have only one name. South-East Asian anthroponymic systems (Indonesia, Burma, Thailand) have been presented by Heikkilä-Horn (2002). For example, people on the Indonesian island of Java usually have only one name. Thus, the only name of Suharto, President of Indonesia in office from 1967 to 1998, is *Suharto* as was his predecessor's only name *Sukarno*. Although Sukarno received the name *Kusno* from his parents when born, he changed it when he was an adult to *Sukarno*; this name refers to the name of the warrior *Karno* from the Indian epic *Mahabharata*. Changing names is also quite common in this culture. Because there are no surnames in the Java naming system, it is impossible to decipher who is whose relative on the basis of names.

Surnames are also unknown in Myanmar – or Burma. However, the Burmese usually have at least two, sometimes even three, names. With the first of these names, we can discover on what day of the week the child was born. For example, the name of a child born on a Thursday will begin with the letter *pa*, *pha*, *ba*, *bha* or *ma* in line with the Indian alphabet, whereas the name of a child born on a Sunday will begin with a vowel. The advice of astrologers is followed in name giving and the name must be suitable for the child's personality. The same as in China, a name aims at guaranteeing a child a prosperous future and sometimes, as a precaution, the astrologer may urge the family, for example, to duplicate the child's name (*Kyaw Kyaw, Mi Mi*).

A name in Burmese culture does not always reveal the gender of the child, nor family relations. People with the same names can be differentiated, for example, by adding the individual's profession, domicile or father's name after the name – hence a kind of byname. The fact that a title depicting the individual's gender, age and status is always in front of the names also helps in distinguishing people from one another.

Surnames, however, are a part of the Thai naming system, but they are generally not used in public. Hence, the Prime Minister of Thailand Thaksin Shinawatra, in office from 2001 to 2006, was usually known in the country as *Thaksin* and by no means as Prime Minister Shinawatra. In order for an individual's identity to be protected, there is rather little use of peoples' official names in Thai culture.

Thai first names, which are traditionally based on Sanskrit, are semantically transparent. These names are usually pleasing and noble in their meaning, such as female names *Sirithida* 'good daughter' and *Thipdevi* 'divine angel' or male names *Weeraphon* 'courageous strength' and *Wittaya* 'knowledge'. Some names can be used as either male or female names, such as *Suchinda* 'good spirit'. Moreover, Thai names, such as *Saengdaw* 'star's brilliance', have become quite popular. However, it is uncommon for Thais to know each other's official names, even after many years of friendship because they call each other only by their unofficial nicknames.

Thais usually receive their own nickname as children for them to use their whole lifetime in place of their official names. There is a limited number of these nicknames and they are usually semantically descriptive, such as *Dääng* 'red', *Uan* 'fatty', *Muu* 'piggy' or *Kob* 'frog'. This name can also be changed and someone may have several different nicknames which are used in various contexts: at home, at school and in working life. Thai children are often only called "mice" hence, by a certain kind of collective term. However, they do use their nicknames amongst each other. Moreover, young women may still be called mice in working life especially when addressing superiors.

In line with African anthroponymy, Asian anthroponymy has changed as a result of Western influence. Today, for example, many Chinese have also taken a Western name for themselves, mostly to facilitate interaction with Europeans and Americans because the Chinese names are usually difficult for them. Because a name's meaning in Chinese culture is an important subject, Western names are often selected on the basis of meaning (*Delicate, Lemon, Ocean, Power*). On the other hand, many Chinese also use general Western names that carry no transparent meaning (*Jane, Mary, Paul, Thomas*). European names are used in the same way in many other Asian countries as well.

Development of European Naming Systems

European Pre-Christian Anthroponymy

Christianity began to spread in Europe in the first centuries of the Common Era but its influence did not reach the whole continent until the 11th century. Before the adoption of Christianity, Europeans had a wide range of anthroponymic systems, however very little is known about them. There have not been many written sources from this time period and information on personal names of those sources in existence is rather random and limited. For example, men's names are mentioned in old documents more than women's names and there are more names of those in a higher social standing than names of the poorer population. Because of the lack of sources, there can never be a perfect reconstruction of a *pre-Christian anthroponymic system*. Nevertheless, some European naming systems are, in this relation, in a better position than others.

There has been an abundance of Ancient Roman and Greek written sources preserved in which there is mention of a great deal of personal names. At the same time, for example, there have been references to Germanic pre-Christian anthroponymy in Greek and Roman sources. This is why a rather good picture of it has been able to be created. Also, Old Scandinavian personal names have been well preserved in runic writings. However, Old Finnish nomenclature has, for the most part, been unknown. There has not been any mention of Finnish personal names in written sources until the 14th century, and even then they were rather limited.

Because the size and population of the Roman Empire was rather large and its government multi-tiered, the Roman anthroponymic system had already also been far developed before the beginning of the Common Era. It differs a great deal from other pre-Christian European anthroponymic systems. The Roman anthroponymic system was a three-name system (*tria nomina*) which included a first name (*praenomen*), a surname (*nomen gentilicium*) and a hereditary byname (*cognomen*). Hence, the name of famous ruler of the Roman State *Gaius Iulius Caesar* had first the first name *Gaius*, then the surname *Iulius* and last, the byname of the Iulius family *Caesar* 'long-haired, full-haired'. The surname referred to a basic unit of Roman society (*gens* 'kin, tribe') whose leader was eldest of the family. This unit not only included the family's forefather and his offspring but also their wives and children, adopted children, protégées and liberated slaves. Sometimes, there was also a special *name of honour* (*cognomen ex virtute*) after these three-part names which often referred to areas conquered by soldiers: *Publius Cornelius Scipio Africanus*. Additional bynames were also used for the indication of the family's different branches and some Romans even had their own individual byname after their names, such as *Caecus* 'blind' or *Barbatus* 'bearded'.

The number of first names was quite limited in the Roman naming system: there were only a few dozen different names. Common names included, for instance, *Primus* 'first', *Quintus* 'fifth', *Octavus* 'eighth', *Lucius* 'brilliant' (or 'born at the rising sun') and *Marcus* 'of Mars, god of war'. Roman surnames included, for example, *Claudius* ← *Claudus* 'lame, limping', *Flavius* ← *Flavus* 'light, fair, yellow' or *Octavius* ← *Octavus* 'eighth'. Names of kinship were usually patronymic, referring to the family's forefather. Common bynames included *Leo* 'lion', *Lupus* 'wolf', *Magnus* 'great', *Paulus* 'small', *Pilatus* 'javelin thrower' and *Urbanus* 'city dweller'. However, the Romans only used one name, usually a byname, in everyday life.

Roman women mostly had two names but their order may have varied. Women's names were usually derived from men's names (*Lucius* → *Lucia*, *Publius* → *Publia*) whereupon there had not been much in the way of special women's names. Hence, the daughter of a father with the name *Marcus Livius Drusus* was *Livia Drusilla*. A female, whose father was *Lucius Attius Atticus* and mother *Valeria Sextina* was thus named *Valeria Attia*. Slaves received names much like bynames, such as *Syrus* 'Syrian' or *Ursus* 'bear'. Additionally, there was a custom in Rome to give slaves Greek names irrespective of citizenship. Because of this, many martyrs of Early Christianity had Greek names even though they were not necessarily Greek.

The three-part naming system of the Roman Empire was used everywhere it was in power and it was also compulsory. However, the gradual collapse of the Empire during Late Antiquity also meant the breakdown of its developed naming system.

The pre-Christian naming system of the Greeks was simpler. In addition to a free citizen's individual name (*Archimedes, Herodotus, Sophocles*), rather well-established patronyms and various expressions referring to a tribe or residence were used. Thus, for example, the name *Themistokles Neokleous Frearrios* means 'Themistokles Neokleous' son of the Frearrios people' and *Demosthenes Demosthenous Paianieus* means 'Demosthenes Demosthenous' son from Paianieus'. However, there was usually only one of the names used daily, the most common of these being the individual's main name. Sometimes, a person was commonly known by his mere byname, such as philosopher *Plato* 'wide-shouldered'; Plato's actual name was *Aristocles*. A slave, however, had only one name which was in the form of a byname.

Greek names were often *two-part names*. For example, *Demosthenes* is made up of name parts meaning 'people' and 'mighty' and *Nicodemus*, the same as *Nikolaos*, made up of parts meaning 'victory' and 'people'. The name *Isidoros* refers to the goddess Isis and 'gift'. Certain name elements were used for the formation of the names, not just any expressions of the language. The two-part nature of these names meant that there was quite a great deal of different names because new names could have been formed from different elements relatively freely. Thus, the need for using established bynames or surnames has not been as great as in such naming systems where a majority of the names are single part names.

The Old Germanic naming system seems to have clearly been based on bearing one name, in other words, every person had only one name. Scholars also believe that the names of the Germanic peoples were originally unique names, whereupon there were no two people of the same name in the community. This is why there was a great deal of different names. Several of these names had been formed from two elements such as, in their current forms, Old High German *Gerhard* ('javelin' + 'hard, strong'), Old English *Edwin* ('rich, fortunate' + 'friend') or Scandinavian *Torbjörn* ('Thor' + 'bear'). There were also single part names used and they were either original or shortened forms of two-part names.

Traditional Germanic names were mostly formed from nouns and adjectives. The later part of a male name was masculine and feminine in a female name, whereas the gender of a name's initial part carried no meaning. Thus, for example, Old High German *Siegfried* and *Hildeger* were male names and *Sieghild* and *Hildegar* were female names. Certain initial parts were also common in male names (*Eber-*) and likewise in female names (*Swan-*). A female name was able to be derived from a male name with the suffix *a*: *Adalbert* → *Adalberta*. *Truncated name forms* were used for many two-part names, such as *Wolfgang* → *Wolf* or *Gertrud* → *Gerta*. Some were presumed to have been originally single part names, such as *Bruno* or *Karl*.

Names of the Germanic peoples were also semantically transparent and there has been a great deal of analysis made on their meanings. According to German onomastician Benno Eide Siebs (1970), the linguistic elements used in Germanic names referred to mythological beings, cult artefacts, animals and plants, natural forces, times of the day, compass points, groups of peoples, social status, colours, friendly or hostile attitudes, social order, warfare and also masculine traits. Typical Old High German names included, for example, *Gertrud* ('javelin' + 'strength'), *Gunhild* ('war' + 'battle') or *Ludwig* ('famous' + 'battle'). According to scholars, the meanings of these two-part names should not be interpreted only as a sum of the meanings of their parts. For example, the Old High German name *Bernhard* does not mean 'strong as a bear' even though its parts in fact mean 'bear' (*bern*) and 'strength' (*hard*) nor does the Old English name *Edgar* mean 'one who defends his property with a javelin' or 'fortunate javelin thrower' even though its parts mean 'rich' or 'fortunate' (*ed*) and 'javelin' (*gar*).

The naming system of the Germanic peoples later changed so that children began to be given names which referred to names of other family members. Names were often created for children by combining their parents' names. If, for example, a father's name was *Hildebrand* and a mother's name was *Gertrud*, their sons' names may have been *Gerbrand*, *Trudbrand*, *Brandger* or *Trudger* and daughters' names *Hildtrud*, *Brandtrud*, *Brandhild* or *Trudhild*. This kind of variation was also typical in Old Norse name giving: The son of a father named *Thorbjorn* may have been *Thorgisl* or *Holmbjorn* and the daughter *Thorborgh*. An even greater change in the Germanic naming system occurred when a child began to be named directly after his grandparents and thus, the name showed to whose kin the child belonged. The thought behind this was also that the grandparents could, in a way, live on in their grandchildren.

Naming children after other people of course meant that names lost their uniqueness and individuality in naming systems when name sharing increased. However, this may not have caused great problems in smaller communities. Moreover, various bynames and nicknames may have been used to differentiate those with the same name from each other, even if it was still not systematic. The use of namesakes and the way to form shorter forms from names led to the fact that Germanic names began to lose their semantic transparency. Names became semantically obscure and after several generations, it was no longer necessarily known what the name originally had meant. Hence, the Germanic naming system gradually lost its original productivity and in the 12th century, the collapse of the system was quite obvious in the case of the naming systems of numerous peoples.

In addition to the Germanic languages and Greek, two-part names have been typical for many other Indo-European naming systems. For example, the Sanskrit name *Vásudattah* is made up of name parts meaning 'good' and 'given'. The Old Slavic name *Borislav* stems from name parts meaning 'battle' and 'honour' and the name parts of *Bogumil* meaning 'god' and 'love'. Similarly, the Celtic name *Toutorix* consists of name parts meaning 'people' and 'mighty' and the name parts of *Caturix* meaning 'battle' and 'mighty'. These naming systems are reminiscent of the pre-Christian Germanic naming systems in many other respects.

Standardisation of Christian Nomenclature in the Middle Ages

The adoption of Christianity had a decisive influence on European anthroponymy. This influence has even been called an anthroponymic "revolution" or "change of paradigm" and it signified the adoption of both names and the principles of name giving. Many scholars, however, have observed that there can be no talk of any "Christian anthroponymy" before the 4th century. Early Christians used ordinary Greek and Latin names as well as those of other languages. They may have also had names of ancient gods or other names referring to pre-Christian cults, such as *Eros, Dionysios, Mercurius* or *Venus*. Conversion and baptising did not thus mean the adoption of new names in the beginning of Christianity nor in the New Testament was it mentioned that those who had converted would have changed their names upon baptising. At that time, baptising was only a ceremony where a person became a member of a Christian parish, not an occasion for name giving.

However, the situation gradually began to change as special "Christian names" became widely used. The term *Christian name* can often be found in onomastic literature, and it is understood to refer to various kinds of names pertaining to Christianity. The term *saint's name* refers to the names of holy figures present in the list of saints of the Catholic and Orthodox Church and *biblical name* refers to any name found in the Bible. We should note that several personal names found in the Bible are also saint's names. Hence, these groups of names partly overlap each other.

Why then did Christian names become widely used? Scholars have suggested that after the acceptance of infant baptism, some Christians may have perceived this ritual as being an occasion where a child could be given a name pertaining to Christianity. This may have then inspired adults to assume new names of Christian origin in their conversion and baptism. The first reliable source on adults adopting new names upon baptism dates from the 6th and 7th centuries. Volker Kohlheim (1996) has classified these early names with relevance to Christianity into five groups:

1. Names signifying Christian ideas and virtues (*Anastasios/Anastasia* 'resurrected', *Felix* 'fortunate', *Victor* 'victor')
2. Names of Christian festivals (*Epifanios/Epifania* 'Epiphany', *Natalis/Natalia* 'Christmas')
3. *Theophoric names*, that is, those that refer to God (*Dominicus* 'belonging to God', *Theodoros/Theodora* 'gift from God', *Theodulos* 'servant of God')
4. Names of biblical characters (*Andreas, Johanna, Paulos, Susanna*)
5. Names of martyrs (*Laurentius, Stefanos, Thekla*)

Part of these names included completely new, created names but many of them were also generally used by non-Christians at that time. Basically, according to Kohlheim, there are two kinds of *religious names*: names which are given according to their semantic content, in other words, those that semantically refer to religion, and names which refer to significant individuals regarding religion, in other words, those with relevance to a founder of religion, his followers or other holy or respected figures. The later of these principles of name giving has been more common within Christianity.

Towards the end of the Roman Empire, names of Christian origin were still quite rare in Europe and they remained uncommon within Western Christianity up until the Early Middle Ages. Hence, special "Christian names" were, for a long time, an exception in the Western Church, not a rule.

Names of Christian origin began to be given in the Eastern half of the Church rather early. In 388, Church Father Johannes Krysostomos already had recommended that the Christians name their children after saints and this eventually became a dominant practice. It became the norm within Eastern Christianity in the 5th century. According to the Orthodox view, this kind of name giving has strong religious significance: the name links a child to the saint he has been named after.

Eastern Christianity early on set off in different directions in its name giving than Western Christianity, which did not adopt the practice of giving names after saints until the Middle Ages, several centuries later. Since the 11th century, when the two main lines of Christianity officially drifted apart from one another, their cultural differences increased even more. The majority of nomenclature in Eastern Christianity includes saints' names of Greek origin but there are also non-Greek saints' names and biblical names amongst it. Over time, these names made their way to all countries that were influenced by the extension of the Orthodox Church, in other words, not only Greece, but also amongst the Slavic peoples of the Balkans and Eastern Europe. The breakthrough of Russian Christianity began in 989 when Vladimir I of Kiev converted to the religion. Orthodox saints' names from Russia found their way to the nomenclature of Karelian and Finnish Orthodox peoples beginning in the 12th century. In addition to Greek and biblical names, there were some preserved, original Slavic names used, such as the aforementioned *Vladimir*, because they were saints' names recognised by the Church.

Because there was no custom to give special names with relevance to Christianity with baptisms prior to the Middle Ages in Western Europe, it is clear that names of Christian origin did not spread out along with the extension of Christianity. These names became more standardised in many Western European countries several centuries later as Christianity did. For example, Christianity began extending to Germany in the 8th century but it was not until the end of the 12th century when its influence began to become more visible in the anthroponymy. However, it was still two centuries later before names of Christian origin became commonplace in Germany. Hence, a great part of Christians in the area bore traditional German names for a long time. Christianity arrived in Scandinavia in the 9th century but it did not start to have an effect on personal names until the 13th century.

The true anthroponymic breakthrough happened in Western Europe in the Middle Ages when people began to be named after saints recognised by the Church. Remembering holy individuals was no new phenomenon in the Middle Ages. Instead, it had begun to develop roughly around 400 CE. Prior to this, beginning in early Christianity, Christians tended to observe dates of the death of sainted individuals – in other words, dates when these individuals moved on to a new life – as common holidays. Naming people after saints, however, began much later.

The adoption of this new way of name giving required that Christianity had already been established as a major religion. By the Middle Ages, the saint cult had also gained strength within the Western Church, through which the thought of using the names of sainted individuals as baptismal names increased. Many traditional anthroponymic systems had also lost their vitality by the Middle Ages and, in a way, internally withered away. Their originally semantically transparent names had become semantically obscure as children began to be given names after other people. At the same time, the number of names being used had also diminished. Hence, the need for new types of names had emerged in Europe.

Some scholars have also pointed out that new names of Christian origin emphasised a person's individual choice and suited it for this "new era". New names also offered parents more possibilities of selection than traditional naming after relatives. On the other hand, the adoption of this new way of name giving was hindered by the thought that the use of a family member's name would transfer this relative's soul to the child. Because traditional beliefs lived long amid medieval Christians, traditional ways of name giving also slowly vanished.

The triumph of saints' names in medieval Europe however tells us something about the strengthening of the Church's grasp on all levels of human life. The adoption of new names symbolised the change of the identity of the whole community and the start of a new period of culture. The use of names with relevance to Christianity has been a way for Christians to be distinguished from the "pagan" culture around them. On the other hand, those who were christened continued to use their traditional names in their own language in many countries within the home, whereupon a certain kind of two-name system was prevalent.

The Roman Catholic calendars of saints, specific to diocese, worked as sources of new names. Children were usually named after a saint whose memorial was close to the child's birthday or which was otherwise important to the family, such as a patron saint concerning the father's occupation or the patron saint of the locality. Moreover, the patron saints of different countries have received many namesakes. This is why *George* is a popular name in England, *Andrew* in Scotland, *Patrick* in Ireland, *Olav* in Norway and so on. The most popular names, however, were those of the disciples of Jesus, apostles and names of other central figures in the New Testament.

Being named after saints became standardised first in Italy, especially in Venice and Ravenna, where there was a strong Byzantine influence. From there, it extended through France to the British Isles, Germany, Scandinavia and other lands. New names were often adopted first in royal families, after which they spread out amongst the common people. The innovation at first travelled from town to town, whereas it arrived later amongst the rural population and nobilities of the countryside. The city bourgeoisie were eager to adopt this new principle of name giving. Names of Christian origin became standard more quickly in female names than male names because there was still an objective to give boys names with relevance to kinship. Hence, for example, the first names referring to Christianity in Scandinavia were given to the daughters of royal families and to the sons of the king and a mistress; possible successors to the throne at that time still received traditional names.

Because new, "Christian names" were of foreign origin, mostly Hebrew, Greek and Latin, they had been incomprehensible to most medieval Europeans. On the other hand, the names' semantic content did not carry any meaning in the new naming system either. In choosing a name, the most important factor was the saint to whom the name referred. That particular saint was regarded as being a protector and divine intercessor for the one being baptised, so strong religious significance was connected to name giving.

Names of Christian origin spread quickly throughout medieval Germany. They already formed a clear majority in many localities in the 15th and 16th century and their share may have risen up to over 90 per cent. The most popular female names were *Margarethe, Elisabeth, Katharina, Anna, Agnes* and *Sophia* and the most popular male names were *Johannes, Nicolaus, Petrus, Michael, Martin* and *Georg*. Many names became phonetically adapted to their new surroundings and became truncated for easy pronunciation: in Germany, *Katharina* became *Katrey, Johannes* became *Hans, Markus* became *Marx, Nicolaus* became *Chlaus* or *Niclas* and so on. In the same way, *Johannes* took different forms in different countries, such as *Giovanni* (Italy), *Jean* (France), *Juan* (Spain), *John* (England), *Johan* (Sweden), *János* (Hungary), *Ivan* (Russia) and so on. On the other hand, many mother tongue names were preserved – but only when they were names of holy people. These included, for example, *Bernhard, Heinrich, Konrad* and *Wolfgang* in Germany and *Edward, Richard, Robert* and *William* in England.

From Bynames to Hereditary Surnames

The adoption of names of Christian origin throughout Europe led to the fact that the number of names used dramatically decreased. Name sharing increased to the point that up to one third of European men were at some point the bearers of the most popular male name, in other words, *Johannes*. People of the same name were rather difficult to differentiate from one another, even in small communities, not to mention cities. At first, efforts were made to resolve the problem so that many various forms of the same root name would be adopted: for example, Johannes would get the forms *Johann, Hannes* and *Hans* in Germany. However, official name forms in church records were still being used so that these other forms would facilitate peoples' identification mostly in daily speech.

However, it gradually became clear that a naming system based on having one name was not sufficient enough for the identification of people in medieval society. The problem was especially great in cities which quickly grew during that time. Hence, a rather new kind of anthroponymic breakthrough started up in medieval Europe and the result was a surname system similar to what it is today. Bynames became a part of the naming system in the first stage of this process. Certain types of bynames, mostly those referring to profession, appearance and residence, started to be used regularly alongside of an individual's own name. These kinds of bynames were, for example, quite common in Scandinavia during the Viking Age (800–1050) and an abundance of these can be found in runic writings of that time.

Later on, bynames changed into hereditary surnames in different countries. In many countries, surnames were created specifically from many various language elements. In regard to the naming system, this development meant that the traditional one-name system, which included an individual name and random bynames along with it, was replaced by a two-name system which consisted of a first name and hereditary surname.

The emergence of a surname system was quite a slow and irregular process throughout Europe. The first surname systems had taken shape on the Italian peninsula in 700 BCE. Many peoples of the area at that time, such as the Sabellians, Latins and Umbrians, started to use patronyms in addition to their individual names, which gradually became hereditary surnames. Later on, Roman surnames (*nomen gentilicium*) began to be formed, in addition to patronyms, directly from Latin individual names and names of places, and surnames became obligatory in that society. With the fall of the Roman Empire, this naming system also fell apart and surnames were in use no later than 400 CE. At the end of Ancient History, Rome began to shift to a one-name system.

However, surnames began to be used again in 800 CE on the Italian peninsula, at first amongst the Venetian patricians. This innovation extended from Italy to France, where surnames became established at the end of the Middle Ages. From France, it travelled to Britain, Germany and other countries. This process began in Germany in the 12th century and lasted for several centuries. There were several extra-onomastic reasons, that is, reasons connected to the general development of culture, which led to the emergence of the surname system in Germany. Hereditary surnames were required because there would be no confusion on hereditary social and financial rights, such as a son's right to his father's profession or property with these names. The administrative systems of medieval society also required the specific identification of people in taxation records and other documents. Surnames also increased the feeling of family cohesion. Another significant factor in the standardisation of surnames is that they were considered fashionable.

The first to adopt surnames in Germany was nobility. This innovation spread out from nobility to the nomenclature of more common social classes of cities and gradually to the common people. It geographically spread out from the south and west to the east and north as well as from large cities to smaller ones, and finally to rural areas. Although surnames were common in the 12th century, for example, in Cologne and Mainz, there was still quite a great deal of Germans without surnames in the 19th century.

The German surname system developed on the basis of traditional bynames. German onomasticians (Seibicke 1982 et al.) have presented several different classifications for them, the main name types include:

1. Surnames derived from personal names (*Althans, Heinzmann, Jürgens*)
2. Surnames referring to place of residence (*Eckmann, Steinhaus, von Goethe*)
3. Surnames referring to descent (*Hesse, Niederländer, Schwabe*)
4. Surnames referring to occupation (*Huber, Schmidt, Wagner*)
5. Surnames derived from descriptive bynames (*Lange, Röting, Schneidewind*)

A similar process also happened in other European countries which, by and large, took several centuries. In addition to the aforementioned name types, a surname system may have also been built upon other well-established byname systems, such as clan names in Scotland.

Name Giving Trends of the Modern Era

At the same time as surname systems developed in different parts of Europe, there were also other great changes happening in anthroponymy. The most significant of these was the secularisation of name giving. Names were no longer given on a religious foundation as clearly as before. As saints' names adopted for religious reasons had originally been established as part of the naming system, they began to be given on other bases as well, such as names referring to family or given after other respected name bearers. Moreover, different trends began to influence the selection of name.

Chivalric poetry especially began to have an effect on name giving in the late Middle Ages. Names from the Knights of the Round Table were adopted in many countries at that time, such as *Arthur* or *Lancelot*. Likewise, works by Dante Alighieri and Francesco Petrarca were also influential which made *Beatrice* and *Laura* quite popular. Beatrice was Dante's beloved in the *Divine Comedy* who guided him through Heaven. Petrarca wrote sonnets for Laura, a woman who he fervently fell in love with after seeing her in church in 1327. The epic poem *Orlando Furioso* (1516), written by Ludovico Ariosto, gave rise to the popularity of the name *Roland* and the plays by William Shakespeare brought out names such as *Edgar* or *Edmund*.

Many names of traditional naming systems were not only preserved in the Middle Ages and the beginning of the modern era because they were introduced as saints' names, but also because they were brought about in the popular literature of the time. Names adopted from literature came into use amongst nobility and from there, extended amongst the people that emulated nobility. As a matter of fact, adopting names of literary characters was particularly quite reminiscent of being named after saints: Many of these epic characters were true role models to Christian knights. Renaissance humanism of the 15th century raised many Greek and Roman names of Ancient History to popularity which had no association to Christian history; instead, they concerned the culture and philosophy of that period in time. These names included, for example, *Achilles, Aristotle, Cicero, Hercules; Cornelia, Diana* and *Lucretia*.

Regardless of the secularisation of name giving, religious name giving continued strong as well. Due to the Reformation, Western Europe had clearly been divided into Catholic and Protestant areas. The Catholics continued to give saints' names to children which still bore a strong spiritual meaning. This practice gradually became established and the Catholic Church made a final decision in the Council of Trent (1543–1563) that anyone being baptised must exclusively be given a Catholic saint's name. Hence, this well-established practice was also officially sealed.

During the Counter-Reformation, or Catholic Revival, new canonised saints of the Church introduced a new nomenclature to the Catholics such as *Aloysius* after Aloysius Gonzaga, *Xaverius* after Francis Xavier, *Ignatius* after Ignatius de Loyola and *Theresia* after Teresa of Ávila. Moreover, names were given with respect to Catholic liturgy, for example *Avemaria*, *Paternoster* and *Pronobis*. The names *Maria* and *Joseph* began becoming popular in Germany in the 16th century, whereas they still were not during the Middle Ages. The name *Joseph* became a typical Catholic name whereas *Maria* was given by both the Catholics and Protestants. The name *Jesus* was given by Christians mostly in the Spanish-speaking Catholic world.

Protestant name giving was clearly different from Catholic naming giving. Because respect for the saints was not important to the Protestants, the conscious naming of children after them had ceased. However, biblical names were favoured – a part of which certainly also included names of Catholic saints. Old Testament names (*Abraham*, *Benjamin*, *Enoch*; *Lea*, *Rebecca*, *Salome*) became especially popular. The popularity of biblical names has been explained by the influence of Martin Luther's translation of the Bible and by the fact that the Protestants emphasised the reading of the Bible as every Christian's right. This naming tradition of the Protestants was also reflected in the first names of such famous men as Benjamin Franklin, Immanuel Kant, Abraham Lincoln and Adam Smith.

The Protestants also emphasised the significance of their mother tongue and created new, semantically Christian, German names in the manner of traditional Germanic names. These included, for example *Christfried* ('Christ' + 'peace'), *Gottlob* ('God' + 'praise') and *Ehregott* ('respect' + 'God'). Christian names of foreign origin were translated into German: *Adam* (← Heb. *adama* 'earth') became *Erdmann*, *Amadeus* (← Lat. 'love' + 'God') became *Gottlieb* and *Timotheus* (Grk. 'fear' + 'God') became *Fürchtegott*. The use of traditional German names was similarly recommended. German Pietists created new, contextually Christian names on the basis of German, such as *Gotthelf* ('God' + 'help'), *Glaubrecht* ('believe' + 'right'), *Leberecht* ('live' + 'right') and *Traugott* ('trust' + 'God'). Moreover, a few traditional Germanic names such as *Gottfried* ('God' + 'peace') received a new Christian interpretation.

Many non-biblical saints' names nearly remained completely out of use in England when the country disassociated itself from the Catholic Church. In place of them, biblical names started to be used. The 16th century Puritans gave their children uncommon biblical names as well, such as

Ebenezer, *Hephzibah*, *Kerenhappuch* or *Obadiah*. They also created new, contextually Christian English-language names such as *Live-well*, *Praise-God*, *Reformation*, *Renewed* or *Sorry-for-Sin* – these indeed never became sustainable, favoured names. Instead, Puritan names such as *Charity*, *Faith*, *Hope* and *Prudence* became quite standard.

Name giving in Europe of the modern age had often been connected to politics as well. France had quite a strong position in the 17th and 18th centuries, which is why French names such as *Antoinette*, *Charlotte*, *Henriette*; *Jean* or *Louis* became popular in many countries. The French Revolution overwhelmed French nomenclature in a special way. Such ideological names as *Egalité* 'equality' and *Vérité* 'truth' became popular, the same as *Rousseau* or *Marat* that had relevance to the central figures of the revolutionary period. Moreover, rather new types of non-Christian names were created based on French: *Tulipe* 'tulip', *Rhubarbe* 'rhubarb'. However, their popularity did not last long. Children were named after dynasty members in the 18th and 19th centuries in many European countries and these names became true, fashionable names. For example, *Fredrik*, *Gustaf*, *Karl* and *Lovisa* rose to popularity in Sweden and the names *Edward*, *Elizabeth*, *Robert* and *William* became standardised in England for the same reason. National romanticism of the 19th century raised the popularity of mother tongue names in several European countries, especially in Protestant areas.

A significant change in European anthroponymic systems was the standardisation of giving multiple baptismal names. The change began in Italy where bearing two names already occurred at the end of the 13th century. From there, this innovation continued its journey to France and Spain, and gradually elsewhere in Europe. The bearing of two names was fairly common in 16th century Germany, especially amongst nobility and in larger cities; however it took some time before this practice spread out to the countryside. Having two names became standard in England through French influence, the same as in Denmark and Sweden via German influence. Sometimes, children were given three names or even more.

It has been suggested that having multiple names was an indication of heightened self-esteem of a higher social class. On the other hand, multiple given names were also useful in differentiating people from one other, such as fathers and sons (*Hans Jacob Schmidt* and *Hans Konrad Schmidt*). Having more than one name also allowed the fact that names could often be given to children on different bases. The Church often limited the number of given names but there were also people that had up to dozens of first names which was a complete status symbol. Many countries adopted the fashionable phenomenon of having multiple names from dynasties. This is what happened, for example, in Sweden, where name combinations *Karl Gustav* and *Ulrika Eleonora* became favoured. These well-established two-name combinations often changed to full compound names (*Eva-Maria*, *Hans-Jürgen*) or two-part names (*Annemarie*, *Karlheinz*).

Film, television and other forms of popular culture have had a strong influence on name giving since the beginning of the 20th century. For example, Margaret Mitchell's novel *Gone with the Wind* (1936) and the film of the same name (1939) made the names of their main characters *Scarlett* and *Rhett* popular. In the same way, film stars Humphrey Bogart and Marilyn Monroe at one time raised their own first names to popularity in different parts of the world. Today, new names are also adopted from Western television series, popular music and the Internet. On the other hand, increased travel as well as different immigrant groups have familiarised Europeans with the names of other cultures. While European first names have become international, they have also become standardised. The same names are often favoured at the same time in many European countries.

Being traditionally named after relatives is still common in many European countries. However, many scholars have noted that appeal or pleasantness have become a more significant principle of name giving than different individual role models. These issues are also associated with the fashion of names: certain types of phonetically structured names are often in fashion at the same time. For example, there had been a name trend in 21st century Germany beginning with *l* and *m* such as *Laura, Leon, Maria* and *Max*; the same as boy's names ending with *as* and *ian* such as *Fabian, Lukas, Niklas* and *Sebastian*. A name trend seems to be developed in society in the same way as fashion phenomena so that name giving is steered by people's subconscious social instinct rather than any specific recognisable factors. Choice of name is always quite a complex process in which several factors have an influence simultaneously.

Stages of Finnish Anthroponymy

Old Finnish Naming System

There is rather little known about the life of the Finnish people before the arrival of Christianity and so consequently, the Old Finnish anthroponymic system is largely vague. However, ancient nomenclature has somewhat been preserved in Finnish place names, earlier bynames and surnames, similarly as in oral folklore. Finnish personal names did not begin to appear in written sources until the 13th century, and even then rather scarcely. Tax lists covering all of Finland existed starting from the 16th century and in church documents from the 17th century.

However, conclusions on Finnish pre-Christian anthroponymy were able to be made on the basis of Baltic-Finnish nomenclature. The oldest written entries on the personal names of the Baltic-Finnish peoples have presumably been in the birch bark documents from Novgorod. Moreover, there has been a great deal of original nomenclature found in early medieval documents concerning the Estonians and Livonians. Later markings were found in the Votic and Ingrian area starting from the 16th century and in 16th and 17th century tax lists. The first extensive overview on this topic was A. V. Forsman's dissertation (1891) which is a pioneering early achievement on Finnish anthroponomastics. The second significant work is German scholar Detlef-Eckhard Stoebke's study on proto-Finnic anthroponymy (1964).

On the basis of research data, it seems that the anthroponymy of Baltic-Finnic peoples would have resembled that of the traditional Germanic one in many respects. It was a system based on having one name, occasionally accompanied by a byname. These traditional individual names were two-part names as the Germanic ones had been. A number of words were used as basic name elements, such as *Hyvä* ('good'), *Iha* ('glad, good spirit'), *Mieli* ('pleasant'), *Päivä* ('sun, day'), *Toivo* ('hope, promise'), *Valta* ('power') and *Vilja* ('grain'). New names were formed from them either by compounding (*Ihamieli, Hyvätoivo, Mielipäivä*) or by derivation (*Hyvä-ri, Hyvä-tty, Mielikkä, Vilja-ttu*). Many of these elements were also used as single-part names (*Hyvä, Iha, Toivo*). Some elements appeared only as the name's later part such as *heimo* (*Ikäheimo* 'age' + 'tribe') and *neuvo* ('advice' *Hyväneuvonen* 'good' + 'advice+ADJ', *Montaneuvonen* 'many' + 'advice+ADJ'). Altogether, scholars have found about twenty basic name elements which were used in the Baltic-Finnic languages. These old personal names have been preserved in Finnish toponymy such as in parish names *Lempäälä* (← *Lempi*), *Nousiainen* (← *Nousia*), *Toivakka* (← *Toivo*) and *Viljakkala* (← *Vilja*).

According to Stoebke, this two-part name type may have originally been Baltic-Finnish. He bases this on the fact that personal names of the Baltic-Finnic peoples are clearly not loans from Germanic names. The nomenclature of the Germanic peoples is contextually much more warlike than that of the Baltic-Finnic peoples. According to Stoebke, Baltic-Finnic nomenclature highlights features such as love, goodness, beauty, joy and hope.

Finnish scholars, such as Viljo Nissilä and Eero Kiviniemi, however have taken the position that the two-part name type of the Baltic-Finnish languages would have been of Germanic origin. For centuries, before the coming of Christianity, Germanic influence had been particularly strong in the Baltic-Finnish linguistic area and personal names could not have been outside of this influence whatsoever. The fact that the distribution of this name type has been clearly emphasised on the Baltic-Finnish languages of the west, however being unknown at all in the anthroponymy of the eastern Finno-Ugric languages, also supports this view. In addition to this name type, numerous Germanic personal names were adopted in Finland during the pre-Christian era, many of which left their mark in Finnish toponymy.

According to early written sources, it would seem that the Old Finnish people may have used other kinds of names than what was previously presented as well. Such *mythological names* with reference to Finnish paganism as *Ahti, Kaleva, Palva, Tapio, Tursas* or *Äijö* have been considered old individual names the same as structural names with suffixes such as *Ampuja* ('shooter'), *Anottu* ('pleaded'), *Laulaja* ('singer'), *Parattu* ('healed') and *Tietävä* ('knowing'). Names with reference to animals, plants and other forms of nature such as *Etana* ('snail'), *Hirvi* ('elk'), *Honka* ('pine'), *Myrsky* ('storm'), *Paju* ('willow'), *Susi* ('wolf'), *Tammi* ('oak') or *Talvi* ('winter') are often also considered individual names.

It is however possible, that many of these names have been bynames rather than true individual names. Bynames seem to have also been included in the Old Finnish anthroponymic system the same as they are included in all known anthroponymic systems. Such old descriptive names as *Mustapää* ('black' + 'head') and *Tervahartia* ('tar' + 'shoulder') have been considered clear bynames. Similarly, the Finns may have already had used patronyms in the pre-Christian era and other bynames with reference to family, the same as bynames with reference to domicile or profession. However, these kinds of names were not hereditary, although a name expressing, for example, domicile or profession remained the same for several generations.

It has been assumed, on the basis of information on other Baltic-Finnish peoples, that Finnish children may have been named after relatives. On this founding, it has been concluded that many Old Finnish names may have lost their semantic transparency during the pre-Christian era when they would not have been comprehensible even to those bearing these names. The epistles of Macarius Archbishop of Novgorod (1534 and 1548) to the Karelians, Ingrians and Votes referred to the fact that a particular person specialised in the care of religious rituals worked as a name giver amongst the Baltic-Finnish peoples.

It is possible that name giving of the Old Finns may have resembled Sámi name giving which was thoroughly described by Norwegian priests in the 18th century. Sámi children were named in a specific order after relatives: the first son received his father's father's name, the next son received his mother's father's name and so on. However, it is impossible to get definite information on the details of Old Finnish name giving or its anthroponymic system. In any case, it is clear that this naming system consisted of a person's main name and various bynames.

FEATURES OF MEDIEVAL ANTHROPONYMY

Christianity began to extend to Scandinavia in the 9th century but the actual anthroponymic breakthrough did not happened there until the 13th century. The development in Finland happened even later. Christianity arrived in Finland from the east and west, at the latest in the 11th century, but it was in existence for a long time alongside Finnish traditional religion. The transition from polytheism to the worship of one god was a slow, centuries-long process for the Finns and a particularly long time was needed for the Christianisation of personal names. Anthroponymy indeed seems to have become Christianised a bit faster in Finland than in other European countries. Such names of Christian origin as *Antti* (*Andreas*), *Lauri* (*Laurentius*), *Martti* (*Martinus*), *Nikki* (*Nikolaus*), *Olli* (*Olav*) and *Paavo* (*Paulus*) were at least already common in Western Finland in the 14th century. Moreover, personal names in 16th century documents concerning Eastern Finland were almost without expectation names of Christian origin. The influence of both Western and Eastern Christianity can also be seen in these names. Behind the eastern border, giving "pagan" names was indeed still common in the 16th century amongst the Karelians, and preserved by the Sámis even longer.

The Christianisation of personal names in Finland was well-founded: traditional Finnish names completely disappeared in practice. One reason for this was that no original Finnish names were preserved at all as saints' names. The only canonised saint on the initiative of the Finns in the Catholic

Church was Bishop Henry, who had an English background. The Finns had also borrowed many personal names, mostly Germanic, before the arrival of Christianity. The Old Finnish anthroponymic system had thus begun to disappear from use prior to the influence of the Christian Church. Those in a position of power in Finnish society had no mother tongue names unlike in Scandinavia where traditional names were preserved even in the names of rulers. Because Finland was under Swedish rule in the Middle Ages, the language of administration was Swedish, used alongside of Latin. Because of this, personal names were also entered in documents in Swedish form and so there were no factors in Finnish society that would have supported the preservation of traditional Finnish names.

Although the Catholic Church has thousands of canonised saints, there were usually 100 to 200 names in different diocesan calendars. The calendar of saints of the Dominican Order was used in the Turku diocese. The oldest known manuscript, in which there is a list of respected saints during the Catholic era in Finland, *Codex Aboensis*, is from the 15th century. In 1488, the Roman Missal *Missale Aboense*, in Latin, was published in Lübeck for the Turku diocese. This missal included the first printed calendar of saints applicable to Finnish life and such names as *Benedictus, Clemens, Henricus, Laurentius, Michael, Petrus, Stephanus, Valentinus; Agatha, Agnes, Barbara, Catherina, Cecilia, Gertrud, Lucia* and *Maria* can be found in it.

Fennicised name forms such as *Antti (Andreas), Heikki (Henrik), Jaakko (Jacobus), Lauri (Laurentius), Martti (Martinus), Mikko (Mikael), Pentti (Benedictus); Katri (Katarina), Kerttu (Gertrud), Kirsti (Christina), Liisa (Elisabet), Marketta (Margareta), Pirkko (Birgitta), Silja (Cecilia)* were adopted from these new saints' names. The Fennicised forms in Eastern Finland were usually Russian influenced. For example, the name *Gregorius* in Eastern Finland took the forms *Riiko, Riiska* and *Rissa* (cf. *Grigorij, Grisha*) whereas the name in Western Finland became *Reko, Reijo* and *Korjus*. Various Fennicised name variants were also necessary in Finland because of the fact that people with the same name needed to be differentiated from one another in daily life. However, non-Finnish name forms were used in official documents.

The most popular male name in Finland and Sweden in the Middle Ages was *Johannes*: its Swedicised name in Sweden was often *Jon* or *Jöns*, and in Finland it was *Juhani* or *Jussi*. The most popular names included Fin. *Olli* / Swe. *Olof, Nikki/Nils, Lauri/Lars, Pekka/Per, Antti/Anders* and *Jaakko/Jakob*. Since the information on Finnish medieval anthroponymy relied mostly on tax lists and other documents in which male names were clearly in the majority, it is impossible to have as much exact information on female names at that time. In the 16th century, there were approximately 30 to 40 different male names being used in the parish of one area and the five most popular may have covered up to over half the men of the parish. 16th century fashionable names included then *Henrik* and *Mats* but the names *Erik, Tomas, Sigfrid* and *Jakob* also gained popularity rather quickly at that time.

Finnish and Swedish medieval anthroponymy also had clear differences which can be explained mostly by different calendars of saints. It is also understandable that the name of the patron saint of Finland, *Henrik* was significantly more popular in Finland than in Sweden. The various differences between localities may have often stemmed from the fact that different parish churches had different patron saints. Wherever a church was dedicated to Jacobus or Laurentius, *Jaakko* and *Lauri* were favoured names. On the other hand, scholars have concluded that medieval Finns have chosen names largely according to living people, not thus directly on the basis of a calendar of saints. This can be pursuant to the fact that the number of names used was much more concise than what was found in calendars of saints. Many names found in lists of saints such as *Ansgarius*, *Hieronymus* or *Tiburtius* were thus never used as personal names.

In addition to individual names of Christian origin, medieval Finns used an abundance of different bynames which were either descriptive of the person or signified his profession or residence. Moreover, patronyms were generally used. In a 1340 letter by Pope Benedict III, which approved the fining of twenty Sääksmäki farm owners, the section of the parties concerned always mentioned their residency but two of them had an additional byname: *Ollj Nivari de Rapalum* ('Olli Nivari of Rapola') and *Nykki Vargh de Voypala* ('Nikki Susi of Voipala', susi 'wolf'). Such names as *Per Böllö* ('owl'), *Lasse Haijkara* ('stork') and *Erich Rotta* ('rat') are present in the Ylä-Satakunta silver tax records (1571). Many of these bynames may have been old individual names or bynames which became homestead names. However, it is not possible to get exact information on this. Descriptive bynames can also be found in the entries *Nicki Rapareisi* ('mud' + 'thigh') and *Wähä Lauri* ('lesser') whereas bynames concerning profession can be found in *olaff kaupamies* ('salesman'), *marti ridari* ('knight'), *Peer Seppä* ('blacksmith') and *Olli Snickar* (Swe. snickare 'carpenter').

The most common way to identify a person in medieval documents was to use a patronym in addition to an individual name: *Henrik Mattson* or *Heikki Matinpoika* ('Heikki son of Matti'). Because this kind of name could easily be given to everyone, and also in Swedish form, they were quite useful in documents in the time of Swedish rule. Usually, the person's residence was added after these: *Hanns Ollsson Lusist*. Sometimes patronyms were recorded in Latin, for example *nicolaus martini* (1478). Moreover, many bynames ending in *nen* were patronymic by nature: for example, *Christer Luckanpoika* ('Christer son of Lucka') is also *Christer Lukahainen* (1640). On the other hand, many bynames ending in *poika* ('boy, son') are not necessarily patronyms but rather they may refer to a place of residence: such as *olaff kivsanpoyca* ('Kiusanpoika' ← 'Kiusa+GEN|boy') is from the homestead of Kiusa in the village of Rautajoki, located in the former municipality of Tyrvää.

True hereditary surnames were not being used in the Middle Ages as randomly as amongst nobility and academics, the same as within cities and the bourgeoisie of German background.

Name Giving in Finland
between the 16ᵗʰ and 18ᵗʰ Centuries

The Protestant Reformation signified the rejection of the worship of saints in addition to many other ecclesiastical reforms. This is why the Protestants both in Germany and other Central European countries began to favour other biblical names, in place of saint's names, the same as mother tongue names. This was a much slower process in Finland than in Central Europe. Although Sweden-Finland had officially shifted over to Lutheranism at the Uppsala Synod in 1593, the Finns still gave their children the same types of names as in the Catholic era at the end of the 16ᵗʰ century, in other words, names of the central, ecclesiastical saints. One reason for this can be that Catholic Church rule in Sweden-Finland completely lost its influence, thus the Lutherans did not have such Catholic counterforce in the Nordic countries which one should have taken distance to by cultural means, as was the case in Central Europe

The Catholic calendar of saints and its nomenclature still regulated Finnish name giving in the 16ᵗʰ and 17ᵗʰ centuries. There was yet a calendar section in Mikael Agricola's Finnish-language prayer book *Rucouskiria* which listed 80 names for commemorative saints' days. They were mostly the same as the names in the previous *Missale Aboense* missal. The same type of nomenclature was also dominant (*Adrianus, Bonifacius, Franciscus, Hieronymus, Valerianus; Barbara, Christina, Euphemia, Margareta, Scholastica*) in the Sigfrid Aronus Forsius almanacs published in the beginning of the 17ᵗʰ century.

Forsius published 23 almanacs altogether from 1608 to 1623. The name lists of these almanacs complied with the nomenclature of the calendar of saints of the Turku diocese. The 1608 almanac was the first one of its kind in Finland, although published in Swedish, and unlike Forsius' other almanacs, many names in Swedish can be found in it such as *Bengt* (*Benedictus*), *Staffan* (*Stephanus*); *Barbro* (*Barbara*) and *Charin* (*Catharina*). It has been suggested that Forsius may have received harsh criticism for these Swedicised name forms and for this reason he may have deleted them from later calendars.

The central memorials of saints were also preserved in German evangelical calendars because people were accustomed to perceive the course of the year with them. The people of Finland had also become acquainted with speaking of, for example, Syys-Matti (*syys* 'autumn'), Talvi-Matti (*talvi* 'winter'), Heinä-Maija (*heinä* 'grass') or Nälkä-Martta (*nälkä* 'hungry') when referring to certain days. Many demotic proverbs were also connected to memorable saints' days such as "Antti joulun alottaa, Tuomas tupaan taluttaa, paha Paavo pois sen ajaa", meaning that the Christmas season will begin on Antti's day (30 November), Christmas will be brought to a cabin on Tuomas' day (21 December) and that it will be driven away on the evil Paavo's day (25 January).

The Protestants in different countries began to adopt other biblical names for the calendars than those featured in Catholic calendars of saints. Moreover, empty pages in the Finnish almanac in the 17ᵗʰ century began to be filled with Old Testament names such as *Adam, Benjamin, Methusalem*;

Ester, Mirjam and *Rebecca*. Since the 17th century, literate Finns became acquainted with these names from ecclesiastical calendars which were appendices to hymn books. Later on, the common people became users of Finnish-language almanacs. The first of these was *Almanach eli Ajan-Lucu* (1705) by Laurentius Tammelin, printed in Turku. From 1749 on, all Finnish almanacs were always printed in Sweden until the end of Swedish rule, that is, until 1809.

Biblical names were still added to 17th century almanacs such as *Aaron, Gabriel, Hesekiel, Moses* and *Zephanias*. The names of dynasty members were also included in these. Hence, the 1721 almanac included, for example, *Ulrika* day (4 July) after Queen Ulrika Eleonora, the 1750 almanac had *Adolf* day (23 June) after crown prince Adolf Fredrik and the 1774 almanac had *Gustav* day (6 June) after Gustav Vasa. International fashionable names such as *August, Emil, Otto; Albertina, Charlotta* and *Fredrika* were also included in calendars. Names in Latin were also changed to Swedish (*Botolphus* → *Botolf, Franciscus* → *Frans*). Hence, the original ecclesiastical calendar of saints began to take the form of the secular name day calendar.

Although it was a few hundred years since the rule of the Catholic Church in Sweden-Finland in the 18th century, approximately three fourths of the nomenclature of the 1790 calendar still included old saints' names. One fifth of the names came from the Bible and they were more or less evenly distributed between the Old and New Testaments. Saints' names and biblical names altogether totalled to nearly 95 per cent. All the names in the calendar were in foreign form and only one fifth were female names.

There are no studies on Finnish name giving in the 17th and 18th centuries concerning the whole population. The nomenclature of almanacs apparently reflected, at least to some extent, the actual name giving of the population. Hellevi Arjava (2005) has investigated name giving in the parish of Kangasniemi in Central Finland between 1684 and 1899. Names of the Old Testament (*Eeva, Saara, Susanna; Abraham, Josef, Samuel*) clearly grew to popularity in this locality in the 18th century the same as dynastical names and other *international names*, that is, names which had been popular in many European countries (*Albertina, Lovisa, Ulrika, Vilhelmina; Axel, Fredrik, Reinhold, Otto*).

Fennisation of Given Names during Russian Rule
When the country became the Grand Duchy of Finland in 1809, the exchange of power gradually began to be seen in Finnish nomenclature as well. Many names of the Russian royal family such as *Alexandra* (1827), *Nicolai* (1827), *Olga* (1868), *Dagmar* (1870), *Georg* (1896), *Mikael* (1901) and *Alexei* (1906) were introduced in almanacs. The number of days of each name was changed to better fit the names of the Russian royal family. Hence, for example the day of *Alexander* was changed from 12 December to 11 September which was the name day of Alexander I according to the Orthodox calendar.

In practice, the influence of Russian rule meant that Finnish nomenclature adopted new names of Russian origin. At the same time, other international influences continued strong. Many international fashionable names were entered in the 19th century almanac such as *Arthur, August, Eugene; Elwira, Flora* and *Josephina*. A major part of these were female names, which was a welcome change because male names previously were clearly in the majority. The naming of women had even been quite one-sided in Finland. For example, out of all baptised females in Kangasniemi between 1700 and 1719, over half were named *Maria* (19 per cent), *Anna* (13 per cent), *Margareta* (13 per cent) or *Katharina* (13 per cent), whereas the dispersion of the most popular male names was much greater; none of these surpassed the 10 per cent margin.

In the 19th century, adopting more than one given name became more and more standardised in Finland. This innovation already began to extend in the country in the 18th century, at first amongst higher class society. This was a model adopted from Sweden, which in turn came from Central Europe. Having multiple names gradually became standard amongst the common people as well, first in Southern and Western Finland. This innovation was, however, rather slowly adopted in Eastern Finland because the Orthodox tradition of name giving there supported giving and bearing only one name. Like many other name innovations, having multiple names first spread out more quickly in girls' names than boys' names. This is because name giving for boys is typically more traditional than it is for girls.

Giving two names was clearly a dominating custom by the end of the 19th century in Southern and Western Finland. Bearing two names rose to 80 per cent in the whole country at the beginning of the 20th century and having three names approximately 15 percent, thus 5 per cent of children had only one name at that time. Regional differences thus gradually evened out.

Along with bearing multiple names, such combinations of names as *Anna Kristiina* and *Maria Elisabet* or *Gustav Adolf* and *Kalle Kustaa* became standard. To the Finnish people, women's combined names in particular were often shortened to compound names (*Maija-Liisa*) and two-part names (*Annastiina*); at that time, a person's latter name may not have been unused in the same way as it is today. Compound names were adopted in official Finnish anthroponymy at the end of the 19th century. However, they did not become standard in male names until after the end of World War II.

The most significant change in 19th century name giving was the Fennisation of the nomenclature which was connected to the national awakening of Finland. The driving thought was that a Finn must have a Finnish first name. Hence, since the mid-19th century, new Finnish names deliberately began to be created either directly on the basis of Finnish (*Arvo* 'value', *Ilma* 'air') or by translating foreign names (*Katarina* → *Siveä* 'chaste', *Victor* → *Voitto* 'victory'). Finnish names were also found in folk poetry as well as the newly published Finnish epic *Kalevala* (names of mythological beings and characters *Ilmari, Kullervo, Väinö; Aino, Kyllikki, Tellervo*).

Suggestions for new names were given in many newspaper articles as well as booklets and calendars. A significant player was, for example, the pen name Arwo Moittivainen that wrote for the Turku newspaper *Sanomia Turusta*. In 1865, under the pen name *Sakki*, Isak Edward Sjöman published

Siveä. Kauno-annakka 1865 which, in addition to fictional material, was an almanac including numerous Finnish names. The names that were in it ended up in the official almanac of the time including *Armas* ('beloved'), *Jalo* ('noble'), *Kielo* ('lily-of-the-valley'), *Mainio* ('excellent'), *Reima* ('brisk'), *Salama* ('lightening'), *Sulo* ('sweet') and *Uljas* ('brave'). Approximately one fifth of Sjöman's suggestions were left outside of the almanac, for example *Apila* ('clover'), *Joutsen* ('swan'), *Kernas* ('wilful'), *Mahla* ('sap'), *Nero* ('genius'), *Reipas* ('brisk'), *Soma* ('pretty'), *Sävel* ('(musical) note'), *Turva* ('safety') and *Ystäwä* ('friend'). Part of Sjöman's names were clear translations such as *Rauha* 'peace' ← *Irene*, *Siveä* 'chaste' ← *Katarina*, *Ohto* 'bear' ← *Ursula* and *Kallio* 'rock' ← *Sten*. At the end of the 19th century, Sjöman's suggested names were taken into the calendars of the oldest adult education organisation in Finland, Kansanvalistusseura, in which new name suggestions were made known to the Finnish people. The 1882 and 1883 calendars were especially notable because the previous calendar names in these were written in Finnish forms, translated into Finnish or replaced by completely new Finnish names.

Moreover, Finnish name forms began to appear in official almanacs. The 1858 almanac already included *Lauri*, *Mauno* and *Paawali* as well as *Martta*, *Ristiina* and *Saara*. There were already around 50 Finnish name forms in the 1890 almanac such as *Heikki*, *Pentti*, *Wilho*, *Yrjö*; *Eewa*, *Katri*, *Siiri* and *Ulla*. The only genuine Finnish name in this almanac was the female name *Aino* (← *ainoa* 'only, sole'), from the national epic *Kalevala*. All others were Finnish forms of international names, such as *Aatto* (*Adolf*); *Alli* (*Alfhild*), *Kerttu* (*Gertrud*) and *Pirkko* (*Birgitta*).

The first great reform of the name day calendar was carried out in 1908. 73 new Finnish names and 59 *pan-European names*, however given a Finnish form, were introduced in the almanac. The principle of the reform was to preserve broadly used names and such uncommon names which were connected to ecclesiastical traditions or demotic commemorative dates. Moreover, there was a demand to increase the share of female names. This reform, which abandoned 150 saints' names, meant a clear secularisation of the Finnish name calendar. New, approved Finnish names for the 1908 almanac were, for example, *Heimo*, *Into*, *Mainio*, *Otso*, *Urho*; *Ilma*, *Lahja*, *Rauha*, *Saima* and *Tyyne*. International and Swedish names included in the almanac of the same year were *Alvar*, *Björn*, *Edvin*, *Holger*, *Valter*; *Adele*, *Ebba*, *Ingeborg*, *Linnea* and *Sylvia*.

The next great reform was seen in the 1929 almanac which took on up to over 200 new names. This reform was considered "the ultimate triumph of nomenclature with Finnish marking or that of Finnish origin" (Kiviniemi 1982). Many Old Finnish names were also now adopted for the name day calendar such as *Arijoutsi*, *Kotivalo*, *Nousia*, *Rautia* and *Utria*. Other Finnish names found in this almanac included *Anelma*, *Hilkka*, *Lauha*, *Ritva*, *Vuokko*; *Aulis*, *Ponteva*, *Tarmo*, *Urmas* and *Veli*. There was also a great deal of Finnish forms of international names. Many of these were well-known names, such as *Leena*, *Liisa*; *Matti* or *Pekka*, which had been used as colloquial, Fennicised forms of official names for centuries.

Moreover, names of notable Finnish men *Aleksi* (Kivi), *Eljas* (Lönnrot), *Juhana Ludvig* (Runeberg), *Juhana Vilhelm* (Snellman) and *Sakari* (Topelius) were placed in the 1929 reformed calendar under their birthdays. Only a few new names of international background were eligible for the calendar: *Anja, Heloisa, Iiris, Leila, Lilli, Meeri, Salli, Taina* and *Harri*. Several Germanic-Scandinavian names were removed from the calendar, many of which were moved to the new Finland Swedish name day calendar. Since the Swedish-speaking population of Finland this year was given its own name day calendar, the Finnish one may have freely become Finnish.

Kustaa Vilkuna was responsible for the new 1950 calendar. He introduced over 100 new names to the almanac which included, for example, *Ari, Ilpo, Jarmo, Kai, Tarvo*; *Arja, Eija, Maarit, Päivi* and *Virve*. Names that wound up being put aside were no longer names of foreign origin but rather mostly such Finnish names that found their way to the 1929 calendar which had not become well-established in use. The next new calendar was completed by Vilkuna in 1973 which was supplemented with over 60 names.

The nomenclature of the 1984 name day calendar was renewed for the first time on the basis of vast Population Register Centre name data. Eero Kiviniemi was responsible for this new calendar. This data has been a basis for later, new calendars by Kiviniemi (1995, 2000, 2005) and Kiviniemi and Minna Saarelma (2010). The most important criterion for bringing new names to the calendar has been the frequency of the name. All in all, the number of names in the Finnish 2010 name day calendar is 834.

Formation of a Modern Surname System

The same as it had happened elsewhere in Europe, social development gradually lead to the adoption of the modern surname system in Finland. The process took several centuries but the actual formative stage of the system began in the mid 1850s and culminated in 1921 in the Surnames Act (*Sukunimilaki*) which came into force that year. The Finnish surname system thus began to take shape during Russian rule in the circumstances where the status of Swedish was still going strong but a Finnish principle had begun to emerge. This era was being labelled by harsh language strife, the fall of social estates, diversifying of social institutions as well as urbanisation and industrialisation. Supporters of the Fennoman movement had the basic idea that every Finn must have a Finnish-language name. A Finnish surname was raised as a symbol of Finnishness the same as Finland's own currency, language, literature and art. At the same time, a national movement represented the adoption of mother tongue last names in Hungary, Estonia and Latvia, for example.

Hereditary surnames were indeed known in Finland in earlier times. They randomly appeared in the Middle Ages amongst nobility and the bourgeoisie of the city with a German background. Surnames were made obligatory for nobility in Sweden-Finland in 1629. The majority of Finnish nobility names were Swedish and they often made reference to a family's coat of arms (*Horn*). They were often two-part names (*Nordenswan*,

Wadenstjerna), many of them included the elements *von* or *af* (*von Alfthan, af Schultén*) or were hyphenated (*Oker-Blom, Stjernvall-Walleen*).

During Swedish rule, Finland had also adopted other byname systems based on social status largely after the Swedish model. Since the 16th century, many priests, for example, and other representatives of the learned elite adopted *intelligentsia names* for themselves. These were often Latin or Greek names such as *Calamnius* (← Kalajoki 'fish' + 'river', Lat. *amnis* 'river') or *Savonius* 'Savonian, one from Savo'. These bynames were not meant to be hereditary. The city bourgeoisie began to adopt new types of Swedish bynames since the 17th century, which were usually two-part names: *Elgman, Lindqvist, Nyström*. Later on, artisans adopted them, the same as others who had a travelling occupation. This kind of name was often a prerequisite for social rise in society together with Swedish language skills. Bourgeoisie bynames became established surnames by the end of the 17th century, however, artisans' names remained nonhereditary until the mid-19th century.

Soldiers of the late 17th century allotment system also had an established naming system. In addition to their own individual name, each foot soldier was given a byname to use which might have been either in Swedish (*Forsström, Hammar, Hilden, Lustig, Svan*) or Finnish (*Kuula* 'bullet', *Tikka* 'woodpecker', *Voima* 'strength'). These names were not hereditary in family but they may have been passed on from soldier to soldier.

Genuine, hereditary surnames emerged in Finland on a national foundation, not just through the influence of Swedish rule. An established, hereditary byname – that is, surname – system was already in use in the medieval, Savo-Karelian region of the burn-beating and hunting culture in Eastern Finland. This system was largely based on names ending in *nen*. They were originally patronymic names (*Nousiainen* 'son of Nousia' ← *Nousia*, *Pentikäinen* 'son of Pentti' ← *Benedictus*) or they referred to the residence of the original bearer (*Sysmäläinen* 'one from Sysmä'), tribe (*Vepsäläinen* 'Vepsian'), profession (*Nahkuri* 'lederer') or character (*Varvas* 'toe'). The emergence of this original system has been explained by the fact that with a surname, a travelling population was able to prove its birthright to hunting and burn-beating grounds conquered by a family. The Western Finland population was a permanent agrarian people and usually either a patronym or something based on an individual byname or homestead name was entered as a byname in church documents. However, these bynames were not hereditary. For example, a homestead name stayed in the family as long as a representative of the family lived there. The cultural boundary between Western and Eastern Finland was quite clear in relation to the use of bynames.

The term *surname* (*family name, last name*; Fin. *sukunimi*, Ger. *Familienname, Geschlechtsname*; Swe. *släktnamn, efternamn*) has often been defined as a hereditary byname which has appeared in the same family for at least two or three generations. However, this definition is by no means perfect because according to it, surnames were, for example, also bynames based on profession in circumstances where a father, his son and grandson all practised the same profession. Sirkka Paikkala (2004) defines a surname thusly:

"A byname is a surname if it is a part of a naming system whose names' functions include the designation of family inheritance as defined by the norms that regulate this naming system". This definition excludes the random inheriting of bynames and covers such consciously adopted surnames which still have not made it to the next generation – or, for one reason or another, will never be inherited.

In Finland, as in many other European countries, the development of the modern surname system began with nobility. This innovation amongst nobility spread amongst clergy, the bourgeoisie and artisans until it reached farm hands and factory workers and finally other inhabitants of rural areas in the early 19th century. On the one hand, earlier, well-established byname systems were the foundation for this new system, on the other hand, it was new types of surname models which began to take shape in the mid-19th century. These were new, nature-themed *Virtanen* ('current+NEN') and *Laine* ('wave') type models that came about in the hundreds at the time and many of which are nowadays the most common Finnish surnames: *Järvinen* ('lake+NEN'), *Koskinen* ('rapids+NEN'), *Lahtinen* ('bay+NEN'), *Mäkinen* ('hill+NEN'), *Nieminen* ('cape+NEN'); *Aalto* ('wave'), *Laakso* ('valley'), *Mäki* ('hill'), *Salmi* ('sound'), *Salo* ('woods') and so on. The interesting thing is that unlike other Nordic countries, there was no adherence to Finnish patronyms or matronyms in its surname system, nor are there any middle names in the Finnish naming system.

Paikkala (2004), who in her dissertation examined the formation of the Finnish surname system, sees this development as a process in which a new surname concept and the name types concerning it as well as old surname and byname systems were integrated into one modern surname system. According to Paikkala, we can see two phenomena that supplement each other in this process. First of all, a new kind of "actual surname" or the *Virtanen* type emerged, which later supplemented the *Laine* type and other new name types, such as those ending in *io* or *iö* (*Saario* 'island+IO') and lexically two-part names, such as *Sinisalo* ('blue' + 'woods'). New Finnish surnames emerged thus on the basis of adopted naming models. Secondly, the function of many old byname systems – such as artisan and soldier names, Swedish patronyms and bynames based on homesteads – expanded, covering the function of a surname.

According to Paikkala, the *Virtanen* type was the first, Finnish-language consciously created surname system through which a new surname concept began to be formed for Finland and which provided the common people with the possibility to reach being equal to other groups who have used bynames. Hence, the surname system socially united the Finnish people and strengthened their national identity.

Finnish surnames can be classified in the following groups according to their background:

1. Surnames based on personal names: *Andersson* (← *Antti*), *Hermunen* (← *Herman*), *Sirkiä* (← *Sergei*), *Tietäväinen* (← *Tietävä*)

2. Surnames based on bynames: *Partanen* ('beard+NEN'), *Suutari* ('cobbler'), *Vänskä* ('Swede')
3. Surnames based on homestead names: *Alatalo* ('lower house'), *Sammallahti* ('moss' + 'bay'), *Vuorela* ('mountain+LA')
4. Names of nobility: *Soisalon-Soininen, Tandefelt, Yrjö-Koskinen*
5. Names of the intelligentsia: *Argillander, Cygnaeus, Gadolin, Savonius*
6. Names of the bourgeoisie and artisans: *Björklund, Lindqvist, Stenberg, Vikman*
7. Soldier names: *Grön, Hammar, Järvelin, Kuula, Rehn, Tapper*
8. Eastern *nen* names: *Holopainen, Kaukonen, Parviainen, Turakainen*
9. Western *Virtanen* and *Laine* type names: *Jokinen* ('river+NEN'), *Lehtinen* ('leaf+NEN'), *Rantanen* ('shore+NEN'); *Laakso* ('valley'), *Niemi* ('cape'), *Salo* ('woods')
10. Other new surnames formed in line with models: *Aarnio, Eloranta, Karanko, Rantala, Saares, Valanne*
11. Translated names of the Fennoman movement: *Kivi* ('stone' ← *Stenvall*), *Oksanen* ('branch+NEN' ← *Ahlqvist*), *Vapaavuori* ('free' + 'mountain' ← *Friberg*), *Virta* ('current, stream' ← *Ström*)

The shift to a uniform surname system was quite a breakthrough in Finnish society: in a few decades, 100,000 Finns adopted surnames for themselves. The press and literature as well as public occasions, university and school all played a role in the extension of this innovation. The key Fennomen of the time, mostly linguists, teachers, politicians and other representatives of the intelligentsia, worked as opinion leaders. Priests and factory foremen, for example, played a role in executing the practicality of this innovation. The *Virtanen* type, which emerged as the heart of the modern surname system, became popular amongst the intelligentsia but reached out more extensively amongst the rural population and, in fact, in areas whose population historically had no established bynames.

The name change of 26 students in 1875 and 1876 was traditionally regarded as being the "first decisive step" of the Fennisation of surnames. However, Paikkala (2004) has shown that the Fennisation of the common people's surnames can be dated earlier than these name change campaigns of the Fennoman intelligentsia or the public press on the issue. The *Virtanen* type effectively reached the countryside in the 1870s and 1880s but this "silent revolution" that happened amongst the people never received any attention. However, the great name change of 1906 and name change campaigns in the 1930s were events that were quite visible in Finnish society. In practice, the standards of the Finnish surname system took shape in a few decades without any official instruction. The 1920 Surnames Act, according to which, "each and every Finnish citizen must be designated with a surname", ultimately made the surname system official.

Given Names and Surnames in 20th and 21st Century Finland

GENERAL FEATURES OF FINNISH GIVEN NAMES

Given names used by the Finns convey a great deal about Finnishness and the history of Finland. Names from several different sources throughout the centuries have been adopted in the language. Current Finnish given names are connected to Old Finnish culture, the Catholic Middle Ages, the era of Swedish and Russian rule and the periods of Finnish national awakening and Finnish independence as well as other cultural currents of different eras. Hence, the linguistic background of Finnish first names is rather diverse. While names of foreign origin have been adopted in Finnish nomenclature, they have often taken a Finnish form and various forms of address and truncations. This is why there often is little resemblance to their original root names (*Liisa* ← *Elisabet*; *Jukka* ← *Johannes*, *Panu* ← *Urbanus*).

An abundance of Hebrew (*Hanna*), Greek (*Teemu* ← *Nicodemus*) and Roman (*Markku* ← *Marcus*) names from the Bible, as well as, for example, Persian (*Esteri*) or Armenian (*Martta*) names can be found amongst Finnish given names. In addition to Greek (*Aune* ← *Agnes*) and Latin (*Julia*) names, Celtic (*Riitta* ← *Birgitta*), Germanic (*Anssi* ← *Anselm*) and Slavic (*Miro*) nomenclature can be found amongst this group. Names of the German and Scandinavian language area have arrived in Finland at different times and from many various sources. A part of these was adopted in the Middle Ages as saints' names (*Olavi* ← *Olav*, *Pertti* ← *Albert*), a part did not come to Finnish nomenclature until the last few decades. Other European nomenclature at different times came from, for example, French (*Loviisa* ← *Louise*), Russian (*Olga* ← Scand. *Helga*), Irish (*Oona*), Estonian (*Salme*) and English (*Harri*). There have been other names that have been adopted in Finnish, outside of Europe and other than biblical names, such as Arabic (*Eleonoora*) and Persian (*Kasperi*) names.

There is a rather large group of Finnish given names that stem from Finnish nomenclature. This includes traditional Old Finnish names, many of which can be found in *Kalevala* and other folk poetry (*Kyllikki*, *Tellervo*; *Jouko*, *Tapio*) and newer nature names (*Kielo* 'lily-of-the-valley', *Pilvi* 'cloud'; *Terho* 'acorn', *Visa* 'silver birch') and other names created on the foundation of the Finnish language (*Hilja* 'silent', *Rauha* 'peace'; *Armas* 'beloved', *Urho* 'hero'). Many names used in Finland are also various, phonetic reformations or adaptations and hybrids of earlier names. This is why their background is often impossible to figure out. These types of names include, for example, *Eija*, *Raili* and *Saila*.

In his book on given names of the Finnish people, *Suomalaisten etunimet* (2006), Eero Kiviniemi had thoroughly investigated Finnish first names from 1880 to 2005. He divides Finnish given names according to their linguistic background and appearance into three main groups: 1) mother tongue names, 2) names of foreign form and 3) Fennicised forms, call names and truncated forms of foreign names. As fig. 7 suggests, the largest group of Finnish given names have included Fennicised forms of names of foreign origin since the 1880s and call names and truncated forms based on them,

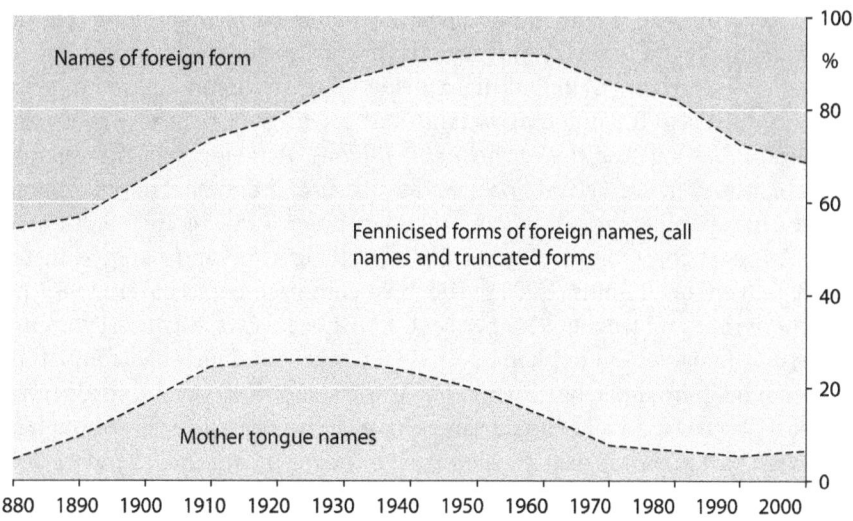

Fig. 7: Finnish given names: mother tongue names, Fennicised forms of foreign names and names of foreign form (Kiviniemi 2006, p. 265).

such as *Leena* (← *Madgalena*), *Maija* (← *Maria*), *Reetta* (← *Margareta*), *Sanna* (← *Susanna*); *Erkki* (← *Erik*), *Heikki* (← *Henrik*), *Matti* (← *Matteus*) and *Pekka* (← *Petrus*). The largest family of Finnish names represent this group, such as *Maija, Maiju, Mari, Marja, Marjatta, Meeri* etc. included in the *Maria* family or *Hannu, Jani, Janne, Juha, Juhani, Juho, Jukka, Jussi*, etc. included in the *Johannes* family.

Non-Finnish name forms, that is, names in non-Finnish form, were rather common in Finland in the beginning of the 20th century but their popularity clearly dwindled upon entering the 1950s. However, their popularity grew again starting in the 1970s. This growth had especially happened at the cost of the core group of Finnish first names, in other words, Fennicised forms and truncated forms of foreign names.

Finnish-language names were at their most popular between the 1920s and 1940s, at a time when the share of male names was approximately 25 per cent and female names roughly 30 per cent. However, after the Winter War and Continuation War, their share declined in beginning the 1970s to approximately 10 to 15 per cent. The popularity of Finnish-language names seems to have again increased in the 21st century as those such as *Aino, Helmi, Pinja; Onni, Pyry* and *Veikka* have become favourites.

Kiviniemi illustrates the linguistic background of Finnish given names with an imaginary group of 100 Finns representing the entire population. Of these, around forty are bearers of biblical names (rather evenly between the Old and New Testaments) and approximately thirty bear ecclesiastical saints' names. The final third is divided into two groups, one side would be some name of a historically important figure or, for example, a literary role model; the names of the other half would not have a clear, personal role model but they would be, for instance, names with reference to nature or names of unclear backgrounds.

According to Kiviniemi's calculations, the Finnish-speaking Finnish population born in the 20th century has approximately 50,000 variant given names – a *variant given name* here means all the written names in different ways, thus also the different variants and spellings of the same root name (*Aleksandra* and *Alexandra*; *Jussi* and *Juhani*). A majority of these names have, however, been given once or a few times and the most popular names are truly popular in comparison to other names. In the 20th century, the 2,000 most common given names were sufficient for up to approximately 98 per cent of all Finns: 1,000 of the most common names covered 98.7 per cent of men and women 97.6 per cent. In the best years, fifty most common first given names of boys had covered 80 per cent and girls had comparable figure of approximately 75 per cent. At the same time, one hundred of the most popular male and female names have always been sufficient enough for a large part of those born. The popularity of a given name has therefore been distributed quite unevenly.

The most popular 20th century female Finnish names (all names)

Maria	*Johanna*
Helena	*Liisa*
Anneli	*Annikki*
Kaarina	*Hannele*
Marjatta	*Tuulikki*

The most popular 20th century male Finnish names (all names)

Juhani	*Kalevi*
Olavi	*Tapio*
Johannes	*Matti*
Antero	*Ilmari*
Tapani	*Pekka*

As Kiviniemi examined the number of Finnish given names for the first time in the early 1980s, the entire amount of various given names came to 34,000; the given names of all of those alive and Finnish-speaking Finnish citizens born in 1965 were included in these figures. The number of names has thus clearly grown since the 1980s. When the number of names given to children annually remained in the numbers between 1,000 and 1,500 until the early 1960s for girls and to the early 1970s for boys, the annual number of names had doubled after this; the increase of the number of girls' names had even been greater than boys' names. The quantitative growth of names is due to the fact that the percentage of unique names from names given annually has multiplied since the 1960s and many of these were compound names. The share of girls' unique names was over 9 per cent and nearly 7 per cent of boys' names in 2005.

Name sharing since the 1970s thus clearly reduced and 50 of the most common names in the 21st century covered only slightly under half of girls and boys annually born. The *top name* or the levelling of the popularity of the most popular given names of each year is one of the clearest trends of the last decades. As, for example, the female name *Sari* in 1966 was given to up to 7.4 girls out of one hundred, the percentage of popular names of each one born each year in the 21st century was under 2 per cent. The same kind of development is also in boys' names, although slightly less distinct.

All in all, name giving has become individualised and diversified. Kiviniemi points out that there has not been such a great and quick change in name selection in about one hundred years as during the last three decades. The standardisation of the giving of more than one given name in the 18th century and the emergence of Finnish given names in the 19th century can mostly be compared to this. The fact that uncommon and even unique names are increasingly sought for children conveys the change of Finnish social values: the need for individual self-determination is extremely powerful in the modern world. General internationalisation and acceleration of information have undoubtedly had an impact on the diversification of nomenclature. Kiviniemi explains the diversification of given names also by the effect of lists of popular first names. As popular names are nowadays known to all, unlike it had previously been, name givers know how to avoid the most common names of all.

Finnish-speaking children born in Finland are nowadays given at least two given names; according to the Finnish Names Act (*Nimilaki*) there can be no more than three names given. There are fewer than two per cent of those born given one name which, in European terms, is rather little. Since the 18th century, the increase of having multiple names has become thus a dominating practice in Finland. The standardisation of giving three given names is a clear trend of the last decades. As those who received three given names in the late 1970s was still approximately 10 per cent of girls and over 15 per cent of boys, there was over 30 per cent of girls with three names in 2005 and over 35 per cent of boys in 2005 (figs 7 and 9). Kiviniemi suggests that one reason for the frequency of boy's having three names is that boys are given hereditary family names more often than girls.

Compound names are always counted as one name in Finland, even though they consist of two different names (*Anna-Mari, Veli-Pekka*). The first common compound name in Finland was the popular *Anna-Liisa* in the 1930s which was followed by *Maija-Liisa, Marja-Liisa* and *Marja-Leena* in the 1940s and 1950s. It had not been commonplace for boys to have compound names until noticeably later than girls, not until after the Winter War and Continuation War. In addition to those mentioned earlier, the most popular Finnish female compound names of Finnish women have been *Sirkka-Liisa, Eeva-Liisa, Anna-Maija, Anne-Mari, Ulla-Maija* and *Marja-Terttu*. The ten most popular male names include *Veli-Matti, Juha-Pekka, Jukka-Pekka, Veli-Pekka, Juha-Matti, Olli-Pekka, Ari-Pekka, Jari-Pekka, Ville-Veikko* and *Vesa-Matti*.

Later on, compound names were created for both genders from virtually any names. The percentage of various compound names from all names in Finland has been extraordinarily large: at least 40 per cent of female names

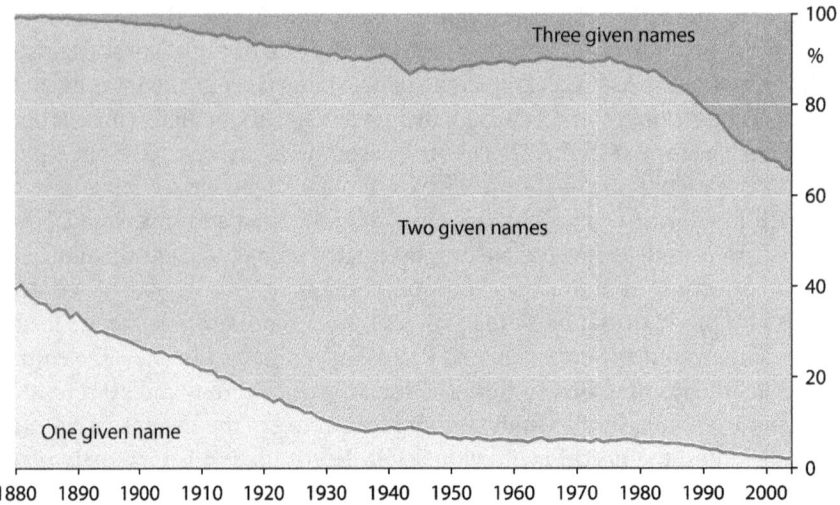

Fig. 8. Percentage of girls receiving one, two and three given names out of those born annually from 1880 to 2005 (Kiviniemi 2006, p. 74).

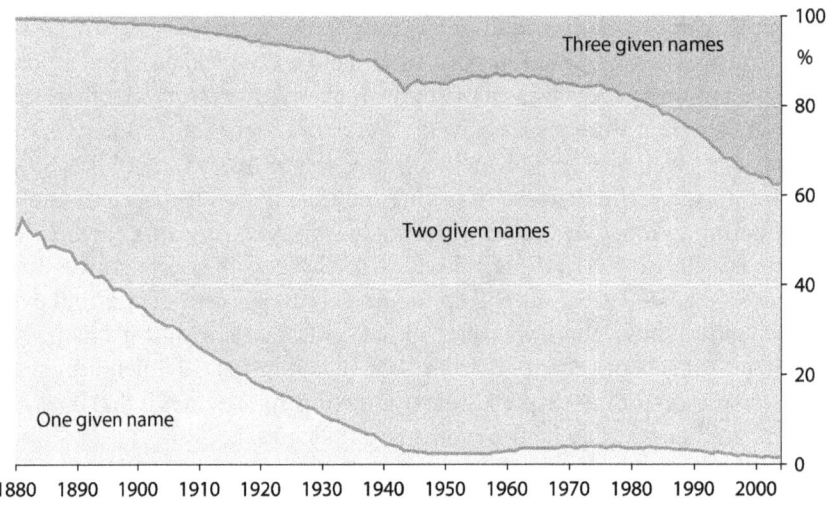

Fig. 9. Percentage of boys receiving one, two and three given names out of those born annually from 1880 to 2005 (Kiviniemi 2006, p. 74).

and slightly less of male names. Since the 1990s, however, the number of compound names has noticeably dropped. Kiviniemi explained this by the fact that individuality is no longer aspired by special compound names but rather by creating or searching for other types of unique names.

It is typical for Finnish given names that first and latter given names are differentiated from one another both quantitatively and qualitatively. If Finnish given names are divided into first and latter given names, over half of the names of each group will only appear in its own group. In practice, these names are often thus either only first names or only second names. It is typical for first given names that they are short, often mono- or polysyllabic (*Päivi, Kai*), whereas the majority of second given names have three (*Marketta, Juhani*) or four (*Eveliina, Katariina*) syllables, sometimes even phonetically heavy, that is, ending in a consonant, bisyllabic names (*Marjut, Tuomas*). Finnish name giving is also regulated by an ideal of the Kalevala meter (trochaic tetrameter), according to which, the heaviest lexical element is aimed at being placed at the end of a name combination. This is why long names by their syllabic structure are common as second given names and short first given names. Moreover, in the standardisation of trisyllabic names, such combinations as *Amanda Elli Aurora* (3 + 2 + 3) or *Eetu Onni Valtteri* (2 + 2 + 3) have become common.

It is also typical that the most common latter given names are notably more commonplace that the most common first given names and simultaneously, their temporal variation is slower. This is due to the fact that second given names are not really used in everyday life so that they are not so often used in the same way as first given names. In the case of second given names, it is more established in boys' name giving than for girls: 20 of the most common boys' second given names covers 59 per cent of all boys' second given names as the corresponding figure for girls is 52 per cent.

In the following lists of the most popular first and second given names, we can easily see how these names differ from one another:

The most popular 20th century female first given names

Anna   *Eila*
Aino   *Leena*
Eeva   *Marja*
Ritva   *Pirjo*
Tuula   *Pirkko*

The most popular 20th century male first given names

Matti   *Juha*
Erkki   *Pentti*
Timo   *Heikki*
Antti   *Pekka*
Kari   *Veikko*

The most popular 20th century female latter given names

Maria   *Johanna*
Anneli   *Annikki*
Helena   *Hannele*
Kaarina *Tuulikki*
Marjatta *Liisa*

The most popular 20th century male latter given names

Juhani	*Kalevi*
Olavi	*Tapio*
Johannes	*Ilmari*
Antero	*Mikael*
Tapani	*Sakari*

The difference between male and female names is not always clear in Finland, although the Names Act states that no boy shall be given a female name and no girl be given a male name. New Finnish given names (*Lahja* 'gift', *Varma* 'certain', *Sulo* 'charm', *Vieno* 'gentle') in the 19th century and the beginning of the 20th century were still problematic but later on, their roles became clear. There are only ten names left (for example *Misa, Oma, Tuisku* and *Venni*) of such names, which after 1960 had been given to either gender at least ten times.

In the case of new, uncommon names, this problem has continuously been encountered. Names of flowers and plants are often perceived as girls' names but other names of nature is more faltering in relation to the distribution of gender. For example, both boys and girls have received the names *Kuu* 'moon' and *Myrsky* 'storm'. The same goes for such names in different roles which occur in different naming systems and which have brought about much to deliberate about. For example, *Nilla* as a female name is a truncation of the Swedish name *Gunilla* but as a male name, it is a Sámi variant of the Greek name *Nikolaos*. The same goes for the Swedish female name *Vanja* (cf. *Anja, Tanja*) but in Russia, it is used as a term of endearment for both men (*Ivan*) and women (*Ivana*). The name *Kim* as a female name is a truncated form of the name *Kimberley* and a truncated form of the name *Joakim* as a male name. Despite these exceptional cases, Finnish given names are rather linked to gender.

Principles of Name Selection

At the same time, as the number of given names in Finland has increased, the principles of name giving have also changed. It has gone from communal name giving to more and more clearly individual name giving, especially since the 1970s.

According to Kiviniemi (2006), typical for 20th century and early 21st century name giving of Finnish people has been that a name common to the parent's generation or their generation preceding them not be selected for a child. This is due to the fact that strong images of their name bearers are often connected to these names. Names in common use at the moment of name giving often also seem too ordinary. However, names (*Adolfiina, Valdemar*) of the name givers' grandparents' generation and the generations prior to them are regarded as being much more novel which is why they are often readily readopted. Fresh and extraordinary options for names can come from name cultures of other countries (*Luka, Miska*) and be new Finnish creations (*Havu* 'conifer needle', *Omena* 'apple'). Truncated forms of earlier names and name forms adapted and combined in other ways can be adopted (*Sakari* → *Saku*; *Minna* → *Minni*, *Lumi* 'snow' + *Kukka* 'flower' → *Lumikukka*) as well as new names created in line with other name models (*Aenna, Rosma, Velveena*).

Hence, there is an aspiration towards fresh and special name options in selecting a name which can also be regarded as being appealing. The preference for a certain name is however quite a complex process which the name giver cannot always specify. Quite often, emotions and chance play a role in it rather than practical points. Factors that are associated with personal images of names are often quite individual and largely unconscious and this is why it can be difficult to analyse. It is clear that, in practice, various criteria for name selection concurrently work and are intertwined with one another. Although the factors connected to name selection cannot usually be able to be thoroughly specified, different name giving principles can indeed be examined and classified on a common level.

The most significant principle of Finnish name giving has been naming after family. It was only a few hundred years ago, when it was a common custom in Finland to give children names from amongst the parents' family. Usually, the names of grandparents were given to the firstborn and those born afterwards were given names of aunts, uncles and other relatives. The thought behind this type of name giving in Finland had been that the life of the grandparents would, in a way, be carried on through the grandchildren. When surnames were not yet in use at the time, naming after family members also signified to which family a child belonged.

Naming after relatives considerably decreased in the 20th century but it is still quite common regarding second given names. For example, over half of Finnish second given names in the 1970s had been chosen according to relatives. Nowadays, when names are given after family members, it is to pay homage towards that specific relative. On the other hand, Kiviniemi emphasises that names appropriate to the style of the time are sought and selected from names of relatives. Hence, the principle of name giving is then more of a novelty and trend of a name connected to family rather than in memory of the person whose name is adopted. As a name is selected, usually from many generations back, the original bearer is often personally unknown to the name giver.

Naming after family is thus a question of when a child is given the name of a living or deceased relative. This name can be given as either the first or second given name and it can be given either as it is or in some form better appropriate to the style of the time. For example, a boy can be named *Eerikki* after his father's father *Erkki* and his granddaughter can be given the name *Eerika*, or a girl can be named *Tuulia* after her mother's mother *Tuulikki*. Sometimes, the same first or second given name can be inherited in the family systematically from father to son – even so that, for example, all male siblings can have the same second given name.

Family connections can also be expressed in other ways. Children may be given names which share some common feature with their siblings or parents. Names may, for example, start with the same letter or phonetic combination (parents *Markku* and *Mirja*, children *Miko* and *Milla*) or end with the same phonetic combination (sisters *Hanna, Jonna* and *Sanna*). In some families, all the children have compound names (*Henna-Riikka* and *Janne-Pekka*) or names that contextually are associated to each other (*Saana* and *Salla*, names of mountains in Lapland). Names of twins are particularly often reminiscent of each other (*Kalle* and *Ville*).

One significant principle of name giving in Finland has also been the naming after personal role models. Role models have included, for example, leading historical figures and politicians (President Urho Kekkonen → *Urho*), religious figures (Lutheran pastor Lars Levi Læstadius → *Leevi*), athletes (hockey player Teemu Selänne → *Teemu*), musicians (Veeti Kallio → *Veeti*) and other "celebrities" of popular culture (first Miss Universe Armi Kuusela → *Armi*) as well as authors and other artists (novelist Aleksis Kivi → *Aleksi*). There can also be fictive role models for names such as characters found in literature (Astrid Lindgren's book *Ronia the Robber's Daughter* → *Ronja*) or pieces of music (*Für Elise* → *Elise*). On the one hand, it is a question of the appreciation of these characters in this type of naming, on the other hand, it is a question of the fact that a pleasant name happened to be found with the publicity of these figures.

Other personal role models may often be the parents' friends and acquaintances, fellow students and teachers, workmates, godparents of the child and other people part of the parents' life. Sometimes, a child may be given a name after another child of the same name. Moreover, it is mostly a question of the fact that in this kind of name giving, an appropriate name may have been found from those of a close circle of people. Should the name of the person concerned not be pleasing to the parents, it would hardly be given to the child no matter how beloved or respected the bearer of the name may be to them.

Parents often say that one criterion for selecting a name is also its phonetic appeal or preference to the name and they want to give a name which sounds pleasant and harmonious. It is clear that a name's appeal is always a matter of personal taste. Someone may think that the name *Hilla* has a nice, gentle ring to it, and someone else may be fond of the vigorous sounding name *Rasmus*. Many kinds of personal images can also be associated with the appeal of names: attractiveness is often adhered to the name of an attractive person. Moreover, a name's semantic content has an effect on the appeal perceived with a name: *Ruusu* ('rose') is an appealing name because a rose is a beautiful flower. Usually a person's taste in names changes along with life – and the changes often follow the changes in name trends. Fashionable names usually are primarily perceived as appealing.

Various practical points are often also associated with name choice. In Finnish, many find it important to give a name to a child that is easy to inflect, pronounce and write. When it comes to inflection in Finnish, it is not enjoyable to have to explain how a child's name is formed, for example, in the genitive: the *i* in the female first name *Lumi* ('snow') does not undergo a vowel change as in the appellative (*Lumin* 'Lumi's', not *lumen* 'of the snow'). There can also be practical problems as a name can be written in several different ways (*Annamari* and *Anna-Mari*, *Nico* and *Niko*, *Tia* and *Tiia*) or if a name's correct pronunciation must be learned separately (*Henrica*: [hɛnrikɑ] not [hɛnri:kkɑ]).

Many name givers also consider if a child's name can be formed into such nicknames or names of ridicule which may perhaps make the child a subject of laughter (*Jukka Antero* → *Akka Juntero* roughly 'bitch redneck'). Parents may similarly contemplate if, for example, a long compound name can work as the child's call name. Many of those selecting a name also emphasise that a name must be short and simple (*Lotta*, not *Charlotta*) because such a name can usually not be shortened. Some also avoid names which are difficult for children who are learning to speak (*Aleksandra*, *Pyry*). Many parents also hope that their child's name will not be too dated; that is, would not just be a fashionable name of the time that would soon be considered old fashioned. On the other hand, some may not wish for a name to be too general so that their child could be easily differentiated from other children, for example, at day care or school.

Names are sought for children in many families of two cultures which would work well in the language and culture of both parents. There are some *multicultural names* in the Finnish name calendar which are included in both the Finnish naming system and the naming system of some other culture. For example, *Laila* would be suitable for a daughter of a Finnish and Arab family, *Veera* for a daughter of a Finnish and Russian family and *Marko* for a son of a Finnish and Italian family. Moreover, many parents of fully Finnish backgrounds may want to give their children names which work elsewhere in Europe such as *Anna*, *Laura*; *Anton* or *Niklas*. Sometimes some may wish to emphasise the internationalisation of names with non-Finnish spellings (*Alexandra*, *Carolina*; *Emil*, *Oscar*).

In the combination of Finnish given names, name givers often also consider how many names a child will need, how the names will suit each other – and how they will fit with the child's surname. Are the names the same in style? Are they phonetically and rhythmically suitable to each other? Again, this is largely a matter or taste.

Moreover, the meaning of the linguistic expression included in the name is often an important issue to parents. Many contemporary parents want to give their children a Finnish-language, semantically transparent name such as *Kanerva* ('heather'), *Ruusu* ('rose'); *Armas* ('beloved') or *Toivo* ('hope'). Some also come up with new names for their children based on Finnish. Sometimes, mother tongue names are associated with the child's moment of birth: for example, a girl born in the spring may be named *Kielo* ('lily-of-the-valley') and a girl born in wintertime may be *Talvikki* ('winter+KKI'). Many Finnish parents choose non-Finnish names on the basis of their original meanings and carefully read their explanations in name dictionaries. Some may want to give their daughter the name *Sofia* meaning 'wisdom' or their son the name *Ilari* because its root name *Hilarius* means 'joyful'.

The day of childbirth or christening can also be a principle of name giving. For example, a boy born on 24 February (name day of Matti) may be given the name *Matti* or a girl christened on 27 May (name day of Ritva) may be given the name *Ritva*. However, this is quite a rare custom today. Sometimes parents consciously select a name whose name day is not close to the child's birthday. Hence, the child's celebratory days would be evenly distributed throughout the year.

Finding a child's name in the name day calendar is sometimes another important criterion for name giving. The parents may want that their child will have his own name day which he can celebrate as he so desires. Because efforts are made to give the most individual names in name selection, the percentage of those without name days of new age groups has grown. As 94 per cent of men and 90 per cent of women born between 1900 and 1959 can find their first given name in Finnish name day calendars, the percentage of boys was 82 per cent and girls 75 per cent of those born between 2000 and 2004. Many Finns with no name day have, however, begun to celebrate their name days on such days which resemble their own names in the calendar either phonetically, semantically or based on the same root name. Some also celebrate their name day according to the Finland Swedish name day calendar.

Principles of name giving may also be connected to the parents' worldview and values. Thus, some families may, for example, only select biblical names for their children such as *Johanna* or *Markus* whereas names of Christian origin would not be approved in some families at all. Such families who have a significant belief in environmental protection may give their children names with a nature theme. Moreover, political values have been reflected in Finnish given names, such as the names *Taisto* ('battle') and *Voitto* ('victory') given during the Finnish Civil War indicate. Other socio-economic factors, spirit of the time, education and different cultural factors also subconsciously have an effect on peoples' taste in names which is really a product of the individual's own cultural background.

Kiviniemi (2006) has made the following list of the most significant principles of Finnish name giving:

1. A name from the family
2. Family connections expressed in some other way
3. Other personal role models
4. The name's appeal or preference towards the name
5. Points concerning the use of the name (lack of problems from different aspects)
6. Meaning of an expression included in the name
7. Birthday or christening day
8. Other selection criteria

Popularity Change of Given Names

Because first names are adopted in the same way as other cultural innovations, their expansion can be described in the same way as the expansion of other cultural phenomena. American scholar Everett M. Rogers presented so-called *diffusion research* in his book *Diffusion of Innovations* (1962) which has been applicable to several different fields of research. According to Rogers, the spread of innovation is a process in which a new idea, object or behaviour over time goes from one member of a social system to another via a channel or channels. Both different social and economic factors and cultural features have an effect on this.

The spread of new phenomena is examined in diffusion research from both sociological and geographical angles. Sociologic diffusion research investigates how and why a person has adopted an innovation whereas geographic diffusion research studies the geographic regularities of the spread of a phenomenon. Both media and personal contacts work as channels for the spread of innovation. Media spreads information effectively to broad groups but personal contacts are best when wanting to change people's opinions.

According to Rogers, the spreading of innovation requires: 1) innovation 2) someone who has adopted the innovation 3) someone who has not yet adopted the innovation and 4) a channel which will link these two persons to each other. Rogers has also divided people into different categories according to which, at which stage they have adopted the innovation. The so-called *innovators* (2.5 per cent) are the individuals who have adopted an innovation. After these are the slightly larger group of *early adopters* (13.5 per cent) who are often educated and socially active and also pose a certain degree of opinion leadership in their community. The next group is the *early majority* (34 per cent) whose members carefully contemplate before adopting an innovation from opinion leaders. After this is the *late majority* (34 per cent) who takes to innovation with suspicion and does not adopt it until it has been generally accepted in the community. The last to adopt an innovation are *laggards* (16 per cent) who are typically conservative and often have little contact to regular communication networks.

This grouping can be applied to name innovation adopters. Eero Kiviniemi however has considered the term *laggard* badly applicable to name givers because in name giving, it is not often a question of adopting innovation at that stage but rather that the child is given, for example, some name previously appearing in the family. The wave-like *innovation curve* is however typical to the spread of nearly all relatively common given names. A good example of this is the popularity change curve of the female name *Eija* (fig 10).

Innovation can also geographically spread in various ways. An innovation spreads from its source or *innovation centre* as a ring-like wave in water in so-called *expansion diffusion*. Adoptors are mostly then in the innovation centre, and their number becomes evenly reduced when moving away from the centre. Innovation spreads from one locality to another hierarchically, that is, from larger centres to smaller ones in a *hierarchal spread*. It has even been stated in onomastics that cities have often worked as pioneers in the case of name innovations. Expansion diffusion and a hierarchal spread often are simultaneous phenomena.

Kiviniemi (2006) has categorised given names of Finnish-speaking Finns between 1880 and 1999 according to their popularity as either names having one *popularity peak* (approximately 75 per cent of the names) or those having two (approximately 24 per cent). There is an abundance of unimodal names in this period because their peak is often so late that it is not possible

4. *Personal Names*

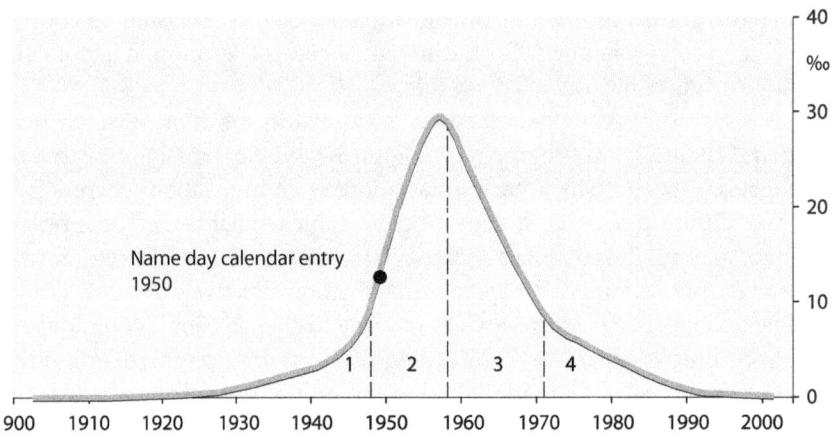

Fig. 10. Selection of the name Eija in Finland from 1900 to 2005 (Kiviniemi 2006, p. 173).

to reach a new peak. Three fourths of bimodal names are such in which the interval of peaks is approximately one hundred years or more, the remainder between 50 and 90 years. A wave-like popularity change is thus also typical for Finnish given names.

There are also so-called *evergreen names*, that is, names which have been rather evenly popular in Finland at different times but they are only a few in number. There were only 15 female and 14 male first given names (e.g. *Eeva*, *Liisa*; *Lauri*, *Olli*) on the level of frequency of at least one per mille during the entire 20th century. This also shows that such names are not really selected for children which are common to the name giver's generation or his previous generation, because strong personal images are often connected to them. The most common of all male and female names of all however seem to be some variant in popularity. For example, the popularity of the name *Anna* has been followed by favourites based on it such as *Anja*, *Anne*, *Anu* and *Anni*.

It has been said that the spreading of new names often differs from the spread of so-called *traditional names* or names that have previously been popular. The popularity of new names often rises more steeply and higher than traditional names and it also usually declines more quickly than the popularity of traditional names. The interval of the popularity peak of new names is also typically longer than that of traditional names. The popularity of traditional names generally does not vanish to the same extent as the popularity of new names. Instead, these names are often preserved in the naming system as more uncommon names.

As new name selections are begun to be sought after one hundred years from a group of old names, a previously common name may rise again to popularity – or not. Rare names usually have historically had better opportunities to come into being new, fashionable names than earlier fashionable names have had because they are better worthy of new ones to name givers. Good examples of this include popular names of the early 21st century *A(a)da* and *Venla*. Many fashionable names also seem to raise other phonetically close names into popularity. Hence, female names such as *Aila, Eila, Laila, Leila, Maila, Oili, Raila, Raili* and *Soile* were popular in the 1930s. Similarly, it is not surprising that *Emma* and *Ella* have both been popular in the 21st century.

Many name favourites may have fluctuated at different rates in different parts of Finland. For example, the traditional Finnish male name *Antti* was simultaneously in some parts of the country on the rise and in other parts on the decline up until the 1930s. It was not until the 1960s when the regional differences regarding the name *Antti* as well as many other names in Finland had balanced out. At the same time, old fashionable names (e.g. *Aili*) may have undergone different popular change curves in different parts of Finland whereas those of new fashionable names (e.g. *Minna*) are quite similar all around. Finnish name giving has thus in the last decades become standard regionally, temporally and quantitatively, which can largely be explained by the influence of media.

The popularity change of second given names differ from that of first given names thus that their waves of popularity are often long and moderate. The reason for this is that these names are used rather little so that they are often unknown to other people. Therefore, many names, such as *Ilmari* or *Olavi*, are quite common and rather consistently popular as second given names whereas they are rare for being first given names or were perhaps only popular at a specific time.

Kiviniemi (2006) has examined the popularity change of given names by dividing the population of those born in the 20th century into to equally large groups: those born between 1900 and 1959 and those born between 1960 and 1999. The 50 most common male and female first given names of these groups indicate that Finnish given names underwent a rather significant reform during the 20th century. The list of girls of the latter half of the 20th century has up to 14 names which had over a 95 per cent occurrence after 1960. There are nine names found in the list of boys whose occurrence was given over 98 per cent in this time period.

The popularity change of given names can also be examined from a perspective of a name trend. Although parents usually aim at finding names for their children that are special and rare, these selections often turn out to be in line with some typical fashion trend to a specific time period. Kiviniemi also speaks of an "invisible sense" when it comes to name selection. On the basis of this, name givers seem to find fashionable name selections for their children as if subconsciously by a certain kind of social instinct. According to the influential Berliner sociologist Georg Simmel, at the turn of the 20th century, fashion is labelled by the dualism of differentiation and imitation: with fashion, efforts are made to individually be distinguished but at the same time with fashion, there is the issue of being identified with others who follow the same trend. Because of this, individuality connected to fashion is usually deceiving. In addition, cyclicality is characteristic to fashion: the beginning, weariness and the end, which a new trend follows again. The standardisation of this phenomenon usually gets a group to reject a trend.

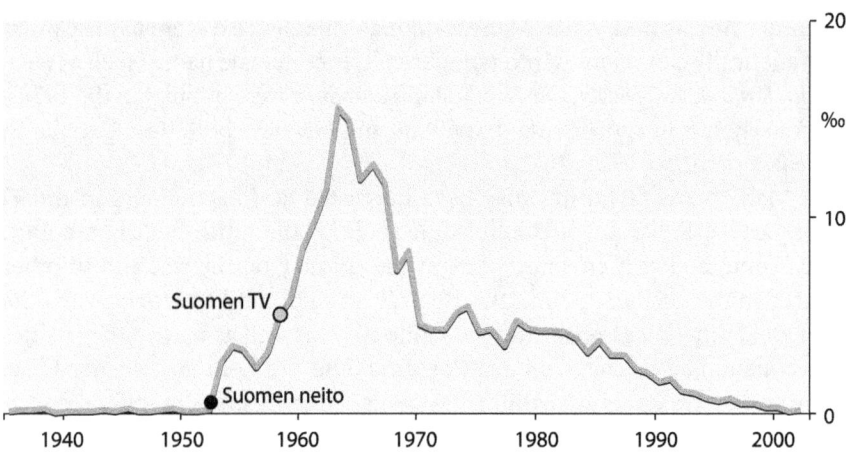

Fig. 11. Teija Sopanen's influence on the popularity of the name Teija in Finland (Kiviniemi 2006, p. 213).

With fashion, the need to be identified with something may be stronger with more people than the need to be differentiated. This is why many name givers consciously provide their children with fashionable names even though they know that these names were popular at the time of name giving: in this case, it is a question of so-called late adoptors. Finnish society in the 1960s and 1970s was still so communal and representative of the same values that the selections of name givers often went straight to the same names – either consciously or unconsciously. For example, up to seven boys out of one hundred received the name *Mika* in 1969. After this, the selection of name has been notably more individual: in 2002, only two boys out of one hundred received the top name *Eetu*.

Moreover, media publicity has an influence on the fashionable trend of given names. Kiviniemi's studies clearly show how, for example, the name *Taina* became common in Finland in the 1960s due to the influence of actress and dancer Taina Elg, how the name *Teija* became popular in the 1950s (fig 11) due to the influence of *Suomen Neito* beauty queen and Finnish television announcer Teija Sopanen and how other beauty queens such as Armi Kuusela, Virpi Miettinen and Satu Östring have had an impact on Finnish nomenclature. New names also found their way from literature in the same way: after the Winter War and Continuation War, the 'Helena' books of the mid-1940s by Aino Räsänen made *Helena*, *Jari* and *Päivi* true fashionable names and the 'Tina' books by Anni Polva brought the name *Tiina* to popularity in the 1960s. Moreover, the influence of athletes can be seen in name giving: for example, sprinter Voitto Hellstén brought the name *Voitto* to popularity again in the 1950s.

The influence of public figures on name trends however is not self-evident but rather it always depends on the name of the person in question. Should the name be quite common, it usually will not get much additional popularity just on the merits of the person. However, a more uncommon

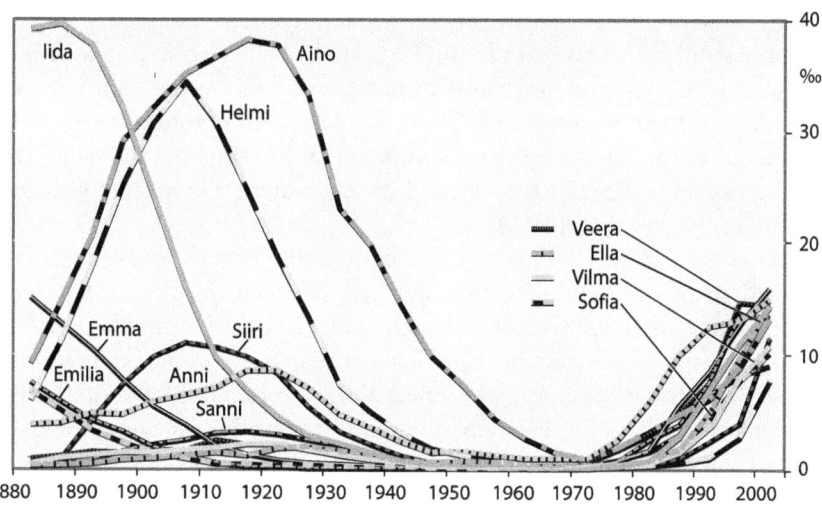

Fig. 12. First given names of girls on the rise and at their peak in 21st century Finland (Kiviniemi 2006, p. 197).

name of a public figure, which is suitable for the style of name of the time, may get increased popularity. These have included, for example, *Viivi* because of Finnish television journalist Viivi Avellan and *Veeti* because of Finnish singer Veeti Kallio. The influence of media publicity on nomenclature is often quite quick but also short-lived.

Kiviniemi however sees the popularity of revived names, in other words old names that became popular again, as a significant trend of name giving in the 1990s and the beginning of the 21st century. These names usually are those or their Fennicised forms that haven't been most common approximately a century earlier (fig 12). Moreover, trisyllabic names (*Aleksi, Matias*) and phonetically heavy bisyllabic names (*Niklas, Rasmus*) have become more popular than before as first given names. Also, rather uncommon and unique names have strongly gained popularity even if they are not naturally visible in lists of common given names.

Kiviniemi's studies reveal that the most common Finnish given names have not had a reform as quickly as it would have been expected in the last decades. After 1950, only ten names had been adopted in Finland which had been given to at least one thousand children. These names are *Janita, Jasmiina, Jessica, Oona, Pinja, Ronja; Jami, Miko, Miro* and *Nico*. New names indeed emerge in abundance all the time but the fact is that they most often end up being uncommon. New names continuously come into Finnish nomenclature by creating new Finnish names, by combining earlier names (compound names), by varying them (derivations and contaminations) and by choosing various spellings.

Name Day Tradition in Finland

The saints had an important position in medieval Catholic culture and their commemorative days were celebrated with great significance. At the time, the saint himself was commemorated, not a person named after him. A more secular name day tradition originated when celebrations were held in honour of significant men of German cities, held on the commemorative days of their patron saints. Thus, the person in question began to be perceived as the one being commemorated and not his patron saint. This celebration of name days soon spread throughout Germany amongst other groups of the population as well.

After the Reformation, both Catholics and Protestants in Germany celebrated name days. The situation however changed during the Counter-Reformation when the Catholic Church made the use of saints' names compulsory for all church members and firmly began to stress the celebration of name days. The Protestants, who rejected the "worshiping of saints" in the Catholic Church, began to celebrate their birthdays in place of name days. Thus, Central Europe was divided in two: the Catholics having a name day tradition and the Protestants having a birthday tradition.

The name day tradition was nevertheless able to reach Denmark through the German Protestants during the Reformation. The custom became standard in the upper class and in cities of Lutheran Sweden in the 17th and 18th centuries but it did not become established in the countryside until the 19th century. It first extended amongst the upper class and in the rural areas of south-western Finland. Name days began to be celebrated elsewhere in the country in the 19th century and the adoption of the tradition was supported by the Finnish name day calendar. The names in this calendar began to correspond rather well to true name giving of the population in the 19th century.

In the 19th century, Finnish name day customs included many traditions that are no longer in practice. These customs included, for example, a name day tree under which gifts were placed or name day dolls made as "spouses" for unmarried men and women. Name day celebrations also included waking up the honouree in the morning with song as well as arranging small coffee gatherings and dances. Sending out name day cards became commonplace in the beginning of the 20th century.

Nowadays, Finns celebrate name days mostly by giving small gifts, sending greeting cards or organising small coffee gatherings. Name day honourees are today also commemorated at the workplace and, in addition to this, name day information is regularly published in many forms of media. In addition to Finland, name days are commemorated as a non-Catholic celebration mostly in Sweden and, for example, in Latvia and the Czech Republic. Name days are still celebrated in Catholic and Orthodox cultures according to ecclesiastic tradition. This kind of celebration can actively be found, for example, in Catholic Poland and Orthodox Greece.

Finnish Surnames

Finnish surnames are made up of various name types both by background and structure. A majority of Finnish surnames are Finnish but there is also a great deal of Swedish names amongst them. There are also names of other nationalities which have been used in Finland over several generations.

Finnish people's surnames have also naturally become international over the last decades through multicultural marriages.

There are approximately 140,000 different surnames currently in the Finnish population as, for example, there were only 75,000 various surnames in 1970. The number of different surnames has thus nearly doubled in only a few decades. This increase can be explained by both international marriages and the strong rise in hyphenated names. In 2006, 72 per cent of married couples adopted the traditional practice of taking the husband's surname but only 7 per cent of marriages were such, where one of the spouses, usually the wife, had a hyphenated name included with their original surname. 20 per cent of married couples preserved their original surnames after marriage, which are mostly birth names of these couples.

In 1998, all of the 127,700 surnames used by Finnish citizens were approximately 40 per cent Finnish, in other words, structurally and phonetically Finnish or Fennicised names. Their bearers made up 77 per cent of the population. Non-Finnish names were 35 per cent and their name bearers made up 22 per cent of the population. Of all the names, 25 per cent were hyphenated but their name bearers made up only 0.6 per cent of the population – the largest part of these hyphenated names are unique or especially rare.

Finnish surnames can typologically be classified, according to their structure, into *root word*, *compound* and *derivational surnames*. Root word surname types includes various Finnish root words (*Koivu* 'birch', *Seppä* 'blacksmith') or are otherwise lexically single part names (*Pentti* ← *Benedictus*, *Rasi* ← *Erasmus*). They can also be young surname forms of a root word nature which have been consciously adopted as surnames (*Aarto*, *Lairo*). Out of all Finnish surnames, 18 per cent includes root word surname types and the percentage of their name bearers makes up 21 per cent of the bearers with a Finnish surname.

A majority of Finnish compound surname types are originally homested names (*Ruohomäki* 'grass' + 'hill', *Saarikoski* 'island' + 'rapids', *Yli-Niemi* 'upper cape'). A part of these also includes Eastern Finnish surnames (*Ikäheimo* 'age' + 'tribe') or specifically names created, that is, so-called adopted as surnames (*Lehmusvaara* 'lime' + 'hill'). This group also includes, for instance, old Southern Karelian names ending in *mies* ('man', *Ahomies* 'glade' + 'man', *Hietamies* 'fine sand' + 'man'), *Matinolli* ('Matti's' + 'Olli') type of surnames based on house names and surnames ending with *poika* ('son'). Compound surname types make up 42 per cent of Finnish surnames and the percentage of their name bearers makes up 17 per cent of the bearers with a Finnish surname, therefore making it the most common structural type of Finnish surname.

Finnish derivational surnames makes up 40 per cent of all Finnish surnames but their bearers make up to 62 per cent of those bearing a Finnish surname. Derivational surnames are thus, on average, clearly the most popular as compared to root word or compound type surnames. The most common of these surname derivations are (the percentages indicate all the surnames of the share of names):

la, lä	21 per cent
nen	9 per cent
mo, mö	2.1 per cent
io, iö	1.8 per cent
ma, mä	1.7 per cent
sto, stö	1.0 per cent

If we examine the popularity of derivational surnames amongst their name bearers, we can note that most Finns have names ending with *nen*: their bearers include up to 47 per cent of the population. Names ending with *la* or *lä* are the second with the most name bearers: 11 per cent.

The most common surnames in Finland in 2011 were:

Korhonen	23,573 people
Virtanen	23,436
Nieminen	21,350
Mäkinen	21,325
Mäkelä	19,580
Hämäläinen	19,284
Laine	18,902
Koskinen	17,943
Heikkinen	17,938
Järvinen	17,071

The most common Finnish surnames are largely represented by nature-themed name models, so called *Virtanen* and *Laine* types, adopted in the formation stage of the Finnish surname system. Of the aforementioned ten most common surnames, representatives of this name type include *Virtanen* ('current+NEN'), *Nieminen* ('cape+NEN'), *Mäkinen* ('hill+NEN'), *Koskinen* ('rapids+NEN'), *Heikkinen* ('Heikki+NEN'), *Järvinen* ('lake+NEN') and *Laine* ('wave'). There are two other surnames ending with *nen* in this list, *Korhonen* and *Hämäläinen* (see page 91 about *Häme*) which are older Savo names and one ending in *lä*, *Mäkelä* ('hill+LA').

Moreover, there are up to 36 names ending in *nen* on the list of the 50 most common surnames. This name type is thus quite marked for Finnish surnames. There are, however, only six names ending in *la* or *lä* on the list (in order of frequency) *Mäkelä*, *Heikkilä*, *Mattila*, *Ojala*, *Hakala* and *Anttila*. Other derivational names in this list are represented only by collective *sto* ending, *Koivisto* ('birch+STO'). There are seven root word name types: *Laine* ('wave'), *Niemi* ('cape'), *Salo* ('woods'), *Kallio* ('rock'), *Laakso* ('valley'), *Lehto* ('grove') and *Nurmi* ('lawn').

WHAT THE LAW SAYS ABOUT FINNS' NAMES

A child in Finland may not be given just any name. Name giving is regulated by law. The first First Names Act (*Etunimilaki*) came into force in the beginning of 1946. In 1985, it was merged with the Surnames Act

(*Sukunimilaki*) and in 1991, the new Names Act (*Nimilaki*) came into force. This law was last revised in 2005.

In the Names Act, it is decreed that a child must be provided with a given name after birth. There may be no more than three given names – a compound name is counted as one name. Given names must be entered in the Population Information System within two months of childbirth. Should the child be christened as a member of the Finnish Evangelical Lutheran Church or the Orthodox Church of Finland, his name can be registered with the local parish. Should the child not be christened, his name must be registered with the local register office of the area where the child resides.

According to the Names Act, a given name which is inappropriate or can otherwise cause an obvious disadvantage cannot be approved. Furthermore, the following types of names cannot be approved:

1. A name which is in form or spelling contrary to Finnish naming practices
2. A female name for a boy or a male name for a girl
3. A surname, unless it is a question of a name ending in *poika* ('son') or *tytär* ('daughter') based on the mother's or father's first name, used after another given name
4. A name which a sibling or step-sibling already has, however it can be used with another given name

A given name that does not fulfil these requirements, however, can be approved according to the Names Act:

1. for a religious reason
2. if the person on the basis of his nationality, family ties or other exceptional factor has a connection to a non-Finnish country and the given name corresponds to the naming practices complied with in the said country
3. if it is considered that there is some other well-founded reason for it

In practice, the Names Act allows for various interpretations and there have been flexible solutions to them. Should problems come up concerning suggested names, the local register offices can request the name board of the Ministry of Justice to provide a statement on them.

Every Finn has the right to change either one or more of his given names once in his lifetime by notification which is submitted to the managing body of the Population Register. Should a person have one or two given names, he can add other names as long as there are no more than three. The same person may discard any of his first names as long as there is at least one left. The order of given names can also be changed. Similarly, a hyphen can either be added to or removed from two names.

The Names Act protects existing surnames and aims at distinguishing given names and surnames from each other. The Names Act also sets spouses to an equal status when a surname is selected when getting married.

Thus, when a marriage takes place, either spouse may adopt the man's or woman's surname for a shared surname or either one can keep his or her own surname. At the same time, either spouse may assume a hyphenated name in which the first part is his or her own surname and the second part his or her spouse's surname. When getting married, spouses may also adopt a completely new, shared surname.

As for children, the Names Act requires that siblings are given the same surname and that the surname of child born both in marriages and cohabitations can be determined on the same bases. A child will always receive the parents' shared surname should they have such a name when the child is born. Should the parents not share the same surname, the parents may together agree on which surname will be given to the child. Should no name be submitted to the authorities or if paternity is not determined, the child shall receive the mother's surname.

Under the Names Act, the changing of a surname is possible. An acceptable reason for a name change is if the use of the surname has resulted in a disadvantage to the person, for example, due to its non-Finnish nature, meaning in standard language or frequency. One can adopt a name which he previously had or which has traditionally belonged to his ancestors for a new surname, should the name change otherwise be deemed appropriate. Moreover, other reasons, such as one's change in life circumstances, can influence the approval of a name change.

Not just any name can be approved as a new surname. The name may not be inappropriate or its use may not cause obvious disadvantage. Without a special reason, a name cannot be approved as a new surname which is:

1. in form or spelling contrary to Finnish naming practices
2. usually used as a given name
3. formed by combining two surnames

A surname which in Finland has been entered in the Population Register System or a name which is normally known to have been established as some Finnish or non-Finnish family's name cannot be approved as a new surname unless there is some special reason for it. Similarly, a name without any special reason cannot be approved as a new surname which coincides with:

1. the name of a foundation, organisation or other community
2. a registered firm name or trade mark or some other protected identifier used in trade
3. a commonly known artist name or pen name

Finnish Unofficial Anthroponymy

Unofficial Bynames in the Finnish Naming System
Various unofficial bynames, which are used together with or instead of a person's official name, have always been known to be included in the Finnish

anthroponymic system. These bynames have been the subject of many Master's theses from Finnish universities (e.g. Elonen 2004, Kiiski 1993, Kurki 1998, Lehtinen 2000, Mustonen 1997, Mäentaka 2001, Paalanen 1992, Pakarinen 1995, Seppälä 1999, Tuomela 2004, Vuola 2001).

At a time when the Finnish surname system was still particularly undeveloped and when first names were a part of the one-sided nomenclature of Christian origin, bynames were required for distinguishing people from each other in their community. In addition to a person's main name, various names with reference to a person's profession, residence, homestead, birth, appearance, character or event were used. If, for example, there were two Mattis in the same village, one could be called *Posti-Matti* ('postman Matti') and the other *Sahuri-Matti* ('Matti the sawyer'), according to these men's professions. These kinds of bynames have been preserved in Finnish folk culture in strict use even after the adoption of the surname system. Hence, a village cobbler may have been later called *Suutari-Niilo*, an aficionado of making distilled spirits *Pontikka-Topi*, sight impaired *Sokea-Jaakko*, nasal-voiced *Huna-Kalle* and a long-winded thinker *Tuuma-Kalle*.

A byname undoubtedly has other functions than the distinction of humans from each other and today, these other functions are the dominant theme in the giving of these names. The confirmation on a communal group spirit is considered an important function of unofficial bynames. The function of derogatory or *pejorative bynames* is to shut a person outside the community – or at least warn him of such a fate. Many names of ridicule even include messages to both the one who has received the name and other community members. They convey the norms and values of the community; that which the community approves of and that which it does not. Some names of ridicule are used when the person concerned is not present. The messages of these kinds of *behind-the-back nicknames* are geared towards the members of the community that hears the name, not the name bearer himself. (Elonen 2004.)

Unofficial bynames are generally also used to show affection between people. Examples of this include pet names for small children (*Anna → Annuliini* 'dear little Anna') and those between lovers (*Nöpönassu* 'snookums', *Mussukka* 'pookie'). A byname can also signify the role of someone in the community (*Pikku-Matti* 'little Matti' and *Iso-Matti* 'big Matti').

Unofficial bynames are often used for making a person's address and speaking about him easier. Additionally, the informality of the speech situation and the unofficial relationship of the user of the name and name bearer are emphasised with them. People's official names can often seem too long and naturally unnecessarily official in every day speech. It is easier and less complicated to wonder "just what is taking that *Pikke* so long" instead of "just what is taking that *Pirjo-Riitta Raatikainen* so long". Sometimes people's names also offer the opportunity to come up with word play and therefore make the practice of communal humour possible (*Myllymäki* 'mill' + 'hill' → *Pyllymäki, pylly* 'bottom, bum').

Unofficial bynames are formed in the Finnish naming system in many different ways. The basis of secondary bynames is people's official names, both given names and surnames. These bynames are formed from given names both by truncating and by different derivational suffixes. Names can be truncated by apheresis (*Marjatta* → *Jatta*), apocope (*Kalervo* → *Kale*) or syncope (*Marjatta* → *Matta*). There is an abundance of different derivations used in forming secondary bynames in Finnish. Typical Finnish derivational suffixes include *de* (*Tuija* → *Tuide*), *is* (*Jukka* → *Jukkis*), *kkA* (*Eino* → *Eikka*), *llU* (*Elina* → *Ellu*), *ppA* (*Timo* → *Timppa*), *sA* (*Tapio* → *Tapsa*), *skA* (*Reino* → *Reiska*), *skU* (*Anne* → *Ansku*) and *ttU* (*Sanna* → *Santtu*). These kinds of hypocoristic forms sometimes become established in official anthroponymy. Hence, for example, *Sami*, *Samu* and *Samppa*, all of which are based on the names *Samuel* and *Samuli*, may be given in the 21st century as official given names.

Moreover, secondary bynames can be formed from surnames by truncating (*Mahlamäki* → *Mahla*, *Näätänen* → *Näätä*) and derivation (*Mäenpää* → *Mäikkä*, *Ketola* → *Ketsu*, *Pokela* → *Poksu*). A name made up of a combination of letters can also be formed from compound names (*Jukka-Pekka* → *Jiipee* [ji: pɛ:]). Sometimes, bynames containing quite new, appellatival expressions can be created from given names and surnames (*Hernesniemi* 'pea' + 'cape' → *Herneaivo* 'pea brain'). These types of names can often be formed on the basis of alliteration (*Noora* → *Norppa* 'ringed seal', *Teemu* → *Temppeli* 'temple'). Secondary bynames can also be formed by rhyming (*Samuli* → *Hemuli* 'Hemulen', a character from the Moomin books, *Ville* → *Ville-Valle*, *Viljanen* → *Hiljanen-Viljanen* 'silent Viljanen') or by some other kind of adaptation (*Laura Kaarina* → *Kaura Laarina* 'like an oat grain bin'). Sometimes, associations that are related to them can be connected to names (*Hannu* → *Hannu Hanhi* 'Gladstone Gander' from Disney comic books and cartoons). A person's byname is often formed from his official name and a descriptive specific part associated with it (*Erä-Jorma* 'Jorma the outdoorsman', *Jousijalka-Ville* 'bowlegged Ville').

Bynames can also be formed independently, that is, in other ways than on the basis of a person's official name. These kinds of names are called primary bynames. The foundation of a primary byname can be, for example, a person's profession (refrigeration engineer: *Lumiukko* 'snowman', product manager: *Intiaanipäällikkö* 'Indian chief'), appearance (*Gandhi*, *Paatintappi* 'boat plug' for a short person), character (*Hönö* 'ditzy, spacey', *Rautarouva* 'iron lady'), behaviour (one who drinks a lot of water: *Kameli* 'camel', one who sings to oneself: *Kävelevä jukeboxi* 'walking jukebox'), speech (*Aikauheeta* for one who constantly says *ai kauheeta* 'how terrible', *Palohälytin* 'fire alarm' for one who has a high pitched voice) or something that the person has done or has happened to him (a man who moved the boundary stone in a dispute with his neighbour: *Kivenpyörittäjä* 'stone roller').

According to their use, unofficial bynames can be classified into private, semi-public and public names. *Private bynames* often include bilateral *reciprocity names*. These kinds of names come about in situations where two friends, siblings, lovers or workmates, who are often in some kind of bantering relationship, begin to call each other by their own nicknames. Moreover, bynames used in family circles are naturally private, in other words, mostly names known in one's own family. Similarly, behind-the-back nicknames can be used by one or two people: for example, a couple may call their neighbour by a name only they know (*Menninkäinen* 'goblin', *Tangokuningas* 'tango king'). Semi-public bynames include names usually used in some community of speakers outside a family, such as at school or the workplace. Public bynames are those which are used in at least two communities of speakers, for example at home, in a group a friends or at the workplace. (Elonen 2004.)

When forming unofficial bynames, it is important that the community approves the name. The approving party is just as significant as the name giver because the approval of the community is a necessary requirement for the fact that the byname must be a part of the community's language use. The principles of naming are always chosen on the basis of an existing nomenclature so that the new names do not differentiate too much from the old names. Hence, giving bynames is more of a choice regulated by the system than complete creative action by the name giver. On the other hand, spontaneity is typical for the formation of bynames: a new name often emerges as if by itself but not without discretion at all. An opinion of the one receiving the name usually does not get heard in the naming nor is there a possibility to change the name by otherwise changing the attitudes of the community.

Bynames of Small Children and Schoolchildren

Children in Finland are given their official name within two months of birth. However, children are often called by different nicknames before this – many times during expectancy. These kinds of names, that is, *foetal* and *newborn nicknames* given to babies before an official name is given, have been studied by Pakarinen (1995).

According to Pakarinen, a majority of foetal and newborn nicknames (61 per cent) are based on other names. Many of these are names which may be given as official names (*Sylvia Santra Kyllikki, Gilbert*) or names which appear in the Finnish naming system as surnames (*Jäppinen, Pöntinen*). Sometimes they refer to a real or fictional role model (singer *Katri Helena*, comic book character *Asterix*). Many foetal nicknames include both male and female names when the sex of the baby is not known (*Hintriikka-Aleksanteri, Milla-Kalle*). These names can also be based on an official name's hypocoristic form (*Emppu* ← *Emilia*, *Valtsu* ← *Valtteri*). They often also include some additional qualifier (*Hoppu-Henkka* 'busy Henkka', *Taavi-vaavi* 'Taavi baby').

Other foetal and newborn nicknames are mostly names based on different appellatives. Many of these are semantically associated with the child (*Mukula* 'kid', *Jälkikasvu* 'offspring'), the child's gender (*Peikkotyttö* 'goblin girl', *Hymypoika* 'smiling boy') or animals or plants (*Omppu* 'apple', *Sittiäinen* 'dorbeetle'). Some of them can be appellatival metaphoric names (*Kultahippu* 'golden nugget', *Moottori* 'motor, engine').

These foetal and newborn nicknames are most often given by the mother and father together (40 per cent) or either the mother (23 per cent) or the father (17 per cent). The name can also be given by some other relative such as the baby's sibling or grandparent. These nicknames given by fathers include, for example, *Juho Kusti*, *Wayne* and *Örvelö*, the ones by mothers include *Hyyryläinen* 'tenant, lodger', *Kirppu-Erkki* 'Erkki the flea'and *Tiitinen*. Names given by siblings include *Mansikka* ('strawberry') as well as *Pikkukisko* (← *pikkusisko* 'little sister') and *Totitonttu* (← *Kotitonttu* 'house gnome') which are formed by children who are learning to speak. Sometimes, the baby can have two nicknames (*Muumipeikko* 'Moomintroll' and *Niiskuneiti* 'Snork Maiden', *Ryysymaria* 'rag Maria' and *Riepupetteri* 'rag Petteri'). Different versions of names can also be used in speech (*Elmeri* and *Emppu*, *Katkarapu* 'shrimp' and *Katkis*). Every tenth foetal and newborn nickname has an effect on the baby's official name, either directly or indirectly (*Pikku Heidi* 'little Heidi' → *Heidi Sofia*, *Aku* 'Donald Duck' → *Iines* 'Daisy Duck').

Nicknames of small children, which are used in addition to their official names both in family and day care, are often pet names or *nursery nicknames*. Vuola (2001), for instance, has examined these types of names. These kinds of terms of endearment are usually based on the child's official name which is varied with different suffixes (*Iida* → *Iidukka*, *Emma* → *Emmukainen*, *Emilia* → *Emppuli*, *Helmi* → *Helmiliini*, *Nelli* → *Nelppu* → *Nelppunen*, *Valtteri* → *Valtsu*). These nicknames can also be based on rhyming (*Enni* → *Enninkäinen-Menninkäinen* 'goblin', *Tommi* → *Tommi-Pommi* 'Tom the bomb'), a form of children's language (*Petteri* → *Peppe*, *Riikka* → *Tiitta*) or some other phonologic adaptation (*Hanna* → *Nanna*). Many different root names have often led to similar forms that can be both girls' and boys' names (*Jonttu* ← *Johanna*, *Jonna*; *Johannes*, *Joni* or *Vilkku* ← *Ville*; *Vilma*). In addition to this, nicknames that are formed like surnames can be derived from first names (*Linda* → *Lindeman*, *Eerik* → *Eerikson*).

Sometimes, children's call names are shorter than their root name (*Emilia* → *Emppu*, *Oskari* → *Osku*), and sometimes clearly longer (*Jere* → *Jeruska*, *Saana* → *Saanukka*). Sometimes an original root form of a child's official name can be used as a term of endearment (*Tea* → *Dorotea*, *Timo* → *Timoteus*). It is clear that attempts are not made to make pronunciation easier with these kinds of forms but rather it is a question of play with the names or being affectionate with them. Small children's two-part names are often shortened both in the family and day care to single part names because of the fact that it would be easier for addressing the children (*Kalle-Matti* → *Kalle*, *Suvihelena* → *Suvi*).

Children's nicknames may also be based on different associations relating to the name (*Jere* → *Jere Jellona*, *jellona* 'lion', *Samuli* → *Setä Samuli* 'Uncle Sam', *Tommi* → *Tommi Taapermanni* → 'Tommi Tabermann', a Finnish poet). They can also be descriptive and refer to the child's appearance (*Rääpäle* 'runt', *Pätkis* 'shorty'), character (*Prinsessa Ruusunen* 'Sleeping Beauty', *Jekku* 'practical joke') or habit or pastime (*Balleriikka*, *Ronaldo*). In a family circle, parents often give their children different bantering names such as *Maisteri Laaksonen* ('Master Laaksonen') for a precocious little boy. A child can also be bantered by using a name form of the other gender that resembles his or her name (*Maria* → *Markku*, *Riikka* → *Riku*).

Unofficial bynames of Finnish schoolchildren have been examined by, for example, Mustonen (1997). These bynames are typically formed from given names with *slang derivational suffixes*, including *Ari* (*Outi* → *Outskari*), *is* (*Mikko* → *Mikkis*), *ke* (*Riikka* → *Rike*), *kkA* (*Henri* → *Henkka*), *kki* (*Jarno* → *Jarkki*), *kkU* (*Sarianna* → *Sarkku*), *ksA* (*Leo* → *Leksa*), *ksU* (*Riikka* → *Riksu*), *kU* (*Johanna* → *Johku*), *nde* (*Lotta* → *Londe*), *pe* (*Sirpa* → *Sipe*), *ppU* (*Teemu* → *Temppu*), *psU* (*Eveliina* → *Epsu*), *sA* (*Riku* → *Riksa*), *skA* (*Maria* → *Marska*), *skU* (*Annika* → *Ansku*), *ssU* (*Johanna* → *Jossu*), *tsU* (*Jere* → *Jertsu*), *ttU* (*Saana* → *Santtu*) and *U* (*Henri* → *Henu*). Similar names in slang form are also formed on the basis of surnames, such as *Hakkarainen* → *Hakkis*, *Honkimaa* → *Honkkari*, *Kuittinen* → *Kuide*, *Pirinen* → *Piksa*, *Romppanen* → *Ropi*, *Silvennoinen* → *Sile* and *Vatanen* → *Vatsku*.

Unofficial names of schoolchildren are often truncated forms of their official names. Finnish given names can be shortened by apheresis (*Eveliina* → *Liina*), apocope (*Eveliina* → *Eve*) or syncope (*Eveliina* → *Eliina*). Similarly, compound names are often truncated to single part names at school (*Sanna-Leena* → *Sanna*, *Lauri-Jaakko* → *Lauri*). In addition to this, surnames can be truncated (*Holopainen* → *Holo*, *Sutinen* → *Suti*). The use of different slang forms and truncating for forming bynames is explained by both the ease of addressing and the trendiness associated with these kinds of name types. Unofficial bynames are a part of the current youthful trends and that is why their structural types vary in the ways of other fashionable phenomena.

Schoolchildren's bynames may also be appellatival adaptations of given names and surnames based on various associations (first names *Juuso* → *Juusto* 'cheese', *Maria* → *Marsu* 'guinea pig', *Mirva* → *Kirva* 'aphid'; surnames *Häikiö* → *Häiriö* 'disorder', *Leskinen* → *Läskinen* 'fatty', *Raekorpi* hail|woods → *Raejuusto* 'cottage cheese'). In most cases, schoolchildren's appellatival bynames are primary by nature and refer to the person's appearance, character, manners or something that has happened to him. These kinds of names either directly or metaphorically describe their referent. For example, the nickname of a blonde, curly haired pupil can be *Karitsa* ('lamb') and a redhead *Porkkana* ('carrot'), a small-sized child may be *Hukkapätkä* ('short stick') and a fat child *Ihratynnyri* ('tub of lard'). A boy who investigates others may receive the name *Colombo* after the detective from the television series of the same name and a talkative girl may get the name *Hölöttäjä* ('blabberer'). A pupil who always says "Emmie ossaa" ("I can't do it") may get the byname *Emmieossaa*. A boy who likes to hunt may be known as *Hirvi* ('elk') and a girl who likes to go horseback riding may be known as *Polle* ('horsey'). Many bynames can be semantically pejorative, that is, abusive, such as *Tyttö-Teemu* (*tyttö* 'girl') for an effeminate boy named *Teemu* or *Yrjö-Kaisa* (*yrjö* 'vomit') for a girl named *Kaisa* who consumes a great deal of alcohol.

Many school-aged children and young people have several different bynames which are used in different contexts. For example, a girl named *Saana* may be called *Saanukka* at home, *Sande* at school and *Tiuhti* ('Thingumy', a character from the Moomin series) in scout camp. Scout names, which have been examined by Kiiski (1993), for example, are reminiscent of schoolchildren's bynames. They are often founded on slang derivations of given names and surnames (*Riina* → *Ride, Vänttinen* → *Väne*) or other forms based on official names (given names *Aarne* → *Arska* → *Turska* 'cod', *Henna* → *Hemuli* 'Hemulen' from the Moomin series, *Mika* → *Mökä* 'loud noise', *Milla* → *Magia* referring to Milla Magia 'Magica De Spell' from Disney comics and cartoons; surnames *Pulkkinen* → *Pulu* 'pigeon', *Ruotsalainen* 'Swede' → *Svedu* 'Swede'). Scout names can also be created in other ways than on the basis of the person's official name, for example, they can be given after role models (*Pikku Myy* 'Little My' from the Moomin series, *Ressu* 'Snoopy') or be created much like descriptive bynames (*Muikku* 'whitefish', *Pulina* 'gab').

BYNAMES OF TEACHERS AND OTHER PROFESSIONAL GROUPS
Bynames in the school world also include nicknames and names of ridicule given to teachers. Their name givers are children and young people but those receiving these names are adults, representatives of a certain professional group. A part of these names is generally known by both the teachers and their pupils but many of these, mainly the names of ridicule are known only by the pupils. These pejorative names are mostly used when the teacher in question is not present, thus they are behind-the-back nicknames. Sometimes, they can be used when the teacher is listening, should the student want to convey negative feelings towards the teacher or his subject. Finnish bynames given to teachers have been studied in theses in, for example, Hämeenlinna, Lammi, Virrat, Parkano, Kankaanpää and Turku. The following examples are mostly from those in Lammi (Lehtinen 2000).

Bynames given to teachers are often bluntly descriptive names. With these names, both negative feelings are expressed and the togetherness of students is strengthened, often through humour. Many bynames given to teachers depict their referent's character traits (*Hanhiemo* 'Mother Goose', *Miss Sunshine*, *Skitso* 'schizo', *Tiukkis* 'nitpicker', *Ääliö* 'moron') or behaviour (*Höpöhöpö* 'nonsense', *Puliukko* 'gutter drunk', *Tuhisija* 'snorter', *Unilääke* 'sleeping pill'). They often also refer to the teacher's appearance (*Kenokaula* 'goosander', *Merilehmä* 'dugong', *Pulloperse* 'bottle-ass', *Puuterinaama* 'powdered face', *Pätkä* 'shrimp, shorty') or dress (*Lederhose, Porno-Irma, Vyölaukkumies* 'fanny pack man'). Moreover, attention can be given to injuries and illnesses (*Mutanttisormi* 'mutant finger', *Veripää* 'blood head'). Subjects taught are seen in the same way in these names given to their teachers (biology: *Sammakko* 'frog', chemistry: *Koeputki* 'test tube', religion: *Hindu*, head teacher: *Apinoiden kuningas* 'king of the monkeys'). Bynames based on both given names (*Urho* → *Urkki*) and surnames (*Hämäläinen* → *Hämis*) are also used for some teachers.

Moreover, other professional groups have colourful practices in adopting nicknames and names of ridicule. These names come about especially in such working communities whose members take part in weekly or monthly trade with each other, such as sailors (Kurki 1998). Old sailors' bynames given in the early 20th century, typically include the person's official name or nickname. They often depict the person's profession (*Silli-Salminen* 'Atlantic herring Salminen'), character (*Hullu-Helmeri* 'crazy Helmeri', *Nuuka-Mäkiö* 'stingy Mäkiö'), appearance (*Isonyrkki-Viku* 'big-fisted Viku', *Kyttyrä-Pena* 'humpback Pena') or manners or pastime (*Henkseli-Heikki* 'suspenders Heikki', *Mandoliini-Matson* 'mandolin Matson'). Newer sailors' bynames given after the 1970s are often metaphoric and they typically do not include the name of the person in question. They also often refer to the person's profession (*Asfaltti-Auvinen* 'asphalt Auvinen'), character (*Vastaranta-Veijo* 'contrarian Veijo'), appearance (*Matti Muotitukka* 'Matti trendy hair') or manners or pastime (*Pieru-Laitinen* 'farty Laitinen'). Unofficial bynames of taxi drivers in Turku have been examined in the same way (Mäentaka 2001).

Moreover, other close working communities, the same as soldiers and prisoners, have similar types of bynames which are based both on people's official names and expressions descriptive of them. For example, the Savonlinna Opera Choir has colourful bynames which include both secondary and primary bynames (Paalanen 1992). Similarly, bynames of professional athletes working in team sports, such as Turun Palloseura (TPS) hockey players of the Finnish SM-liiga, have been studied (Seppälä 1999). What is interesting is that the bynames given by active fans of this team are quite different from the bynames used by the hockey players themselves. For example, amongst the players, Mikko Eloranta of TPS is known by the names *Kuli, Atte, Jarno, Kohno, Kulli, Määräilijä* ('dictator'), *Serve* and *Skrobot*. Fans, however, have given him such names as *Kuli, Mikke, Työmyyrä* ('eager beaver'), *Linda, Elo, Muuri* ('wall'), *Predator, Terrieri* ('terrier'), *Mikkis, Miksa, Eltsu, Isi* ('daddy'), *Luupää* ('bone head'), *Maalikunkku* ('goal king'), *Mela* ('prick, dick'), *Miki, Mikkie, Miku, Rantsu* and *Xena*. (The names in these lists are in order of frequency.) It is easy to note that these bynames are mostly based on the person's given name and surname and also descriptive of him in various ways. The name *Linda* is explained by the fact that Eloranta was dressed up like blonde violinist Linda Lampenius for his bachelor party. New names all the time emerge in the fan base on the basis of the players' behaviour in the game.

In addition to work communities, Finnish adults use bynames naturally given in the home, both by spouses and children, the same as in groups of friends or pastimes such as in choirs, hunting groups or various organisations. These bynames are often names descriptive of the person in many ways but mostly people in these leisure time groups are called by their given name or surname (*Riitta, Hietanen*) or a secondary byname based on their given name (*Ari → Arska, Riitta → Ritu*).

Naming Systems of Linguistic Minorities

Finland Swedish Personal Names

There are many different linguistic minorities in Finland whose anthroponymy differs quite much from that of the majority of the population. These include, for example, Finland Swedes, Sámi and Finland's sign language minority. Finland Swedes are the country's largest linguistic minority; they make up 5.5 per cent of the entire population. All in all, there are nearly 300,000 Swedish speakers with Swedish knowingly being one of Finland's two official languages. Marianne Blomqvist (1993, 2006), in particular, has studied the anthroponymy of the Swedish-speaking population of Finland.

It is known that Swedish-speaking settlement has been on the coasts of Finland since the Viking Age, but according to the latest studies, it has not been continuous. There was a clear break in this settlement, particularly in the 11th century, but a new group came to Finland from Sweden in the 12th century. The oldest Swedish population still bore Scandinavian names of the Viking Age, such as *Helga, Sigrid; Gudmund* or *Thorsten*. When the status of Christianity became established, the nomenclature became Christianised. Hence, the most popular names, for example, in 15th century Jakobstad, on the western coast of Finland, were *Jöns, Per, Oluf, Anders* and *Lasse*.

Finland Swedish name giving during Swedish rule mainly complied with the name giving trends of the mother country – the same as in Finnish-language name giving. For example, female names ending in *a* and *ina*, derived from male names, became standard in the 18th century (*Augusta, Fredrika; Albertina, Vilhelmina*). At the same time, dynasty names became popular and bearing two names became standard (*Ulrika Eleonora, Carl August*). In addition to Sweden, an influence from other European countries, especially France and Germany, was seen in Finland Swedish name giving.

Name giving of the Finnish and Swedish speaking population however began to differentiate from one another in the 19th century when Finns, who were inspired by nationalism, began to give their children Finnish names (*Aino, Saima; Armas, Väinö*) and the Swedish-speaking population favoured Scandinavian names (*Astrid, Ingrid; Gunnar, Sven*). The most common Finland Swedish female names between 1881 and 1981 included *Maria, Margareta, Elisabet, Linnea, Helena, Anna, Sofia, Elisabet, Ingeborg* and *Alice*. The most common male names were *Erik, Karl, Johan, Johannes, Mikael, Vilhelm, Anders, Henrik, Gunnar* and *Valdemar*.

In 2010, the popular given names (first given names) of Finland Swedish girls were *Amanda, Elin, Ida, Ella, Emma, Wilma, Saga, Agnes, Ellen* and *Olivia*. The top on the boys' list included *Oliver, Elias, Anton, William, Alex, Emil, Lucas, Liam, Alexander* and *Kevin*. Nowadays, there is quite a strong international influence in Finland Swedish nomenclature. More exotic names can be found in groups of given names such as *Chiara, Savannah, Zafira; Bruce, Demian* and *Lennon*.

Finland Swedes, for the most part, have Swedish surnames. We should however note that many fully Finnish-speaking families still have Swedish surnames – not all Finns got to Fennicise their surnames in the name changing campaign of the early 20th century. Some Swedish-speaking families preserved their Swedish surnames but decided to become Finnish-speaking. Thus, for example, roughly half of those named *Andersson* in Greater Helsinki are today Finnish-speaking. On the other hand, many Swedish speakers today have a Finnish surname (e.g. writers *Johannes Salminen* and *Henrik Tikkanen*). We therefore cannot make an assumption on a person's – or even their ancestor's – mother tongue on the basis of their surname.

Surnames of the Swedish-speaking population often emerged, much like the surnames of the Finnish-speaking population, on the basis of the merging of various byname systems. Behind these names include names of nobility (*af Hällström, Munsterhjelm*), intelligentsia (*Castrenius* → *Castrén, Wegelius*), bourgeoisie (*Borgström, Ekman*), soldiers (*Glad, Kullberg*), homesteads (*Bertils, Nygård*) and patronyms (*Johansson, Karlsson*). The most common Swedish surnames in Finland in 2003 included (in this order): *Johansson, Lindholm, Nyman, Karlsson, Lindström, Andersson, Eriksson, Lindroos, Lindqvist* and *Lindberg*.

Finland Swedes naturally use unofficial bynames as well, both secondary bynames derived from official names and primary names in many ways descriptive of the person. Bynames – or nicknames – derived from given names include, for example, *Annika* → *Anki, Gunilla* → *Nilla, Viveka* → *Vickan; Björn* 'bear' → *Nalle* 'teddy bear', *Per-Erik* → *Pärre* and *Stig* → *Stigo*. Bynames derived from surnames include *Chydenius* → *Kyssen, Nylund* → *Nylle* and *Träskman* → *Träskis*. Bynames descriptive of the person include, for example, *Lots-Erik* ('nautical pilot') and *Näsan* ('big nosed').

Sámi Personal Names

There are approximately 8,000 Sámis included in the population of Finland, nearly half of which reside in the Sámi areas of Northern Finland. The rest reside in different parts of the country, mostly in Greater Helsinki or in other larger cities. According to data collected in the Sámi districts, just under a half of Sámi people speak Sámi as their mother tongue whereas according to the Finnish Population Register Centre, it is less than one fourth. The difference here is due to the fact that registering a mother tongue has been the responsibility of the Sámi people. It has been possible to enter Sámi as a mother tongue since 1992. The 1991 Language Act (*Kielilaki*) allowed for Sámi name giving and obliged the authorities to adopt Sámi letters. The letters *á, đ, č, ŋ, š, ŧ* and *ž* were thus adopted in 1999. The Language Act reform entered into force at the beginning of 2004 and it safeguarded the rights of the Sámi people to maintain and develop their language and culture as well as use the Sámi language with the authorities.

The Sámi people of Finland have two different naming systems: there is a naming system which includes an official given name and surname which identifies the person in writing and the Sámi people's own naming system which identifies a person orally. In everyday conversation, Sámi people generally refer to one another with an expression in which a specific part precedes the person's first name that includes one of his parent's names as well as possibly a grandparent's name. This specific part can also refer to the person's residence, profession or spouse. For example, a person whose official name is *Elin Inga Ester Lukkari* may be known by the Sámi call name *Mákká Jovsset Elle*, that is, 'Elle of Jovsset of Mákká'. The given name in this traditional naming system is the person's main name and all the other ones are bynames. The system does not know actual surnames but some families have their own terms which are used like other bynames, for example *Biennáš*, *Bihtoš* and *Vulleš*. There are both Sámi and Finnish names in the official surname stock of the Sámi people. Typical names include, for example, *Aikio*, *Magga*, *Näkkäläjärvi* and *Valkeapää*.

A majority of Sámi official given names include foreign names either in the form of other languages or adapted to Sámi. Moreover, mother tongue names have somewhat been used. In 1997, the University Name Day Almanac (*Yliopiston nimipäiväalmanakka*, almanakka.helsinki.fi/english.html) was published which, for the fist time, included a name day calendar of Sámi names collected by Pekka Sammallahti. There are 564 names in this calendar, 60 per cent being male names and 40 per cent female names. A majority of the names in this calendar are foreign names adapted to Sámi but there are also traditional Sámi names from folk tales amongst them. Male names such as *Ahkemiella*, *Beahkká*, *Duoŋgi*, *Mielat* and *Sárrajuoksa* and female names such as *Álehttá*, *Gáhteriinná*, *Hilbmá*, *Sivnne* and *Vuohkku* can be found in this calendar.

In name giving, the Sámi people have traditionally favoured names found in family circles. The use of Sámi names became standardised in the 21st century, for example, nearly half of Sámi children born in 2002 received a mother tongue name. It is understandable that the confirmation of a Sámi identity is desired with Sámi-language names.

Between 1990 and 2002, the most common names given to Sámi children were nearly without exception Finnish. All the names of girls in the list of popular names were (in this order) *Maria*, *Kristiina*, *Sunna*, *Maarit*, *Inka*, *Laura*, *Pauliina*, *Anni*, *Elina* and *Elli*. Popular boys' names were *Matias*, *Aslak*, *Johannes*, *Mikael*, *Antti*, *Jere*, *Johan*, *Juhani*, *Oskari* and *Petteri*. Some of the most popular girls' first given names were *Sunna*, *Inka*, *Laura* and *Maria* and those of boys were *Jere*, *Áilu*, *Johan* and *Matias*. Of these male names, *Áilu* (*Áillohaš*) was artist Nils-Aslak Valkeapää's Sámi name.

Personal Names in Sign Language
There are also personal names in Finnish anthroponymy used by sign language users. There are approximately 5,000 deaf people included in this language group as well as their close friends and relatives, together roughly 10,000 people. Sign language today has an officially recognised standing as one of Finland's linguistic minorities.

A signed name is usually associated with a child along with christening. It may have been given to an infant during his first days of life or even before birth. In addition to this, the child will receive a given name and surname as required by Finnish law after birth. Finnish deaf people previously have not received a signed name until going to school; the name givers were mostly other deaf pupils. Many deaf people have not learned sign language until school because only approximately one tenth of deaf children have deaf parents.

Giving signed names at home started to increase in the 1980s, the same as the child's education in sign language became standard. The fact that deaf parents more often give names of their own language to both their deaf and non-deaf children than before is evoked by the boosting of sign language users' self-esteem. A mother tongue name is regarded as a primary symbol of belonging to this language group; it socialises the individual in his community.

Names in sign language are produced in the same way as other language elements, in other words, by hand, body and mimicry, but without sound. A large part of Finnish sign language names, approximately 70 per cent, is descriptive, that is, depictive of its bearer. These names are usually based on the appearance or typical behaviour of the name bearer. If there is, for example, a scar on a person's neck, his signed name can be *Forefinger grazing the neck twice*. A person with a crooked nose can be *Forefinger and middle finger pressing straight against the tip of the nose* and someone who constantly squints his eyes can be *Forefinger making small circles on the cheekbone*. Many names are contextually pejorative and these are especially given in school. Names given to children by the parents are however more appealing. They often reflect the parents' wishes or include references to previous deaf generations.

Personal names in sign language are often clearly different from other signed words. Approximately two thirds of personal name signs are produced, for example, in the face which, as a signing area of the body, includes only one fourth of other parts of the lexicon. As the articulation place of other parts of sign language, the common, non-domineering hand appears four times less common in nomenclature. Moreover, personal names are nearly 90 per cent one handed as under half of other signs are produced with one hand. Signed names are often quite prototypical and they clearly are included amongst names, in the same way, as for example, *Liisa* or *Matti* are recognised as personal names in Finnish.

Names in sign language can also be based on a person's official given name or surname. For example, a woman with the name *Marja* (*marja* 'berry') may be named 'berry' in sign language or a person whose surname is *Jokela* ('river+LA') or *Jokinen* ('river+NEN') may be given a signed name meaning 'river'. The propriality of a translated name is signified with a special element produced by the lips. These names are especially given to those people outside of the sign language community. When there is no semantically close sign available, a person's official name may be produced by fingerspelling. Names produced in this way are left marginal due to an alien spelling: they are only used if there is no other alternative.

Päivi Rainò (2004), who in her dissertation has studied personal names in sign language, has noted that Finnish signed names are in a state of change from descriptive expressions to more abstract signs which function as identifying etiquettes only. At the same time, there is a shift from unique names to polyreferential names in this naming system: more and more names thus have many bearers. Hence, a certain kind of onomasticon from signs applicable as names is being formed in the language.

5. Animal Names

In this chapter, the reader will be provided with a general overview of how animals are perceived to comprehend language and, above all, names. It covers how names are structurally and officially given to cats, dogs, cattle and horses in Finland as well as explores the unofficial name variants of these animals.

Do Animals Use Names?

Are humans, *homo sapiens*, the only species that use proper nouns, that is, proper names? Scholars have attempted to answer this question in several ways. It seems that many animal species have at least learned names used by humans. For example, a dog will recognise its own name given by its owner and is able to come to the place when it is called by that name. Simultaneously, a dog is able to recognise other names of animals and people as well as places by human speech. A dog may, for example, know where it is going when its owner says "Come on! Let's go to Central Park!"

Moreover, we believe that animals in a close relationship with other people can recognise names. In the past, for example, cattle in Finland were called home from the pastures on a summer evening by shouting out each name of the cow and the calling expression *ptrui*. Cows have responded by mooing and trotting off towards the caller after the bellwether.

The opinions on the linguistic abilities of domestic animals vary and there has been much consideration on what the "understanding" of names ultimately means in the case of different species. Is it truly a question of the fact that an animal understands a name as a linguistic expression with reference to an individual or does it just learn to recognise its master's voice and react to it in an expected way? Although familiar domestic animals even understand names on some level, they are not known to create names or use them in their mutual communication.

Linguists and biologists have also studied the cognitive and linguistic capabilities of apes, mostly chimpanzees. Since speech formation is physiologically impossible for these animals, attempts have been made to teach them different kinds of sign and symbolic languages. A keyboard with images or plastic arbitrary symbols corresponding to different words connected to a computer-controlled speech synthesiser has been used as an aide for this. With these aides, chimpanzees have learned to construct simple sentences, creative questions and even convey something about what has happened in the past. However, their comprehension of human speech has remained quite limited.

In some studies, chimpanzees have learned sign language. For example, in the 1960s, the chimpanzee named Washoe learned to form rather complex signed sentences such as "Please give me that hot smoke" when she wanted a cigarette. Chimpanzees have also invented new signs and learned to teach them to each other. In addition to this, they have also learned to use signed names, both their own and the names of others. The sign language of a gorilla by the name of *Koko* was examined in an American study in the 1970s. Koko was reported to have learned approximately 600 signs during the study, out of which several were names. Koko herself named a few humans and animals that were important to her by her own initiative. For example, she had given a man named *Al* a signed name meaning 'leg' and a small kitten a name meaning 'lips'. (Patterson & Linden 1986.)

Moreover, studies carried out amongst dolphins have produced interesting results. According to researchers (Janik et al 2006) at the University of St Andrews in Scotland, bottlenose dolphins give themselves "individual names" and use them systematically in communication with other dolphins. The use of these kinds of referential expressions is necessary in circumstances in which dolphins do not see each other but want to tell each other where they are. According to the study, it is not a question of the fact that dolphins would only recognise the sounds of different individuals and distinguish them from each other but instead, dolphins' "names" are based on conscious changes of the frequency of sound. The identifying expression a dolphin gives itself may be, for example, a whistling type of sound *wee-o-wee-o-wee-o-wee*. The researchers presume that young dolphins first learn the names of others in the pod and then create names to differentiate themselves from the others.

The individual names of dolphins are thus amazingly reminiscent of human personal names. These names are formed by modulating sounds in various ways. In the same way as humans understand the name *John* or *Peter* as utterances of different people, dolphins also understand each other's names, according to this study, even when they are produced by dolphins others than the name bearer. We can assume that this type of research will continue in different parts of the world and may produce new and interesting results.

In addition to biologists and linguists that have studied the linguistic abilities of animals, onomasticians have also taken an interest in the names of animals. However, the subjects of investigation have usually been names which humans have given to various animal spices, not so much the recognition and use of names linked to the linguistic capabilities of animals. Some onomasticians have shown enthusiasm in investigating the taxonomic terms of different species such as, for example, the "names" of birds (*yellow wagtail, snowy owl*). However, these names have not been considered names in Finnish onomastics (*keltavästäräkki, tunturipöllö*) but rather seen as terms because they classify, not identify, their referents.

As it has been stated in chapter 4, names of animals cannot be considered personal names in Finnish onomastics because they do not refer to people or human-like beings. Instead, animal names form their own name category in the same way as personal names, place names and commercial names. Similarly as with personal names, animal names can be categorised into official and unofficial names. For example, a pedigree cat or dog usually has both official registered names and unofficial call names differing from them, and sometimes even numerous terms of endearment or names of ridicule based on them. Not all animal species, which have been given names by humans, have these types of official and unofficial names. Instead, only one call name might be used.

Humans have traditionally given names to animals with which they have some sort of personal relationship, either financially or emotionally. These are domestic animals that live in close interaction with humans such as cats, dogs, cows and horses, and sometimes even sheep, pigs, roosters, hens and other animals included in agriculture. The smaller the group of animals is, the more likely each one will be named. Thus, sheep will easily get names on a farm should there only be a few, whereas those of a heard of a few hundred will not usually be named. The decisive factor to this is, as in other types of naming, the reason they are needed: such an animal will get a name when there is a need to speak of it as an individual. There is usually a situation behind the official naming of animals in which the utilisation of the animal requires different registration, for example, for farming (animal husbandry, dairy production) or competition (harness racing, cat and dog shows).

There has been a great deal of Master's theses carried out at various Finnish universities on the names of animals. Subject of investigation have been cat, dog, cattle and horse names. Marianne Blomqvist (2011) has also published a book on the names of domestic animals, used by Swedish-speaking Finns over the centuries. In addition, Minna Saarelma (2011, 2012) has written popular books on dog and cat names, which also include the official name day calendars for these animals for 2012, published by the Almanac Office at the University of Helsinki. Moreover, one Finnish dissertation has been written on horse names (Kalske 2005).

Cat and Dog Names

People living in the urban environment have mainly given names to their pets such as cats, dogs, guinea pigs, mice, parakeets, parrots and turtles – even snakes and rats. Names given to pets are reminiscent, in many respects, of people's nicknames: by nature, they are almost without exception affectionate or, at the least, casual names. They also have features which make them typical for certain species.

Finnish Master's theses on cat names (Keinänen 2009, Laine 1997, Sarkkinen 1997) have clearly highlighted the fact that these names are often onomatopoetic and refer to a cat's meowing, purring, hissing or growling. They typically begin with an *M*, usually contain the phonemes [i], [r] and [s] and are also usually short. The most popular syllabic types are CVCCV (*Misse, Mörri, Sissi*) and CVCV (*Mökö, Nöpö*). Moreover, different Finnish terms referring to cats (for example meaning 'kitty' and 'pussy') such as *katti, killi, kissi, miiru, mirri, kisu, kis-kis* and *kolli*, can be seen in cat names (*Katti-Matti, Kisuliini, Miirulainen*). The names can also describe the animal's appearance (*Pörrö* 'fluffy', *Söpö* 'cute', *Tuhkis* 'ashen', *Viiru* 'stripped'), character or behaviour (*Lady, Nössö* 'sissy', *Vinku* 'whine') or position in the family or litter (*Junnu* 'junior', *Peipi* 'baby', *Sisko* 'sister'). Sometimes they refer to some event that has happened to the cat (one that was found: *Mooses* 'Moses').

Nearly half of cat names, however, are commonly known Finnish personal names, both first names (*Elvis, Otto, Veera*) and surnames (*Lipponen, Möttönen, Tossavainen*). This tells us that pets are seen as human beings and that is why people wish to personify them with names. These names often refer to familiar public figures (*Jasseri* ← *Arafat, Picasso*) or fictive role models (*Asterix, Hamlet*). Many cats also have other kinds of terms of affection or names of ridicule based on call names (*Manta → Mantukka, Tasmanian tuholainen* 'Tasmanian devil'). A majority of cat names are unique but approximately every tenth can have a name which is reasonably common for Finnish cats. Sometimes, the same cat names of a litter are associated with one another either phonetically or contextually and form a kind of naming system (*Aatu, Eetu* and *Iita*; *Hewey, Dewey* and *Lewey*).

The naming of pedigree cats however follows specific name formation rules. The official name of pedigree cats includes a *cattery name* in the genitive (ending in *n* in Finnish) and the cat's own name (*Karvatassun Jooseppi* 'hairy|paw+GEN Jooseppi'). In addition, these cats usually have an unofficial call name as well which is often based on their official name (*Amaryllis → Ami, Daidalos → Daidu, Narcissus → Narsku*).

Dog names – both purebreds and mixed breeds – have been studied in theses by, for example, Anttila (1993), Lehman (2010), Tuomisto (1992) and Vaattovaara (1996). Purebred dogs in Finland have an official *registered name* which includes a *kennel name* and the animal's own name (*Swordmaker's Elegant White*). Names of kennels are registered names under international protection. They are company names which must be sellable and attractive to the breeders. Names of kennels must be no more than 15 characters long and they often refer to the country which the breed of dog is from (Saluki: *El Hamrah*, Siberian husky: *Nunivak*). Today, a majority of names of kennels are in English (*Fidelity, Foxruns, Luminous*), with Finnish names clearly in the minority (in the genitive, *Aijanpihan* 'Aija+GEN|yard+GEN', *Haukkukallion* 'bark|rock+GEN', *Rapatassun* 'dirt|paw+GEN').

Puppies in kennels are often systematically named, for example, by a name beginning with the same letter or the same name associated with a similar theme (flowers, gems). Call names of pedigree dogs are often formed on the basis of this official name (*Cassandra → Kassu, Fuji San Lord Jasu*

Maro → Jasu, Nobleman → Noba). However, mixed breed dogs only have a call name and possibly, in addition to this, various nicknames.

It is typical of Finnish dog names that they are formed with different derivational suffixes such as *ki* (*Niki, Piki*), *kke* (*Jakke, Vikke*), *kkU* (*Jekku, Haukku*), *lla* (*Bella, Stella*), *ppe* (*Jeppe, Puppe*) or *ssU* (*Ressu, Tessu*). The name must be short and easy to pronounce so that it functions in calling the dog. Dog names can also describe the animal's appearance (*Jellona* 'lion', *Laku* 'liquorice', *Tiny*), character or behaviour (confident: *Brasse*, vivacious: *Vili*) or refer to its breed (Samoyed *Sami*, terrier *Terri*) or some event (born during a blizzard: *Tuisku* a Finnish personal name also meaning 'blowing snow'). Dogs are also often named after familiar public figures (*Kofi* ← *Kofi Annan, Senna* ← *Ayrton Senna*), fictive characters (*Rin Tin Tin, Ransu* a dog puppet on the Finnish children's television series Pikku Kakkonen) or other role models. Many Finnish dog owners today can find a name for their pet in dog name day calendars sold in book stores. The name lists for these calendars, as well as for those for cats and horses, have been collected by Marianne Blomqvist and Minna Saarelma. The Almanac Office of the University of Helsinki owns the copyright to these calendars.

Dogs are often also given nicknames based on their call names (*Dinah → Dinsku, Piki* 'pitch (from tar)' → *Pikipoika* 'pitch boy'). Moreover, other terms of endearment and names of ridicule are commonly used (*Höpönassu* 'pookie', *Punkero* 'fatty', *Täystuho* 'total destruction').

Cattle Names

Finnish cattle names have been studied in theses by, for example, Vatanen (1993) and Viitala (1995). The topic has also been published in the book *Ystävä, Hyvä ja Äpyli – nämäkin lehmännimiä* (1997) and also the name day calendar for cows *Navetan nimipäivät* (Blomqvist & Vuorinen 1996) – Finnish name day culture thrives strong amongst cows in Finland.

Cows have been significantly beneficial in Finnish agriculture and they may have been given names for as long as they have been considered domestic animals. The oldest known *cattle names* are from the Late Proto-Finnic period. Because of this, some similar cattle names are known in Finland and Estonia such as Finnish *Hellikki* and Estonian *Hellik*. The earliest written entries of cattle names are from the 18th century (*Mielicki, Tähiki*).

Traditional Finnish cattle names often describe the animal's appearance (*Kaunike* 'beautiful+KE', *Kirjo* 'speckled', *Punikki* 'red+KKI'), character or behaviour (*Herukki* 'trickling+KKI', *Lypsikki* 'milking+KKI') or time of birth (Whitsunday or *helluntai* in Finnish: *Heluna, Talvikki* 'winter+KKI'). Moreover, nature names have been popular for cows (*Kukka* 'flower', *Orvokki* 'violet'). Names ending in diminutive *kki* (*Mansikki* 'strawberry+KKI', *Muurikki* 'cloudberry+KKI') have especially been common and often considered prototypical for Finnish cattle names.

Since the 1950s, cattle control guidelines (1957) have strongly had an influence on the names of cows. These guidelines require milking cows to have names. The recommendation is that calves born in a certain year are always given names beginning with the same letter. The names are given to calves when they are one to two months old when they are registered. However, name giving at farms that are not included in this cattle control is freer.

The recommendation of having the same letter starting these names has led to the fact that many current cattle names are contextually meaningless (*Amuli, Hissa, Illa, Juula, Lollo, Roppi, Ylä, Ämmy, Örri*). On the other hand, descriptive names that characterise the cow are also still given (appearance: *Lumikki* 'snow+KKI': 'Snow White', *Soma* 'pretty', behaviour: *Tomera* 'energetic', *Vilkas* 'vivacious'). The names often are also connected to nature (flowers: *Kielo* 'lily-of-the-valley', *Leinikki* 'buttercup', fruits and berries: *Omena* 'apple', *Puolukka* 'lingonberry', other plants: *Papu* 'bean', *Tilli* 'dill', animals: *Leivo* 'lark', *Uikku* 'grebe', natural phenomena: *Usva* 'mist, fog', *Viima* 'strong, cold wind'). Many of the names are abstract (*Haave* 'dream, wish', *Yllätys* 'surprise') and often contextually positive (*Ilo* 'joy', *Lysti* 'happy'). The names can also refer to, for example, sounds (*Kuiske* 'whispering', *Suhina* 'rustling') or mythological beings (*Keiju* 'faerie', *Onnetar* 'Lady Luck').

Sometimes, cattle names are associated with common food and drink (*Puuro* 'porridge', *Rusina* 'raisin') or brand names and various goods (*Eloveena* based on the Elovena brand of Finnish oat products, *Lelu* 'toy'). Common female names and nicknames (*Jaana, Kikka, Pipsa, Sohvi*) are rather common, the same as various human terms (*Pimu* 'chick (young woman)', *Suttura* 'hooker', *Tuttava* 'acquaintance'). Nowadays, cows are often named after public figures; these names are found both on television and other media (*Melina, Pamela, Samantha*). Moreover, names ending in *kki* are popular (*Emmikki, Maarikki*), the same as names ending in *kka* or *kkä* (*Leijukka, Unnukka*) and *na* or *nä* (*Ipana, Rosina*).

All in all, cows in Finland are hence given names of other proper names and appellatives appearing in language as well as meaningless *quasi names*. In studies, name givers often emphasise that the cattle name must be appealing, light and soft sounding, thus "cow-like".

Horse Names

There has been one dissertation written about the nomenclature of horses in Finland: *Suomessa syntyneiden hevosten nimistö* by Marja Kalske (2005). In addition to this, Finnish horse names have been studied in theses by, for example, Honkanen (2001), Kuukasjärvi (1997), Partanen (2000) and Villikka (1997).

Nearly every homestead in Finland once had its own horse. Traditional *horse names* generally depicted the animal's appearance, especially its colour (*Liina* 'flax, linen', *Pilkku* 'spot', *Rusko* 'brown', *Tähti* 'star', *Valko* 'white') or character, either observed or aspired (*Tarmo* 'energy', *Vilkku* 'blink'). In addition, common names of people have been used such as *Heikki* or *Pekka* as well as typical "horse-like" names meaning 'horsey' such as *Poku* or *Polle*. These names were usually only used orally.

Nowadays, the naming system of Finnish horses includes the animal's official registered name, a call name and additionally possibly used nicknames and names of ridicule. Official registered names are given within one month of the foal's birth and are registered with the Finnish Trotting and Breeding Association, Suomen Hippos ry. These names must be unique and suggestions for a name may not always necessarily be approved. The name must either be Finnish or Swedish, no more that 15 characters long and may not be inappropriate. The name may not, for example, advertise a product or include profanity or dialectical or slang words.

Usually, registered names of Finnish horses are compound names, one part referring to the horse's gender and the other being the horse's name. Patronymic and matronymic names include, for example *Hopan Hessu*, *Jaanen-Sälli*, *Maikin-Poika* and *Valtin-Antti*, in which the name's initial part refers to the colt's parent. Mares' names are sometimes formed with the feminising ending *tAr* affixed to the parent's name (*Sitko* → *Sitkotar*). The name can also be a combination of the parents' names (*Pirva* ← father *Varvi*, mother *Pilkuke*, *Hilseri* ← father *Ponseri*, mother *Hilo-Tyttö*). Moreover, derivational endings or other structural elements used in names may be hereditary (*Kerskari* ← *Tuikari*). Two-part *genealogical names* became standard in the 1960s and are nowadays dominant.

The name of the horse in the official name is again usually descriptive of the animal (*Keikari* 'dapper man', *Sopu* 'harmony') or includes a personal name (*Aapeli*, *Valma*) or some other name (*Tarina* 'story', *Valopiste* 'point of light'). Names of harness racing horses often refer to, for example, speed and acceleration (*Lento* 'flight', *Sprintter*, *Vauhti* 'speed', *Vire* 'light breeze').

Horse call names are those used everyday which is why they are usually shorter than their official names. They are usually formed on the basis of their registered names by truncation (*Aro-Hanski* → *Hanski*, *A.T. Pikku-Nikko* 'little Nikko' → *Nikko*, *Huimapää* 'wild head' → *Huima* 'wild', *Jehutar* → *Jehu*, *Kuuman Kipinä* 'hot spark' → *Kipinä* 'spark', *Ukulele* → *Uku*) or by various slang suffixes (*Pika-Viesti* 'fast message' → *Pikis*, *Tähtihetki* 'star moment' → *Tähtäri*, *Tytön Yllätys* 'Tyttö's surprise' → *Ylläri*). A registered name can also be altered to a more Finnish form (*Gertrud* → *Kerttu*, *Pepper* → *Pippuri*) or it can be replaced by a more familiar expression that is phonetically reminiscent of it (*Eroosio* → *Eetu*, *P.K. Askare* → *Asko*, *Vilhaus* → *Ville*). Many horse call names are based on associations conjured by the registered name (*Pensseli* 'paint brush' → *Suti* 'brush', *Sähinä* 'hiss' → *Sähkö* 'electricity', *Tulisuudelma* 'kiss of fire' → *Pusu* 'kiss').

In addition to secondary call names stemming from registered names, Finnish horses also have primary call names which characterise the animal's appearance (*Blondi* 'blondie', *Musti* 'blackie', *Peikko* 'goblin'), character or behaviour (*Hörhö* 'crackpot', *Mahti* 'power', *Potku* 'kick'), gender (*Likka* 'girl', *Poju* 'boy, lad') or age (*Nestori*, *Vaavi* 'baby'). Sometimes, the call name can be a name which has not been approved as the horse's official name (*Vaapukka* dial. 'raspberry').

Nicknames of horses, which are studiously used in the stables, are often based on their call names (*Hyrinä* 'hum' → *Hyrtsi*, *Kirppu* 'flea' → *Kirppulainen*, *Putte* → *Putikka*, *Santeli* → *Santeli-Manteli* 'Santeli almond'). They can also be primary nicknames descriptive of the animal. These are generally affectionate by nature (*Lellikki* 'fondling', *Pikku-Prinsessa* 'little princess', *Söpöliini* 'cutie pie') but they can also be pejorative (appearance: *Jättimarsu* 'giant guinea pig', *Köriläs* 'hulk', age and gender: *Jätkä* 'dude, lumberjack', *Papparainen* 'little old man', character and manner: *Ahmatti* 'glutton', *Riiviö* 'rascal, fiend', *Äkäpussi* 'shrew').

6. Commercial Names

In today's globalising and economically driven world, commercial nomenclature is one of the newest and enthusiastically examined topics of research in onomastics. This chapter deals with the economy and the global market and how company names, brands, trade marks and product descriptions fit in. Names other than those in the economy are also examined from a commercial perspective. The chapter thoroughly covers the history, legality, structure and functions of Finnish company names along with the latest trends in commercial naming and research of the subject.

Commercial Nomenclature as a Topic of Research

Names and Trade

Commercial nomenclature can be defined from a financial perspective: *commercial names* are names whose function is to direct the choices of consumers and investors and that have economic objectives in their use. There is usually a juridical owner of a commercial name who defines its rights and limitations of use. The owner of a company name is usually the same as its referent, that is, the company, but the referent of a company name and the owner of the name can also be two different entities. One, but not the only function of a commercial name is to represent the monetary yield of its owner. Commercial names are also different from many other names in that the names themselves can be a subject of trade. Commercial names thus have monetary value.

A great deal of money is increasingly being spent for the creation and development of different names in world economy. The development of names is often entrusted to outside specialists, that is, to businesses familiar with advertising and marketing. Businesses that produce commercial names may charge large amounts of money for names intended for the international market. However, money invested for the creation of names is only a fraction of the sum that the owners end up using for making the names known. A commercial name is meant to be seen, and visibility costs money.

Why then are names used for commercial purposes? What makes a name such that it has significant weight in trade? Why is a name considered to be a part of the marketing strategy of products in the market? Why, as they say, does a "good name sell"? The answer can simply be found in the heart of a proper name: a name identifies its referent, singles it out, makes it unique and distinguishes it from all others. All of these factors are also objectives of marketing. A company or product with a name aims at being singled out from a group of all similar others of the same kind. A name is a linguistic way for this task to be carried out. Due to their fundamental character, names include a great deal of informational and emotional significance associated with their referents, so that with a name, people's images about the referent can be modified. With a name, the referent can be expressed in a positive light, should it so be desired. When a name catches on to positive images, these images draw in people who are ready to use money also in order to acquire them.

With names, paradoxical, commercial competition can indeed veer away from its purpose. As more and more referents get their own name and the number of various names is continuously on the rise, a result of this is an inflation of commercial names. As efforts are made to create similar positive images for all these names, they no longer are distinguished from one another. New names must then be created in order to get the attention of the consumer. Commercial names would no longer have an impact on us as strong as before because we would not understand the "spirit of the game": we know that with names, there are objectives to influence us. In a way, respect towards names has vanished and because of this, they can easily be changed even though the referent would completely remain the same. A continuous conflict between the underlying reason behind commercial naming and the competitive outcomes with names leads to the fact that commercial nomenclature is the most vulnerable name category to radical changes and experimentation with linguistic boundaries. It also guarantees the fact that marketing professionals – and onomasticians of commercial names – will have much to deal with.

Types of Commercial Names

Commercial names normally refer to the names of businesses and various products. In daily language use, different commercial name categories often overlap and it is not always clear what it really means when we speak of company names, product names or brands. When we wish to examine commercial nomenclature, the differences between these concepts must be defined.

In international onomastics, especially in German onomastics, commercial names (Fin. *kaupallinen nimi*, Ger. *Wirtschaftsname*, Swe. *kommersiellt namn*) are sometimes also called *ergonyms*. However, this term has not been established in Finnish onomastics. The concept of ergonym is broader than commercial names because, aside from names of commercial businesses and products names, it also includes all non-commercial institutions, such as schools, cultural places, churches, different administrative fields and organisations.

A *company name* (Fin. *yritysnimi*, Ger. *Unternehmensname*, Swe. *företagsnamn*) is an expression which consistently refers to a certain business. With this name, a company is identified and its activities distinguished from other companies. A company is a financial unit whose purpose is to purchase inputs, merge them in the production process and sell acquired assets for the acquisition of income. There are different kinds of companies in Finland: the most common forms of business include limited companies, limited partnerships, general partnerships and private traders. All businesses are thus not companies (e.g. private traders) nor, on the other hand, can all companies in the strictest sense of the word be considered businesses that practise economic activity (e.g. housing cooperatives). A specific visual form, a *logo*, is often also created for a company name. The use of a logo is limited to visual factors such as letterheads, advertisements and packaging. This is why logos are not central subjects for a linguistic, onomastic study.

The referent of a company name is abstract but the name can be used for concrete commercial property, a commercial building or business area. In this way, the semantic field of the name extends from its core meaning to subjects closely related to it, in this case, the place where the business is run (*He lives quite close to **Fortum***). The issue at hand is a metonymic, that is, relational association – the same phenomenon occurs when, for example, a statue's surroundings are also referred to by the name of the statue (*Our meeting place is **Havis Amanda***). This kind of name can, in a way, be considered polysemic: the meaning of the name has been extended so that it covers referents that are closely related to one another.

A *trade mark* is a registered sign with reference to a certain product group of a specific manufacturer. The sign can also include text and patterns. A trade mark can also be a form of packaging (a Coca-Cola bottle) or some sound (an ice cream truck's theme song). An important function of a trade mark is to distinguish the products or services of the owner of the sign from other similar types of these products or services, in other words, it signifies the origin of the product or service. It thus functions as a tool in advertising and marketing. Licences can also be granted for trade marks so that all products sold with specific trade marks will not necessarily be the products of the owner of the trade mark (*Barbie* pyjamas). A trade mark is not quite precisely first and foremost a linguistic expression. In Finnish business marketing, for example, there is an emphasis on not inflecting a Finnish trade mark in language use according to normal Finnish grammatical rules. Instead, the owners of trade marks prefer that an appellative be added to its context so that it can be inflected. As a whole, a registered trade mark is not a name nor a term but rather a phenomenon outside of linguistics.

A *product name*, however, is an element of language. It is an expression included with a trade mark or some other linguistic expression referring to the concept of a manufactured or developed product for commercial use. For example, ***Benecol*** *was created as a result of long product development* is an appropriate sentence. It is often difficult to differentiate a trade mark and product name from one another but the difference is quite clear regarding onomastics: a product name is a proper name whereas a trade mark is not. However, many times, there is a desire to emphasise the fact that a product name has been registered as a trade mark. Then, the term *trade mark* can be used in onomastics when it is referring to a name included in the trade mark.

All product names are not a part of a trade mark. A product type can also be identified with a product name from a broader product group expressed with a trade mark. For example, instant porridge in individual packets by the product name *Hetki* ('moment') is sold under the Finnish *Elovena* (a brand of Finnish oat products) trade mark. Individual products, such as a certain toothpaste or cough drop, are normally also identified with long names with multiple parts, which include both a trade mark and product name, and in addition to these, they can have, for example, a word signifying the type of product (*toothpaste, cough drop*). The expression may also include the name of the company and a qualifier which can describe, for example, the flavour of the toothpaste, such as *Unilever Pepsodent® Junior toothpaste Mild Mint*.

By commercial names, many people primarily mean brands. The term *brand* partly overlaps with a *company name* and a *trade mark*. It is a widely known, financially valuable name which includes an image of the surplus value offered by the products. A brand usually refers to many product groups and is often based on a company name or its registered trade mark. Brands are bought and sold and their worth can dramatically rise higher than the worth of the actual production plant and the professionals working there. A brand is, above all, a name and, from the owner's perspective, this name has a key, unique role: everything else from packaging to the manufacturer and marketing can change but the name of the brand will stay the same. A name is the core of a brand.

When we speak of product names and brands, we should remember that product names are used quite often in situations with reference to products as if they were representatives of their class. Should we say *This car dealer sells Fords*, the word *Ford* is used in the same way as *dandelion* in the sentence *The child is picking dandelions*. In this kind of context, the expression referring to the product is not an identifying name but rather a classifying appellative. The fact that, in this case, the word is usually written with a capital letter may make the interpretation more indistinct.

A summarisation of the characteristic features of certain types of commercial nomenclature is presented in the following table. There can be, to some extent, some variability in the way the terminology is used in the field and it even can be internationally incoherent. In Finnish commercial nomenclature, the terms used are *tavaramerkki, tuotenimi, tuotemerkki* and *brändi* and in English, *trade mark, product name* and *brand name*. In Swedish studies, they use the terms *varumärke, varumärkesnamn* and *produktnamn* and in German studies, the terms *Warenmarke, Produktname* and *Markenname*. All of these terms are used in a way that cannot, at this point in time, be seen as established in any of these aforementioned languages. When examining a study, we should thus be precise in what is meant by the terms being used.

Table 1: Comparison of a company name, product name, trade mark and brand.

	Company Name	**Product Name**	**Trade Mark**	**Brand**
A proper noun	x	x		x
Function	identifies the company	identifies the product concept	signifies the product's origin	identifies the whole product grouping of a certain company and signifies the surplus value of the products
Appellatival use is common		x		x
Can be inflected in Finnish language use	x	x		x
Linguality/ visuality	language element; if visualised = logo	language element	can include language, patterns, sound, forms	language element which usually has a certain visual form

Factors Taken into Account in Examining Names

Commercial names are associated with business communication in the business world, that is, the kind of image the company conveys about itself. A company can be profiled by visual and verbal means. One visual means is, for example, a logo which refers to the established appearance of the name of the company (e.g. typography, relationship of letters). The contents which the company conveys about itself are expressed by verbal means. In addition to content itself, lingual choices, such as what language will be used or how it will be used, are important as well as the company's naming policy: what will be named and what kinds of names will be used.

Naming policy is connected, for instance, to the organisational structure and marketing of the company. Companies can make various decisions on the use of names. In addition to an actual company name, the firm can have auxiliary legal names with which it identifies certain parts of its activities (*Nokia corporation*: *Nokia Mobile Phones, Nokia Internet Communications, Nokia Networks* etc.). For the choice for product marketing, there is either a product image solution, whereupon the name of the company does not aim to be made known but a trade mark is created for the products (*Procter & Gamble*: *Pampers, Pringles, Fairy, Ariel* etc.), or a business image solution whereupon the company consistently gives its products its own name. Attempts are made to form a brand from the company's name in the latter solution (*Canon, Fazer, Nokia, Shell*). Naming policy can also be practised by merging both solutions whereupon the company name is used as a tying umbrella name to products, each one having their own trade mark (*Kellogg's Rice Krispies®*, *Kellogg's Special K®*).

When examining commercial names, it is important to recognise their connection to the language use of the financial world, especially the language of marketing and advertising. It is also important to recognise their connection to visual factors. Commercial names do not exist separately from a commercial context. Instead, they fulfil demands set by the business world. At the same time, however, they are examined as part of a broader cultural circle and a part of language use. The economy is a system created by people, and common cultural features have an effect on the financial world. Certain types of texts are typical for the language use of the financial world in addition to which, factors such as a specialised vocabulary, unique metaphors and style all label the language of economy. A presentation on statistical figures and precise concepts are often characteristic to this language but, on the other hand, many types of texts of the financial world, such as advertisements, include an extremely emotive vocabulary. All of this may also be seen in the nomenclature.

In the study of commercial nomenclature, what kinds of functions the names work in must be taken into account. There are many functions set for names in the financial world. The key factor is that a name distinguishes; a name must be sufficiently distinguished from others. Similar companies or similar products cannot have the same or even similar types of names. On the other hand, some have intentionally – and unlawfully – succeeded in creating names for their companies and products which are reminiscent of known brands, and thus get to ride on the ready-made reputation of these brands. It is typical for many commercial names that, in one way or another, they carry some information, for example, on the company's field of activity or the type of product. Several commercial names aim at creating positive images and appeal to the emotions and thus attract clients to make purchasing decisions. Names are created to be used so that in their formation we can also think about different practical points: the name's length, how it is written, how it is pronounced, its visual appeal or the name's various operative surroundings. The function of a name can also be the integration of the company or product in some specific cultural circle or certain production or services sector.

In many ways, commercial nomenclature differs from traditional onomastic topics, place names and personal names, as a subject of research. Many commercial names are *official*, names registered by authorities. There are also such commercial names that are not registered by the authorities and which are consequently *unofficial*. These include, for example, unofficial truncations used for official company names or other commercial names such as *Stokka* (← *Stockmann Oyj Abp*).

There is an aspiration for every commercial name to include various messages to various recipients. Merely identifiability is not sufficient as a function of a name in commercial nomenclature. Instead, commercial names are carefully planned, taking the language community, financial world and advertising requirements into consideration. Official and unofficial commercial names are thus always coherently created for public, and largely for written use through various established decision-making processes. Since the departure in the definition of a commercial name is its ownership and commercial value, such spontaneous names of business or products originated in the language community, for example, the Fennicised slang forms *Mäkkäri* (← *McDonald's Corporation*), and *Pösö* (← *Peugeot*) are not really included in commercial nomenclature but rather in unofficial urban or cultural nomenclature.

It has been categorically stated at times in onomastics that a name carries no meaning because it functions only in a referential relationship. However, everyone knows that it is not insignificant what the context of an expression, the meaning of a product name with reference to a certain drink, for example, is. Its importance does not only remain in the circumstances of naming but instead, the meaning is continuously present when the name is being used. These contexts of expression are exploited in marketing: a Finnish consumer is probably more likely to adhere to a beer bottle that has the name *Karhu* ('bear') on it rather than one that has the name *Pupu* ('bunny') or *Lehmä* ('cow'). These expressive meanings are not quite as strongly present in the linguistic circumstances of place names and personal names, although they are perhaps in existence behind them and may come forth in certain situations.

Commercial names structurally differ from many other names as well. There is quite a great deal of variation in their structure and the vocabulary used in them. These names are more complex than place names and often seem to include many different elements which is why the syntactic segmentation of single part and compound names used in toponomastics does not work in such a way in commercial nomenclature. The order of name elements and name parts may be syntactically significant in commercial nomenclature but it is not as systematic as it is in place names.

Due to the aforementioned reasons, research methods have been exclusively developed for the study of commercial nomenclature. The structure of these names is examined by dividing them into name parts but not in the same way as for place names. Instead, these name parts are defined on a *functional-semantic basis*. The name parts of commercial names each have their own function based on the semantic content of the part in the name as a whole. In this way, for example, long, official company names can be divided into meaningful parts, whose arrangement and internal structure can be examined further: in the name *Kukkakauppa Floora tmi Anna Lindberg*, there is a part signifying the form of business, that is, its corporate identifier (*tmi* ← *toiminimi* 'legal name, trade name'), a part signifying the business concept (*Kukkakauppa* 'flower shop'), the actual naming, that is, its identifying part (*Floora* 'flora') and a supplementary part that provides additional information (*Anna Lindberg*, the name of the owner). (Sjöblom 2006.) Long product descriptions can similarly be divided up into functional parts: the name of the company, a trade mark, the name of the product, the type of product and the supplementary part providing further information can all be separated in these names.

It is possible to examine the semantic content of a commercial name when we start off by looking at the meaning relationship the expressions that make up the name have to the referent of the name itself. They can express something direct about the referent, for example, convey what field of activity or who the owner of the business is (*Rakennusliike Virtanen* 'construction company Virtanen') or what the manufactured product is at hand and by whom (*Mattilan leipomon Ruisleipäset* 'Mattila bakery's rye bread'). They can also express something about the referent through indirect, metaphoric or metonymic association. A metaphoric relationship is a question of, for example, when a product name of a car is *Firebird*. As for a metonymic relationship, this would be if a barbershop's name would contain the word *scissors*. Many commercial names include expressions which are not real words of any language. These elements can, however, include recognisable parts from some words or names, whereupon a large group of different meaning associations can get compressed into one name element: for example, the expression *Medilab* in a company name is based on a compressed meaning relationship, which probably conjures an association of the medical field (*medical, medicine* etc.) and a laboratory. Quite many commercial names have been formed so that they are not in any way semantically connected to their referent. In this case, the meaning relationship is disconnected.

The study of the structure and meaning of commercial names always requires the analysis of their functions alongside of them. As it has previously been stated, commercial names have been planned to function in a commercial context where the perspectives of marketing, location, advertising and consumers must be taken in to account. Multiple senses, especial visuality, are in a close connection to commercial nomenclature so that the account of visual points is important although it cannot be the main purpose of linguistic onomastics (Sjöblom 2010).

RESEARCH TRADITIONS OF COMMERCIAL NOMENCLATURE
Globally speaking, the study of commercial nomenclature is quite new and there have only been rather few of these studies carried out. Interest in the field is on the rise which is proven by more and more presentations at international onomastic conferences and by articles that have appeared and are being published in scholarly journals. The first international symposium concentrating on commercial nomenclature called Names in the Economy was organised in 2006 in Antwerp, Belgium. Numerous scholars interested in company names, product names and brands as well as other themes tangential to commercial nomenclature convened together at this symposium to contemplate questions on the subject. Afterwards, symposiums have been held every few years.

Up until now, a large part of studies concerning commercial nomenclature has been carried out from a marketing perspective. Naming issues are associated with the research of marketing communication and management as well as so-called design management philosophy. Moreover, anthropologists and cultural geographers as well as law specialists have dealt with names in their research. However, linguistic studies on commercial nomenclature, especially articles, have already been available to some extent. The most key subject in these articles is brands which provide an opportunity to approach both company and product nomenclature simultaneously. Since brands are based either on company names or trade marks, the difference between company names and brand names has not necessarily been highlighted in all the studies whatsoever. The confusion of terminology and set of concepts may, to some extent, complicate the familiarisation of sources of the field. Studies only concentrated on company names or unequivocally on product names have been published less.

Mostly individual researchers of different parts of the world have carried out studies on commercial nomenclature (more detailed information on these sources can be found in the bibliography at the end of this book). A large part of these studies have been published in Europe and in Northern America but there has been interest in commercial nomenclature in all the other continents as well. In Europe, studies on commercial nomenclature have been carried out in German-speaking areas since the 1970s. Some of the first steps were taken in East Germany where Rosemarie Gläser and her colleagues took an interest in the language use of the financial world, especially regarding nomenclature and terminology. At Gläser's hand, the research plan *Fachsprachenonomastik*, in which product names and trade marks are included as just one of its subjects, came about at the University of Leipzig. Its other areas of research included various taxonymic terms (e.g. *Anemone pulsatilla*) and proper nouns as constituents of terms of professional language (e.g. *Darwinism*). This line of research seems, however, to have taken a backseat nowadays.

There are currently many other onomasticians in German-speaking areas with their sights firmly set on the research of commercial nomenclature. Monographs on the field of commercial nomenclature are quite uncommon but one of them was published by Cristoph Platen in 1997 which focused on European product names. Its materials covered, for example, a literary overview of research carried out thus far on product names. In addition, numerous other researchers in German-speaking areas have published articles on commercial nomenclature (e.g. Angelika Bergien, Gerhard Koss, Ludger Kremer, Julia Kuhn, Elke Ronneberger-Sibold, Holger Wochele, Antje Zilg).

Moreover, commercial nomenclature has, to some extent, been considered in the Nordic countries as a part of so-called other nomenclature. A Nordic symposium was held in 1991 which included other topics than personal names and place names. Presentations at the symposium had been published in a text by the name of *Övriga namn* (1994) and it contained several articles concerning the names of businesses and product names. The theme was picked up in a collection of articles published in 2002 called *Avgränsning av namnkategorier*. Nordic scholars' interest in commercial nomenclature has mainly been associated with the broader research field of urban nomenclature, often examining names of businesses as a part of toponymy. So far, the only monograph carried out on company names is the dissertation covering a Finnish collection of company names by Paula Sjöblom, published in 2006.

There is an abundance of research on commercial nomenclature in English and in many other languages, for example in Russian and Italian. There is at least one dissertation on the genericisation of brand names, in other words, the transformation of these names to appellatives, for example, how the automobile name *Jeep* became the appellative *jeep* (Clankie 2002). Several publications include individual articles whose themes often are more limited, concentrating on one location, business or product. Individual articles have been published in journals of onomastic sciences and other publications but there are also publications in existence presenting a collection of research findings on commercial nomenclature (e.g. Names in Commerce and Industry 2007, Onoma 43/2008, People, Products and Professions 2009).

Factors that Determine Name Giving

LAWS AND GUIDELINES

When commercial names are created, merely the opinion of the name giver and creativity is not sufficient. Many factors outside of the name giver can have an influence on naming. Different sections in laws and authoritative guidelines as well as advertising, marketing and business strategy perspectives must be taken into account when creating a name.

Finnish law does not interfere too much with the linguistic form of commercial names. There are, however, certain requirements enacted to ascertain distinctiveness. The function of legislation is to safeguard ownership and name protection issues especially pertaining to the use of commercial names. The most important laws steering commercial name giving in Finland include the Trade Names Act (*Toiminimilaki*, 1979), which regulates company names, and the Trade Marks Act (*Tavaramerkkilaki*, 1964), which regulates trade marks.

According to the Trade Names Act, a Finnish trade name (*toiminimi*) is a "name which an entrepreneur uses in his or her activities". The law guarantees the possessor of the trade name the exclusive rights to its use which means that no other entrepreneur may use it and no other name can even be confused with it. Exclusive rights to a trade name can usually be achieved by registering the name with the Finnish Trade Register (*Kaupparekisteri*) but a private trader can also get exclusive rights to his trade name just by establishing it for his own use.

A trade name in Finland can also have a registered *parallel company name* (*rinnakkaistoiminimi*) which means that the name has carefully been translated into another language. For example, the Swedish name *Pargas blomsterhandel Ab* can also have its parallel company name in Finnish *Paraisten kukkakauppa Oy* ('Parainen flower shop ltd'). This rule concerning two or more languages is the only one which the Trade Names Act presents on the lingual form of names.

A Finnish firm which has a trade name can practise a part of its business under another name which is called an *auxiliary company name* (*aputoiminimi*). For example, *Burger-In Oy* practices its business as a fast food restaurant under the auxiliary company name *Hesburger* and its business as a café under the auxiliary company name *Hesecafe*. Another example is *Talentum Oyj* which publishes a magazine under the name the auxiliary company name *Talouselämä* ('financial world'). Auxiliary company names are also official.

In addition to a trade name and auxiliary company name, a so-called *secondary identifier* (*toissijainen tunnus*) can be used, as protected under Finnish law, which can be, for example, a contortion (for example, the secondary identifier *Stokka* in addition to the trade name *Oy Stockmann Ab*) but also a pattern, an image or even a theme song. Exclusive rights to a secondary identifier have been received when it has been demonstrably established as such that the business is recognised by it on the market. Secondary identifiers are not officially registered, as they are unofficial commercial names.

As it has previously been stated, the Trade Names Act sets the company name requirements concerning the fact that two similar firm names cannot exist nor may businesses of the same field have two firm names that may possibly be confused with one another. There may not be, for example, two businesses with one named *Besstion* and the other *Bestion*. A trade name may not be confused with some other trade mark. For example, the trade name *Kahvikauppa Kulta-Katriina* ('coffee shop golden Katriina') would not be approved because it would be confused with the well-known Finnish coffee trade mark *Kulta-Katriina* ('golden Katriina'). A trade name must not go against good taste; for instance, profanity or a vulgar or racist expression would not be permitted. The name may not be misleading either.

The law also defines how a Finnish corporate identifier, such as the acronyms *oy* (← *osakeyhtiö* 'limited company, Ltd') or *oyj* (← *julkinen osakeyhtiö* 'public limited company, plc'), must be entered in the name of a company. The main principle is the fact that the form of business must be visible in the name. Should it be a question of a Finnish limited partnership, the name must contain either the full word *kommandiittiyhtiö* or the acronym *ky*. A Finnish cooperative must have the words *osuuskunta* or *osuus* or the acronym *osk* in its name. In addition to the corporate identifier, a Finnish housing cooperative (*asunto-osakeyhtiö*) must also contain the company's place of business such as *As Oy Helsingin Merihelmi*, ('housing cooperative Helsinki sea pearl') or *Asunto Oy Vähänkyrön Merihelmi* ('housing cooperative Vähäkyrö sea pearl'). A private entrepreneur's trade name requires no corporate identifier but the abbreviation *tmi* (← *toiminimi*) may be included. The expression *avoin yhtiö* is not required in a Finnish general partnership, provided the name of the company indicates the form of business. For example, the names *Lahtinen & Co* and *Lahtinen & Kilpi* convey that there is more than one entrepreneur whereupon it is not a question of a private trader. On the other hand, when a Finnish name is lacking a corporate identifier, it cannot be associated with a limited company or limited partnership because noting these identifiers in these forms of businesses is compulsory. The only option is thus a general partnership. Moreover, there are no corporate identifiers in auxiliary company names.

The Finnish Trade Register, which operates under the Finnish National Board of Patents and Registration (*Patentti- ja rekisterihallitus*), provides clearer and more detailed guidelines on what kinds of company names can be registered that what can be found in the sections in the Trade Names Act. These guidelines can easily be found on the webpages of the National Board of Patents and Registration in English, Finnish and Swedish (www.prh.fi). According to the law, the requirement on sufficient individuality means that a company name cannot be just a general word which describes the quality of activity or marketable product nor merely a general place name. For example, such expressions as *Osakeyhtiö Markkinointi* ('limited company marketing') or *Auto Oy* would not be approved as a trade name. Such a name as *Nokia Oy* would no longer be approved under current regulations due to the fact that it is based on a place name (the town of Nokia in central Finland).

A common given name or surname would also not be approved as a trade name. So, such company names as *Timo tmi* or *Nieminen Oy* would not be possible. However, the identifying name of the company's owner can be approved as a company name: *Timo Nieminen Oy* or *T. Nieminen tmi* would be acceptable as long as similar names have not previously been registered. Similar guidelines concern combinations of letters only or merely a number, so *2001 Ky* or *XR Oy* as such are not acceptable as company names.

If the owner, however, wishes to have the aforementioned types of elements for the name of his company, something additional to verify the identification of the whole name can be added to the words, names or combinations of letters and numbers to act as an aide. Even though *Auto Oy* will not work, *Kuusiston Auto Oy* ('Kuusisto car ltd') would sufficiently be an identifying name. Instead of *XR Oy*, the name *XR-palvelut Oy* ('XR services ltd'), for example, could be registered. Similarly, phrases (e.g. *hyvää yötä* 'good night') which by themselves would not be sufficient enough as a company name could be linked to a word that signifies the field of business, whereupon the name would be identifying: *Motelli Hyvää yötä Oy* ('motel good night ltd') would be a valid company name.

The Trade Register recommends taking general correct spelling rules into consideration in the formation of the name's linguistic form but the register authorities do not really oversee the compliance of these rules. Generally speaking, however, the first letter of the name in a registered company name, as in all proper nouns, is written with a capital letter. Names otherwise variably follow spelling norms of the language.

The age of the Internet and internationalisation have certainly changed the environment of company names in many ways. However, *domain names* thus far have not been approved as registered trade names but they must be understood as their own category that has their own rules and requirements. In the best case scenario, they are reminiscent of the name of the company, which has a website where visitors are taken to, but different requirements other than the form of the company name influence their formation.

According to the Trade Marks Act, a Finnish trade mark can be a regular word or name and, as it has previously been stated, it can also be a pattern or, for example, a form of packaging. However, here we will concentrate on those regulations and guidelines of the Trade Marks Act and the authorities, those that concern the linguistic elements of a trade mark, in other words, the actual product name.

Exclusive rights are also given to trade marks and no other entrepreneur may use a trade mark owned by another in his activities without permission. A trade mark may not be confused with another of the same field of business or type of goods. However, such trade marks will not interfere with each other that refer to completely different types of goods. Hence, for example, *Karhu* ('bear') can either be a trade mark of the Finnish beer or sports equipment.

Exclusive rights to a trade mark do not give the owner the right to typically limit the use of comparable common or proper nouns in the language. No one, thus, may limit the lingual use of the name *Karhu* or the appellative *karhu* with their ownership. However, the law provides the owner of the trade mark the right to request, for example, the mention of the word's use as a registered trade mark in dictionaries or websites. This protects the owner's rights in such cases where a developed product name extends to general use, a classifying meaning. For example, in addition to the definition of *kännykkä* as 'mobile phone' in the Finnish Language Office (*Kielitoimisto*) dictionary, there is an acknowledgement of the fact that the word had been a registered trade mark of Nokia Oy.

The regulations concerning the confusion of a trade mark also spreads out to other areas than other trade marks. A trade mark cannot be another entrepreneur's name, trade name, auxiliary company name or secondary identifier. It also cannot be anyone's name of an artistic piece of work included with copyright protection, a name of a registered plant variety or other comparable name which is already previously owned by another.

Finnish trade mark rights can be achieved either by establishing or registering the symbol. Establishment means that the symbol is regularly used as an identifier of certain products of the same manufacturer and it must be commonly known through this symbol. Registration does not generally provide any stronger protection than establishment but it is easier to be indicated by registration and the possibility of registration already exists before a trade mark can begin to be used. In other words, by registering, it is possible to reserve a trade mark for one's own use. As trade marks, unregistered product names can be considered official names in onomastics when they are used as officially registered names.

The National Board of Patents and Registration of Finland provides – the same as for trade names – excellent guidelines in English, Finnish and Swedish on the formation of trade marks, with examples. The legal requirement for the distinguishing features of a trade mark results, for example, in the fact that it may not be such a word which describes the product in question. This kind of descriptiveness would thus limit the possibilities of others that provide similar products to market theirs. So, *Apple* works as a symbol of the computer but would not, for example, as a symbol of an apple pie. These limitations also concern, for example, words depicting the product's quality (*Hyvä 'good'), price (*Halpa 'cheap, inexpensive'), place of manufacturing (*Ruotsi 'Sweden') or date or establishment (**1991*).

The character ® is often attached to registered trade marks but its use is not compulsory. However, the symbol may not be used, should the trade mark not be registered in Finland or in the EU. In this case, the character ™ can be used.

The National Board of Patents and Registration of Finland upholds the Trade Mark Register and one can apply for registered trade marks from the Trade Mark Database, located on its webpages. The trade mark can also be registered across the European Union. The Office for Harmonization in the Internal Market (Trade Marks and Designs) of the European Union runs this registration which maintains the EU trade mark database. The database also includes information on trade mark applications that are in the middle of being processed or, for one reason or another, that have been rejected or cancelled.

COMMERCIAL OBJECTIVES

Commercial nomenclature is, above all, affected by commercial objectives which include the search for a form for a name that will serve different marketing purposes. Naming is a part of business communications, that is, what kind of image the company outwardly reveals about itself in regard to marketing. Significant concepts of this include identity, profile and image. The company's *identity* involves the company's personality: what the company truly is. The *profile* is the image the company sends out, in other words, how the company wishes to outwardly appear. The *image* is what the company portrays about itself to its stakeholders or target audience. It is based on attitudes and how the messages the image sent out has been interpreted. Images have an especially strong influence on people's behaviour, why the construction of images in business life is important and the images may be financially formed to be more valuable than the products themselves.

Companies and products can be profiled by visual and verbal means. Names are included in verbal means. In a way, names symbolise the identity of a company or product. They immediately trigger many different images which are associated as being characteristic of the name's referent. A name can express what the company does and in which area of business the company operates or it can link the business to a specific country or locality. It can also function as an umbrella of various companies, product groups or products such as well-known major brands such as *Sony* or *Adidas*.

Regarding the company's image, it is usually considered important that names used in a company, alongside of other factors, will build a unified totality. Every new name and product name must be appropriate to other existing nomenclature, the company's style and strategic solutions. Should a company strategically decide to start emphasising environmental concerns, it could be beneficial to also make future naming solutions on the basis of this strategy: perhaps elements will start to be used in names which will bring a clean environment to mind (for example, words with reference to nature). When it is strategically sensible for a Finnish company to start emphasising Finnishness, components with a *Kalevala* (the Finnish national epic) theme, for example, can be chosen for the names.

From a marketing perspective, the target audience, that is, the group of people for whom the products or services of the company in question has been planned, must be taken into consideration. When the target audience is the pensioner population, names are selected in a different way than when the client base is primarily teenagers. A hairdressing salon named *Salón Lady* surely would attract a different kind of clientele than one named *Studio Rasta*.

In regard to marketing, a commercial name is good when it supports the company's financial objectives. Name giving and name change are purely economic issues. Human perspectives are indeed influential because people do use names, however language and the language community are not an absolute value in the planning of a company's naming policy. They are only tools for achieving the main objective – financial utility. Changing names, a great deal of which has been publicly spoken about in the last years, can be wise if the utilities of the expensive process of change are estimated to be greater than the disadvantages. All commercial names have some marketing value. On the other hand, it is apparent that names are quite often changed without taking the essential strength of proper nouns into account: over time, a large set of images can be linked to a well-established name, these images being an essential part of the marketing value of a commercial name. When a name is changed, the new image must be built from scratch because the images conjured by the new name would only be associated with the name's linguistic form. All of the images associated with the old name, which have been built up during the name's history, would be wiped clean. In turn, great marketing efforts would be required to choose those subjects from the old name that would be desired to be associated with the new name, and then the combination of the new form and the old meanings would work out. Should, a company name with an honourable history be widely known, it may be short-sighted to abandon a name that seems old fashioned at a certain time just because of some new business activity or internationalisation. It is usually an easier and less expensive solution to construct new meanings on top of the old name than to create all the meanings for a new name completely from square one.

Besides laws and authoritative provisions, standard spelling rules and guidelines of the Finnish Language Board mostly may have an influence on commercial name giving. In practice, however, commercial names often break language norms in many ways. The visual form of a name, which can be used as a marketing aide, is also considered in name planning. Spelling contrary to the norm, such as beginning with a lower-case letter, the writing of compound words as two separate words, or different special characters, are planned for logos. In developing them, it has not necessarily been considered how the name will look as part of the text or how it will sound as part of spoken language. Sometimes, these factors that are contrary to norms, and the contradiction to visual and articulated forms, can be consciously used as power tools.

Commercial names are basically a part of the standard language of the language community which everyone must be able to use within the framework of commonly agreed rules. Ownership to a name should not mean the ownership to a certain kind of language use. Should commercial names be required to be written with exceptional spelling, there may be difficulties in regular communication as a result. On the recommendation provided by the Finnish Language Board in 2000, it has been stated that spellings in compliance with standard guidelines will be applied to the writing of company names in straightforward texts and that names will be inflected according to the normal, grammatical rules of Finnish. These recommendations have been noted to be applicable to product names as well. The board provided a recommendation in 2004 which primarily concerned the formation and spelling of the names of educational institutions, but at the same time also other organisations. These guidelines similarly follow the spirit of those that were given in 2000, however they are still not fully sufficient nor necessarily always make the work of economics journalists dealing with spelling problems and other requirements of commercial names in texts any easier. There are clearly certain general factors contrary to norms in commercial names which seem to be included in their basic features. For example, writing different words within a company name starting with a capital letter can in Finnish often be connected to the structure of the company name: functional name parts are distinguished from each other with capital letters.

In addition to identification, names always also have an advertising function: the name must grab someone's attention. One way to do this is to deviate from spelling rules or other features associated with standardised language. This kind of deviation featured in attention-getting objectives in commercial and commercially toned names is called an *attractor* (see e.g. Kremer 1998). These deviations are included mostly in logos and advertisements. It is desirable that names would be written according to standard norms in other language use, such as in newspaper articles and other texts. Sometimes, non-standard elements of names may indeed unintentionally be due to the ignorance or carelessness of the creator of the name.

The following is a list of non-standard elements found in Finnish commercial names:

Lowercase or capital letter?
- Beginning with a lowercase letter (*marimekko*)
- A word other than the first beginning with a capital letter (*Yliopiston Apteekki* 'university pharmacy', standard form *Yliopiston apteekki*)
- A whole word written in capital letters (*AURA-instituutti* 'Aura institute')
- Capital letters in the middle of a word (*Kemira GrowHow*)

Compound Words
- Compound parts written separately (*SKV Kiinteistönvälitys* 'SKV reality', standard form *SKV-kiinteistönvälitys*)
- A collocation written as a compound (*Tervesuu Hammaslääkäriasemat* 'healthy mouth dentist offices', standard form *terve suu*)
- Non-standard use of a hyphen (*Ilta-Sanomat* 'evening messages', standard form *Iltasanomat*)
- Missing a hyphen (*Valiojogurtti*, 'Valio yogurt', standard form *Valio-jogurtti*)

Other Exceptions
- Non-proprial use of punctuation marks (*Hasse!*)
- Special or misspelled abbreviations (*A.I.K.A. mainos* 'T.I.M.E. advertising')
- Avoidance of genitive and other inflectional cases (*Turku Energia* 'Turku energy', standard form *Turun energia* 'Turku+GEN energy')
- Combining expressions from various languages (*Kontio Strong*, kontio 'bear')
- Use of non-Finnish letters (*Parturi-Kampaamo Yxkax* 'barber shop lickety-split', standard form *yks kaks*)
- Misspelled words (*Kampaamokauppa Hairlekiini* 'salon shop hairlequin', standard *harlekiini* 'harlequin')

History of Commercial Naming in Finland

Personal names and place names have existed as linguistic categories for centuries. In comparison to this, the emergence of commercial nomenclature can more or less be dated to recent history. There had not been a need for commercial nomenclature before society began to develop toward free commerce and the mutual competition of merchants. There were indeed signs of the fact that commerce was strengthened with identifying names given to businesses and products, especially early in Central Europe in particular, but there was not much commercial nomenclature appearing in Finland before the 19th century. In regard to the understanding of the development stages of Finnish commercial nomenclature, it is important to become acquainted with the social circumstances in which these names emerged.

Before the 19th century, a mercantile economic policy was dominant in Finland. A strict social division of work prevented competition. The bourgeoisie of the cities had the exclusive rights to commerce, and artisan occupations and professions had been organised as guilds which took on a limited number of entrepreneurs. In practice, these professions thus had a trade monopoly, so knowing the name of the merchant or artisan only was sufficient for the recognition – so far as recognition was by and large necessary – of trade and products. At the same time, however, the bourgeoisie in power and nobility may have had so-called trading firms which were conglomerates of the time. They simultaneously practised, for example, shipping, lending and trade. These trading firms were also known by the name of their owner.

The 18th century was a time of the rise of the European bourgeoisie, especially in Great Britain. Trade, seafaring and industry developed, the status of factory workers gained strength and the best of the bourgeoisie achieved nobility by their wealth. Hence, the borders between different estates balanced out. The same development extended to the Nordic countries as well. The top of the Swedish bourgeoisie was represented by wholesalers and trading firms in Stockholm. Ironworks was a significant source of income. Finland could not avoid these influences because Finnish cities had trade relations with Stockholm and directly with Western Europe.

The iron industry and a growing lumber industry, driven by exporting, had a central role in the change of the financial world of 18th century Finland. A bourgeoisie that became an ironworks proprietor, and similarly a farmer, stepped outside of his own class. A commercial and industrial chain was built around sawmills which was contrary to official trade policy. When, at the same time, the rural peasants began to practise business that previously was a part of bourgeoisie activity, a change in the financial structure gradually occurred. Little by little, small changes opened up possibilities to the rise of free commercialism.

Many economic historians place the turning point of the Finnish financial world to the 1840s, at time when the economy and international trade grew and the structure of the economy clearly changed. The issue of free trade also rose to publicity in the 1840s in J. V. Snellman's newspaper *Saima* and in the newspaper *Kanava*. The level of education rose and a flood of new inventions came to the North. The 1860s was considered the decade of the Finnish industrial revolution. In this decade, the country adopted its own currency, the Finnish mark, which gave the Bank of Finland (*Suomen Pankki*) better opportunities to advance funds for industry. The decree given on joint-stock companies (*Osakeyhtiöasetus*), came into force in 1864 and was significant in regard to trade. Through this law, many new joint-stock companies were established in Finland.

The decree on livelihood (*Elinkeinoasetus*), was established in 1879 and provided Finnish citizens the right to practise any profession or economic activity without any legislative restrictions. Instead of pre-determined regulation, power was given to competition to determine who would succeed. Society gradually changed to being more commercial than before because the people who went to factories and other businesses outside the home earned more money than before. This income was used to purchase different consumables. What would have better lifted the standard of living than a new oil lamp or sewing machine, and what would have saved time better than a bicycle or a ready-made suit? Urban trade in Finland became specialised – book shops, grocery stores, photography studios emerged – and the first department stores were seen at the end of the 19th century.

According to Sjöblom (2006), the aforementioned urbanisation launched by industrialisation and the growth of consumption in Finland is also the first significant reason for the emergence of commercial nomenclature. As there was a greater desire to purchase goods and services, naturally more shops and other businesses were required to fulfil these needs. The number of businesses grew and so it was no longer easy to distinguish them from one another. The need then to differentiate businesses from one another with precise expressions came about. At the same time, when product selection grew, similar products were available, however produced by different manufacturers. One's products may have been perceived better than another's and these needed to be distinguished from each other whereupon identification was possible with names.

Another reason for the emergence of commercial nomenclature can be found in business activity itself. The following factors describe how people's thinking on business activity developed this category which was able to be expressed by linguistic means:

a) An entrepreneur and business in the old system were really one and the same: a merchant was behind the counter and sold his own products. The goal was just to make ends meet. A shop was the same as the merchant and it was passed on to his children. Now, in a new stage, businesses themselves became targets of commerce and they could be bought and sold. This phenomenon confirmed the thought that business in itself is an entity existing separable from the entrepreneur.

b) At the same time, the nature of businesses also changed. Alongside of concrete products, abstract products (such as insurance) and services (such as steamboat travel) began to be sold. Enterprise became diversified and it had not been understood in the same way as before. A name formed this kind of business of abstract products into a manageable unit.

c) The conceptualisation of a business as its own independent being was made easy because of the fact that new legislation (the aforementioned *Osakeyhtiöasetus* 1864 and *Elinkeinoasetus* 1879 and also the decree on trade names, *Toiminimiasetus*, 1896) and the establishment of the Finnish Trade Register formally confirmed the identity of businesses. These factors distinguished businesses from a person who practised business activity.

The third reason for the emergence of commercial nomenclature was the expansion of the foreign concepts of advertising and marketing to Finland. At first, eager advertisers were namely non-Finnish businesses, especially insurance companies. Finnish merchants gradually began to provide information about their products in newspapers because the understanding was that fierce competition required more and more visibility. Visual advertising also extended to Finland. Signs with names of the shops were affixed outside of the establishments. Images in par with attention-getting foreign models gradually started to be used in newspaper advertisements. The fact that names of businesses and products were written the most visible way possible with a larger font than other advertisements, for example, was common in advertising. When a name was repeated over and over again in advertising, people began to unite businesses, products and names to each other and got used to the thought that commercial referents have a name.

Earlier in this book, the concept of the temporal strata of nomenclature was mentioned and the fact that names, originating from many periods, are used at the same time. Now, there are asynchronous names of course used in company names, albeit in its entirety from a relatively short time. On the other hand, company names clearly form strata in which hereditary structural types of names from different periods can be seen. These structural types have developed in the following way:

Before the mid-19th century, there really had been no need to name companies and products in Finland. Instead, it was enough to speak of the people who practised trade or manufactured products. Of course, the person was referred to by a personal name and that name included all of the meanings associated with the name bearer, including his activities and business. If there was a need to speak namely of some person's firm or factory, descriptive, appellatival expressions were used. The following are examples of how writings or advertisements were available in the Finnish newspapers *Suometar* and *Uusi Suometar*:

(1) ... *kustannettu* **Kivipiirtäjältä Herra Liewendahl'ilta** *Helsingistä* (Suometar 1847)
...*charged by* **Stone Etcher Mister Liewendhal** *of Helsinki*
(2) *Mustia kauroja suuremmissa ja pienemmissä joukoissa ostaa Helsingissä* **kauppias A. F. Wasenius**. (Uusi Suometar 1869)
Black oats in bigger and smaller batches bought by **merchant A. F. Wasenius** *in Helsinki.*
(3) *Eilen illalla kello 9 ilmoitettiin* **puuwillatehtaassa** *hätäsoitolla, walkean olewan walloillaan.* (Uusi Suometar 1869)
There was an alarm at the **cotton factory** *yesterday at 9 o'clock in the evening due to a fire.*

Little by little, when Finnish business began to be perceived as an independent subject, from a person to a distinctive entity, identifying expressions began to be used to speak about it. The first types of company names were flexibly similar as previously used expressions but their context indicated that they were more like proper names. Thus company names were at first informative and descriptive such as *Johnson & Sidorow*, *Waseniuksen Kirjakauppa* ('Wasenius' book shop'), *Helsingin Punssi- ja Wiinikauppa* ('Helsinki punsch and wine shop') and *Wärtsilän tehdas* ('Wärtsilä factory'). The first company names which were not primarily informative were created just at the end of the century. Instead, they aimed at arousing positive images. The first new types of names including metaphoric and metonymic elements came about, such as *Wakuutus-osakeyhtiö Kaleva* ('insurance company Kaleva') and *Henkivakuutus-Osakeyhtiö Suomi* ('life insurance company Finland'). These appealed to people supporting the modern principle of Finnishness with their freshness and national imagery.

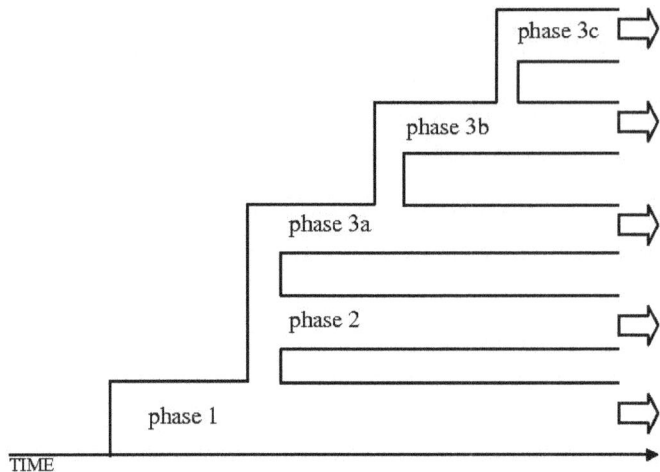

Fig. 13: Types of company names appearing in Finnish (Sjöblom 2006).

During their history, company names have become diversified: these initial name types are still possible but the objective of arousing attention requires inventing more and more various names. Company name types such as *Kallen veneverstas* ('Kalle's boat workshop') are traditional, certain prototypes of names but many such name types, which had not occurred yet in the 19th century at all, have been dominant in contemporary nomenclature. It remains to be seen what kinds of new name types the future will bring.

The aforementioned stratification of name structures is drawn up by the figure above (fig. 13) which shows the appearance of different name types in language. In stage 1, only a personal name which referred to the entrepreneur had been used for business activity. According to stage 2, appellatival expressions descriptive of the business activity had come about and, simultaneously, proper names referring to the business itself started to be used which, however, were strongly reminiscent of appellatival expressions (3a). In stages 3b and 3c, new types of company names had appeared in the language, first there were names metaphorically utilising words of the language and later meaningless quasi words and acronyms. All these different ways to refer to a specific company are still present; the structures, as it were, have not changed but rather they have diversified.

Finnish product names seem to have not emerged until a bit after the emergence of the category of company names. This is due to the simple fact that the first product names included the manufacturer's name, either a personal name or company name. In early expressions referring to products, the manufacturer's name seems to have appeared only in the genitive form (the Finnish case ending *n*) so their connection to descriptive appellatives was still fixed (*Amerikkalaiset Singerin Alkuperäiset ompelukoneet* 'American original Singer's sewing machines'). However, advertising that stirs the imagination came into the picture in product names perhaps faster

Plate 2: The Singer trade mark can be seen in a sewing machine advertisement featured in Uusi Suometar, 29 September 1880. (Source: The Historical Newspaper Library of the National Library of Finland)

than company names. As many had manufactured products for advertising outside of Finland, a product name referring to its origin was often quite strange and exotic sounding to Finnish consumers. People became used to the fact that the names of these products were perhaps not comprehensible or informative. The category of product names had emerged, at the latest, in the stage when an expression referring to the origin of the product no longer necessarily had been in the genitive but instead, typographic means, such as quotation marks or capital letters, were used to mark the word as a name (*Patenteerattu "ROBEY"-höyrykone* 'patented "ROBEY" steam engine').

The origin of products began to be advertised more frequently beginning in the early 1870s which can be seen in examples 4 to 8, taken from the newspaper *Uusi Suometar* between 1874 and 1879. Usually, the product of a factory or manufacturer was provided in the advertisement (examples 4 to 6 and 8). Mention of the manufacturer guaranteed the quality of the product. The first actual product names (example 7 and plate 2) appear in advertisements of the late 1870s in which foreign products were mentioned. The first time the genitive case was not marked was in 1879 (plate 3).

(4) *Rääwelin paahdettua sikuria, Herrain Rettig & Kump:in Tupakkia* (1874)
   Rääwel roasted chicory, Messers Rettig & Co's Tobacco

(5) *R. Hornsbyn & Pojan Niitto- ja Leikkuukoneita myypi Lars Thuring* (1876)
   R. Hornsby & Son's Mowers and Reaping Machines sold by Lars Thuring

Plate 3: Robey has also been typographically designated as the name of the product in this advertisement featured in Uusi Suometar, 12 March 1879. (Source: The Historical Newspaper Library of the National Library of Finland)

(6) *Kokkolan Tulitikkutehdasyhtiön hywintunnettuja tulitikkuja myypi täällä ainoastaan – – Parwiainen & Winter.* (1876)
Well-known matches of the Kokkola Matchstick Factory Company sold here only by – – Parwiainen & Winter.

(7) *Hyviä Elmén Rusinoita varrettomia tukuttain 30 p:iin naul. myypi C. M. Eskolin* (1878)
Delicious stemless Elmén Raisins, a gross for 30 pennies a pound, sold by C. M. Eskolin

(8) *Juuston juoksutinta Tukholman Teknillisen tehtaan valmistamaa ta'attua prima tavaraa* (1879)
Cheese rennet produced by Stockholm Technical Factory first class goods

Upon entering the 20th century, products were already given their own names which no longer were associated with the name of the manufacturer. The first Finnish tractor, the *Kullervo*-moottorivetäjä (*Kullervo* a tragic hero

MOOTTORIVETÄJÄT

Kullervo-moottorivetäjä

Plate 4: Kullervo-moottorivetäjä from 1918. (Source: Hankkijan arkisto.)

from *Kalevala* and a male name, *moottorivetäjä* the old word for 'tractor') from 1918, manufactured by Turun Rautateollisuus ja Vaunutehdas Oy, an iron and tram factory in Turku, is an example of this (plate 4).

Company Names

STRUCTURAL DESCRIPTION OF COMPANY NAMES

We will take a closer look at company names, their structure, meanings and functions in the following section with examples. The example companies here, for the most part, do not really exist. These names have been invented on the foundation of models of real company names, altering the vocabulary. It has already been stated earlier that when examining names, dividing them into structural parts is required. The familiar division of place names into name parts is not quite applicable to the examination of company names because company names often include various other elements and because while the order of these elements may be syntactically significant, they are not syntactically quite the same as in place names. It is better to define the name parts of company names on a functional-semantic basis, in other words, on the basis of function and meaning.

As previously stated, Finnish company names can be divided into four different name parts: a *corporate identifier*, a *part signifying the business concept*, an *identifying part* and a *supplementary part*. Not all of these appear in most company names but there are such names in which we can distinguish all four name parts: for example, the name *Kauneushoitola | Päivänpaiste | tmi | Tarja Tappurainen* ('beauty health centre | sunshine | private trader

| Tarja Tappurainen', the name parts differentiated by vertical bars) first includes the part signifying the business concept, then the identifying part, then the corporate identifier and finally the supplementary part.

The order of name parts in company names is rather free but not arbitrary. Certain name parts have a tendency to be situated at certain points in the name. Changing the order of parts may alter their special role in the entirety of the name, so the order of name parts sometimes will affect the how they will be interpreted. For example, it is natural to interpret the word *Puistopalvelu* ('park services') in the name *Puistopalvelu | Mäkinen | Oy* as the part signifying the business concept but in Finnish, the order could also be altered to *Mäkinen | Oy | Puistopalvelu*. In this case, the same word situated after the corporate identifier seems to have less stress regarding the whole name which is why it would be classified as a supplementary part.

The *corporate identifier* is compulsory in Finnish company names, except for in names of private traders and general partnerships. Its form is quite standard: the part can either be a whole word signifying the form of business (for example *aktiebolag* Swe. 'limited company', *toiminimi* 'trade name', *julkinen osakeyhtiö* 'public limited company') or its acronym (for example *AB*, *tmi*, *Oyj*). There can be variation, to some extent, in the written form of these acronyms. The corporate identifier is usually placed right at the front or end of the name. An exception to this order is the part signifying the business concept which can sometimes be placed ahead of the corporate identifier, e.g. *Musiikki | Oy | Forte fortissimo* ('music | ltd | Forte fortissimo'), and the supplementary part which often is placed right after it, such as *Rokkisradio | Oy | Lappeenranta* ('rock music radio | ltd | Lappeenranta', in Lappeenranta in South-Eastern Finland). There can be more than one corporate identifier in names whereupon they are always of different languages, for example *Oy | Bonbon | Ab* or *Aktiebolaget | Bonbon | Oy | Ltd*. The most typical thing is that the corporate identifier is an acronym placed at the end of a limited company, for example *Rovaniemen Karkkitukku Oy* ('Rovaniemi candy wholesale ltd', in Rovaniemi in Northern Finland) and placed at the beginning of private trade names, for example *Tmi Namihimo* ('private trader treats craving').

The *part signifying the business concept* is found in a company name on a semantic basis. It conveys the business concept of the company, that is, what it produces, in what way and who is doing the production. This semantic foundation however is not sufficient enough alone to show some name element as this part because the identifying or supplementary part can often also convey something about the business concept of the company. The part signifying the business concept must additionally be a word neutral in tone in relation to the referent of the name, in other words, it may not include any tone in style deviating from standard language, uncommon word choice nor bear very affective meanings. For example, both parts in the name of the candy shop *Makeispuoti Tikkarigalleria* signify something about the business concept of the company but only the first word *Makeispuoti* ('sweets shop') is tonally neutral whereas one product group sold is highlighted in the latter part *Tikkarigalleria* ('lollypop gallery') and, in addition to this, the

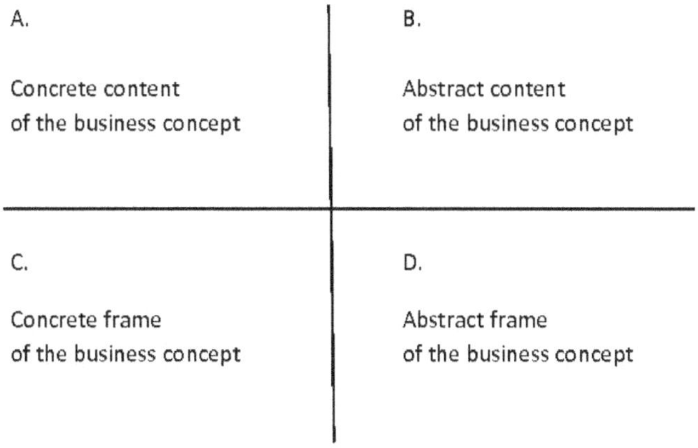

A.	B.
Concrete content of the business concept	Abstract content of the business concept
C.	D.
Concrete frame of the business concept	Abstract frame of the business concept

Fig. 14. The semantic fields of the part signifying the business concept.

uncommon word *galleria* ('gallery') is used in comparison to its referent as the principle component of the compound word. *Makeispuoti* is thus the part signifying the business concept and *Tikkarigalleria* is the identifying part of the name.

It is possible to describe the semantics of the part signifying the business concept in more detail by grouping their parts according to if they express something about the actual products or services of the company (*business concept content*) or the framework or operation of the company's activities (*business concept frames*). The word signifying the content of the business concept can be semantically quite concrete such as *auto* ('car') or *kello* ('watch, clock') or, on the other hand, it can be fully abstract such as *palvelu* ('service') or *suunnittelu* ('planning, design'). In the same way, words that signify the frames of the business concept can be divided into concrete ones such as *kukkakauppa* ('flower shop') or *tilitoimisto* ('accounting office') or abstract ones such as *teollisuus* ('industry') or *yhtymä* ('group'). There is a sliding boundary between concrete and abstract expressions. Hence, the semantic content of the business concept can be understood by a four-field image (fig. 14) whose horizontal coordinator shows the semantic concreteness/abstractness of the name part and the vertical coordinator shows to what extent the name part signifies the business concept through content or frames.

According to research (Sjöblom 2006), just under half of the registered company names in Finland include a part signifying the business concept. The number is clearly greater, if only those names, which include even the smallest amount of Finnish, are considered. This is at least partly due to the fact that the part signifying the business concept is quite often Finnish although there may otherwise be non-Finnish elements in a name. The industry and form of business will have an influence on how the business concept will be expressed in the name of the company.

A company name can never be formed by a part signifying the business concept alone because under the Trade Names Act, a neutral word descriptive of the company's activities is not sufficiently identifying. In addition to this, there must always be one part which identifies the name. Merely *Yrityspalvelut Oy* ('business services ltd'), thus, would not do as a name but *Karkkilan Yrityspalvelut Oy* would. In this case, the name includes the identifying name part *Karkkilan* (the town of Karkkila in the genitive), the part signifying the business concept *yrityspalvelut* and the corporate identifier *oy*.

The *identifying name part* is, in essence, the actual name of the company. In practice, merely the identifying name part, which is thus always a compulsory part, is sufficient enough in many cases for recognising a company. Instead of the aforementioned *Makeispuoti Tikkarigalleria*, we could indeed identifiably speak of *Tikkarigalleria* alone. This, however, is not always the case, such as in the aforementioned example *Karkkilan Yrityspalvelut Oy*. This kind of name is only usable when the identifying part and the part signifying the business concept form a whole image.

The semantic content of the identifying name part can be quite diverse. The linguistic elements that the name part includes and their meanings are strongly associated with messages which the name passes on to language users. We will discuss the meanings included in company names in more detail later. Here, however, we will divide identifying name parts using mostly formative criteria:

The identifying name part can include the following types of elements:
- A personal name (***Matti Möttönen** Oy*, *Studio **Veera***)
- A place name (***Oulun** vuokra-auto Oy* '**Oulu** rental car ltd', ***Kaivopuisto** Trading Oy*)
- Other proper nouns, such as an imaginary person, character or place name, animal name, name of celestial body, ship name, etc. (*Oy **Jupiter** Ab*, ***Mustin** murkina Oy* '**Musti's** grub ltd')
- An expression bearing lexical meaning (***Poutapäivä** Power Production Oy* '**fair weather day** Power Production ltd', *Lähettipalvelu **Vikkelät kintut*** 'courier service speedy feet')
- A quasi word (***Avidox** Oy*)
- An acronym or number (***MRS**-Hieronta Oy* '**MRS** massage ltd', *Tmi Pukuompelimo **4 Men*** 'private trader suit tailor **4 Men**')

The identifying name part can include many words, so elements from many other groups than one of those listed above can be associated with it. Out of the abovementioned examples, the identifying part of *Mustin murkina Oy* includes, in addition to the proper noun *Musti* (a dog name 'blackie', in the genitive case), an expression bearing lexical meaning *murkina* ('food, grub'), and the identifying part of the name *Tmi Pukuompelimo 4 Men* in addition to having a number, carries the lexical expression *men* (in word play of 'four men' or 'for men'; *Pukuompelimo* '(men's) suit tailor').

The most common identifying name parts in Finnish company names are such elements which bear lexical meaning. As we add all of the classes of proper nouns together, we use proper nouns as elements of identifying name parts almost as much as expressions that bear lexical meaning. Quasi words, that is, words which are not part of any real language, are also common because they are used more than any single group of common nouns and almost as much as personal names and place names together. Acronyms and numbers as elements of identifying name parts are less used but, nevertheless, are not uncommon.

A small group of Finnish company names include, in addition to the abovementioned described factors, a certain kind of extra, explanatory element, without which the name may seem completely identifying and sufficient. This *supplementary part* provides information on the owner of the name or the industry, domicile or geographic area of its referent. The supplementary part is usually placed at the end of the name, sometimes even after the corporate identifier. It is particularly common that a non-Finnish company, registered in the Finnish Trade Register, would identify its activities in Finland with a supplementary part signifying the name of the country *Suomi* or *Finland*. Private traders may sometimes supplement their trade name with their own personal names (*Optikko Sinisilmä tmi* **Iris Kukkanen** 'optician blue eye private trader **Iris Kukkanen**').

What then are the typical structures of Finnish company names? Is there a prototype or are there prototypical company names? We can say "yes" to the latter question because Finnish company names essentially seem to follow the same types of structural models in relation to the name parts and their order. Efforts are made to have the number of name parts as small as possible, which means having one or two name parts depending on if the corporate identifier in the name is compulsory or not. Indeed, the identifying name part appears in all company names. Including a part signifying the business concept in a name is quite common as previously stated. Private traders who need not use a corporate identifier quite often include a part signifying the business concept in the name which normally is located before the identifying part but can also appear right after it.

A prototypical name of a limited company would first include the identifying part, which is made up of an expression bearing lexical meaning, a proper noun or quasi word, and then after this part, the acronym *Oy* (*Bonbon Oy*). Should a part signifying the business concept be included in the name of a limited company, its position is prototypically located between the identifying part and the corporate identifier (*Bonbon Production Oy*, *Suonenjoen mansikkaleivos Oy* 'Suonenjoki strawberry pastry ltd'). The prototypical company name of a private trader includes an identifying part only (*Tekstinikkari* 'text carpenter') or one with a part signifying the business concept preceding it (*Mainostoimisto Tekstinikkari* 'advertising agency text carpenter'). Should this kind of name include a corporate identifier, it is prototypically located at the beginning (*Tmi Mainostoimisto Tekstinikkari*). There are no absolute regulations on the number of name parts or their order but rather it is a question of prototypes which, in real data, vary in different ways.

Determining Language in Company Names

The fact that quite often two or sometimes even more different languages can be used in the same name is also connected to the understanding of structural parts of contemporary company names. Language users indeed take note of change in language but it is not always possible to believe that two elements of different languages in a name can have different functions. A change in language nearly always happens at the boundary of name parts. Another factor perceptible about multilingual company names is that name parts which have an informative function (the part signifying the business concept or the supplementary part) are always either in Finnish or English in Finnish company names, in some rare cases also in Swedish. By its informative value, a language which is believed to be understood by everyone is chosen for the most important name part. The use of English in these name parts indicates the general idea that all Finns understand English. The second issue is the question of if these English name parts are even understood. It has been stated, at least in European studies, that a large part of consumers do not necessarily understand the percentage of English in slogans and advertisements (Gerritsen et al 2000). English words thus appearing even in company names may not completely be understood – also in Finland.

People are generally quite interested in what language company names truly are and if they are any language at all. There is no simple answer to this question because defining the *linguistic origin* of names can be difficult. We cannot always find an unambiguous interpretation of company names because many proper nouns and quasi words, as well as words from different languages which can be quite similar in form, can appear in these names. Also, the fact that not all speakers are in the same way conscious about the language of the names nor may they know the language that well must be taken into consideration. If a name includes, for example, a Romany word (there is a Romany minority in Finland), many Finns most likely would not recognise the word as Romany and many might even imagine it to be a completely invented word.

A key issue in the study of company nomenclature (and commercial nomenclature in general) is to analyse the linguistic origin of the names because the influence of the internationalisation and globalisation of culture can clearly be seen in commercial names. Because of this, regardless of difficulties, attempts must be made to create certain principles according to which, the linguistic origin of the names can be defined. In the following, we should remember that regardless of the principles presented, there are always individual cases in which a researcher ends up making a conclusion on the basis of his own subjective opinion or ends up leaving his conclusion wide open.

We start off from the name as a whole when defining the linguistic origin of company names. However, the corporate identifier is the exception and can be left outside of the investigation; after all, it is almost always Finnish (or sometimes Swedish or English) regardless of what language the name otherwise is. Other elements appearing in the name can be either some known language or an invented language which we shall call a *quasi-language*. Not all of the elements appearing in names can clearly be connected to one specific language. As the linguistic origin of company names are examined, it is first best to investigate if the name has neutral elements regarding language. These neutral elements include internationalisms, personal names referring to the company owner, commonly known and internationally used place names, other internationally known names and also acronyms.

Internationalisms are words which, in form and meaning, are identical in many European languages. It is difficult to say which language is perceived by the speakers or even the name givers regarding these words. Internationalisms appearing in these kinds of names include, for example, *ateljé, bar, café, centre/center, photo/foto, info, internet, kebab, market, media, pasta, pizza, pub, studio* and *taxi*. The name *Fotostudio Anna*, for example, could be Swedish but it could also be Finnish because, after all, the personal name *Anna* is known in Sweden, Finland and many other countries as well. The name can linguistically be defined as being international on this basis.

Personal names referring to the owner of the company can certainly be such that they can easily be connected to a certain language (for example, many indeed consider *Matti Möttönen* to be a Finnish name). However, they are neutral regarding language because of the fact that they have no meaning concerning the conceptualisation of the language of the name: even if the name giver would like to give an English or German name to his business, his own name cannot be changed to the same language even though it would be included in the company name.

Company names can also have proper nouns which do not refer to the owner. If this kind of name is internationally known, it would then be linguistically neutral regarding the company name as a whole. For example, the name *Kauneussalonki Torino* ('beauty salon Torino') is a Finnish name on this basis, *Kauneussalonki Beautiful Torino* is a name including Finnish and English and *Bella Torino* is an Italian name.

The linguistic origin of acronyms is often difficult to determine and so a useful strategy is to consider them neutral in linguistic terms. *JRE Oil Co. Oy* would thus be an English name due to the word *oil* whereas *JRE-yhtiöt Oyj* ('JRE companies plc') would be a Finnish name.

Company names can be linguistically grouped by how many languages, be they one or two or more, are included or by how they function in relation to linguistic origin in quite the same way in different parts of the Western world. Names made up of only one language are called *monolingual* names, those of two or more languages or some true language and a quasi-language are *multilingual* names and the third group made up of *universal* names. Universal names can further be divided into three groups: 1) Names including international and neutral words only 2) Names that are completely a quasi-language 3) Names including only the name of the owner.

The language of the financial world is globally English. This is notoriously due to globalised marketing through the Internet and other channels of information. English is a common language of communication and considered to be a universal language. English has extended from the business language between companies to advertising aimed at consumers and its influences on commercial nomenclature have been observed in different parts of the world. English is also a common language in Finnish company names, even though Finnish-language names are still the majority. On the other hand, Swedish, which was common to Finnish company names one hundred years ago, is now virtually left to the sidelines.

Quasi-lingual words have become more common in company names and rather large businesses are increasingly adopting or changing a name which is actually not any language. There are, however, often familiar elements in these invented names and so they are rarely completely independent from real language. As a name is formed on the bases of such elements as *com*, *edu*, *fin*, *inter*, *lex*, *medi*, *tek*, *web* and so on, it is not difficult to find connections to their origin which can often be found in English, Latin or Finnish. These types of elements are like blocks with which an appropriate tower can be built. They have a common, recognisable form and meaning and they can be affixed to one another rather freely.

Latin is a language which is abundantly utilised in company names, as well as in product names. As the mother of many European languages and as a language that has given a great deal of vocabulary to many non-Indo-European languages, it is useful in names whose purpose, in addition to an identifying function, is to arouse various semantic associations in the listeners. This is because many Latin words are, at the least, comprehensible to many people. There are more extensive images on Western culture and civilisation that are associated with Latin; it is a historic-politically neutral language which exudes cogency and scholarship and, in line with certain opinions, masculinity.

It is good to remember that Finnish company names are also becoming international in that more and more different languages are being used as elements in them. Italian, Spanish, French and German are such languages which arouse certain types of images, which is how they find their way to company names. Foreign entrepreneurs in Finland with their various languages also have an impact on the spectrum of languages. Just 50 years ago, a company name in Chinese would have been extremely exceptional whereas today, a countless number of these kinds of names exist in 21st century Finland.

The multilingualisation of commercial language use and, at the same time its nomenclature as well, has been observed in research done in other countries. English in particular, but also other foreign languages, find their way in a similar fashion to Japanese, Russian, German and Dutch commercial language and nomenclature. Loulou Edelman (2009), who has studied the language included in all kinds of signs in the main business street of Amsterdam, has observed that the names of shops and products on signs in particular has an increased share of English and other foreign languages in relation to Dutch. Provided proper names would not be counted amongst them at all, there would be a much more Dutch image from the linguistic scenery of the central shopping area of Amsterdam. Angelika Bergien (2005) has noted in her study of the company names of the former East German Sachsen-Anhalt that nearly half of the names include at least some non-German element, particularly English or French. In general, prestige languages, that is, languages which people stereotypically have a positive image of, would rather be used. In this socio-onomastic study, the opinions of consumers on company names were also examined. Regarding non-German elements, there were rather large differences in the opinions between respondents aged between 20 and 30 and those between the ages of 40 and 50: older consumers shunned these elements notably more often than the younger ones.

Semantic Description of Company Names

As we have said, it is important that a commercial name arouses various connotations. These associations can, in a certain way, be considered the meaning of the name. The meaning of a company name does not refer to a classifying, conceptual meaning because a proper noun does not have such a meaning nor does it mean, in this context either, the etymology of the name or the principles of naming. These, however, are of course possible to examine too. In regard to a language community, a company name and commercial names usually have meaning which includes different semantic connections which the name's form arouses in the minds of the speakers. A part of these connections is subjective, a part common to many language speakers. These kinds of common associations are included in the name's linguistic meaning not just a part of subjective world knowledge.

The theoretical background to onomastics has been covered in the first chapter of this book where the research trend of cognitive linguistics was introduced. The difference of this kind of research to earlier linguistic perspectives is mainly that meaning has been brought out to the core of a language system. From this perspective, it is natural to justify that proper names are also included in the structuring of meanings in language in the same way as other words. It has been noted that the meaning of proper nouns can be described according to what kind of relationship the form of the expression has to cognitive domains that are aroused in our minds by the referent.

When examining company names, we should focus on key topics that businesses, as we think of them as referents, include, such as industry, owner, location, size, area of activity and so on. When we know what referent the name is referring to, the form of the name (a company name) is, in one way or another, connected to the characteristics of its referent (a company). In our minds, this connection is a semantic relationship, and with this relationship, the meaning of the name can be determined. The different name parts of a company name can function in different meaning relationships.

The linguistic form of a name or name part can directly convey subjects about the business: the name may, for example, refer directly to the owner of the company or its industry (*Einar Pinnalan polkupyöräkorjaamo* 'Einar Pinnala's bike repair shop'), in which case the name has a *direct meaning relationship* to its referent.

The form of a name or name part can also be in an *indirect meaning relationship* whereupon the words appearing in the name are connected to the referent through some kind of association, most commonly metonymically or metaphorically. A *metonymic*, that is relational, association means that a word appearing in a name is connected to a conceptual field in which the referent is included. With metonymy, we can emphasise a part of a whole. The name of the hairdressers *Rajut rastat* ('fierce Rastas') is metonymic because a Rastafarian hairdo has a conceptual point of contact to the business where the hairdressing takes place. By highlighting a certain hairstyle in the name, it emphasises certain characteristics of the business at the same time. A *metaphoric*, that is, comparative association means that a word appearing in the name represents a conceptual field where structural points of contact can be found in a conceptual field represented by the referent. A typical metaphor in company names is the comparison of an intellectual working or service company to a person that does physical work or a place such as *Ohjelmatoimisto Telkkariverstas* ('event agency TV workshop'), or to compare the business to some ideal or spacious setting such as *Päiväkoti Satumetsä* ('day care fairy tale forest') or *Grilli-kioski Nakkiareena* ('snack bar hot dog arena'). There are countless other metaphors that can be used. An indirect meaning relationship can also be founded on other kinds of associations, for example, the arousal of certain moods or *symbolism* (*Hate Music Oy*, *Ekokauppa Kyyhky* 'ecoshop dove').

The semantic connections of a name or name parts to the referent, however, are not always that clear. Names in particular that include quasi words are such that as they are, they cannot arouse direct associations any better or worse than indirect ones. Still, recognisable parts of words or names are often compressed in them through which, direct or indirect semantic connections can be found. Semantic connections are therefore more complicated and often more subjective than the aforementioned cases but they still may include a great deal of common meanings to language speakers. This is called a *compressed meaning relationship* because several different semantic contents have been condensed in the expression. An example of this is *Finteknorex* whose elements can refer to, for example, Finnishness (*fin*), technology (*tekno* 'techno-') and royalty (Lat. *rex*) – sometimes there may be other ways to perceive this.

When the phonetic form of the name as it is does not arouse any image concerning the business, then it is a question of a *disconnected meaning relationship*. The semantic connection between the form and the referent of the name has been completely disconnected and gradually only such associative meanings – not thus linguistic meaning – which originate from the traits of the referent become linked to the name. For example, an acronym as the identifying part of a name is often exactly this, unless the acronym already has some commonly known meaning (compare, for example, the acronyms *STH* and *DNA*).

Certain scholars (e.g. Herstatt 1985; Bergien 2006) have separated *primary*, that is, literal meanings of company names and *secondary*, that is, meanings of company names pertaining to products into two different types of meanings. When a new company name is created, the important function of the primary meaning helps the consumer learn the secondary meaning. When the secondary meaning has been learnt, the primary meaning can, in a way, be forgotten. A real example of this dominating state taken by the secondary meaning is *Benetton*, whose primary meaning is the surname of the founders of the company. Not many would ever think that this is the primary meaning. Instead, the name *Benetton* only brings certain types of products to mind. This changing process of meaning takes time and is a matter of fact connected to the building of the brand. In creating a brand from a company name, the secondary meaning needs to be brought out so that the primary meaning that pertains to the name itself remains in the back of people's minds.

Social and Cultural Functions

In addition to linguistic meaning, the *interpersonal function* between products and consumers is fundamental in regard to company names and other commercial names. Certain scholars are of the opinion that a name's functions are even more fundamental than the name's form (e.g. Bergien 2006) whereas others believe that the form, meaning and functions work together and are equally important (Sjöblom 2006).

A company name can simultaneously have several social and cultural functions. These functions occur in a social context where the names emerge and where they are used. Socio-cultural functions are closely linked to the aforementioned meaning relationships but there is reason to keep them separate from the meaning of the name which is itself a phenomenon concerning language. Function is a phenomenon which pertains to the use of language. The more functions a name works in, the better and more useful it often is regarding the business itself.

Company names have at least the following types of functions: An *informative* company name provides people with information on the business. A direct meaning relationship is always informative but a name or name part based on an indirect or even compressed meaning relationship can also be informative when it reveals something, for example, about the industry of the business.

Persuasiveness has been considered just one of the most important functions of commercial nomenclature. A persuasive name easily creates an image on an approachable, qualified, servicing, economic company or one that includes other types of positive traits. A *persuasive function* steers people's behaviour and builds an image of the business together with other communications of the company. We should however remember that persuasiveness is ultimately a subjective experience: emotional value aroused by expressions included in the name is the issue at hand. A name can be persuasive in many different ways: it can exude safety, arouse curiosity, entertain, directly answer the needs of the customer or it can be humorous or aesthetically pleasing. Sometimes, persuasiveness can also mean the limitation of clientele. For example, in some people's opinion, an expression can seem unapproachable but others may find it insightful and appealing.

A *practical function* emphasises the name's instrumental value. A name must distinguish the company from others, it must be easy to inflect (in Finnish, for example) and it can perhaps be easily formable as an appealing, visual logo. Practicality is also promoted by the name's placement in the beginning point of the alphabet. Sometimes the fact that the part signifying the business concept is placed first in a name may be practical in various alphabetical catalogues. Thus, for example, all hotels or salons will be found consecutively in the same place.

An *integrative function* pertains to the fact that a name indicates the company's connection to, for example, a specific geographic area or certain culture. The name can certainly include direct reference to the locality where the company operates but a name can also indirectly integrate the business to a specific area, for example, by choice of language or dialect. It has been stated in international studies that businesses aimed at the local market receives an abundance of names pertaining to the local language or dialect than those geared towards a broader market (van Langevelde 1999). It has also been pointed out that many consumers truly appreciate the fact that a regional identity can in some way be seen in a company name (Bergien 2005). Certain kinds of expressions, such as *international*, can work in an integrative function. At the same time, an integrative function concerns the fact that a name can follow naming models of other companies of the same field. We can see that, for example, many hairdressers, construction companies or advertisement agencies have the same types of names. A name, which does not differentiate much from names of other businesses of the same field, integrates the business amongst other businesses of their own industry.

An *individualising function* unites company names to personal names. In a certain way, a company name has deep, metaphoric meaning: it personifies the business, creates a human actor from it. A personal name has a strong individualising function: it makes its bearer something unique, provides it the value of an individual as a member of a community. The same is done by a company name, and names which are founded on a compressed or disconnected meaning relationship and which already are structurally reminiscent of (female) personal names, are especially strong (*Elixia*, *Edita*, *Ikea*, *Nordea*, *Sonera*).

A company name can also have other functions, but the aforementioned five may be the most important regarding a language community. With regard to social and cultural functions outside of language, how company names, in themselves as a part of commercial language use, reflect but also build up a surrounding culture must be highlighted. For example, after the fall of the Soviet Union, the speedy change that occurred in the economic environment of Russia had attracted scholars to examine how commercial names reflected these repercussions. This subject was approached by Alexei Yurchak (2000) and Sergei Gorajev (2007). The observations of these scholars show that names have expectedly become westernised thusly, that foreign languages are used in them and efforts are made to arouse many kinds of associations with them. A previously public space can be privately conquered with names. On the other hand, Russia has not borrowed the Western language of market economy directly. Instead, a new naming culture was born out of the encounter of the old Soviet system and new Western influences. By giving new names to businesses which dominate a public space that before was owned by the government, a certain kind of *performative function* is simultaneously realised: there is indication to the legal owners of the space, the current leaders, private entrepreneurs, of the social reality and balance of power are defined.

Brands, Product Names and Trade Marks

Commercial names may sometimes refer to subjects which would not really exist without a name – name thus are, in a way, an essential part of the creative process. Entrepreneurs imagine their businesses to operate a bit like authors imagine the events in their books. This thought links the creation of commercial names to the creation of literary names. Names have a certain function that brings forth images in the company's activities the same way as names have an important function regarding the story in a book. A company name can also be invented as if to be put in a desk drawer, to be set aside for sale or to be later adopted. In this case, a name can exist before a referent or the name can create the referent for itself. The same phenomenon is often also seen in the case of products: the building of images begins before the products are even manufactured. When developing a new product (material or immaterial), an identifying name immediately provides the product with some added value.

Brands are all about the fact that rather than selling a mere product or service, the experiential world built around the product is also sold. A brand is an image of added value offered by a product or service. The image gradually emerges in these communicative circumstances where a certain name is systematically used, aiming at some certain objective. In this, we can speak about the building of a brand: the foundation is a name (normally a name of a company or trade mark) on top of which, as if brick by brick, stories that produce added value, different experiences based on the senses, emotions and so on are constructed. Success in building a brand and keeping the brand afloat all comes down to how durable the building materials are. This means that the images and promises the brand includes are based on reality.

The Interbrand consultancy, among others, has published lists on the world's most prestigious brands. Those that are regarded as good brands are well-known by consumers and opinion leaders and they are at the top of the industry in their own field. The best brands create a consistent identity based on language, sight, hearing and touch. Consumers all around the world always experience brands in the same way. In addition to a common, global message, local culture must also be taken into consideration in the marketing of this brand (for example, *McDonald's* in Finland sells a *McRuis* 'McRye' which is a hamburger on dark, Finnish rye bread instead of a regular hamburger bun, which would hardly be available in Paris). A brand cannot be a brand without its emotive side. By appealing to the values and emotions of the consumer, a brand guarantees his loyalty.

As a linguistic sign, a brand differs from company names structurally but not by its semantic content. Brands are structurally simpler than company names, often only one word long or an acronym. They are usually made up of a company name's identifying part, so they include similar language elements as company names: quasi words, personal names, expressions bearing lexical meaning, place names, other proper nouns and acronyms. Being a brand is also mainly something other than a lingual phenomenon but yet there are also linguistic requirements to it. For a brand to be built from a name, it must be rather short, easy to pronounce and remember. Moreover, a *slogan* is particularly associated with a brand (*Nokia. Connecting people*).

All brands do not emerge on the basis of a company name but rather they are constructed around product names and trade marks as well, such as *Fairy* and *Dr Pepper*. In addition, there is a desire for brands in other areas than traditional trade. Many cities and provinces build up a brand from their names (we can speak of, for example, the brand *Lapland*). Brands are created out of names of different events (*Ruisrock, Pori Jazz, New York Marathon, Vasaloppet*), the same as television programmes (*Idols* the Finnish version of *American Idol, Talent* the Finnish version of *America's Got Talent*). Efforts are made to make brands out of people involved in entertainment in particular but also in politics. A name, commercial products and non-commercial values and experiences are merged together in being a brand. When *Lordi* soft drinks, *Joulupukki* ('Santa Claus') coffee, *Angry Birds* toys or *Helsinki* t-shirts are sold, brands are made.

Especially in large cities, but also on a small scale, companies are interested in fortifying their brand by purchasing urban space and providing various places with their name or the name of their product. There have been strong objections to this latter mentioned type of intrusion of commercialism in a public area and, for instance, various anti-advertisement campaigns have questioned this phenomenon. There have been ponderings on how long we shall allow commercialism to dominate our environment and even ourselves. (Klein 2001.)

The linguistic structure and semantic contents of brands are interesting in relation to the brand's imaginary world, which however is largely based on extralinguistic factors.

In regard to onomastics, product names and trade marks are just as interesting and their structure may well be made up of multiple parts.

The conceptual difference between a product name, trade mark and brand has been covered in the beginning of this chapter. Products are usually identified with an expression comprising of multiple parts and which we shall use the term *product description* for this concept. Product descriptions are made up of multiple parts and can include the following: the name of the manufacturer (company name), a trade mark, a product name, an appellative signifying the type of product and a qualifier. For example, the order of the product description *Leaf | Iso | SISU® | Pastilli | Tuhti Hedelmä* is: company name, product name ('big'), trade mark ('perseverance, guts'), appellative signifying the type of product ('pastille'), qualifier ('hearty fruit'). The word *Iso* and the trade mark *SISU* really form an indivisible product name in this example. *Iso* is not actually a part of the trade mark. The product name, along with the trade mark, is the core of the product description. Providing there is no separate product name, the linguistic element of the trade mark corresponds to the product name. The following table shows examples of different product descriptions:

Table 2: The structure of a product description.

COMPANY NAME	TRADE MARK	PRODUCT NAME	TYPE OF PRODUCT	QUALIFIER
Unilever	*Pepsodent®*	*Junior*	*toothpaste*	*Mild Mint*
GlaxoSmithKlein	*Odol®*	*N'ICE*	*Zahnpflege-Bonbons*	*Mint-Menthol*
Cloetta Fazer	*Pantteri®* 'panther'	*Yö mix* 'night mix'	*mixed candies*	*Jumbo*
	Lumene®	*Quick & Chick*	*Nail Polish*	*Horizon*
	Nokia	*N73*		*Music Edition*
Valio	*Benecol®*		*energy drink*	*raspberry*
Daimler-Chrysler	*Mercedes-Benz*	*S 600*		*Sedan*

In many cases, the name of the manufacturer is the foundation of the product description, whereupon it is seen less in the product name (*Lumene* ← *Lumene Group*, *Nokia* ← *Nokia Oyj*). The trade mark symbol ® is not always used even though it would be a question of a registered trade mark (*Nokia*, *Mercedes-Benz*). The actual product name is missing from the *Valio Benecol* example in which the trade mark *Benecol* also functions as the name of the product but in which, to some extent, the appellative signifying the type of product *energy drink* is also contextually like a name. The product name often designates a certain series of products and with the aid of the type of product and qualifier, individual product types can be differentiated from them. The qualifier can include various lexical or numeric descriptions about the product's technical qualities, those picked up by the senses or other characteristics and sometimes it can even be rather long.

Christoph Platen (1997), who has studied product names (trade marks), has noted that the modern human comes into contact with approximately 300 product names a day. According to Platen, product names are totalities in which linguistic and marketing perspectives come together so that both are taken in to consideration when examining them. The fact that product names also have other meanings than just the identification of their referents is characteristic of these names. Thus, similar factors concerning meaning and function largely concern product names as they do in company names.

In Platen's words, product names can be found on the field of conflict between arbitrariness and motivation. Product names are united with company names by the compliance of certain prototypical models: analogy is always to some extent a steering factor in name giving.

Platen divides elements included in product names into three groups which are then split up into sub-groups. Platen's division, though slightly modified from the original, with examples, is as follows:

1) Words of a real language
   - appellatives and other lexemes (*Golf, Camel, Elle*)
   - proper names (*Wasa, Mont Blanc, Brigitte*)
2) Creative formations
   - phonetic or orthographic modifications of words (*X-tra*)
   - derived words (*Yougurette, Nutella*)
   - compound words and collocations (*Dentagard, Ultra Pampers*)
   - sentences and phrases (*Nimm Zwei, After Eight*)
3) Quasi words
   - acronyms (*Haribo* ← Hans Riegel Bonn)
   - "arbitrary" formations (*Elmex*)

The meanings of product names can be examined from the same kind of perspective as in the meanings of company names, in other words, by analysing what kinds of meaning relationships between the form of the name and its referent are aroused in the language speaker. The perspective can indeed also be etymological whereupon what the motivation, that is, the principles with which a name's elements has been chosen at the moment of name giving has been, is primarily examined. In considering etymologies, it is best to be grounded and not get too easily eager to come to imaginary interpretations. Every interpretation should be confirmed by asking the owner of the product name directly for the real motivation or by comparing various sources (company histories, dictionaries, encyclopaedias, Internet searches and so on). Many expressions presumed to be arbitrary or fantastical names may turn out to have had quite simple motives. For example, the name of the chocolate bar *Mars* is based on the surname of company's founders Frank and his son Forrest Mars. The mythological sounding name *Ikea* is an acronym which consists of the first letters of the founder Ingvar Kamprad and the homestead (Elmtaryd) and village (Agunnaryd) where he was born. Many names have knowingly included many different motivations: for example, *Nylon* is a contamination which, according to one explanation, is based on the names *New York* and *London* but, on the other hand, includes elements of the words *vinyl* and *cotton*, and also has other explanations to the name.

Product names are perhaps even more susceptible to take elements from foreign languages than company names. Elke Ronneberger-Sibold and Paola Cotticelli Kurras (2007) have compared elements of German and Italian origin from the beginning of the 20th century to the mid-1970s. The reproduction of English-language elements can clearly be seen in both of these materials and especially the expansion of language in the Italian materials. The meaning of English-language elements in German product names has also been examined by Werner Brandl (2007). According to his preliminary results, the percentage of product names both including English and completely English has simultaneously multiplied as the percentage of purely German and other kinds of language combinations have diminished. English is thus a clearly attractive language but Brandl asks what these English elements must be for them to be appealing in the opinion of Germans. On the one hand, what kinds of images are associated with English and, on the other hand, what kinds are associated with German? It is apparent that different languages are appropriate for different products in different ways.

Product names are a part of a language's vocabulary and susceptible to similar changes as other words in the language. A great concern to the owners of product names is their genericisation into a common noun, that is, an appellative – a phenomenon which happens in the case of other proper nouns (for example, the Finnish male names *Uuno* and *Yrjö* → *uuno* 'idiot' and *yrjö* 'vomit'). When becoming generic, a product name loses its identifying function. According to Shawn Clankie (2002), this happens as a result of a series of gradual grammatical and semantic changes: a temporary, metonymically used name in a general sense by some speaker gradually becomes a collectively used appellative. When becoming a part of the lexicon, the vocabulary of a language, the name ultimately loses its original connection to the product completely. For example, the word *walkman* is no longer really known as a product name. There are many reasons for genericisation. It particularly happens if the name's referent in a way represents a new conceptual class which has no appellative to describe it. At the same time, one reason can be that the product name is shorter or otherwise more practical to use than an appellative already in existence. The general familiarity of a product name certainly promotes its genericisation the same as how much there is a need to use the expression that describes the type or product in question in the communication of the language community.

On the Border Areas of Commercial Nomenclature

Western people have internalised marketing thinking so thoroughly that it has dominated our entire sphere of life. In one way or another, nearly everything is commercial: when we are searching for a job, we must market ourselves, and when we are at work, we must sell our skills to both the employer and "clients" which today include for example, in addition to customers of traditional trade, patients in need of medical care, people in search of social aid, students at educational institutions or children and their parents at day cares. A politician markets his ideas to voters, a performance or creative artist must find the right market. The productivity of universities is measured and even culture and art are spoken of as a product.

The commercialisation of our sphere of life has also had an impact on nomenclature because many name categories that have already been in use, such as the names of housing cooperatives, public organisations, books, television programmes or animal names, have also begun to receive commercial tones. New name categories have also emerged which at least have, unless there is always a commercial foundation, a commercial function: names of various events, electronic games, performer names, names of trade centres and so on.

Finnish housing cooperatives (*asunto-osakeyhtiö*, acronyms *asunto oy* or *as. oy*) have been studied by Marianne Blomqvist (1997), Taina Kettunen (1999) and Paula Sjöblom (2000a). Housing cooperatives are companies whose goal is not the acquisition of financial gain. Their names thus are not originally based on commercialism although they do practise economic activity. Many names of old housing cooperatives founded at the turn of the 20th century are even quite ideological (*Työväen Asunto Oy Riento* 'workforce housing cooperative hasten', *Asunto-osakeyhtiö Valpas* 'housing cooperative alert') and as such they once highlighted the ideals of the housing cooperative activities or bases of the shareholders (housing cooperative of workers, housing cooperative of the Karelians). The time of accelerated construction and apartment production that begun in the 1950s often led to schematic names based on a street address, for example *As. Oy Koulukatu 14* ('housing cooperative 14 school street'). A bit later on, variation to the nomenclature emerged by exploiting the toponymy existing in the residential area (Tampere neighborhood *Amuri → Asunto-oy Amurinmäki* 'housing cooperative Amuri hill'). After construction and housing production had changed more clearly into business only, the names of the housing cooperatives changed: efforts were made to arouse positive associations with the names and themes of the name were often selected from elsewhere than the nomenclature of the neighbourhood. A good example of this includes the names of the Vuosaari ('flow|island') housing cooperatives in Helsinki *Vuohelmi* ('flow|pearl') or *Helsingin Swingi* ('Helsinki swing').

Commercialisation also touches upon names of various educational institutions. Private educational institutions are not the only ones that wind up competing for students but also many institutions maintained by public funds vigorously market their "products", in other words, their degree programmes. As there is a desire to utilise all possible ways in marketing, it often ends in changing an old name into something believed to be more sellable. The result is a group of names of educational institutions which sometimes are reminiscent of each other perhaps a bit too much (*Diak*, *Humak* and *Hamk*). A name's semantic connection to education has been faded out completely. Models of commercial nomenclature are also followed as names of various public commercial establishments have been eager to change. For example, the Finnish Government Printing Centre (*Valtion painatuskeskus*) became *Edita*, the Finnish Post (*Posti*) became *Itella* and the Finnish Roads Enterprise (*Tieliikelaitos*) became *Destia*. These kinds of name changes usually arouse lively public debate.

Moreover, animal names today have been influenced by commercialism. This especially concerns kennel and breeder names of cats and dogs and also stable names for horses. The function of these names is not only to identify the animal but also to indicate its breeder and pedigree. The name is the breeder's advertisement and a certain kind of product guarantee quite the same way as a trade mark acts as a guarantee of a product. The breeder name, however, does not make the name a commercial product name completely nor certainly make the animal merely some sort of product; after all, animals differ from manufactured products, as they are quite different as living beings. Everyone knows that a name per se does not necessarily guarantee, for example, the success of the animal in a cat or dog show or a horse's success in a harness race. There are guidelines provided by the Finnish Kennel Club for dog kennels which, for instance, limit the name to no more than 20 characters and to have no more than two words. Similar kinds of guidelines do not exist for horse names in Finland but one study (Kalske 2005) shows that Finnish stable names are often made up of two parts, one of which conveys the name of the stable and the other, the horse's own name. The part indicating the stable can be a word (*Pinewood*), a collocation (*Black Horse*) or an acronym (*SG*). Examples of these kinds of horse names include *Pinewood Wild West*, *Black Horse Romanus* and *SG Oh'Boy*.

Ships and boats have been given names for quite a long time. Vessels have often been identified by female names and, moreover, christenings reminiscent of people's name giving ceremonies give us reason to believe that one function of the name is personification. Today, however, many names of cruise ships, ice breakers and cargo ships have more and more of a commercial function as well. The name has an owner, the shipping company, and many of these names are reminiscent of company names just like animal names that have a commercial tone. Quite often, there is some reference, for example, to the shipping company that owns the vessel in these names. In the typical fashion of commercial names, English elements are used in ship names and, depending on the type of vessel, their semantic contents include strength (*Otso* 'bear', *Urho* 'hero'), speediness (*Tallink Superfast*), beauty (*Silja Serenade*) or other qualities highlighting positive factors. Some studies on ship names include those by Ole-Jørgen Johannessen (2005) and Anita Schybergsson (2009).

Rather new name categories with a commercial tone include, for example, names of various commercial and other events as well as popular culture artist names. A great deal of money often revolves around fairs, sporting events and many cultural activities. In terms of their objectives, these events today are highly commercial, even though the content itself would essentially seem to be completely non-commercial. The number of events grows all the time and competition for people's time increases faster and faster. A name is a part of the marketing of these events the same way as it is for companies. In the best case, the name of a regularly repeated event is made to become a brand. Examples of these kinds of brands include *Neste Oil Rally Finland*, *Rio Carneval* and *Cannes Film Festival*.

An *artist name* is a name which a professional in the field of culture uses in his or her artistic work. Those who have artist names include musicians (Gordon Sumner: *Sting*), authors (Eric Blair: *George Orwell*) and so on. Moreover, other public figures in their activities are known by a different name (Vladimir Ilyich Uljanov: *Lenin*; Edson Arantes do Nascimento: *Pelé*). Many socially influential figures have been known by another name or a *pseudonym* (former president of Finland Urho Kekkonen: *Pekka Peitsi*). These names have not originally been used for commercial reasons but the commercialisation of popular culture in particular has shifted the function of artist names and pseudonyms to a more commercial direction.

The term *stage name* can also be used for an artist name in popular culture, especially for musicians and can be given to both individuals and various line-ups. The music business is a growing industry in which great amounts of money are being exchanged. Commercialism is inevitably a part of today's music world, albeit against the will of many musicians. This phenomenon concerns pop music in particular but classical music can hardly escape this completely. For a long time now, popular musicians have used stage names (*Alice Cooper, Lady Gaga, Paleface*), and simultaneously various musical groups have received names for a long time (*The Beatles, Abba*). There is, thus, a naming tradition, but today, the vision of a record company often influences the names. For example, in Finland, some band names (*Gimmel, Jane, IndX*) have been created through the format of the television programme Popstars. These names are built on a purely commercial foundation.

Names emerging in the sphere of pop and rock music do not seem to have any boundaries whatsoever. There can be an aim at just about any kind of association with these names and there is a great deal more variation in them than in other commercial and commercially toned names. However, certain tendencies associated with a music genre can be observed in these names. For example, Finnish schlager and tango music is stereotypically connected to names such as *Ari Aalto & Atlantic* or *Hymyhuulet* ('smiling lips'), whereas heavy metal music is connected to names referring to death, metal and the colour black (*Apocalyptica, Metallica, Black Sabbath*). Language play (*Yrjöpensas* after George Bush ← *yrjö* 'George' or 'vomit' and *pensas* 'bush', *Ultra Bra* containing the Swedish word *bra* 'good' or 'brassiere'), astonishing references (*Tasavallan Presidentti* 'President of the Republic', *Eläkeläiset* 'pensioners', *Apulanta* 'fertiliser') and intertextuality (*Children of Bodom* after the Lake Bodom murders, *Shakespears Sister* referring to Virginia Woolf's *A Room of One's Own*) are often characteristic of band names. A name that looks like a combination of a first name and surname is also common (*Jemson Green, Jethro Tull, Pelle Miljoona*). In the same fashion as artists and bands in the music business promote record sales and the popularity of their live shows with good names, performers and artists in various other fields can build a product name for themselves: Finnish authors (*Rosa Liksom*), comic strip artists (*Juba*), performance artists (*Irma Optimisti*), porn stars (*Rakel Liekki* 'flame'), television and radio hosts (*Peltsi*). Commercialism is more or less present in all artist names. Stage names in Finnish popular music have been studied by Ilari Hongisto (2006).

So then, what about other personal names other than artist names? Can first names serve commercial purposes? This question is not as strange as it perhaps may seem at first glance because studies (Kiviniemi 2006) have shown that upon entering the end of the last century and in this century, the number of unique names given to Finnish children has been on the rise. More and more parents wish to give their children a name which others would not have. Books on rare names and names which no one yet has but would work as a first name have been published to help parents find a name. There are also various websites to help in naming problems weighing on mothers and fathers. The endeavour to give a child a unique name without a doubt brings the same objectives to mind that influence the fact that every business, every product and every race horse will get a name that is different from all others and which cannot be confused with any other name. It is hardly directly imagined that a unique or very rare name is commercial but perhaps, in one way or another, there is an aspiration to help the child be successful later in life. A special name always sticks in our minds. A completely other matter concerns world news that has sometimes reached Finland that parents might name their children after some luxury brand. This kind of naming, however, would not even be possible according to Finnish legislation.

Finally, let us take a look at Internet domain names which are not actually subjects of onomastic research but are in a certain way still associated with commercial nomenclature and the formation of commercial names. While it is often connected to some proper noun, a *domain name* can mostly be compared to a postal address; it is a more humane form of an actual, technical website address. In Finland, domain names are granted by the Finnish Communications Regulatory Authority. An article on Finnish domain names was written by Mari Voipio (2001).

The meaning of a business's domain name has grown together along with the commercialisation of the Internet. A domain name that is easy to remember guarantees that the business can be found on the web where there is no centred directory, regardless of various search providers. Acquiring a good domain name is a part of a company's marketing strategy. A domain name also has symbolic value: on some level, it at least indicates that the company in question is taken seriously. Since the competition of businesses on the web is often much easier than traditional methods, a domain name can bring a business more requests for quotations than before and, through this, the opportunities for trade as well.

The same kinds of factors that are required of a good company name are actually required of a good domain name. It must be rather short so that it would be easy to write. When it is reminiscent of the name of a business or trade mark, it will be easy to remember or guess even if no one would ever have heard of it. The fact that it would be difficult to write it wrong must be taken into consideration in the selection of a domain name. A name which best describes the business activity is considered better than most alternatives. For example, if there would be a Finnish company called *Pro-Delicias Ky*, a candy shop under the auxiliary company name *Karkkisirkus* ('candy circus'), it would be more practical for it to have *karkkisirkus.fi* for its domain name than *prodelicias.fi* which would, for Finns, be more difficult to remember and also prone to be written wrong. Provided the business wishes to build a brand or even create some kind of business image, it is usually not recommended to adopt a regular appellative as a domain name even if it would be easy to remember (*herkku.com* 'treat.com').

The standardisation of Internet use has without a doubt had an influence on the name selections of businesses, especially in countries where just the name of the business or part of it would do for a domain name. Finnish businesses primarily headed towards being a webstore may favour English and avoid the letters *ä* and *ö*. The Nordic countries have represented a rather rigid approach to domain names but nowadays, the rules have become more lenient. Earlier, when only a name in its exact registered form would be acceptable, long domain names such as *hallituskadunhammaslaakaripiste.fi* ('governmentstreetdentistpoint.fi') came about that would have a greater likelihood for spelling errors and greater difficulty in international use. For this reason, many Finnish businesses aim at adopting a shorter name which would also be easer as a domain name.

The use of domain names also completely makes way for a new kind of company name type, so-called dot-com company names which end in *.com* such as *Amazon.com*. However, it does not seem that this trend will become that permanent. Moreover, these kinds of names are virtually not seen in Finland at all.

The development of Finnish company names and product names is already a difficult task due to many regulations and guidelines that, in addition, the question of what kind of domain name a company or trade mark can get to use must nowadays be taken into consideration. The difficulty particularly lies in the fact that perhaps the best possible domain name may not be used because someone else already owns it; or then again it can be used by paying a fortune for it. Trade is practised with domain names and at its worst we can even speak of speculation and theft. These kinds of website disputes are settled by the worldwide copyright and trade mark organisation WIPO (World Intellectual Property Organisation).

7. Names in Literature

This final chapter explores names featured in literature, mainly in fiction. The reader will understand the creation, categorisation and functions of character names and fictive place names. It also covers the translation and study of names in literature. Finally, the reader will gain insight into Finnish literary onomastics and will become familiar with its cultural and social aspects as well as translation in Finnish literature.

Names in Fiction

Literary onomastics usually refers to the onomastic research of fiction although proper names indeed occur in non-fiction as well. The function of proper names in non-fiction is rather clear: there is typically reference to various, real world referents with these names, such as places, people, animals, businesses and so on. The use of names in these texts, regarding the writer, is an economic and practical solution: when a referent can be identified with a name, it does not need to be described by complicated explanations. The function of proper nouns in fiction is, however, more diverse and therefore cannot be interpreted only by their referential relationship.

Proper nouns in the novels, short stories and poems of various authors have been given consideration for some time now in comparative literature. Along with the analysis of a certain novel, there may have been reference to how the names of the central characters in the book carry various additional meanings connected to the plot of the story and open up new possibilities for interpretation to the novel. However, these kinds of considerations have been rather random and vague. Moreover, there has been little systematic examination of names and naming systems included in fictive texts.

The study of literary onomastics has increased in the past years both in Finland and elsewhere in the world. Consequently it nowadays has its own place at international onomastic conferences and many onomasticians with a linguistic background have specialised in the study of names in literature. Names in works of such authors as Samuel Beckett, G. K. Chesterton, Charles Dickens, Fjodor Dostojevski, James Joyce, Nikolai Leskov, J. K. Rowling or

William Shakespeare have been subjects of research. In addition to this, the nomenclature of medieval romances, folk tales and children's literature as well as the translation of names in literature have been of special interest to scholars. In practice, these studies have mostly focused on personal names; after all, a person and his psyche are key topics in the study of literature. To some extent, place names and other nomenclature included in literature have of course been studied as well. Literary onomastics is thus a multidisciplinary area of research in which the perspectives of literature, translation and onomastics are merged together – and in which perspectives of other areas are required, such as cultural research and history.

What kinds of names then appear in fiction? Names in literature can be divided into two main groups: fictive names and non-fictive, or authentic, names. *Fictive names* refer to referents which only exist outside the real word, that is, in the imagination of the author – and the reader. These kinds of referents include, for example, imaginary characters and places created by the author for his book. We should note that a name in literature is also fictive when some other referent, referred to by the same name, happens to be in the real world. For example, the main character's name *Matti Virtanen* in Kari Hotakainen's novel *Juoksuhaudantie* (*Trench Road*, 2002) refers to a fictive Matti Virtanen and not a real world Finnish man with the same name.

Sometimes, fictive names only appear in this kind of literature and are created by the author especially for his book. They are usually reminiscent of real world nomenclature to the extent that the reader will recognise them as names of certain kinds of referents but they can also be quite special. For example, G. K. Chesterton played with such personal names in his texts as *Bunchoosa Blutterspangle* and *Splitcat Chintzibobs*. Special names are especially found in science fiction and other fantasy books and with these names, the boundaries of language may consciously be tested. Sometimes, names in books are borrowed from other fictive texts (*Hamlet, Don Quixote*). Loaned names thus refer to the fictive world of another book and its events.

In addition to fictive names, *non-fictive* or *authentic names*, which have reference to people, places and other referents of the real word, can occur in fiction. Some novel may, for example, be located in Paris having the names of true Parisian streets, restaurants or cafés – but there can be fictive names alongside of them. At the same time, there may be references to authentic, real word people in these kinds of novels, such as French politicians or artists. It is also typical for several novels that the main character and his circle of friends represent the fictive world whereas the story's broader environment of events represents some real world environment – which the author, however, can describe as he pleases, even intentionally one-sidedly or by distortion. However, the environment of a book in the fantasy genre, and also its nomenclature, is usually completely fictive – although it is often reminiscent, at least to some extent, of real world environments. It has often been noted that many stories located in a society on alien planets or the distant future are in fact about our own society and its problems.

With regard to the real world and its nomenclature, literary nomenclature can be classified on the basis of the aforementioned into the following name types:

1. *Authentic names*, that is, names which have referents existing in the real world and reference is made to them with these names
2. *Realistic but non-authentic names*, that is, names which are possible in the real world but refer to fictive referents
3. *Invented* or *coined names*, that is, names created by the author himself which refer to fictive referents and the kind which do not occur in real world nomenclature
4. *Loaned names*, that is, names that refer to fictive referents loaned from another literary tradition, which do not occur in real world nomenclature

It is clear that an author names the characters and other referents according to his own views and the literary requirements of his book. On the other hand, the author must take the reader into consideration; the reader will ultimately interpret the naming world, not only in regard to the content and structure of the book, but also from his own world image and experiences. Several different levels are merged in the names of literature both inside and outside the book. This is why they have been categorised as diverse narrative, stylistic and literary tools both linguistically and culturally (Bertills 2003).

When an author begins to name characters, places and other referents in his text, the naming systems of his own mother tongue as well as other languages he knows will be in the background. On the foundation of this cultural information, using his artistic creativity, he will build up a nomenclature which may be reminiscent of a great deal of existing naming systems or he will differ from them quite significantly. It is typical that both the form of the name and its content are quite often strongly motivated. The author's selected or invented names always form a naming system or *onomastic landscape* in texts against which individual names should be examined. A new name will often receive its literary meaning only in relation to other names appearing in the same text. On the other hand, literary onomasticians emphasise that the names should always be interpreted in a literary context as well – thus, as part of the story as a whole, not as a separate entity from it.

It has been noted that many authors have given special consideration to the naming of their characters. For example, it has been said that Charles Dickens (1812–1870) was thoroughly obsessed with the formation of personal names – or the careful selection and adaptation of ready-made names – in his books. The names in Dickens' books are often semantically transparent. For example, the barrister's dismal assistant in the novel *Our Mutual Friend* (1884–1885), whose employer never knew if he was deep in thought or contemplating murder, was named *Blight*. Dickens also played a great deal with names and made his characters play with them as well. He often gave groups of people, for example, the same types of names such as those appearing in the barrister's imaginary client list *Mr Aggs, Mr Baggs, Mr Caggs, Mr Faggs, Mr Gaggs* and *Mr Boffin*. Dickens' names often also include hints to the fates of his characters. For example, the pseudonym *Handford* was used for the person after being saved from being thrown into a river. This pseudonym has been interpreted to refer to *Handforth*, a place name referring to a duck pond. (Casotti 1998.)

Moreover, the personal names in G. K. Chesterton's detective series are often descriptive. These books include, for example, *Sir Isaac Hook* who likes to fish, a wealthy family with the surname *Bankes* and a man with a white hat and hair named *Art Alboin* (Lat. *albus* 'white'). The name of the murderer in Chesterton's story is *Welkin* 'cloud, sky, heaven'; he murders his victims in the highest storey of a house located on a high mountain. The name of this central person is associated directly with the core theme of the book. (Sobanski 1998.) A great deal of descriptive names can also be found in medieval romances. For example, the king by the name of *Wonder* in the book *Roman van Walewein* had the ability to perform many kinds of miracles.

With the semantic transparency of personal names, it is easy for authors to include various information in their text that characterise the person or are otherwise associated with the content of their books. These names often describe the physical or mental qualities, character traits or behaviours of the name bearer. The content of a name can also signify social roles or relationships between the characters, or prophesise the name bearer's fate. These types of names are often easily put across to the reader, especially in children's literature. Their interpretation can also sometimes be quite challenging and only after careful name analysis of the whole book can we come to a conclusion on them.

However, those making interpretations cannot be sure if the semantically transparent names created or selected by the author include intentional messages or not, unless the author has explained their background in some other context. In any case, the reader may find a considerable part of the names to be mystical and obscure. The fact that the text is not easily self-evident but instead it leaves space for the reader's own associations and different possibilities for interpretation is at the heart of literature. Another interesting factor includes those characters or referents that have not been named. Being unnamed and opaqueness are often quite significant in the interpretation of the book.

Besides semantic transparency, personal names can include additional information in other ways. The author can, for example, emphasise the inclusion of a character to a certain group by selecting his name which is characteristic to the group. Thus, a foreign character will often have a name referring to his nationality (a German gentleman *Müller*, a Swedish lady *Svensson*), a representative of a certain religion will have a name referring to this religion (the Jewish surname *Goldstein*, the Catholic first name *Joseph*) and a person of a certain social group will have a name characteristic to this group (a maid *Miina*, a daughter of an estate *Charlotta*). Similarly, a person's normalcy can be described with a common name whereas the speciality of a name often refers to the fact that the character is in some respect extraordinary.

A character name can also be phonetically motivated. For example, it can be phonetically reminiscent of the person in the book by other key words. For instance, the young student *Burrows* described by G. K. Chesterton is "*b*ig and *b*urly" and he has "*b*rown hair" and a "*b*road *b*ack". Character names phonetically and structurally reminiscent of each other may also include a clue to the fact that the people may be in some special relationship with each other. Chesterton's books have, for example, the brothers *Herbert* and *Harry Druce* as well as the gentlemen of the same philosophy *Wain*, *Crake* and *Blake*. On the other hand, special names can refer to characters' opposing characteristics.

Names can also include references to other characters in literature, in other words, they can be intertextual. This kind of name includes, for example, the name of Chesterton's contradictory private investigator *Dr Hyde* which refers to Robert Louis Stevenson's book *Strange Case of Dr Jekyll and Mr Hyde* (1886) in which *Dr Jekyll* and *Mr Hyde* represent the good and evil sides of the same person. Similar references to real world people are also common. For example, the first name of the aforementioned Sir Isaac Hook has been explained to refer to the writer of the fishing classic *The Compleat Angler* (1653), Izaak Walton. The use of these types of names often includes comic and satirical elements. (Sobanski 1998.)

Name changes of characters in novels often reflect changes happening in their phases of life, identity or psychological development. Hence, the main character of a book can have a different life in a different phase of life. For example, in Jhumpa Lahiri's novel *The Namesake* (2003), the main character, an American of Indian origin searching for his identity, is *Gogol* (named after his father's favourite Russian author) and later is known as *Nikhil* or *Nick*. Moreover, the kinds of names used for a person in different contexts – such as official names, nicknames or pejorative names – tell much about the relationships between characters and their changes. The personal names in fictive works can also tell us – in addition to many other details – what date the book or its time period is associated with. For example, *Liisa Matintytär*, an outdated patronymic name, represents a completely different time in Finnish nomenclature than the name *Janita Saaristo*, which is a modern combination of a first name and a surname. When authors create an image of a time period, they will often exploit information on the popularity change of names.

Moreover, place names in fiction often include different types of information supporting the content of the book. Authentic place names usually help pinpoint the story to a specific country, region or town – and fictive ones to some imaginary environment. Semantically transparent place names can also characterise the place, for example, by giving it information about typical flora or fauna (*Tamminiemi* 'oak cape', *Kettumetsä* 'fox forest') or refer to something that has occurred at the place (*Surmavuori* 'death mountain'). Similarly, they can support the creation of the mood of the book: there are often "frightening" place names in thrillers (*Huuhkajavuori* 'eagle-owl mountain', *Synkmetsä* 'gloomy forest'). Sometimes, place names in literature include various associative connections to names of places in existence and in this way will get some additional, sometimes even humorous, meaning.

Fictive place names often also form their own toponymic system. The names of this system are usually structurally reminiscent of real world nomenclature. It is also typical that in the creation of names in literature, the same or at least similar name formation rules are used as in the creation of real world nomenclature – although these rules can be freely broken. In terms of the context of the text, the breaking of these rules is usually seen as being significant, sometimes also comical.

Names in fiction also always function as a dynamic part of the text and are in interaction with other elements that construct the content of the book and carry the story. As a result, they have a narrative, story-telling function. Names therefore have a very central role in the interpretation of texts. However, different authors and individual books differ a great deal from each other in this respect. Some authors use names on many levels and rather ambiguously, whereas the nomenclature used by others offers a great deal less to be analysed.

Names appearing in fiction have several different influential functions and on different levels of the text. The functions of these names have been classified in different sources in many different ways. This classification, which is partly overlapping and in no way completely perfect, may however cover the chief functions of names in fiction:

1. *Identifying function*: the name refers to a fictional or non-fictional person, place or other referent and distinguishes it from other representatives of the same type
2. *Fictionalising function*: the name makes its referent a fictional person, place or other referent
3. *Localising function*: the name refers to a specific time period or place
4. *Social function*: the name refers to a social class or the identity and role of the person in his community
5. *Descriptive function*: the name describes the person, place or other referent and thus gives additional information on the referent in question
6. *Associative function*: intentional associations supporting the content of the text are linked to the name for real world or fictional persons, places or subjects
7. *Affective function*: the name reflects different emotive states and creates the emotional atmosphere of the book
8. *Ideological function*: the name refers to the ideology concerning the referent in question or supports the ideological message of the book
9. *Classifying function*: persons, places and subjects of the book are classified into various sub-groups semantically, contextually or structurally with the same type of names or similar names

10. *Narrative function*: the name functions as a fundamental element in the telling of the story
11. *Humorous function*: the reader is entertained and amused with linguistic play concerning the name.

Translating Names in Literature

There is a clear principle concerning the translation of proper nouns in Finnish pragmatic texts: as a general rule, names are not translated. This is due to the fact that in non-fictive texts, proper nouns only have an identifying function. They function as etiquette-like sensors of the referent, carrying no semantic content which would require translation. For this reason, names of people are usually not translated in pragmatic texts. However, there are exceptions to this which include only the names of certain rulers and popes which traditionally have Finnish-adapted name forms such as *Carl XVI Gustaf → Kaarle XVI Kustaa* or *Ioannes Paulus II → Johannes Paavali II*. The same concerns well-established name forms adapted for Finnish for place names: *Cape of Good Hope → Hyväntoivonniemi, Stockholm → Tukholma*. These name forms have come about because all expressions functioning as names do not sit well in Finnish and they can result in pronunciation or spelling problems to its language users. These kinds of translated names and adapted names have become established Finnish name forms and there are a number of sources available for the regular Finnish language user to help find out which form is correct or recommended.

However, the translation of fictive texts is a much more complicated issue. There are both translated and untranslated names and it is usually the translator who decides if there is a need for a translation or not. There are four possible strategies for the translation of names in literature:

1. *Loan* or loaning the original foreign language name as it is to the target language
2. *Translation* or translating the original foreign language name into the target language
3. *Adaptation* or phonetically adapting the original foreign language name in the target language
4. *Replacement* or replacing the original foreign language name by some other name or appellatival expression

We can also take a *partial loan, partial translation, partial adaptation* or *partial replacement* into consideration. These pertain to names which are made up of more than one part whereupon only part of the name is loaned as it is, translated, adapted to the target language or replaced by another name or expression.

All of these strategies are variably used in many fictional works. In some books, the principle has been to only use those proper nouns which would be translated in pragmatic texts, while all the names wind up being targets of translation in others. Which strategy a translator chooses depends on both the nature of the book – especially the functions of the proper nouns in the text – and its readers.

There are four levels in the text which the translator must take into consideration. The text's formal side is represented by its grammatical and stylistic levels and the side containing meaning is represented by its semantic and pragmatic levels. Since their importance varies in different texts, the translator must carefully consider how the nomenclature of the translation will work on all these levels when dealing with proper nouns. Has the style of the name been preserved after it has been translated? Is the name's semantic significance so important that it would be evident also in the translation? Will the reader understand what the name of the original text refers to or should a completely new equivalent, appropriate for the culture of the target language, be created for it?

Many translators end up considering how much they can deviate from the strategies of the original text and if they should be loyal to the author or to the reader. The translated text must always be in proportion to the recipients of the target language and their cultural knowledge. It is clear that the main function of the text must nevertheless be preserved. Being faithful to the original text, the translation must be able to pass on information (*informative function*), emotions (*affective function*) and different activity and behavioural models (*imperative function*).

Associative, secondary mental images or connotations linked to names are often more important than their actual meanings. Many names and words, in addition to their referential relationship or denotation, also have either positive or negative emotions. At the same time, different informational connotations are linked with names. These connotations are not merely personal; they are often also firmly cultural. How can they be preserved in translation – or replaced by connotations concerning the target language? Will the translation emotively, and by its informational connotations, coincide with the original name form?

Names untranslated in fiction are often authentic names, that is, names which refer to referents existing in the real word. At the same time, should there be commonly known people or places mentioned in the book, the same name forms will be used for them than those that would otherwise used in the target language: thus *Paul Newman* in novels translated into Finnish would be *Paul Newman* and not, for example, *Pauli Uusimies*. Similarly, name forms adapted to the target language found in daily language use are used for place names and other names with reference to the real world (*Paris → Pariisi, La Tour Eiffel → Eiffelin torni*). The translation strategy in the case of these kinds of names is thus usually a loan or an adaptation.

However, fictional names, that is, names which refer to fictive referents, are often translated – or untranslated. Of these names, realistic but non-authentic names, that is, those which could be possible in the real world but refer to fictive referents, can simply be untranslated. Since these kinds of names often function as expressions of nationality or social class of their bearers as they are, a translation is unnecessary. With original names, an air of authenticity is preserved in the translation: if a novel takes place in Scotland, it is natural that its nomenclature will typically be Scottish. Should a realistic but non-authentic name with reference to a fictional character be semantically transparent and its meaning essential regarding the interpretation of the book, the translator may select name translation for his strategy.

Invented names created by the author himself are often translated, especially when they are semantically transparent and significant regarding the interpretation of the book (*Pippi Långstrump* → *Pippi Longstocking*). Should the original name not be semantically transparent but its phonetic makeup arouses certain kinds of associations, the translator may aim at adapting the name so that these associations will be aroused in the readers of the target language. Unless this works, he may replace the name completely with another name in the target language. Translators often lean on appellatival expressions when the referent of the original name is alien to the readers of the target language. If, for example, a Finnish text was about a person eating a *Suffeli* (a Finnish chocolate bar), the translator may replace this with an appellative with reference to a chocolate bar. Loan names, that is, names referring to fictional referents borrowed from another literary tradition (*Hamlet*, *Odysseus*), are not usually translated because they are usually known. Well-established name forms however are used for many of these (*Orlando Furioso* → *Raivoisa Roland*).

Names in children's literature and fairy tales are notably translated more often than in names in adult literature. This is due to the fact that names in children's books are often semantically transparent and can easily be interpreted. On the other hand, the fact that children have less knowledge than adults about other cultures and their naming systems is a reason for translating. Just like their names, efforts are made to adapt other contents and language of children's books to a child's world. Because names in children's books must be easy to pronounce, foreign names are often replaced with the familiar nomenclature of the target language – except if the character in question or other referent represents a specific nationality. It is also easier for small children to identify with literary characters if they have familiar names. Because of this, the children *Wendy*, *John* and *Michael* in J. M. Barrie's *Peter Pan* (1904) are known as *Leena*, *Jukka* and *Mikko* in the Finnish translation. The internationalisation of Finnish culture tells us that many names in children's books today are not translated. For example, Lewis Carroll's *Alice's Adventures in Wonderland* (1865) was translated in 1906 and 1972 in Finland under the title *Liisan seikkailut ihmemaassa* (*Alice* → *Liisa*) but it was translated again in 1995 by Alice Martin under the title *Alicen seikkailut ihmemaassa* in which the main character's name *Alice* is preserved.

There has been quite a great deal of research done on the translation of names in fiction in different countries in the past years. These studies have produced interesting results because the problems concerning name translation reveal what kinds of functions proper nouns have in fiction. Translations of children's literature have especially been the subject of investigation and, in the past years, literary onomasticians have meticulously taken to, for example, the analysis of the names in the different translations of J. K. Rowling's *Harry Potter* books.

Translations have been studied (Nykiel-Herbert 1998) in South Africa of certain English-language narratives to other languages of the country (Xhosa, Zulu, Sotho, Peli, Tswana, Venda, Tsonga and Afrikaans). Various strategies have been used in these translations where the cultural contexts of the target language have been carefully taken into consideration in many ways. English personal names are often translated into Zulu (*Violet* → *Thandeka*) whereas the original names in other translations have been preserved or adapted in the local language (*Alfred* → *Aleferete*). The study has shown that it is easier for African children to identify with characters that have a familiar African name. On the other hand, translators must see to it that translated or untranslated names will not result in misunderstood social or political messages of the stories. Nomenclature of children's books translated into German, for example, has been examined in the same way. Scholars have also emphasised that preserving foreign language names increase children's familiarity with names and so translation is not always the right solution. Names can therefore function as tools for internationalisation in children's literature as well.

Finnish Literary Onomastics

There has been relatively little study of literary onomastics in Finland. One dissertation that discusses the nomenclature of children's literature (Bertills 2003) has been completed on the field as well as a few theses. The subjects of research have mostly included names found in Finnish literature (e.g. Pentti Haanpää, Tove Jansson, Eeva Joenpelto, Kalle Päätalo, F. E. Sillanpää, Anni Swan, Mika Waltari) but to some extent, the nomenclature of foreign authors have been examined as well (e.g. Selma Lagerlöf, Astrid Lindgren, A. A. Milne, J. R. R. Tolkien). In addition, personal names found in Finnish primers have been studied in the same way.

The personal names in Kalle Päätalo's Iijoki series, for example, have been examined from a sociolinguistic point of view. These names form a cohesive anthroponymic system in which each name type has its own function concerning different social situations. For example, surnames are mostly used at logging area and timber rafting work sites. Similarly, different names are often used when speaking directly to a person and also behind someone's back. The abundance and expressiveness of anthroponymy is typical to Päätalo's books. His characters have several nicknames and bynames which are used in different circumstances of speech. For example, reference to a character named *Reino Kurtti* is made with names such as *Reke, Rentti, Reino, Kurtti, Kurtti-Reino, Kurtti-Reke, Kurtti-Rentti, Rentti-Kurtti, Kurtin poika* 'son of Kurtti' and *Mehtä-Sakun poika* 'son of forest Saku'. All of the personal names in Päätalo's novels have three basic functions: identification, expressing social relationships and temporary emotional charges and creative play with linguistic elements.

Moreover, the anthroponymy in Pentti Haanpää's books have been examined from a sociological perspective (Sirviö 1976). The study has analysed how the personal names of different social groups – such as lumberjacks, criminals, soldiers, homestead masters and a higher social class – differ from one another. There are both common Finnish names (surnames *Aalto, Lehikoinen, Varis*) and Haanpää's own invented names (surnames *Höröläinen, Lompalo, Rantaräty*) found in his nomenclature. Moreover, Haanpää introduces colourful bynames (*Kylpyhullu-Kemppainen* 'bath-mad Kemppainen', *Metso-Kasperi* 'wood grouse Kasperi', *Yksisilmä-Kunelius* 'one-eyed Kunelius'). Character names in Anni Swan's young adult books have been examined in the same way (Tikkala 2005). These names clearly show a person's social status, in other words, if he is of a higher social class, middle class, working class or a part of the farming population. Thus, nobility in the books have foreign names such as *Ottilia Von Sumers* or *Henrik Gyllenheim* and peasants have Fennicised name forms such as *Hiski Riepponen* or *Manta Kustaantytär*. The people belonging to different social classes are addressed in different ways in different situations. The names used by Swan also reflect cohesion of the characters (siblings *Ritva* and *Risto* or *Liisi* and *Lotti*) as well as naming trends of different time periods.

The personal names of causerie writer Olli's (otherwise known as Väinö Albert Nuorteva) collections in the 1960s have also been a topic of research (Metsämuuronen 1991). Olli uses both commonly known names (first names *Helmi, Kalle, Vihtori*; surnames *Niemeläinen*; nicknames *Arska, Osku*) and rare ones (first names *Adalia, Eemu*; surnames *Apunen, Orvas, Tätilä*) and even his own invented names (first names *Oino, Lissy, Millvaukee*; surnames *Salokitara* 'woodland guitar', *Muikkukehto* 'whitefish cradle') in his causeries. The names Olli gives are often in some way descriptive of their bearers. For example, a private thinker *Olotilanne* ('state of being') and an angry person named *Murahdus* ('grunt') are found in these texts. The fact that Olli's personal names are an essential factor in the structure of the comedy of his causeries is clear. Furthermore, it is characteristic of the names featured in Kirsi Kunnas' children's books to be multilayered, onomatopoeic and to have word play. For example, the names of the rabbits *Pupu Suputtaja Puppeli* and *Pupu Paaputtaja Papuli* (*pupu* 'bunny') refer to the verbs *puputtaa* 'nibble', *supattaa* 'whisper' and *paapattaa* 'babble' (Raivo 2001).

The personal names in Tove Jansson's Moomin books have also provided interesting material for those examining literary onomastics (Bertills 1995, 2003). The characters in the series have Swedish-language names with a clear meaning (*Snorken* from *snokig* 'snooty', *Misan* from *miserabel* 'miserable') and names whose phonetic makeup is reminiscent of certain words used in the language. For example, the names *Moomintroll* (Swe. *Mumintroll*), *Moominmamma* (Swe. *Muminmamman*) and *Moominpappa* (Swe. *Muminpappa*) containing *moomin/mumin* conjures images of something small, round, soft and kind (cf. *mamma, mommy, mummy*). In translating these names, however, their original meanings or associations linked to them are not always preserved. For example, *Hemuli* is merely the Finnish form of the original name in Swedish *Hemulen*, which is based on an old legal Swedish term *hemul* 'a seller's obligation to prove his rights to sell certain goods'. The Hemulens are responsible attendants in Moominvalley that do not do anything for fun but rather for gain. Moreover, fictive character names in Walt Disney animated films have been examined in the same way (Pearl 2007).

Problems concerning the translation of names in literature have been raised in many theses. For example, the study (Klockars 1987) that examined proper nouns in the translation of the Antti Tuuri's novel *Pohjanmaa* (1982) in Swedish *En dag i Österbotten* (1985) shows that the translator cannot always find a good equivalent. A majority of personal names of this book, located in Finnish-speaking Southern Ostrobothnia, have appropriately not been translated, although, at the same time, some have been adapted to Swedish as needed (evangelist *Luukas* → *Lukas*; surname *Sarliini* → *Sarlin*). However, the name *Hurja-Hilja Riipinen*, for example, was given the Swedish form *Enorma-Norma Riipinen*, although this well-known historical figure of the right-wing Lapua Movement of the 1930s, activist *Hilja Riipinen*, is the case at hand. The translator has not translated Finnish-language place names into Swedish even when they refer to Swedish-speaking places (*Koivulahti* – *Kvevlax*) or large cities that have an official Swedish name in Finland (*Savonlinna* – *Nyslott*). However, the Finnish-language *Vaasa* paper in this Swedish translation is called *Vasabladet* even though there is a Swedish newspaper of the same name published in Finland completely dissimilar to this. In this case, the translator should know both the culture of where the book originally appeared or is about and the culture of the readers of the book very well. In a similar fashion, the character names *Bill* and *Bull* (the cats in Gösta Knutsson's Peter-No-Tail books) known to the Finns as *Pilli* and *Pulla* as well as *Piff* and *Puff* (the Disney chipmunks *Chip* and *Dale*) known in Finnish as *Tiku* and *Taku* have appeared in the Finnish translation of Anders Jacobsson and Sören Olsson's Swedish-language Bert middle-grade fiction books. (Ahlö 2005.)

The nomenclature of J. K. Rowling's Harry Potter books has been a challenging task to translators. Place names in these books have usually been given Finnish translations so that they represent Finnish place name types (*Knockturnalley* → *Iskunkiertokuja*, *Stoatshead Hill* → *Kärpänpäänmäki*). However, the names of foreign wizarding schools have not been translated (*Beauxbatons*, *Durmstrang*). Under half of the personal names in these books have been translated into Finnish; sometimes the person's entire name (*Vindictus Viridianus* → *Kosto Onsuloinen*, from the Finnish saying *kosto on suloinen* 'revenge is sweet') and sometimes just part of the name (*Boris the Bewildered* → *Boris Böllämystynyt*). Not all of the names of the pupils at wizarding school have been translated because the translator did not want to highlight other types of pupils there. Moreover, Rowling's animal names have been translated into Finnish (cat *Snowy* → *Tuisku*, dog *Fluffy* → *Pörrö*) as well as names of products (hair potion *Sleekeazy* → *Iisisiliä*, newspaper *Witch Weekly* → *Me Noidat* 'us witches', a play on the title of the Finnish women's magazine *Me Naiset* 'us women'). According to the study of these names (Karppinen 2003), each Finnish translation is accurate and case-specific. A similar, multilayered nomenclature that is also challenging for the Finnish translator can be found in J. R. R. Tolkien's fantasy books *The Lord of the Rings* (Mentula 2006).

Bibliography

Aalto, Tiina 2002: Osoitteena Osmankäämintie: tutkimus eräästä ryhmänimistöstä. [Multiple naming schemes: street naming using plant names.] – *Virittäjä* 106 pp. 208–222.

Aikio, Ante 2008: The study of Saami substrate toponyms in Finland. – *Onomastica Uralica 4* pp. 159–197.

Ainiala, Terhi 1997: *Muuttuva paikannimistö*. [A changing toponymy.] Finnish Literature Society Publications 667. Helsinki: Finnish Literature Society.

Ainiala, Terhi 2000: Paikannimistön muuttuminen. [A change in place names.] – *Virittäjä* 104 pp. 355–372. Helsinki: Society for the Study of Finnish.

Ainiala, Terhi 2001: Paikannimistön keruun tavoitteet ja tulokset. [The objectives and results of toponymy collecting.] – Kaija Mallat & Terhi Ainiala & Eero Kiviniemi (eds.), *Nimien maailmasta* pp. 7–22. Kieli 14. Helsinki: University of Helsinki Department of Finnish.

Ainiala, Terhi 2003: Kaupunkinimistön tutkimuksen perusteet. [The study of urban names.] – *Virittäjä* 107 pp. 207–225.

Ainiala, Terhi 2004: Kadunnimet opastajina ja sivistäjinä: kesän 2002 keskustelun tarkastelua. [Street names as guides and educators: an investigation of a conversation in summer 2002.] – *Virittäjä* 108 pp. 106–115.

Ainiala, Terhi (ed.) 2005: *Kaupungin nimet: kymmenen kirjoitusta kaupunkinimistöstä.* [Names in the city: ten writings on urban nomenclature.] Kotimaisten kielten tutkimuskeskuksen julkaisuja 134. Helsinki: Finnish Literature Society.

Ainiala, Terhi 2006: Helsingin nimet. [Names in Helsinki.] – Kaisu Juusela & Katariina Nisula (eds.), *Helsinki kieliyhteisönä* pp. 100–122. Helsinki: University of Helsinki, Department of Finnish Language and Literature.

Ainiala, Terhi & Komppa, Johanna & Mallat, Kaija & Pitkänen, Ritva Liisa 2000: Paikannimien käyttö ja osaaminen – nimitaito Pälkäneen Laitikkalassa. [Knowledge and use of place names in Laitikkala in the parish of Pälkäne.] – *Virittäjä* 104 pp. 330–354.

Ainiala, Terhi & Pitkänen, Ritva Liisa 2002: Paikannimistöntutkimuksen valinnat: etymologioista sosio-onomastiikkaan. [Choices in toponymastics: from etymology to socio-onomastics.] – *Virittäjä* 106 pp. 231–240.

Ainiala, Terhi & Saarelma-Maunumaa, Minna 2006: Nimistöntutkimus yhä monitieteisempää. [Onomastics an increasingly multidisciplinary research subject.] – *Virittäjä* 110 pp. 99–107.

Ainiala, Terhi & Vuolteenaho, Jani 2005: Urbaani muutos ja kaupunkilaiset identiteetit paikannimistön kuvaamina. [Urban change and the identities of city dwellers described by toponymy.] – *Virittäjä* 109 pp. 378–394.

Alanen, Timo 2004: *Someron ja Tammelan vanhin asutusnimistö: nimistön vakiintumisen aika.* [The oldest settlement names of Somero and Tammela: a time of establishing nomenclature.] Somero: Oy Amanita Ltd.

Alanen, Timo & Kepsu, Saulo 1989: *Kuninkaan kartasto Suomesta 1776–1805.* [The king's atlas of Finland.] Finnish Literature Society Publications 505. Helsinki: Finnish Literature Society.

Alford, Richard D. 1988: *Naming and identity: a cross-cultural study of personal naming practices.* New Haven: HRAF Press.

Alhaug, Gulbrand & Saarelma, Minna 2007: Eeva Törmänen eller Eva Dørmenen? Møte mellom finsk og norsk namnesystem i Noreg. [Encountering the Finnish and Norwegian naming system in Norway.] Digital publication, University of Tromsø, Munin/ NORNA 2007: http://hdl.handle.net/10037/1228.

Arjava, Hellevi 2005: *Alpiini ja Otteljaana: kangasniemeläisten etunimet 1684–1899.* [Alpiini and Otteljaana: given names of the people of Kangasniemi between 1684 and 1899.] Suomi 190. Helsinki: Finnish Literature Society.

Avgränsning av namnkategorier. Rapport från NORNAs tjugonionde symposium på Svidja 20-22 april 2001. [Defining name categories. Report from the 29th NORNA symposium in Suitia.] Eds. Terhi Ainiala & Peter Slotte. Tallinn: Institute for the Languages of Finland & Kirjakas.

Bauer, Gerhard 1985: *Namenkunde des Deutschen.* [Names of the Germans.] Bern – Frankfurt am Main – New York: Peter Lang.

Bergien, Angelika (2007): In search of the perfect name – prototypical and iconic effects of linguistic patterns in company names. – Ludger Kremer & Elke Ronneberger-Sibold (eds.): *Names in Commerce and Industry: Past and Present* pp. 259–272. Berlin: Logos.

Bergien, Angelika (2008): Global and regional considerations in the formation of company names. Atti del XXII Congresso Internazionale di Scienze Onomastiche, Pisa, 28 agosto - 4 settembre 2005. Vol II, pp. 289–297. Pisa: Edizioni Ets.

Bertills, Yvonne 2003: *Beyond identification: proper names in children's literature.* Åbo: Åbo Akademis Förlag.

Blanár, Vincent 1991: Das antroponymische System und seine Funktionierung. [An anthroponymic system and its function.] – Eeva Maria Närhi (ed.), *Proceedings of the XVIIth International Congress of Onomastic Sciences. Helsinki 13–18 August 1990.* Vol. 1 pp. 208–215. Helsinki: University of Helsinki and Institute for the Languages of Finland.

Blomqvist, Marianne 1993: *Personnamnsboken.* [Personal name dictionary.] Loimaa: Finn Lectura.

Blomqvist, Marianne 1997: Names of mansion blocks in Helsinki. – Ritva Liisa Pitkänen & Kaija Mallat (eds.), *You name it: perspectives on onomastic research* pp. 237–246. Studia Fennica, Linguistica 7. Helsinki: Finnish Literature Society.

Blomqvist, Marianne 2002: *Dagens namn.* [Name of the day.] Pieksämäki: Schildts Förlags AB.

Blomqvist, Marianne 2006: *Vad heter finlandssvenskarna?* [Finland Swedes: what are their names?] Skrifter utgivna av Svenska folkskolans vänner, Volym 177. Helsingfors: Svenska folkskolans vänner.

Blomqvist, Marianne 2011: *Våra fyrfota vänner har också namn.* [Our quadruped friends also have names.] Skrifver utgivna av Svenska folkskolans vänner. Volym 190. Helsingfors: Svenska folkskolans vänner.

Blomqvist, Marianne & Vuorinen, Anitta 1996: *Navetan nimipäivät.* [Cattle shed name days.] Helsinki: Valio.

Brandl, Werner 2007: Buy English? Changes in German product naming. In: Ludger Kremer & Elke Ronneberger-Sibold (eds.): *Names in Commerce and Industry: Past and Present*, 87–98. Berlin: Logos.

Casotti, Francesco M. 1998: Naming and misnaming people/characters in *Our Mutual Friend*. – W. H. F. Nicolaisen (ed.), *Proceedings of the XIXth International Congress of Onomastic Sciences. Aberdeen, August 4–11, 1996*. Vol. 3 pp. 347–351. Aberdeen: University of Aberdeen.

Clankie, Shawn 2002: *A theory of genericization on brand name change*. Studies in Onomastics 6. Edwin Mellen Press.

Coseriu, Eugenio 1987: *Formen und Funktionen: Studien zur Grammatik*. [Forms and functions. Studies on grammar.] Tübingen: Max Niemeyer.

Cotticelli Kurras, Paola 2007: Die Entwicklung der hybriden Wörtschöpfungen bei den italienischen Markennamen. [The development of hybrid word creations in Italian product names.] In: Ludger Kremer & Elke Ronneberger-Sibold (eds.): *Names in Commerce and Industry: Past and Present*, 167–185. Berlin: Logos.

Dalberg, Vibeke 1985: On homonymy between proper name and appellative. – *Names* 33 pp. 127–135. New York: The American Name Society.

Edelman, Loulou 2009: What's in a name? Classification of proper names by language. – E. Shohamy and D. Gorter (eds.): *Linguistic landscape: Expanding the scenery* pp. 141–154. London and New York: Routledge.

Forsman, A. V. 1891: *Pakanuudenaikainen nimistö: tutkimuksia Suomen kansan persoonallisen nimistön alalla. I.* [Nomenclature of pagan times: studies on the topic of personal names of the Finnish people.] Suomi. Kirjoituksia isänmaallisista aineista. Helsinki: Finnish Literature Society.

Gardiner, Alan 1940: *The theory of proper names: a controversial essay*. London: Oxford University Press.

Gerhards, Jürgen 2003: *Die Moderne und ihre Vornamen. Eine Einladung in die Kultursoziologie*. [Given names of a modern time. An introduction to cultural sociology.] Wiesbaden: Westdeutscher Verlag.

Gerritsen, Marinel & Korzelius, Hubert & van Meurs, Frank & Gijsbers, Inge 2000: English and Dutch commercials: not understood and not appreciated. – *Journal of advertising research* July–August pp. 17–31. New York: Advertising research foundation.

Gorjaev, Sergei (Forthcoming): The name and the game: product- and company names of the anthroponymic origin in the modern Russian language. (Symposium presentation. Names in the Economy 2, Wien 2007.)

Harling-Kranck, Gunilla 1990: *Namn på åkrar, ängar och hagar*. [Names of fields, meadows and corrals.] Skrifter utgivna av Svenska litteratursällskapet i Finland 565. Helsingfors: The Society of Swedish Literature in Finland.

Harling-Kranck, Gunilla 2006: Kaupunkinimistö. Kaupunkiasutus ja kadunnimet Ruotsissa ja Suomessa. [Urban nomenclature. Urban settlement and street names in Sweden and in Finland.] – Gabriel Bladh & Christer Kuvaja (eds.), *Kahden puolen Pohjanlahtea: ihmisiä, yhteisöjä ja aatteita Ruotsissa ja Suomessa 1500-luvulta 1900-luvulle* pp. 207–258. Historiallinen arkisto 123:1. Helsinki: Finnish Literature Society.

Heikkilä-Horn, Marja-Leena 2002: Kaakkoisaasialaiset nimet. [Southeast Asian names.] – Pirjo Mikkonen (ed.), *Sukunimi? Etunimi? Maahanmuuttajien nimijärjestelmistä*. Kielenkäytön oppaita 3. Kotimaisten kielten tutkimuskeskuksen julkaisuja 114. Helsinki: Institute for the Languages of Finland.

Helsingin kadunnimet. [Helsinki street names.] Second, corrected printing. (First printing 1971.) Helsingin kaupungin julkaisuja 24. Helsinki: City of Helsinki 1981.

Helsingin kadunnimet 2. [Helsinki street names 2.] Helsingin kaupungin julkaisuja 32. Helsinki: City of Helsinki 1979.

Helsingin kadunnimet 3. [Helsinki street names 3.] Edited by Jyrki Lehikoinen. Helsinki: City of Helsinki nimistötoimikunta 1999.

Herstatt, Johan D. 1985: *Die Entwicklung von Markennamen im Rahmen der Produktneuplanung.* [The development of brand names within the framework of product re-planning.] Frankfurt: Lang.

Huldén, Lars 2001: *Finlandssvenska bebyggelsenamn: namn på landskap, kommuner, byar i Finland av svenskt ursprung eller särskild svensk form.* [Finland Swedish settlement names: Finnish provinces, municipalities and villages whose names are of Swedish origin.] Skrifter utgivna av Svenska litteratursällskapet i Finland 635. Helsingfors: The Society of Swedish Literature in Finland.

Husserl, Edmund 1929: Phenomenology. – *Encyclopaedia Britannica.* Vol. 17 pp. 699–702. Chicago – London – Toronto: Britannica.

Häkkinen, Kaisa 2004: *Nykysuomen etymologinen sanakirja.* [Etymological dictionary of contemporary Finnish.] Helsinki: WSOY.

Iso suomen kielioppi. [The large grammar of Finnish.] Auli Hakulinen (main ed.), Maria Vilkuna, Riitta Korhonen, Vesa Koivisto, Tarja Riitta Heinonen & Irja Alho. Finnish Literature Society Publications 950. Helsinki: Finnish Literature Society 2004.

Itkonen, Terho 1961: *Nimestäjän opas.* [Name collector's handbook.] Tietolipas 21. Sanakirjasäätiön nimistöjaoksen julkaisuja 1. Helsinki: Finnish Literature Society.

Itkonen, Terho 1997: *Nimestäjän opas.* [Name collector's handbook.] Third, revised printing. Apuneuvoja suomalais-ugrilaisten kielten opintoja varten XIII. Helsinki: Finno-Ugrian Society.

Janik, V. M. & Sayigh, L. S. & Wells, R. S. 2006: Signature whistle shape conveys identity information to bottlenose dolphins. – *Proceedings of the National Academy of Sciences of the United States of America* 103 (21) pp. 8293–8297.

Kalske, Marja 2005: *Suomessa syntyneiden hevosten nimistö.* [Nomenclature of horses born in Finland.] Publications of the Department of Finnish and General Linguistics of the University of Turku 73. Turku: University of Turku.

Karikoski, Elin Vanja 1996: Finske slektsnavn i Sør-Varanger. [Finnish surnames in Southern Varanger.] – *Studia anthroponymica Scandinavica* 14 pp. 83–108.

Karikoski, Elin Vanja 2001: Ruijafinske slektsnavn i endring. [Ruija Finnish surnames in change.] – Gunilla Harling-Kranck (ed.), *Namn i en föränderlig värld. Rapport från den tolfte nordiska namnforskarkongressen, Tavastehus 13–17 juni 1998* pp. 154–164. Studier i nordisk filologi 78. Helsingfors: The Society of Swedish Literature in Finland.

Karsten, T. E. 1921, 1923: *Svensk bygd i Österbotten I, II.* [Swedish settlement in Ostrobothnia.] Svenska litteratursällskapets skrifter 155. Helsingfors: Svenska litteratursällskapet.

Kepsu, Saulo 1981: *Pohjois-Kymenlaakson kylännimet.* [Village names in northern Kymenlaakso.] Finnish Literature Society Publications 367. Helsinki: Finnish Literature Society.

Kepsu, Saulo 1990: Valkealan asuttaminen. [The settlement of Valkeala.] – *Valkealan historia* I pp. 89–456. Valkeala: Valkealan kunta.

Kepsu, Saulo 1990: Toponymie des Dorfes Kepsu. [Toponymy of the village of Kepsu.] – Heikki Leskinen & Eero Kiviniemi (ed.), *Finnish Onomastics: Namenkunde in Finnland.* Studia Fennica 34 pp. 61–83. Helsinki: Finnish Literature Society.

Kepsu, Saulo 2005: *Uuteen maahan: Helsingin ja Vantaan vanha asutus ja nimistö.* [To the new land of Uusimaa: old settlement and nomenclature of Helsinki and Vantaa.] Finnish Literature Society Publications 1027. Helsinki: Finnish Literature Society.

Kepsu, Saulo 2008: Espoon vanha asutusnimistö. [Old settlement names of Espoo.] – Kaija Mallat, Sami Suviranta & Reima T. A. Luoto (ed.), Kylä-Espoo. Espoon vanha asutusnimistö ja kylämaisema pp. 9–156. Espoo: Espoon kaupunki.

Kiviniemi, Eero 1971: *Suomen partisiippinimistöä: ensimmäisen partisiipin sisältävät henkilön- ja paikannimet.* [Finnish participle names. Personal and place names with the first participle.] Finnish Literature Society Publications 295. Helsinki: Finnish Literature Society.

Kiviniemi, Eero 1975: *Paikannimien rakennetyypeistä*. [On structural types of place names.] Suomi 118: 2. Helsinki: Finnish Literature Society.

Kiviniemi, Eero 1977: *Väärät vedet: tutkimus mallien osuudesta nimenmuodostuksessa*. [Bending waters: a study of the role of models in name formation.] Finnish Literature Society Publications 337. Helsinki: Finnish Literature Society.

Kiviniemi, Eero 1978: Paikannimistö systeeminä. [Toponymy as a system.] – Eero Kiviniemi (ed.), *Nimistöntutkimus ja paikallishistoria* pp. 73–89. Paikallishistoriallisen toimiston julkaisuja n:o 2. Helsinki.

Kiviniemi, Eero 1979: Nimistöntutkimus. [Onomastics.] – *Otavan suuri ensyklopedia* 12. Helsinki: Otava.

Kiviniemi, Eero 1980: Nimistö Suomen esihistorian tutkimuksen aineistona. [Names as research material of Finnish prehistory.] – *Virittäjä* 84 pp. 319–338.

Kiviniemi, Eero 1982: *Rakkaan lapsen monet nimet: suomalaisten etunimet ja nimenvalinta*. [The many names of our beloved children: Finnish given names and name selection.] Espoo: Weilin+Göös.

Kiviniemi, Eero 1985: Rautalammin varhaishistoriaa paikannimistön näkökulmasta. [An early history of Rautalampi from a toponymic perspective.] – Jukka Kukkonen (ed.), *Rautalammin kirja* pp. 99–130. Jyväskylän yliopiston kotiseutusarja 20. Rautalampi: Rautalammin kunta.

Kiviniemi, Eero 1990: *Perustietoa paikannimistä*. [Place names basics.] Suomi 148. Helsinki: Finnish Literature Society.

Kiviniemi, Eero 1991: Analogisk namngivning och den toponomastiska teorin. [Analogical name giving and toponomastic theory.] – Gordon Albøge, Eva Villarsen Meldgaard & Lis Weise (ed.), *Analogi i navngivning. Tiende nordiske navneforskerkongres, Brandberg 20–24 maj 1989* pp. 111–120. NORNA-rapporter 45. Uppsala: Norna-förlaget.

Kiviniemi, Eero 1993: *Iita Linta Maria: etunimiopas vuosituhannen vaihteeseen*. [Iita Linta Maria: a guide to given names for the new millennium.] Helsinki: Finnish Literature Society.

Kiviniemi, Eero 1999: Studenter som namnforskare. [Students as onomasticians.] – Mats Wahlberg (ed.), *Den nordiska namnforskningen: i går, i dag, i morgon. Handlingar från NORNA:s 25:e symposium i Uppsala 7–9 februari 1997* pp. 255–262. NORNA-rapporter 67. Uppsala: Norna-förlaget.

Kiviniemi, Eero 2006: *Suomalaisten etunimet*. [Given names of the Finns.] Finnish Literature Society Publications 1103. Helsinki: Finnish Literature Society.

Kiviniemi, Eero & Harling-Kranck, Gunilla & Slotte, Peter & Pitkänen, Ritva Liisa 1977: Der Namenbestand an der finnisch-swedischen Sprachgranze. [Nomenclature on the Finnish Swedish linguistic border.] – *Onoma* 21 pp. 426–429.

Kiviniemi, Eero & Mustakallio, Sari (eds.) 1996: *Nimet, aatteet, mielikuvat: kolme näkökulmaa etunimiin*. [Names, ideologies, images: three perspectives on given names.] Kieli 11. Helsinki: University of Helsinki Department of Finnish.

Kiviniemi, Eero & Pitkänen, Ritva Liisa & Zilliacus, Kurt 1974: *Nimistöntutkimuksen terminologia. Terminologin inom namnsforskningen*. [Onomastic terminology.] Castrenianumin toimitteita 8. Helsinki: Finno-Ugrian Society.

Klein, Naomi 2001: *No logo*. London: Flamingo.

Kohlheim, Volker 1996: Die christliche Namengebung. [Christian name giving.] – Ernst Eichler & Gerold Hilty & Heinrich Löffler & Hugo Steger & Ladislav Zgusta (ed.), *Namenforschung – Name Studies – Les noms propres: ein internationales Handbuch zur Onomastik – an international handbook of onomastics – manuel international d'onomastique*. Volume 2 pp. 1048–1057. Berlin: Walter de Gruyter.

Kohlheim, Volker 1998: Towards a definition of the onymic system. – W.H.F. Nicolaisen (ed.), *Proceedings of the XIXth International Congress of Onomastic Sciences. Aberdeen, August 4–11, 1996.* Vol. 1 pp. 173–178. Aberdeen: University of Aberdeen.

Koivulehto, Jorma 1987: Namn som kan tolkas urgermansk. [Names interpreted as Proto-Germanic.] – Lars Hulden (ed.), *Klassiska problem inom finlandssvensk ortnamnsforskning* pp. 27–42. Svenska litteratursällskapets jubileumssymposium på Hanaholmen 4–6 oktober 1985. Studier i nordisk filologi 67. Skrifter utgivna av Svenska litteratursällskapet i Finland 539. Helsinfors: The Society of Swedish Literature in Finland.

Kremer, Ludger 1998: Unternehmensname: Aspekte ihrer namenkundlichen Betrachtung. [Company names: an onomastic investigation.] – W. F. H. Nicolaisen (ed.), *Proceedings of the XIXth international congress of onomastic sciences. Aberdeen, August 4–11, 1996.* Vol. 1 pp. 186–193. Aberdeen: University of Aberdeen.

Kripke, Saul 1972: Naming and necessity. – Donald Davidson & Gilbert Harman (ed.), *Semantics of natural language* pp. 253–255. Dodrecht: Reidel.

Kunze, Konrad 2003: *dtv-Atlas Namenkunde: Vor- und Familiennamen im deutschen Sprachgebiet.* [First and last names in the German linguistic area.] 4., überarbeitete und erweiterte Auflage. München: Deutscher Taschenbuch Verlag.

Laapotti, Marjukka 1994: *Lahden paikannimistö.* [Toponymy of Lahti.] Lahti: Lahden kaupunki.

Lakoff, George 1987: *Women, Fire, and Dangerous Things. What Categories Reveal about the Mind.* London: University of Chicago Press.

Lampinen, Arja 1999: Iloisa Sisko ja Reima Veikko – miten kaksosten nimet muodostavat parin. [Iloisa Sisko and Reima Veikko – how names of twins form a pair.] – *Sananjalka* 41 pp. 81–105.

Van Langendonck, Willy 1995: Name Systems and Name Strata. – Ernst Eichler & Gerold Hilty & Heinrich Löffler & Hugo Steger & Ladislav Zgusta (ed.): *Namenforschung – Name Studies – Les noms propres: ein internationales Handbuch zur Onomastik – an international handbook of onomastics – manuel international d'onomastique.* Volume 1, pp. 485–489. Berlin: Walter de Gruyter.

Van Langendonck, Willy 2007: *Theory and typology of proper names.* Berlin: Mouton de Gruyter.

van Langevelde, Ab 1999: What's in a Frisian business name? Regional identification in private enterprise in the Netherlands. – Ab van Langevelde (ed.), *Bilingualism and regional economic development* pp. 57–73. Groningen: Rijksuniversiteit Groningen.

Lehikoinen, Laila 1988: *Kirvun talonnimet: karjalaisen talonnimisysteemin kuvaus.* [Kirvu homestead names: an account of the Karelian homestead naming system.] Finnish Literature Society Publications 493. Helsinki: Finnish Literature Society.

Leino, Antti 2007: *On toponymic constructions as an alternative to naming patterns in describing Finnish lake names.* Studia Fennica, Linguistica 13. Helsinki: Finnish Literature Society.

Lempiäinen, Pentti 2004: *Suuri etunimikirja.* [The big dictionary of first names.] Third, revised printing. Helsinki: WSOY.

Liao, Chao-chih 2000: *A sociolinguistic study of Taiwan-Chinese personal names, nicknames, and English names.* Taichung: Feng Chia University.

Louhivaara, Maija 1999: *Tampereen kadunnimet.* [Tampere street names.] Tampereen museoiden julkaisuja 51. Tampere.

Malinowski, Bronislaw 1945: *The dynamics of culture change: an inquiry into race relations in Africa.* New Haven: Yale University Press.

Mallat, Kaija 1997: Interpreting place-names. – Ritva Liisa Pitkänen & Kaija Mallat (eds.), *You name it. Perspectives on onomastic research* pp. 97–106. Studia Fennica Linguistica 7. Helsinki: Finnish Literature Society.

Mallat, Kaija 2007: *Naiset rajalla: kyöpeli, Nainen, Naara(s), Neitsyt, Morsian, Akka ja Ämmä Suomen paikannimissä*. [Women at the boundary: *Kyöpeli, Nainen, Naara(s), Neitsyt, Morsian, Ämmä* and *Akka* in Finnish Place Names.] Finnish Literature Society Publications 1122. Helsinki: Finnish Literature Society.

Mallat, Kaija & Ainiala, Terhi & Kiviniemi, Eero (eds.) 2001: *Nimien maailmasta*. [On the world of names.] Kieli 14. Helsinki: University of Helsinki Department of Finnish.

Mikkonen, Pirjo (ed.) 2002: *Sukunimi? Etunimi? Maahanmuuttajien nimijärjestelmistä*. [Surname? Given name? On the naming systems of immigrants.] Kielenkäytön oppaita 3. Kotimaisten kielten tutkimuskeskuksen julkaisuja 114. Helsinki: Institute for the Languages of Finland.

Mikkonen, Pirjo & Paikkala, Sirkka 2000: *Sukunimet*. [Surnames.] Revised edition. Helsinki: Otava.

Mill, John Stuart 1906: *A system of logic: ratiocinative and inductive*. New impression. London: Longmans, Green & co.

Mills, A. D. 2001: *Oxford dictionary of London place names*. Oxford: Oxford University Press

Modéer, Ivar 1933: *Småländska skärgårdsnamn: en studie över holmnamnen i Mönsterås*. [Names of the Archipelago of Småland.] Skrifter utgivna av Gustaf Adolfs akademien för folklivsforskning 1. Uppsala: Lundequistska bokhandeln.

Mustakallio, Sari 1996: Sisko ja sen veli. *Veli-, Veikko-, Veijo- ja Sisko*-nimien leviäminen. – Eero Kiviniemi & Sari Mustakallio (eds.), *Nimet, aatteet, mielikuvat. Kolme näkökulmaa nimiin* pp. 13–97. Kieli 11. Helsinki: University of Helsinki Department of Finnish

Müller, Horst M. 2003: Neurobiologische Grundlagen der Sprache. [Neurobiological basics of language.] – Geo Rickheit & Theo Herrmann & Werner Deutsch (ed.), *Psycholinguistik: Ein internationales Handbuch* pp. 57–80. Handbücher zur Sprach- und Kommunikationswissenschaft 24. Berlin: Walter de Gruyter.

Namenforschung: ein internationales Handbuch zur Onomastik – Name Studies: an international Handbook of Onomastics – Les noms propres: manuel international d'onomastique. 1. Teilband. Ed. Ernst Eichler et. al. Handbücher zur Sprach- und Kommunikationswissenschaft 11, 1. Berlin: de Gruyter, 1995.

Namenforschung: ein internationales Handbuch zur Onomastik – Name Studies: an international Handbook of Onomastics – Les noms propres: manuel international d'onomastique. 2. Teilband. Ed. Ernst Eichler et. al. Handbücher zur Sprach- und Kommunikationswissenschaft 11, 2. Berlin: de Gruyter, 1996.

Names in Commerce and Industry: Past and Present. Ludger Kremer & Elke Ronneberger-Sibold (eds.). Berlin: Logos.

Nicolaisen, W. F. H. 1997: Names and words – yet again. – Marianne Blomqvist (ed.): *Ord och några visor tillägnade Kurt Zilliacus 21.7.1997* pp. 199–203. Meddelanden från institutionen för nordiska språk och nordisk litteratur vid Helsingfors universitet.

Nissilä, Viljo 1939: *Vuoksen paikannimistö I*. [Toponymy of Vuoksi I.] Helsinki: Finnish Literature Society.

Nissilä, Viljo 1962: *Suomalaista nimistöntutkimusta*. [Finnish onomastics.] Finnish Literature Society Publications 272. Helsinki: Finnish Literature Society.

Nissilä, Viljo 1975: *Suomen Karjalan nimistö*. [Finnish Karelian nomenclature.] Karjalaisen Kulttuurin edistämissäätiön julkaisuja. Joensuu: Karjalaisen Kulttuurin edistämissäätiö.

Nissilä, Viljo 1980: Germaanisen nimiaineiston etymologista ryhmittelyä Suomen nimistössä. [Etymological grouping of a corpus of Germanic names in Finnish nomenclature.] – *Viipurin suomalaisen kirjallisuusseuran toimitteita* 4 pp. 131–194. Helsinki: Finnish Literary Society of Vyborg.

Nuorgam, Ánne 2004: Saamenkielisistä nimistä. [On Sámi-language names.] – *Yliopiston nimipäiväalmanakka 2005 – Universitetets namnsdagsalmanacka 2005 – Universitehta nammabeaivealmmenáhkki 2005* pp. 76–77.

Nykiel-Herbert, Barbara 1998: Applied onomastics: translations of personal names in South African books for children. – W. H. F. Nicolaisen. (ed.): *Proceedings of the XIXth International Congress of Onomastic Sciences. Aberdeen, August 4–11, 1996.* Vol. 3 pp. 366–372. Aberdeen: University of Aberdeen.

Nyström, Staffan 1998: Names in the mind: aspects of the mental onomasticon. – W. F. H. Nicolaisen (ed.), *Proceedings of the XIXth international congress of onomastic sciences. Aberdeen, August 4–11, 1996.* Vol. 1 pp. 229–235. Aberdeen: University of Aberdeen.

Närhi, Eeva Maria 1990: The onomastic central archives – the foundation of Finnish onomastics. – Heikki Leskinen & Eero Kiviniemi (eds.), *Finnish Onomastics. Namenkunde in Finnland.* Studia Fennica 34 pp. 9–25. Helsinki: Finnish Literature Society.

Ojansuu, Heikki 1920: *Suomalaista paikannimitutkimusta 1: tähänastisen tutkimuksen arvostelua.* [Finnish toponomastics 1: a review of research to date.] Turku: Otava.

Onoma. Journal of the International Council of Onomastic Sciences.

Paikkala, Sirkka 2000: Nimistönsuunnittelu kunnissa 1999. [Name planning in municipalities 1999.] – Sirkka Paikkala (ed.), *Kaavanimien hätäkaste. Nimistönsuunnittelu kunnissa 1999.* Kotimaisten kielten tutkimuskeskuksen julkaisuja 113. Institute for the Languages of Finland and Association of Finnish Local and Regional Authorities.

Paikkala, Sirkka 2004: *Se tavallinen Virtanen: suomalaisen sukunimikäytännön modernisoituminen.* [The ordinary Virtanen: the modernisation of Finnish surname practices from the 1850s to 1921.] Finnish Literature Society Publications 959. Helsinki: Finnish Literature Society.

Paikkala, Sirkka & Pitkänen, Ritva Liisa & Slotte, Peter 1999: *Yhteinen nimiympäristömme: nimistönsuunnittelun opas.* [Our shared name environment: a guide to name planning.] Helsinki: Institute for the Languages of Finland and Association of Finnish Local and Regional Authorities.

Pamp, Bengt 1994: Övriga namn och andra: ett forsök till gruppering av egennamn. [Other names: An attempt at grouping proper names.] – Kristinn Jóhannesson & Hugo Karlsson & Bo Ralph (eds.), *Övriga namn. Handlingar från NORNA:s nittonde symposium i Göteborg 4–6 december 1991* pp. 49–57. Uppsala: NORNA-rapporter 56.

Patterson, Francine & Linden, Eugene 1986: *Koko – puhuva gorilla.* [The Education of Koko 1981]. Helsinki: Otava.

Paunonen, Heikki & Paunonen, Marjatta 2000: *Tsennaaks Stadii, bonjaaks slangii? Stadin slangin suursanakirja.* [The big dictionary of Helsinki slang.] Helsinki: WSOY.

Paunonen, Heikki & Paunonen, Marjatta 2010: *Stadin mestat. Ikkunoita Helsingin ja sen asukkaiden historiaan ja menneisyyteen.* [Stadi Sites. Windows to the history and past of Helsinki and its residents.] Helsinki: Edico.

People, Products and Professions. Choosing a Name, Choosing a Language. Eva Lavric & Fiorenza Fischer & Carmen Konzett & Julia Kuhn & Holger Wochele (eds.) Sprache im Kontext 32. Frankfurt/M.: Peter Lang.

Pipping, Hugo 1918: *Finländska ortnamn.* [Finnish place names.] Skrifter utgivna av Åbo Akademi kommitté 7. Helsingfors: Schildts.

Pitkänen, Ritva Liisa 1985: *Turunmaan saariston suomalainen lainanimistö.* [Finnish loan names of the Turunmaa archipelago.] Finnish Literature Society Publications 418. Helsinki: Finnish Literature Society.

Pitkänen, Ritva Liisa 1996: Viljelijän kylä – kalastajan saaristo: ammatti nimitaidon taustana. [A farmer's village – a fisher's islands: profession as a backdrop to toponymic competence.] – Ritva Liisa Pitkänen, Helena Suni & Satu Tanner (eds.), *Kielen kannoilla: Kotimaisten kielten tutkimuskeskus 20 vuotta* pp. 102–118. Kotimaisten kielten tutkimuskeskuksen julkaisuja 86. Helsinki: Institute for the Languages of Finland.

Pitkänen, Ritva Liisa 2004: Onomastic research and teaching in Finland. – *Onoma* 39 pp. 29–43.

Platen, Christoph 1997: *"Ökonymie": zur Produktnamen-Linguistik im europäischen Binnenmarkt*. [The linguistics of product names in Europe.]Tübingen: Max Niemeyer.

Pöyhönen, Juhani 1998: *Suomalainen sukunimikartasto*. [The Finnish surname atlas.] Finnish Literature Society Publications 693. Helsinki: Finnish Literature Society.

Pöyhönen, Juhani 2003: *Suomalainen sukunimikartasto II. Karjalaiset nimet*. [The Finnish surname atlas II. Karelian names.] Finnish Literature Society Publications 922. Helsinki: Finnish Literature Society.

Rainò, Päivi 2004: *Henkilöviittomien synty ja kehitys suomalaisessa viittomakieliyhteisössä* (CD). [The emergence and development of personal name signs among Finnish sign language users.] Deaf Studies in Finland 2. Helsinki: Finnish Association of the Deaf.

Rogers, Everett M. 1962: *Diffusion of innovations*. New York: Free Press.

Ronneberger-Sibold, Elke 2007: Fremdsprachliche Elemente in deutschen Markennamen: ein geschichtlicher Überblick. [Foreign elements in German product names: a historical overview.] In: Ludger Kremer & Elke Ronneberger-Sibold (eds.): *Names in Commerce and Industry: Past and Present*, 187–211.Berlin: Logos.

Russel, Bertrand 1956: Lectures on logical atomism. – Robert C. Marsh (ed.), *Logic and knowledge*. London: Georg Allen & Unwin.

Räisänen, Alpo 2003: *Nimet mieltä kiehtovat: etymologista nimistöntutkimusta*. [Fascinating names: etymological onomastics.] Finnish Literature Society Publications 936. Helsinki: Finnish Literature Society.

Saarelma-Maunumaa, Minna 2003: *Edhina ekogidho – Names as links: the encounter between African and European anthroponymic systems among the Ambo people in Namibia*. Studia Fennica, Linguistica 11. Helsinki: Finnish Literature Society.

Saarelma, Minna 2006: *Nimipäiväjuhlat*. [Name day celebrations.] Helsinki: Kirjapaja.

Saarelma, Minna 2011: *Koirien nimipäiväkirja – Bella, Niksu vai Romeo?* [A dog's name day book – *Bella, Niksu* or *Romeo?*] Helsinki: Minerva Kustannus Oy.

Saarelma, Minna 2012: *Kissojen nimipäiväkirja – Viiru, Nöpö vai Kassinen?* [A cat's name day book – *Viiru, Nöpö* or *Kassinen?*] Helsinki: Minerva Kustannus Oy.

Saarikalle, Anne & Suomalainen, Johanna 2007: *Suomalaiset etunimet Aadasta Yrjöön*. [Finnish first names from Aada to Yrjö.] Helsinki: Gummerus.

Saarikivi, Janne 2006: *Substrata Uralica: studies on Finno-Ugrian substrate in northern Russian dialects*. Tartu: Tartu University Press.

Saxén, Ralf 1910: *Finländska vattendragsnamn*. [Finnish hydronyms.] Skrifter utgivna av Svenska litteratursälskapet i Finland 92. Helsingfors: The Society of Swedish Literature in Finland.

Schybergson, Anita 2009: *Kognitiva system i namngivningen av finländska handelsfartyg 1838–1938*. [A cognitive system in the naming of Finnish merchant vessels.] Nordica Helsingiensia 17. Helsingfors: Institutionen för nordiska språk och nordisk litteratur, Helsingfors universitet.

Searle, John 1969: *Speech acts: an essay in the philosophy of language*. Cambridge: Cambridge University Press.

Seibicke, Wilfried 1982: *Die Personennamen im Deutschen*. [Personal names of the Germans.] Sammlung Göschen 2218. Berlin: Walter de Gruyter.

Seppänen, Anni-Marja 2005: Jyväskyläläisen yliopisto-opiskelijan nimimaisema. [The onomastic landscape of the University of Jyväskylä student.] – Terhi Ainiala (ed.), *Kaupungin nimet: kymmenen kirjoitusta kaupunkinimistöstä* pp. 126–150. Kotimaisten kielten tutkimuskeskuksen julkaisuja 134. Helsinki: Finnish Literature Society.

Siebs, Benno Eide 1970: *Die Personennamen der Germanen.* [Personal names of the Germans.] Wiesbaden: Dr. Martin Sändig oHG.

Sirén, Hanna 2005: Nähdäänkö Nälkälaaksossa vai Jurrilassa? Asenteet ja huumori pirkkalalaisten nuorten epävirallisissa paikannimissä. [See you in Nälkälaakso or Jurrila? Attitudes and humour in the unofficial place names of Pirkka youth.] – Terhi Ainiala (ed.), *Kaupungin nimet: kymmenen kirjoitusta kaupunkinimistöstä* pp. 110–126. Kotimaisten kielten tutkimuskeskuksen julkaisuja 134. Helsinki: Finnish Literature Society.

Sjöblom, Paula 2000: *Soma, Kärsä-Pähkinä ja Junavahti*: turkulaisten asunto-osakeyhtiöiden nimet. [Soma, Kärsä-Pähkinä and Junavahti: names of Turku housing cooperatives.] – *Virittäjä* 104 pp. 373–392.

Sjöblom, Paula 2002: Firmanamn som namnkategori. [Company names as a name category.] – Terhi Ainiala & Peter Slotte (eds.): *Avgränsning av namnkategorier. rapport från NORN:.s tjugonionde symposium på Svidja 20–22 april 2001* pp. 89–100. Helsinki: Forskningscentralen för de inhemska språken.

Sjöblom, Paula 2006: *Toiminimen toimenkuva: suomalaisen yritysnimistön rakenne ja funktiot.* [A firm name's job description: the structure and functions of Finnish company names.] Finnish Literature Society Publications 1064. Helsinki: Finnish Literature Society.

Sjöblom, Paula 2007: Finnish company names: structure and function. – Ludger Kremer & Elke Ronneberger-Sibold (eds.): *Names in Commerce and Industry: Past and Present* pp. 297–306. Berlin: Logos.

Sjöblom, Paula 2008: Namnens tolkning som en kognitiv process: exemplet kommersiellt namnförråd. [The meaning and interpretation of names as a cognitive process: commercial names.] – Guðrún Kvaran & Hallgrímur Ámundason & Jónína Hafsteinsdóttir & Svarar Sigmundsson (eds.): *Nordiska namn – namn i Norden. Tradition och förnyelse,* pp. 419–424. Norna-rapporter 84. Uppsala: Norna-förlaget.

Sjöblom, Paula 2009: The linguistic origin of company names in Finland. – Eva Lavric & Fiorenza Fischer & Carmen Konzett & Julia Kuhn & Holger Wochele (eds.): *People, Products and Professions. Choosing a Name, Choosing a Language* pp. 289–295. Sprache im Kontext 32. Frankfurt/M.: Peter Lang.

Sjöblom, Paula 2010: Multimodality of company names. – *Onoma 43 (2008)* pp. 351–380.

Sjöblom, Paula 2011: A cognitive approach to the semantics of proper names. – *Onoma 41 (2006)* pp. 63–82. Uppsala: International Council of Onomastic Sciences (ICOS).

Slotte Peter 1976: Ortnamns räckvidd; namnbruk och namnkunnande. [A range of place names; use and knowledge of names] – Vibeke Dalberg & Botolv Helleland & Allan Rostvik & Kurt Zilliacus (ed.), *Ortnamn och samhälle: aspekter, begrepp, metoder* pp. 125–140. NORNA-rapporter 10. Helsingfors: The Society of Swedish Literature in Finland.

Slotte, Peter, Kurt Zilliacus & Gunilla Harling 1973: Sociologiska namnstudier. [Sociological name studies.] – Kurt Zilliacus (ed.), *Synvinklar på ortnamn* pp. 97–181. Skrifter utgivna av Svenska litteratursällskapet i Finland 454. Meddelanden från folkkultursarkivet 1. Helsingfors: The Society of Swedish Literature in Finland.

Sobanski, Ines 1998: The onymic landscape of G.K. Chesterton's detective stories. – W.H.F. Nicolaisen (ed.), *Proceedings of the XIXth International Congress of Onomastic Sciences. Aberdeen, August 4–11, 1996.* Vol. 3 pp. 373–378. Aberdeen: University of Aberdeen.

Šrámek, Rudolf 1972/1973: Zum Begriff "Modell" und "System" in der Toponomastik. [The concepts of "model" and "system" in toponomastics.] – *Onoma* 18 pp. 55–75. Leuven.

Stoebke, Detlef-Eckhard 1964: *Die alten ostseefinnischen Personennamen im Rahmen eines urfinnischen Namensystems.* [Old Baltic-Finnic personal names within a Proto-Finnish naming system.] Nord- und osteuropäische Geschichtsstudien. Band IV. Hamburg: Leibnitz-Verlag.

Suomalainen paikannimikirja. [Dictionary of Finnish place names] Kotimaisten kielten tutkimuskeskuksen julkaisuja 146. Helsinki: Karttakeskus and the Institute for the Languages of Finland. 2007.

Toropainen, Ritva 2005: *Oulun paikannimet – mistä nimet tulevat.* [Oulu place names – where names come from.] Oulu: Oulun yliopistopaino.

Turun katuja ja toreja. Nimistöhistoriaa keskiajalta nykypäivään. [Turku street and market squares. A history of nomenclatures from the Middle ages to today.] Sanna Kupila & Marita Söderström (eds.) Turku: Turun museokeskus 2011.

Vahtola, Jouko 1980: *Tornionjoki- ja Kemijokilaakson asutuksen synty. Nimistötieteellinen ja historiallinen tutkimus.* [The origins of settlement in the Torne and Kemi River Valleys. An onomastic and historical study.] Studia Historica Septentrionalia 3. Rovaniemi: Pohjois-Suomen Historiallinen Yhdistys.

Vahtola, Jouko 1983: En gammal germansk invandring till västra Finland i bynamnens belysning. [Old Germanic migration to western Finland in the analysis of village names.] – *Historisk tidskrift för Finland* 1983 pp. 252–279. Helsingfors: Historiska föreningen.

Valtavuo-Pfeifer, Ritva 1998: *Terrängnamn i Svenskfinland.* [Finland Swedish topographic names.] Skrifter utgivna av Svenska litteratursällskapet i Finland 615. Helsingfors: The Society of Swedish Literature in Finland.

Vandebosch, Heidi 1998: The influence of media on given names. – *Names* 46 (4) pp. 243–262. New York: The American Name Society.

Vatanen, Osmo 1997: *Ystävä, Hyvä ja Äpyli – nämäkin lehmännimiä.* [*Ystävä, Hyvä* and *Äpyli* – these too are cattle names.] Vantaa: Suomen kotieläinjalostusosuuskunta.

Vilkuna, Kustaa 2005: *Etunimet.* [Given names.] Ed. Pirjo Mikkonen. Helsinki: Otava.

Voipio, Mari 2001: Internetin verkkotunnukset. [Internet domains.] – Johanna Komppa & Kaija Mallat & Toni Suutari (eds.), *Nimien vuoksi* pp. 146–168. Kielen opissa 5. University of Helsinki Department of Finnish.

Vuolteenaho, Jani & Ainiala, Terhi 2005: Urbaanin paikannimistön haasteita: kielitieteen ja maantieteen tieteenalatraditioista arkiseen käyttönimistöön Helsingin metropolialueella. [Challenges of urban toponymy: from disciplinary traditions of linguistics and geography to the daily use of nomenclature in the metropolitan area of Helsinki] – *Alue ja ympäristö* 1/2005 pp. 4–18.

Willems, Klaas 2000: Form, meaning, and reference in natural language: A phenomenological account of proper names. – *Onoma* 35 (2000) pp. 85–119.

Wilson, Stephen 1998: *The means of naming: a social and cultural history of personal naming in Western Europe.* London: UCL Press Limited.

Wittgenstein, Ludwig 2009 [1953]: *Philosophical Investigations.* 4th edition, P.M.S. Hacker and Joachim Schulte (eds. and trans.). Oxford: Wiley-Blackwell.

Yli-Kojola, Maria 2005: Kurvinpussi vai Torikatu? Kouvolalaisten mielipiteitä kadunnimistä. [How Kouvola residents feel about their street names.] – Terhi Ainiala (ed.), *Kaupungin nimet: kymmenen kirjoitusta kaupunkinimistöstä* pp. 178–201. Kotimaisten kielten tutkimuskeskuksen julkaisuja 134. Helsinki: Finnish Literature Society.

Yliopiston nimipäiväalmanakka – Universitetets namnsdagsalmanacka – Universitehta nammabeaivealmmenáhkki. [University name day almanac.] Volumes 1996–2008. Helsinki: University of Helsinki.

Yurchak, Alexei 2000: Privatize your name. Symbolic work in a post-Soviet linguistic market. – *Journal of Sociolinguistics* 4 pp. 406–434. Oxford: Blackwell.

Zelinsky, Wilbur 2002: Slouching toward a theory of names: a tentative taxonomic fix. – *Names* 50 pp. 243–262. New York: The American Name Society.
Zilliacus, Kurt 1966: *Ortnamnen i Houtskär*. [Place names in Houtskär. An overview of the composition of nomenclature] Studier i Nordisk filologi 55. Skrifter utgivna av Svenska litteratursällskapet i Finland 416. Helsingfors: The Society of Swedish Literature in Finland.
Zilliacus, Kurt 1972: Nimistötieteellisten synteesien aikaa. [An era of onomastic syntheses] – *Kalevalaseuran vuosikirja* 52. Nimikirja pp. 360–383. Helsinki: WSOY.
Zilliacus, Kurt 1980: Ortnamnsförråden vid språkgränsen i Finland. Presentation av ett forskningsprojekt. [Toponymy in the linguistic border in Finland. Introducing a research project.] – Thorsten Andersson & Eva Brylla & Allan Rostvik (ed.), *Ortnamn och språkkontakt. Handlingar från NORNA:s sjätte symposium i Uppsala 5–7 maj 1978* pp. 317–349. NORNA-rapporter 17. Uppsala: Norna-förlaget.
Zilliacus, Kurt 1989: *Skärgårdsnamn*. [Archipelago names.] Skrifter utgivna av Svenska litteratursällskapet i Finland 558. Helsingfors: The Society of Swedish Literature in Finland.
Zilliacus, Kurt 1997: On the function of proper names. – Ritva Liisa Pitkänen & Kaija Mallat (ed.), *You name it: perspectives on onomastic research* pp. 14–20. Studia Fennica Linguistica 7. Helsinki: Finnish Literature Society.

Unpublished Theses

Aarnio, Liisa 1984: Kalle Päätalon Iijoki-sarjan henkilönnimet: sosiolingvististä tarkastelua. [Personal names in Kalle Päätalo's Iijoki series: a sociolinguistic investigation.] Master's thesis. University of Joensuu.
Ahlö, Malin 2005: Erisnimien kääntäminen kahdessa Bert-kirjassa: kulttuuri- ja taustatietoerojen vaikutus kääntäjän ratkaisuihin. [Translating proper nouns in two Bert books: the impact of cultural and background differences on the translator's solutions.] Master's thesis. University of Vaasa.
Ahtola, Grete 2007: Helsingin yliopiston opiskelijoiden käyttämiä epävirallisia paikannimiä. [Unoffical place names used by University of Helsinki students.] Master's thesis. University of Helsinki.
Anttila, Elina 1993: Koirien nimet ja nimeämistavat. [Names and naming practices of dogs.] Master's thesis. University of Helsinki.
Bertills, Yvonne 1995: Muumikirjojen henkilönnimet ja muminismit sekä niiden käännökset. [Personal names and Moominisms from the Moomin books and their translations] Master's thesis. Åbo Akademi University.
Elonen, Tuula 2004: Pohjan kunnan epävirallinen henkilönnimistö: nimien antaminen, käyttö ja funktiot. [Unofficial anthroponymy in the municipality of Pohja: name giving, use and functions.] Master's thesis. University of Turku.
Eskeland, Tuula 1994: Fra Diggasborra til Diggasbekken: finske stednavn på de norske finnskogene. [From Diggasborra to Diggasbekken: Finnish place names in the Finnskogen area of Norway] Disertation. Oslo: University of Oslo.
Eskelinen, Riikka 2008: Kaupunkinimistön funktiot. [The functions of urban nomenclature.] Licentiate thesis. University of Helsinki.
Hongisto, Ilari 2006: Apulantaa Waltarilla. Populaarimusiikin suomenkielisten esittäjännimien semantiikkaa. [Apulanta with a side of Waltari. The semantics of Finnish-language artist names in popular music.] Master's thesis, University of Turku.
Honkanen, Anita 2001: Suomenhevosten kutsuma- ja lempinimistä. [On Finnish horse call names and nicknames.] Master's thesis. University of Jyväskylä.
Karbin, Tiina 2005: *Vuokki, Kolari, Mustis* ja muut: tutkimus paikannimien käytöstä Helsingin Vuosaaressa. [*Vuokki, Kolari, Mustis* and others: an investigation on the use of place names in Vuosaari, Helsinki.] Master's thesis. University of Helsinki.

Karppinen, Hanna 2003: Harry Potter -kirjojen suomennoksissa käytetyt uudissanat. [Neologisms used in the Finnish translations of the Harry Potter books.] Master's thesis. University of Tampere.

Keinänen, Minna 2009: Kissoille annetut henkilönnimet. [Personal names given to cats.] Master's thesis. University of Helsinki.

Kiiski, Päivi 1993: Kotona *Meerikkä*, koulussa *Ämmä*, partiossa *Tiuhti*: kuopiolaispartiolaisten kutsumanimet. [*Meerikkä* at home, *Ämmä* in school, *Tiuhti* in the scouts: Call names used by scouts in Kuopio.] Master's thesis. University of Helsinki.

Klockars, Britta 1987: Erisnimet käännösongelmana. [Proper names as a problem in translation.] Master's thesis. University of Vaasa.

Korttila, Anne 2003: *Rehti Putterista Parsapellon Pätiäisiin*: Aku Ankka -sarjakuvalehden erisnimien tarkastelua. [From *Rehti Putteri* to *Parsapellon Pätiäinen*: An investigation of proper nouns in Aku Ankka comic strips.] Master's thesis. University of Helsinki.

Kurki, Elina 1998: *Poiju* ja *Piru-Sunkvisti*: merimiesköllit kahden aineiston valossa. [*Poiju* and *Piru-Sunkvisti*: unofficial bynames of seamen analysed through two sets of data.] Master's thesis. University of Turku.

Kuukasjärvi, Neena 1997: Suomenhevosten nimistä. [On Finnish horse names.] Master's thesis. University of Oulu.

Laine, Heidi Mariia 1997: Kissojen nimet ja nimeämistavat. [Names and naming practices of cats.] Master's thesis. University of Helsinki.

Lampinen, Arja 1997: Ristimänimien valinta ja nimenannon uudennokset Jyväskylässä 1766–1930. [Choice of christening name and innovations of name giving in Jyväskylä from 1766 to 1930.] Licentiate thesis. University of Turku.

Lehtinen, Auli 2000: *Kana*, *Koeputki* ja *Kuparikypärä*: opettajien lisänimien synnyn ja käytön tarkastelua. [*Kana* ('chicken'), *Koeputki* ('test tube') and *Kuparikypärä* ('copper helmet'). An investigation on the emergence and use of teachers' bynames.] Master's thesis. University of Turku.

Mentula, Mikko 2006: *Klonkku*, *Reppuli* ja *Hallavaharja*: fiktiivisten erisnimien muodostus, merkitykset ja funktiot J. R. R. Tolkienin teoksessa *Taru sormusten herrasta*. [*Klonkku*, *Reppuli* and *Hallavaharja*: Formation, meanings and functions in the Finnish translation of J.R.R. Tolkien's Lord of the Rings.] Master's thesis. University of Turku.

Metsämuuronen, Saila 1991: Henkilönnimet Ollin 1960-luvun pakinakokoelmissa. [Personal names in Olli's collections in the 1960s.] Master's thesis. University of Helsinki.

Mustakallio, Sari 1995: Sisko ja sen Veli: *Veli-*, *Veikko-*, *Veijo-* ja *Sisko-*nimien leviäminen. [A Sister and her Brother: The extension of the names *Veli*, *Veikko*, *Veijo* ('brother') and *Sisko* ('sister').] Master's thesis. University of Helsinki.

Mustonen, Raija 1997: Joensuun peruskoulun yläasteiden oppilaiden lempinimet lukuvuonna 1994–1995. [Nicknames of upper level comprehensive school pupils in Joensuu in academic year 1994–1995.] Master's thesis. University of Joensuu.

Mäentaka, Samuli 2001: Turkulaisten taksinkuljettajien köllinimet. [Unofficial bynames of Turku taxi drivers.] Master's thesis. University of Turku.

Paalanen, Johanna 1992: *Kale*, *Kelpo* ja *Suudelniilo*: lempinimet yhteisössä. [*Kale*, *Kelpo* and *Suudelniilo*: Nicknames in a community.] Master's thesis. University of Helsinki.

Pakarinen, Elisa 1995: *Tiuku Helinä* ja *Teho Ensio*: lasten työnimet. [*Tiuku Helinä* and *Teho Ensio*: Foetal and newborn nicknames.] Master's thesis. University of Helsinki.

Partanen, Katriina 2000: *Kultapoju* ja *saunapalvi*: hevosten lempinimet ja nimeämistavat. [*Kultapoju* and *saunapalvi*: nicknames and naming practices of horses.] Master's thesis. University of Helsinki.

Pearl, Leonard 2007: Hahmonimet hahmottumassa: Disney-piirroselokuvissa esiintyvien suomenkielisten henkilönnimien sananmuodostus, rakenne ja merkityssuhteet. [Character names taking shape: Word formation, structure and meaning relationships of Finnish-language personal names in full-length, animated Disney feature films.] Master's thesis. University of Turku.

Raivo, Maria 2001: Henkilönnimet Kirsi Kunnaksen lastenkirjoissa. [Personal names in children's books by Kirsi Kunnas.] Master's thesis. University of Turku.

Saarinen, Janne 2006: Suomen paikkakuntien epäviralliset nimet. [Unofficial names of localities in Finland.] Master's thesis. University of Jyväskylä.

Sarkkinen, Tarja 1997: Kissan kutsumanimien äänteelliset piirteet ja nimeämisperusteet. [The phonetic features and priniciples of naming of cat call names.] Master's thesis. University of Oulu.

Seppälä, Tiina 1999: *Toke, Muurahainen* ja *Tarzan* – Aniksen joukkuekaverit: Turun Palloseuran jääkiekkoilijoiden lempinimet katsomossa ja kentällä. [*Toke, Muurahainen* and *Tarzan* – Anis'teammates: Turun Palloseura hockey players' nicknames in the stands and on the ice.] Master's thesis. University of Turku.

Sirviö, Teija 1976: Pentti Haanpään käyttämät henkilönnimet teoksissa I–X. [Personal names used by Pentti Haanpää in his collection of books Teokset 1–X.] Master's thesis. University of Helsinki.

Tiitola, Ulriikka 1992: Nimitaidosta ja paikannimien säilymisestä Kangasalan Saarikylissä. [On toponymic competence and preservation of place names in the Saarikylät region of Kangasala.] Master's thesis. University of Tampere.

Tikka, Kaisa 2006: Paimion Vistan koululaisten leikkipaikannimiä. Katsaus leikkipaikannimien syntymiseen ja käyttöön. [Schoolchildren's names for places of play at the Vista school in Paimio. A look at the emergence and use of names for places of play.] Master's thesis. University of Turku.

Tikkala, Saara 2005: Nimet ja mielikuvat: Anni Swan nuorisokirjojensa henkilöhahmojen nimeäjänä. [Names and images: Anni Swan as a name giver of characters in her young adult books.] Master's thesis. University of Helsinki.

Tuomela, Marjo 2004: Laihialaisten miesten etunimiä ja lempinimiä kolmella vuosikymmenellä. [Given names and nicknames of Laihi men in three decades.] Master's thesis. University of Vaasa.

Tuomisto, Anna-Stiina 1992: Koirien nimistä ja nimeämisestä. [Dog names and naming] Master's thesis. University of Turku.

Vaattovaara, Heidi 1996: Suomen bokseri- ja rottweilerikennelnimet sekä kennelnimien nimenantoperusteet. [Boxer and Rottweiler kennel names in Finland and the principles of naming for kennel names.] Master's thesis. University of Jyväskylä.

Vatanen, Osmo 1993: *Lakka Hillantytär* ja *Ursula*: pohjoiskarjalaisten karjantarkkailutilojen lehmännimistöä. [*Lakka Hillantytär* and *Ursula*: Cattle nomenclature of North Karelian dairy farms.] Master's thesis. University of Joensuu.

Viitala, Tarja 1995: Lehmännimiä Jämsässä. [Cattle names in Jämsä.] Master's thesis. University of Jyväskylä.

Villikka, Minna 1997: Suomenhevosten nimistä ja nimeämisperusteista. [On Finnish horse names and their priciples of naming.] Master's thesis. University of Joensuu.

Vuola, Sanna 2001: Kalannin ja Laitilan lasten puhuttelunimet. [Children's call names in Kalanti and Laitila.] Master's thesis. University of Turku.

Index

A
acculturation process 137
adaptation 97, 106, 261
affective function 121, 260, 262
affective meaning 33
analogy 36, 40, 55, 79
annexe 76
anthroponomastics 23, 124
anthroponym 23, 124
anthroponymic system 125
anthroponymy 23, 124
appellative 13
artefact name 24, 66
artisan name 135
artist name 135, 252
association 32
associative function 260
associative name 77
attractor 225
authentic name 256, 257
auxiliary company name 220

B
bachelor name 131
baptismal name 131
behind-the-back nickname 134, 191
biblical name 149
birth name 131, 138
bourgeois name 135
brand 213, 245
breeder name 205, 251
byname 130, 132, 134

C
call name 134
cat name 205
categorical meaning 26
categorisation 25, 27
cattery name 205
cattle name 206
Celtic name 135
christening name 131
Christian name 149
clan name 125
classification model 24
classifying function 15, 260
code name 132
cognitive domain 34
cognitive linguistics 34
coined name 257
collective personal name 129
commemorative name 101
commercial name 210
common noun 13
company name 212
comparative name 77
compound name 36, 71, 135
compound surname 187
compressed meaning relationship 217, 242
confirmation name 131
connotation 32
contrastive name 78
corporate identifier 233, 234
cultivation name 24, 66
culture name 24, 66

D
dance name 140
deappellatival 68
deep structure 34
definite 29
denotation 32
deproprial 68

derivational surname 187
derogatory-protective name 138
descriptive byname 130, 133
descriptive function 260
designating name part 73
diffusion 137
diffusion research 180
direct meaning relationship 75, 241
direct naming 75
disconnected meaning relationship 217, 242
dog name 205, 251
domain name 221, 253
double name 135
double-barrelled name 135

E
ellipse 83
endonym 19
epexegesis 83
ergonym 211
ethnonym 135
etymological meaning 32
etymological research 45
etymology 16, 86
evergreen name 182
exonym 19
expansion diffusion 181

F
family name 131, 167
fashionable name 135
female name 135
Fennicised name form 160
fictionalising function 260
fictive name 256
first given name 131
first name 24, 131
first name system 125
foetal nickname 132, 133, 193
folk etymology 33
folk linguistics 58, 118
foreign language name 135
forename 131
full annexe 76
function 17
functional name part 216
functional-semantic (analysis) 216

G
genealogical name 208
generation name 134
generative linguistics 34
generic element 37

generic part 37, 71
generic part annexe 76
genericisation 249
given name 131
group name 103

H
hierarchal spread 181
homonym 31
horse name 207
humorous function 261
hunting name 140
hydronym 24, 66
hyphenated name 131, 135
hypocorism 133
hypocoristic byname 132, 133

I
identification 124
identifying 20
identifying (name) part 233, 236
identifying function 260
identifying meaning 32
identity 18, 20, 223
ideological function 260
imperative function 262
indirect meaning relationship 77, 242
indirect naming 77
individual name 130
individual personal name 129
individualising function 244
inductive naming 76
informative function 123, 243, 262
initiation group name 134
initiation name 140
innovation 137
innovation centre 181
innovation curve 181
integrative function 244
intelligentsia name 167
international name 163
internationalism 239
interpersonal function 243
invented name 257

K
kennel name 205, 251

L
laggard 181
last name 131, 167
latter given name 131
legal name 214
lexical meaning 32

linguistic origin 238
literary name 135
loan name 21, 95, 257
localising function 260
logo 212

M

macronym 21
macrotoponym 66
maiden name 131
main name 130
male name 135
married name 131
matronym 130
meaning 31
metaphoric meaning relationship 217, 242
metaphoric name 77
metonymic meaning relationship 217, 242
metonymic name 78
metonymic transference 33, 78
micronym 21
microtoponym 66
middle name 131
milk name 143
monarch name 135, 139
monolingual name 239
monoreferential 15
mother tongue name 135
multicultural name 179
multilingual name 239
multiple names 130
mythological name 158

N

name 13
name category 23
name change 129
name cluster 76
name density 70
name district 56, 112
name element 36, 233
name formation model 21
name formation rule 36
name formation suffix 77
name giver 127
name giving ceremony 126
name of abuse 133
name of address 134
name of comparative transference 78
name of honour 146
name of ridicule 129, 133
name part 36, 37, 73, 233

(name) part signifying the business concept 233, 234
name planning 99
name sharing 128
name strata 22
name typology 35, 36
names of educational institutions 225
namesake 139
namesake relationship 128
naming model 168
naming system 21, 130
narrative function 261
nature name 23, 66, 135
newborn nickname 132, 133, 193
nickname 129, 133
nobility name 135
non-fictive name 256
nursery nickname 132, 133, 194

O

official byname 132
official commercial name 215
official personal name 126
official place name 65, 99
onomasiology 23
onomastic landscape 257
onomasticon 35
onomastics 13
opaque name 31
opposing name 78
ox name 140

P

pan-European name 165
parallel company name 219
parallel form 85
parallel name 85
paraphrase 74
partial adaptation 97, 261
partial loan 261
partial replacement 261
partial translation 261
patronym 128, 130
pejorative byname 133, 191
pen name 132, 143
performative function 245
persona 130
personal name 23, 130
personification 20
personifying 20
persuasive function 243
pet name 132, 133
place name 23, 63
planned name 35, 99

political name 135
polyreferential 30
polysemy 33, 78
popularity change 135
popularity peak 181
posthumous name 143
practical function 119, 244
praise name 140
presuppositional meaning 26
primary urban name 105
primary byname 132
primary matronym 130
primary name 33
primary patronym 130
principle element 71
principle of name giving 127
principle of naming 35, 46, 74
private byname 192
product name 212, 247
proper name 13
proper noun 13
prototype 28
proverbial name 140
pseudonym 132, 252
public name 128

Q
qualifier 247
quasi-language 239
quasi name 207

R
reciprocity name 192
reduction 83
referent 15
regional monograph 46
registered name 205, 208
religious name 143, 149
revived name 135
root name 76, 135
root word surname 187

S
saint's name 135, 149
Scandinavian name 135
scout name 132
secondary byname 132, 133
secondary identifier 220
secondary matronym 130
secondary meaning 242
secondary name 33, 106
secondary patronym 130
secret name 125, 129

semasiology 23
settlement name 24, 66
ship name 251
signed name 200
single name 130
situational variation 115
slang derivational suffix 195
slang place name 105
slogan 246
social function, sociocultural function 120, 243, 260
social name 140
social variation 115
socio-onomastics 56, 110
solider name 135, 140
specific element 37
specified name 76
specific part 37, 71
stage name 187, 252
standardisation 18
stratum, stratification 22, 229
substrate name 50, 95
suffixation 84
supplementary (name) part 233, 237
surface structure 34
surname 24, 131, 167
surname system 125
symbolic unit 34
syntactic-semantic 53, 72
systematic name 140
systematic naming 128

T
teknonymy 129
temporal strata 92
temporary name 138
term of endearment 133
thematic name 103
theophoric name 149
top name 135
topographic name 24
topographic word 16, 71
toponomastics 23, 64
toponomy 23, 63
toponym 23, 63
toponymic competence 111
trade mark 212
trade name 216, 219
traditional (given) name 182
traditional place name 65
transcription 64
translated name 135
transparent name 31, 126

truncated name 135
truncated name form 147
two-part name 147

U
unique name 126, 135, 253
unisex name 135
universal name 239
unofficial byname 24, 131, 132
unofficial commercial name 215
unofficial place name 105

urban name 99
user-specific variation 115

V
variant given name 172
variation name 78

W
wandering name 140
weekday name 140

Studia Fennica Ethnologica

Memories of My Town
The Identities of Town Dwellers and Their Places in Three Finnish Towns
Edited by Anna-Maria Åström, Pirjo Korkiakangas &
Pia Olsson
Studia Fennica Ethnologica 8
2004

Passages Westward
Edited by Maria Lähteenmäki & Hanna Snellman
Studia Fennica Ethnologica 9
2006

Defining Self
Essays on emergent identities in Russia Seventeenth to Nineteenth Centuries
Edited by Michael Branch
Studia Fennica Ethnologica 10
2009

Touching Things
Ethnological Aspects of Modern Material Culture
Edited by Pirjo Korkiakangas, Tiina-Riitta Lappi & Heli Niskanen
Studia Fennica Ethnologica 11
2009

Gendered Rural Spaces
Edited by Pia Olsson & Helena Ruotsala
Studia Fennica Ethnologica 12
2009

LAURA STARK
The Limits of Patriarchy
How Female Networks of Pilfering and Gossip Sparked the First Debates on Rural Gender Rights in the 19th-century Finnish-Language Press
Studia Fennica Ethnologica 13
2011

Where is the Field?
The Experience of Migration Viewed through the Prism of Ethnographic Fieldwork
Edited by Laura Hirvi & Hanna Snellman
Studia Fennica Ethnologica 14
2012

Studia Fennica Folkloristica

PERTTI J. ANTTONEN
Tradition through Modernity
Postmodernism and the Nation-State in Folklore Scholarship
Studia Fennica Folkloristica 15
2005

Narrating, Doing, Experiencing
Nordic Folkloristic Perspectives
Edited by Annikki Kaivola-Bregenhøj, Barbro Klein & Ulf Palmenfelt
Studia Fennica Folkloristica 16
2006

MÍCHEÁL BRIODY
The Irish Folklore Commission 1935–1970
History, ideology, methodology
Studia Fennica Folkloristica 17
2007

VENLA SYKÄRI
Words as Events
Cretan Mantinádes in Performance and Composition
Studia Fennica Folkloristica 18
2011

Hidden Rituals and Public Performances
Traditions and Belonging among the Post-Soviet Khanty, Komi and Udmurts
Edited by Anna-Leena Siikala & Oleg Ulyashev
Studia Fennica Folkloristica 19
2011

Mythic Discourses
Studies in Uralic Traditions
Edited by Frog, Anna-Leena Siikala & Eila Stepanova
Studia Fennica Folkloristica 20
2012

Studia Fennica Historica

Medieval History Writing and Crusading Ideology
Edited by Tuomas M. S. Lehtonen & Kurt Villads Jensen with Janne Malkki and Katja Ritari
Studia Fennica Historica 9
2005

Moving in the USSR
Western anomalies and Northern wilderness
Edited by Pekka Hakamies
Studia Fennica Historica 10
2005

DEREK FEWSTER
Visions of Past Glory
Nationalism and the Construction of Early Finnish History
Studia Fennica Historica 11
2006

Modernisation in Russia since 1900
Edited by Markku Kangaspuro & Jeremy Smith
Studia Fennica Historica 12
2006

SEIJA-RIITTA LAAKSO
Across the Oceans
Development of Overseas Business Information Transmission 1815–1875
Studia Fennica Historica 13
2007

Industry and Modernism
Companies, Architecture and Identity in the Nordic and Baltic Countries during the High-Industrial Period
Edited by Anja Kervanto Nevanlinna
Studia Fennica Historica 14
2007

CHARLOTTA WOLFF
Noble conceptions of politics in eighteenth-century Sweden (ca 1740–1790)
Studia Fennica Historica 15
2008

Sport, Recreation and Green Space in the European City
Edited by Peter Clark, Marjaana Niemi & Jari Niemelä
Studia Fennica Historica 16
2009

Rhetorics of Nordic Democracy
Edited by Jussi Kurunmäki & Johan Strang
Studia Fennica Historica 17
2010

Studia Fennica Anthropologica

On Foreign Ground
Moving between Countries and Categories
Edited by Minna Ruckenstein & Marie-Louise Karttunen
Studia Fennica Anthropologica 1
2007

Beyond the Horizon
Essays on Myth, History, Travel and Society
Edited by Clifford Sather & Timo Kaartinen
Studia Fennica Anthropologica 2
2008

Studia Fennica Linguistica

Minimal reference
The use of pronouns in Finnish and Estonian discourse
Edited by Ritva Laury
Studia Fennica Linguistica 12
2005

ANTTI LEINO
On Toponymic Constructions as an Alternative to Naming Patterns in Describing Finnish Lake Names
Studia Fennica Linguistica 13
2007

Talk in interaction
Comparative dimensions
Edited by Markku Haakana, Minna Laakso & Jan Lindström
Studia Fennica Linguistica 14
2009

Planning a new standard language
Finnic minority languages meet the new millennium
Edited by Helena Sulkala & Harri Mantila
Studia Fennica Linguistica 15
2010

LOTTA WECKSTRÖM
Representations of Finnishness in Sweden
Studia Fennica Linguistica 16
2011

TERHI AINIALA, MINNA SAARELMA & PAULA SJÖBLOM
Names in Focus
An Introduction to Finnish Onomastics
Studia Fennica Linguistica 17
2012

Studia Fennica Litteraria

Changing Scenes
Encounters between European and Finnish Fin de Siècle
Edited by Pirjo Lyytikäinen
Studia Fennica Litteraria 1
2003

Women's Voices
Female Authors and Feminist Criticism in the Finnish Literary Tradition
Edited by Lea Rojola & Päivi Lappalainen
Studia Fennica Litteraria 2
2007

Metaliterary Layers in Finnish Literature
Edited by Samuli Hägg, Erkki Sevänen & Risto Turunen
Studia Fennica Litteraria 3
2009

AINO KALLAS
Negotiations with Modernity
Edited by Leena Kurvet-Käosaar & Lea Rojola
Studia Fennica Litteraria 4
2011

The Emergence of Finnish Book and Reading Culture in the 1700s
Edited by Cecilia af Forselles & Tuija Laine
Studia Fennica Litteraria 5
2011

Nodes of Contemporary Finnish Literature
Edited by Leena Kirstinä
Studia Fennica Litteraria 6
2012

www.ingramcontent.com/pod-product-compliance
Lightning Source LLC
Chambersburg PA
CBHW080801300426
44114CB00020B/2793